Infrastructure Financing in India

Infrastructure Financing in India

Trends, Challenges, and Way Forward

KUMAR V PRATAP

Senior Economic Adviser, Ministry of Commerce and Industry, Government of India

MANSHI GUPTA

Deputy Director, Ministry of Finance, Government of India

OXFORD
UNIVERSITY PRESS

Great Clarendon Street, Oxford, OX2 6DP,
United Kingdom

Oxford University Press is a department of the University of Oxford.
It furthers the University's objective of excellence in research, scholarship,
and education by publishing worldwide. Oxford is a registered trade mark of
Oxford University Press in the UK and in certain other countries

Published in the United States of America by Oxford University Press
198 Madison Avenue, New York, NY 10016, United States of America

British Library Cataloguing in Publication Data

Data available

Library of Congress Control Number: 2023943980

ISBN 978-0-19-888493-4

DOI: 10.1093/oso/9780198884934.001.0001

Foreword

Economists and policymakers recognize clearly that infrastructure investment is necessary for growth and development. The economic model that India is pursuing post the pandemic, in fact, places infrastructure investment as the centrepiece of India's economic strategy for inclusive economic growth. India recognized very early that the Covid-19 pandemic will engender severe supply-side shocks from lockdowns, night curfews, and other economic restrictions that adversely impact supply chains across the board. India, therefore, has pursued the Hicks-Samuelson accelerator-multiplier model for economic growth, which places capital expenditure as its centrepiece. This is in stark contrast to the Keynesian prescription of a pure demand-side push through revenue expenditures that the rest of the world has pursued.

As the private sector becomes exceedingly risk-averse during a crisis and shies away from investment, Government of India's capital expenditure has been enhanced by about 35 per cent in Budget 2021/22 to Rs.5.54 trillion, most of which would be directed towards infrastructure investment and help India accelerate the V-shaped recovery that has manifested over the last year and build on the double-digit GDP growth that is expected this year.

The book, *Infrastructure Financing in India: Trends, Challenges, and Way Forward*, is about facilitating infrastructure financing to help India attain its ambitious infrastructure goals as captured in the recently launched National Infrastructure Pipeline, the *Gati Shakti* Master Plan, and the National Monetization Pipeline. Key takeaways from the book are as follows. First, compliance with the environmental, social, and governance (ESG) criteria of institutional investors would make infrastructure assets more attractive to this class of investors and thereby facilitate long-term infrastructure financing without any asset–liability mismatch. At the same time, such compliance will also make for more sustainable provisioning of infrastructure. Second, user charges in infrastructure sectors should at least cover operation and maintenance expenses of infrastructure assets. Such a levy of user charges would enable sustainable financing of infrastructure, improve governance of infrastructure assets, while also generating resources for expansion of infrastructure services to the very poor. Third, monetization of brownfield assets enables more efficient provisioning of infrastructure services while also facilitating more greenfield investments. The Government of India is already in the process of implementing many of these recommendations to ensure that infrastructure investments propel the growth of the Indian economy.

The most popular method of implementing private infrastructure projects is through project financing. My own research, in the context of large investment projects, shows that project finance offers a contractual and organizational substitute for investor protection laws. Project finance enhances debt capacity by making cash flows verifiable through contractual arrangements and enforcement of these contracts. As such, maintaining the sanctity of contracts is important for attracting private investment, a theme that has also been underlined in the book.

Another notable contribution of the book is the need for internalizing the externalities generated by large infrastructure projects such as metro rail to make them financially viable through value capture finance. The book includes twenty case studies that provide apt learnings to researchers, teachers, and students—be they MBAs or Masters in Public Policy—alike. This book will also be useful to policymakers and infrastructure finance professionals who want to have a deeper understanding of infrastructure financing in India.

The book has been written by two serving officers of the Indian Economic Service (IES). A key mandate of the service is to contribute to better policymaking. The book furthers this endeavour and sets the path for other members of the service to follow the lead provided by the authors of this book. Writing, providing inputs to policy, publishing books and articles in peer-reviewed journals are important to the IES to achieve its mandate.

I commend the authors for providing rich insight into infrastructure financing and comprehensive exposition of its various facets. I am confident that the book will find wide readership.

New Delhi

Dr Krishnamurthy Subramanian
Executive Director, IMF
17th Chief Economic Advisor (2018–2021), Government of India

Preface

India has embarked on a massive infrastructure building plan in the form of the first-ever National Infrastructure Pipeline (NIP), the implementation of which would be crucial for maintaining her position as the fastest-growing large economy in the world. Making a financing plan for the NIP is important for it to be implemented as planned.

This book is an attempt to look at both the traditional and innovative ways in which the NIP can be financed. Conventionally, there are four major sources of financing for infrastructure: gross budgetary support, internal and extra budgetary resources of the public sector, multilateral and bilateral loans, and private investment. However, because of the Covid-19 pandemic, most of these traditional sources of finance are quite stretched and so the government has been emphasizing private infrastructure investment, which is also suffering from risk aversion. The book captures this story in a number of chapters, including a chapter especially dedicated to the impact of Covid-19 on infrastructure and its financing.

In this environment of fiscal stress and increased risk, the book emphasizes a number of non-traditional financing sources like reasonable user charges, which would not only ensure adequate operation and maintenance of infrastructure assets leading to their sustainability, but also improve accountability (and therefore, governance) in the provisioning of these services. In addition, the book lays major emphasis on making infrastructure more compliant with ESG norms, with the objectives of providing more sustainable infrastructure services and opening up the vast pool of institutional resources (from pension, insurance, and sovereign wealth funds) for infrastructure investment. This emphasis on ESG compliance would be opportune as institutional investors are looking to diversify their asset holdings (and infrastructure assets are attractive as they provide long-term steady returns that have low correlation with business cycles) to be better able to honour their liabilities. ESG compliance would also help India overcome the traditional trade-off between growth and the environment. The book discusses asset recycling and value capture finance as additional avenues for sustainable infrastructure financing.

In terms of the enabling environment for infrastructure investment, it is felt that the sanctity of contracts and addressing regulatory risk are crucial. Infrastructure investments are long term and in the nature of sunk costs. Therefore, the sanctity of contracts, which is part of the institutional framework for promoting infrastructure investment, needs to be upheld and authorities should not give in to opportunistic demands aimed at destroying this sanctity. Similarly, India has seen a plethora of infrastructure regulatory institutions in recent times, which, however, have not mitigated regulatory risk much. These issues are discussed at length and with evidence in the book with the objective of mainstreaming them in discussions on infrastructure financing.

The book also looks to contribute to some of the ongoing debates on infrastructure financing in India, including the use of sovereign foreign-currency borrowings for financing infrastructure, the necessary conditions for the success of the fledging development finance institution that India has created recently, a new credit-rating metric for infrastructure projects given that the Loss Given Default in such projects is much lower than that for projects more generally, and the need for creating a 3P India institution on the lines of similar institutions in other major private-infrastructure-promoting countries like the United Kingdom, Australia, and Canada.

In order to make the subject intelligible and evidence-based, the book has twenty case studies and in-depth examples, both Indian and global, illustrating its major conclusions. Apart from helping students of infrastructure and its financing and practitioners in their jobs, we also hope to stimulate research interest in the contemporary infrastructure financing reality and its challenges in India and across the globe. We recognize that the field of infrastructure financing is an evolving one and new knowledge is being created as innovations are tried out around the world. The extent to which this book informs the stakeholders—in government, the private sector, and academia—in making better decisions and encourages further research in infrastructure financing would, therefore, be the litmus test of the value of our efforts.

New Delhi, India

Kumar V Pratap
Manshi Gupta

Acknowledgements

We express our gratitude to several people who helped us shape this book. We apologize in advance to those whom we would doubtless fail to mention despite our best efforts.

We, particularly Dr Pratap, owe a massive debt of gratitude to the late Shri Gajendra Haldea, who kindled in him the love for infrastructure and public–private partnerships that have been the main preoccupations of his life since the time he started working with him. Shri Haldea took great pains to uphold the public interest which has been a model for Dr Pratap and which is also reflected in some of the chapters in the book. Shri Subhash Chandra Garg, the then Finance Secretary and Dr Arvind Subramanian, the then Chief Economic Advisor mentored Dr Pratap in his dream job of Joint Secretary (Infrastructure Policy and Finance), DEA, Ministry of Finance where he worked on financing the National Infrastructure Pipeline, which is the main theme of the current book. Special thanks are also due to Shri Lok Ranjan, Secretary, Ministry of Development of North Eastern Region and Dr Rajesh Chakravarti, Dean, Management Development Institute, Gurgaon for their support. Dr Pratap's association with the Indian Institute of Management IIM Shillong and the Indian School of Business (ISB), Mohali and Hyderabad have helped coalesce the material into its present shape. He would like to thank IIM Shillong and ISB for the opportunity. Dr Pratap would also like to thank the current batch of students at IIM Shillong and the five batches of students at ISB for the questions and discussion that have helped make the arguments in the book more robust.

We would like to acknowledge the extraordinary support we received from Dr T. V. Somanathan, Finance Secretary, Government of India, Marie Lam-Frendo, CEO, G20 Global Infrastructure Hub, Australia, and Sujoy Bose, MD and CEO, National Investment and Infrastructure Fund, India for devoting their time to read parts of the manuscript. We would also like to thank Dr Krishnamurthy Subramanian, former Chief Economic Advisor and currently Executive Director, IMF, for being very generous in the foreword to our book. We are grateful to our colleagues in the government who provided assistance in the form of data and guidance. We would also like to thank our families, who would have missed us for long hours and on holidays, without whose support the book would never have been completed.

Dhiraj Pandey of Oxford University Press shepherded the project in the most encouraging manner.

We alone remain responsible for the errors and shortcomings that we are sure have crept into and remained in the book despite our best efforts. We can only appeal to the readers' indulgence and kind feedback here.

Kumar V Pratap
Manshi Gupta

Contents

Figures

Tables

Boxes

Abbreviations

AAI	Airports Authority of India
ABFL	Aditya Birla Finance Limited
ABS	asset-backed securities
ACI	Airports Council International
ADB	Asian Development Bank
ADIA	Abu Dhabi Investment Authority
ADR	American Depositary Receipts
AERA	Airport Economic Regulatory Authority
AIF	Alternate Investment Fund
AIFI	All India Financial Institution
AIFL	Aseem Infrastructure Finance Limited
AIIB	Asian Infrastructure Investment Bank
ALM	asset–liability mismatch
AMRUT	Atal Mission for Rejuvenation and Urban Transformation
ARI	Asset Recycling Initiative (Australia)
ASEAN + 3 region	ASEAN members plus China, Japan, Republic of Korea
ASQ	Airport Service Quality
AT&C	aggregate technical and commercial (losses)
AUM	assets under management
BAM	brownfield asset monetization
BBNL	Bharat Broadband Network Limited
BE	Budget Estimate
BHEL	Bharat Heavy Electricals Limited
BII	British International Investment
BMRC	Bangalore Metro Rail Corporation
BNDES	Banco Nacional de Desenvolvimento Econômico e Social (Brazil)
BNEF	Bloomberg New Energy Finance
BoB	Bank of Baroda
BOO	Build-Own-Operate
BOOT	Build-Own-Operate-Transfer
BOT	Build-Operate-Transfer
BRICS	Brazil, Russia, India, China, and South Africa
BROT	Build-Rehabilitate-Operate-Transfer
BRSR	Business Responsibility and Sustainability Report
BRT	Bus Rapid Transit

BSE	Bombay Stock Exchange
BTC	Baku-Tbilisi-Ceyhan
CA	Concession Agreemet
CAG	Comptroller and Auditor General
CAGR	compound annual growth rate
CDO	collateralized debt obligation
CE	credit enhancement
CERC	Central Electricity Regulatory Commission
CFA	Central Financial Assistance
CGAM	Core Group of Secretaries on Asset Monetization
CGIF	Credit Guarantee and Investment Facility
CIL	Coal India Limited
CMIE	Centre for Monitoring Indian Economy
CPI	Climate Policy Initiative
CPP	Calling Party Pays
CPPIB	Canada Pension Plan Investment Board
CPSE	central public sector enterprise
CPSU	central public sector undertaking
CRAR	capital to risk (weighted) assets ratio
CRIF	Central Road and Infrastructure Fund
CSO	civil society organization
CWC	Central Warehousing Corporation
CWCNSL	Continental Warehousing Corporation (Nhava Seva) Ltd.
DBFM	Design-Build-Finance-Maintain
DBFOT	Design-Build-Finance-Operate-Transfer
DDP	Designated Depository Participant
DET	Department of Education and Training
DFC	Dedicated Freight Corridor
DFCCIL	Dedicated Freight Corridor Corporation of India Limited
DFI	development finance institution
DIAL	Delhi International Airport Limited
DII	domestic institutional investor
DISCOM	distribution company
DMRC	Delhi Metro Rail Corporation
DNB	Danajamin Nasional Berhad (Malaysia)
DPIIT	Department for Promotion of Industry and Internal Trade
DPR	detailed project report
DSCR	debt service coverage ratio
EC	environmental clearance
ECB	external commercial borrowing
EDFC	Eastern Dedicated Freight Corridor
EESL	Energy Efficiency Services Limited
EIA	Environmental Impact Assessment

EIB	European Investment Bank
EIRR	economic internal rate of return
EL	Expected Loss
EMDE(s)	Emerging Market and Developing Economies
EMP	enhanced monitoring period
EoDB	Ease of Doing Business
EP	Equator Principle
EPC	Engineering-Procurement-Construction
EPE	Eastern Peripheral Expressway
EPF	employee provident fund
EPFO	Employee Provident Fund Organization
ESG	environmental, social, and governance
ETC	electronic toll collection
ETV	Embassy Tech Village
EV	electric vehicle
FAR	floor area ratio
FATF	Financial Action Task Force
FCI	Food Corporation of India
FDI	foreign direct investment
FEM (NDI) Rules	Foreign Exchange Management (Non-Debt Instrument) Rules 2019
FIDIC	International Federation of Consulting Engineers
FII	foreign institutional investor
FIRR	financial internal rate of return
FoF	Fund of Funds
FPE	for-profit enterprises
FPI	foreign portfolio investment
FSB	Financial Stability Board
FSI	Floor Space Index
FY	financial year
G20	Group of Twenty
GAIL	Gas Authority of India Ltd
GB	gigabyte
GBP	Green Bond Principles
GBS	gross budgetary support
GDP	gross domestic product
GDR	Global Depository Receipts
GFANZ	Glasgow Financial Alliance for Net Zero
GGEF	Green Growth Equity Fund
GGR	Gender Gap Report
GIIN	Global Impact Investing Network
GNPA	gross non-performing assets
GoI	Government of India

GP	General Partner
GQ	Golden Quadrilateral
GRESB	Global ESG Benchmark for Real Assets
G Sec	government security
GSM	Global System for Mobile Communications
GST	goods and services tax
GW	gigawatts
HAM	hybrid annuity model
HC	high court
HEFA	Higher Education Funding Agency
HFE	Hero Future Energies
HIPL	Hindustan Infralog Private Limited
HML	Harmonized Master List of Infrastructure Subsectors (India)
HNI	high-net-worth individual
HPCL	Hindustan Petroleum Corporation Limited
HSD	high-speed diesel
HUDCO	Housing and Urban Development Corporation
ICCT	International Council on Clean Transportation
ICE	internal combustion engine
ICMA	International Capital Markets Association
ICR	interest coverage ratio
ICT	information and communication technology
IDBI	Industrial Development Bank of India
IDF	infrastructure debt fund
IDPL	Infrastructure Development Projects Limited (L&T)
IEBR	internal and extra budgetary resources
IECV	initial estimated concession value
IES	Indian Economic Service
IFC	International Finance Corporation
IFC	infrastructure finance company
IFCI	Industrial Finance Corporation of India
IIFCL	India Infrastructure Finance Company Limited
IIG	India Investment Grid
IM	investment manager
IMF	International Monetary Fund
IMM	impact measurement and management
IMSC	Inter-Ministerial Steering Committee
IndAS	Indian Accounting Standards
InvIT	infrastructure investment trust
IOSCO	International Organization of Securities Commissions
IPA	Infrastructure and Projects Authority (United Kingdom)
IPCC	Intergovernmental Panel on Climate Change
IPO	Initial Public Offer

IR	Indian Railways
IRCON	Indian Railway Construction Company
IRCTC	Indian Railway Catering and Tourism Corporation
IRDA	Insurance Regulatory and Development Authority
IREDA	India Renewable Energy Development Agency
IRFC	Indian Railway Finance Corporation
IRGD	interest rate–growth differential
IRIS+	Impact Reporting and Investment Standards
IRSDC	Indian Railway Station Development Corporation
ISP	internet service provider
ISTS	Inter-State Transmission System
ITU	International Telecommunication Union
IUC	interconnection usage charge
JICA	Japan International Cooperation Agency
JNNSM	Jawaharlal Nehru National Solar Mission
JNPT	Jawaharlal Nehru Port Trust
JR	Japan Railway
JVC	joint venture company
KIIFB	Kerala Infrastructure Investment Fund Board
KPI	key performance indicators
KSEB	Kerala State Electricity Board
L&T	Larsen & Toubro
LCR	London and Continental Railways
LCS	Limited Concession Scheme
LFI	lead financial institution
LGD	Loss Given Default
LIBOR	London Inter-Bank Offered Rate
LP	Limited Partner
LPVR	least present value of revenues
MB	megabyte
MCA	Model Concession Agreement
MDB	multilateral development bank
MEIL	Megha Engineering and Infrastructure Ltd
MMRDA	Mumbai Metropolitan Region Development Authority
MNRE	Ministry of New and Renewable Energy
MoEF	Ministry of Environment and Forests
MoR	Ministry of Railways
MoRTH	Ministry of Road Transport and Highways
MPPA	million passengers per annum
MRA	Metro Railway Administration
MRI	magnetic resonance imaging
MRTS	mass rapid transit system
MSRDC	Maharashtra State Road Development Corporation
MSW	municipal solid waste

MTF	Medium-term Framework
MTNL	Mahanagar Telephone Nigam Limited
MTOE	million tonnes of oil equivalent
MTR	mass transit rail
MWCI	Manila Water Co. Inc.
MWSI	Maynilad Water Services Inc.
MWSS	Metropolitan Waterworks and Sewerage System
NABARD	National Bank for Agriculture and Rural Development
NaBFID	National Bank for Financing Infrastructure and Development
NAFED	National Agricultural Cooperative Marketing Federation of India Ltd
NARCL	National Asset Reconstruction Company Limited
NBFC	non-banking financial company
NCEPC	National Committee on Environmental Planning and Coordination
NDB	New Development Bank
NDC	Nationally Determined Contribution
NEMMP	National Electric Mobility Mission Plan
NGFS	Network for Greening the Financial System
NHAI	National Highways Authority of India
NHB	National Housing Bank
NHDP	National Highways Development Program
NIDP	National Infrastructure Delivery Plan (United Kingdom)
NIIF	National Investment and Infrastructure Fund
NIIF IFL	NIIF Infrastructure Finance Limited
NIP	National Infrastructure Pipeline
NMP	National Monetization Pipeline
NPA	non-performing asset
NPO	non-profit organization
NPS	National Pension System
NPV	net present value
NRHM	National Rural Health Mission
NRW	non-revenue water
NSE	National Stock Exchange
NTP	National Telecom Policy
NTPC	National Thermal Power Corporation
NVG	National Voluntary Guidelines
O&M	operation and maintenance
ODA	official development assistance
OMD	Operate–Maintain–Develop
OMDA	operation, management, and development agreement
OMT	Operate-Maintain-Transfer

OTPP	Ontario Teachers' Pension Plan
PAT	perform–achieve–trade
PAT	profit after tax
PBI	Project Bond Initiative
PCE	partial credit enhancement
PCS	public charging station
PD	Probability of Default
PFC	Power Finance Corporation
PFI	private finance initiative
PFP	privately financed project
PFRDA	Pension Fund Regulatory and Development Authority
PGCIL	Power Grid Corporation of India Limited
PIB	Press Information Bureau
PM	project manager
PM-KUSUM	Pradhan Matri Kisan Urja Suraksha Evam Utthaan Mahabhiyan
PPA	power purchase agreement
PPF	Public Provident Fund
PPF	project preparation facility
PPI	Private Participation in Infrastructure
PPP	public–private partnership
PRC	People's Republic of China
PSA	power supply agreement
PSC	public-sector comparator
PSE	public-sector enterprise
PSU	public-sector undertaking
PT SMI	PT Sarana Multi Infrastruktur (Indonesia)
R+P	Rail Plus Property Model
RBI	Reserve Bank of India
RE	renewable energy
REC	Rural Electrification Corporation
REIT	real estate investment trust
RfP	Request for Proposal
RfQ	Request for Qualification
RG	restricted group
RIL	Reliance Industries Limited
RITES	Rail India Technical and Economic Service Limited
RJIL	Reliance Jio India Limited
RLDA	Rail Land Development Authority
RoE	return on equity
ROSCO	Rolling Stock Company
RPO	renewable purchase obligation
SAR	South Asia Region

SBD	standard bidding document
SBI	State Bank of India
SDF	station development fee
SDG	Sustainable Development Goal
SDL	State Development Loan
SE Asia	South-East Asia
SEBI	Securities and Exchange Board of India
SEC	Securities and Exchange Commission
SECI	Solar Energy Corporation of India
SERC	State Electricity Regulatory Commission
SLR	statutory liquidity ratio
SOF	Strategic Opportunities Fund
SPPD	solar power park developer
SPV	special purpose vehicle
SRI	socially responsible investment
SSE	Social Stock Exchange
SWF	sovereign wealth fund
TAMP	Tariff Authority for Major Ports
TCFD	Task Force on Climate-related Financial Disclosure
TCX	Currency Exchange Fund
TIF	tax increment financing
TOC	train operating company
TOD	transit-oriented development
TOT	Toll-Operate-Transfer
TPC	total project cost
TRAI	Telecom Regulatory Authority of India
UDAY	Ujjwal Discom Assurance Yojana
ULB	urban local body
UMPP	ultra-mega power project
UMREPP	ultra-mega renewable energy power park
UNEP FI	United Nations Environment Programme Finance Initiative
UNPRI	United Nations Principles for Responsible Investing
VCF	value capture finance
VGF	viability gap funding
VRR	Voluntary Retention Route
VSNL	Videsh Sanchar Nigam Limited
WCED	World Commission on Economic Development
WDFC	Western Dedicated Freight Corridor
WNS Europe	Western, Northern, and Southern Europe
WPI	Wholesale Price Index
YoY	year-on-year
ZCB	zero coupon bond

About the Authors

Kumar V Pratap is passionate about infrastructure and public–private partnerships. Currently, he is Senior Economic Adviser in the Government of India. Earlier, he has worked with the Prime Minister's Office (as Deputy Secretary) and Ministry of Finance (as Joint Secretary, Infrastructure Policy and Finance) at New Delhi, and the World Bank in Washington, DC.[1]

He has made seminal contributions in formulating the asset monetization policy of the Government of India as well as the 'electronic auction of coal' and the 'competitive bidding of coal blocks' policies. He also contributed extensively to the G20 Principles for Quality Infrastructure Investment adopted by the G20 leaders in 2019.

He was Member Secretary of the task force that prepared India's first National Infrastructure Pipeline. In the past, he was part of the task force for setting up a road regulator, and the Chair of the Committee writing the Model Concession Agreement for PPPs in the Urban Water Supply sector. He led the Indian delegation at the G20 Infrastructure Working Group meetings. He is currently on the Board of Directors of the North Eastern Development Finance Corporation (NEDFi) and was earlier on the Board of Directors of ONGC Videsh Limited, India Infrastructure Finance Company Limited (IIFCL), IRSDC, Indian Railway Finance Corporation, AIIB (Beijing), and New Development Bank (Shanghai).

He has written a book, *PPPs in Infrastructure: Managing the Challenges*, published by Springer (Singapore) in 2018. He has also published with Oxford University Press, the World Bank, University of Melbourne, *Economic and Political Weekly*, SAGE journal *Vikalpa*, and the popular press including *Economic Times*, *Business Standard*, and *Financial Express*.

He was a visiting professor at the Indian School of Business (Hyderabad and Mohali) from 2013 to 2017 teaching a strategy and policy elective on 'Infrastructure and the Private Sector'. He has also lectured at the

---

[1] Views expressed in the book are those of the authors and not of the Government of India.

University of Michigan (Ann Arbor), London School of Economics, Singapore Management University, Lee Kuan Yew School of Public Policy (Singapore), Duke University, University of Maryland, World Bank (Washington, DC), IMF (SARTTAC), Indian Institute of Management (IIM, Ahmedabad), IIM (Lucknow), IIM (Indore), IIM (Shillong), National Academy of Administration (Mussoorie), and National Institute of Public Finance and Policy (Delhi).

He is a recipient of University of Maryland's John J. Sexton and doctoral fellowships, a letter of appreciation from the Indian Prime Minister, the National Talent Search Examination (NTSE) scholarship, the University of Melbourne's Emerging Leaders Fellowship, and the Schulich Business School's (Canada) Sustainable Infrastructure Fellowship.

He has an MBA from IIM, Lucknow (1987) and a PhD from the University of Maryland, College Park, United States (2011).

Manshi Gupta is Deputy Director in the Infrastructure Policy and Planning Division of Department of Economic Affairs, Ministry of Finance. She is a part of Indian delegation at the G20 Infrastructure Working Group meetings under G20 Finance track. She has earlier worked as Assistant Professor in the Department of Economics, Shri Ram College of Commerce, Delhi University. She represented India in the Third Meeting of the Infrastructure Financing and Public–Private Partnership Network of Asia and the Pacific organized by UNESCAP. She has a Master's in economics from the Delhi School of Economics.

Introduction

Infrastructure is critical to a society's growth and development. It pushes the production possibility curve outwards by increasing productivity, facilitates the delivery of public services, enables rapid information-sharing and communication, assists mobility of goods and people, creates opportunities for all segments of society, including unserved and underserved communities, thus enabling inclusive growth. By paving the way for new industries and growth centres to emerge, it is also a crucial aid to structural transformation and export diversification.

Investment in infrastructure has become even more important because of its role in creating jobs, helping address climate change, and aiding countries to recover from the Covid-19 pandemic. Infrastructure has long been underfunded in India and the pressure will grow with climate change and population growth. India spent only 5.6 per cent of her GDP on infrastructure in the period 2010–2015, while fast-growing countries of East Asia in their fast-growing phases have spent around 7–8 per cent of their GDP on infrastructure. India's infrastructure financing landscape continues to lag behind her infrastructure aspirations and needs. India's infrastructure goals are discussed in Chapter 1, which outlines the country's first-ever National Infrastructure Pipeline (NIP, 2020). NIP aims at infrastructure investment of Rs.111 lakh crore (about US$1.5 trillion) in the six-year period from financial year (FY) 2019/20 to FY 2024/25. While the NIP is technically feasible, for NIP targets to actually be realized, would require a number of policy changes, infrastructure reforms, new financial instruments and institutions.

India not only needs new and more efficient infrastructure, but will also require significant investment in existing infrastructure to improve resilience to diverse threats such as pandemics, malicious cyber-attacks and climate change. Chapter 2 looks at sources of infrastructure finance. Because of the fiscal resource crunch accentuated by the high-priority

Infrastructure Financing in India. Kumar V Pratap and Manshi Gupta, Oxford University Press.
© Kumar V Pratap and Manshi Gupta 2024. DOI: 10.1093/oso/9780198884934.003.0001

demands of the Covid-19 pandemic, there is increased reliance on the private sector for infrastructure provisioning, exemplified by the opening up of new sectors to such investment, like railways (railway stations), social infrastructure (health, education, solid waste management, water and wastewater treatment and supply), and even strategic sectors (medical and industrial use of radio isotopes).

Underinvestment in infrastructure in general and social infrastructure in particular is also driven by low user charges. User charges have traditionally been low, especially in publicly provided infrastructure services like water, power, health, and education, and not even enough to recover operation and maintenance (O&M) expenses of infrastructure assets. Reasonable pricing of infrastructure services is essential for their financial viability, the environmental and resource use efficiency of natural resources, and also to promote ownership and accountability, and therefore improve governance, of infrastructure assets. Chapter 3 discusses reasonable user charges for sustainable infrastructure financing.

Chapter 4 discusses the financing of economic and social infrastructure, focussing especially on challenges in financing social infrastructure and the strategies to overcome them. The Manila Water Company case for water supply, and the numerous education and health public–private-partnership (PPP) projects in Australia and the United Kingdom show that private participation in social infrastructure is possible for mutual benefit to the private and public sectors. Impact investment, social stock exchange, and so on, will also play a part in popularizing private investment in social infrastructure.

Too often, infrastructure financing may lack transparency, leading to ill-informed investment decisions, that create unsustainable debt burdens, ultimately threatening economic stability and exacerbating the challenges faced by the vulnerable populations. In India this has been manifested in declining asset quality of infrastructure and the associated problem of non-performing assets (NPAs) in banks. Chapter 5 discusses project finance or non-recourse financing and explains why this is the preferred method for implementing projects by the private sector. It allows companies to raise finances on the basis of the cash flows generated by the project, with no recourse to the balance sheet of the project sponsor. This enables project sponsors to undertake a number of infrastructure projects and accelerate infrastructure investment.

Chapter 6 discusses ways to augment infrastructure financing through innovative strategies like brownfield asset monetization (BAM) and value capture finance. BAM or asset recycling involves unlocking capital through the monetization of de-risked brownfield assets. In this way, BAM can lead to a virtuous cycle that generates resources for more greenfield infrastructure investment. An important policy recommendation for BAM to achieve its objective is that the government should allow transfer of resources garnered through BAM to the same entities that make their assets available for BAM (as opposed to these resources getting into the Consolidated Fund of India). What this means is that if National Highways Authority of India (NHAI) makes its completed road projects available for BAM, the resources so garnered should also go to NHAI for new projects or retiring its debt. This would incentivize BAM. The chapter also gives details of the National Monetization Pipeline (NMP) launched by the Government of India in August 2021. Value capture finance is associated with internalizing the externalities generated by large public investments, like in metro rail, to improve the financial viability of these projects. This chapter also discusses metro rail financing in India and lessons that can be learnt from Hong Kong metro for sustainable financing of metro rail projects.

Banks are the main source of debt finance for private infrastructure projects in India and the world. However, when banks finance infrastructure, they face the associated issue of asset–liability mismatch (ALM) as bank liabilities are short term, while infrastructure assets are of a much longer duration. Chapter 7 discusses how we can move from bank finance to bond finance through credit enhancement and infrastructure debt funds. There is utility in moving from bank financing of infrastructure to bond financing (this will also address the ALM issue), especially after cash flows have stabilized in the operational phase of projects.

Infrastructure financing gap can be closed through increased institutional investment (from pension, insurance, and sovereign wealth funds) into infrastructure. Globally, institutional investors have large assets under management to service their long-term liabilities. They are looking for stable returns over the long term. Hence, institutional investment into infrastructure would align their interests with those of governments without ALM. Chapter 8 discusses this priority of governments the world over to channel institutional investment into infrastructure. However, in the case of India, domestic institutional investors have not been investing much on infrastructure. The chapter will explore the reasons for this, also suggesting policy measures, for domestic institutional investors to invest in infrastructure (as foreign, mainly Canadian pension funds, are major investors in Indian infrastructure). This chapter also discusses the importance of infrastructure projects aligning with the environmental, social, and governance (ESG) norms, increasingly being used by these investors for their investments. Compliance with the ESG norms of institutional investors would not only make infrastructure assets attractive to this class of investors, but also make for more sustainable provisioning of infrastructure. In this context, the chapter discusses the role of India's own sovereign wealth fund, the National Investment and Infrastructure Fund (NIIF), to facilitate such investments.

Key priorities relating to infrastructure in the coming decades would be climate- and disaster-resilient infrastructure, digital connectivity, and gender equity. Economic competitiveness and prosperity will largely be driven by how well countries harness their digital and technology sectors and transition to clean energy to provide environmentally sustainable and inclusive growth for their people. Chapter 9 discusses environmentally and socially responsible infrastructure finance. The chapter expands on the Equator, Carbon, and Climate Principles, and also the green bond, climate bond, and social bond avenues for financing infrastructure projects. This chapter also discusses the perceived trade-off between growth and environment, while deliberating on whether exploitation of renewable energy (through the case study of Solar Energy Corporation of India Ltd.) is the silver bullet that side-steps this trade-off to enable sustainable development. Finally, the chapter elaborates on the large gender gap in infrastructure, which is a major social concern that limits desirable and inclusive outcomes from infrastructure investments.

Infrastructure financing generally implies sunk costs, which increases risks for private investors from arbitrary behaviour by stakeholders. Therefore, it is necessary to preserve sanctity of contracts and also mitigate regulatory risk. These are important prerequisites for sustainable financing of infrastructure projects. Chapter 10 discusses these generic issues for sustainable infrastructure financing. Sanctity of contracts needs to be upheld for assuring a stable institutional framework. This will also enable fairness of outcomes to stakeholders—the government, the private sector, and the users. Allowing post-contract changes in the obligations of the private sector through renegotiation of contracts will promote more aggressive bidding and threaten the private participation in infrastructure regime of the country. The chapter also looks at infrastructure regulation in India to evaluate whether some of the decisions taken by infrastructure regulators are increasing regulatory risk. This discussion leads to a case for other regulatory options like 'regulation by contract' and multi-sectoral regulators, rather than creating independent sectoral regulators for each sector that is opened up for private participation. These will ensure that infrastructure development is carried out in a transparent and sustainable manner to lead to desired outcomes for countries and communities.

The Covid-19 pandemic has highlighted that unequal access to infrastructure has disproportionately affected low- and middle-income households in terms of both lives and livelihoods. Chapter 11 discusses the Covid-19 pandemic and its impact on infrastructure and its financing. Implementation of India's first NIP (2020) has been impacted adversely at least in the first two years (FYs 2020 and 2021) as public sector resources were constrained because of the high-priority expenditures associated with the pandemic and private-sector investments suffered from increased risk. Even after relative normalcy and appearance of infrastructure green shoots in the midst of the pandemic, it is unlikely that the lofty targets of the NIP would be achieved.

The last chapter (Chapter 12) of the book discusses some questions related to infrastructure financing like the need for a new development finance institution (DFI) in India, which has since been set up. India has a long history of DFIs and lending to infrastructure was almost exclusively their preserve. However, an assessment of the performance of these institutions reveals a mixed bag. Due to the ongoing difficulties in infrastructure financing in India, it has been suggested that India needs a new DFI on the lines of BNDES of Brazil and the China Development Bank. The chapter highlights some issues so that the new DFI is able to fulfil its mandate, while also making a reasoned case for strengthening the existing DFIs in the country. The chapter also tries to answer some other pertinent questions such as whether there is a case for sovereign borrowings in foreign currency for infrastructure finance, the need for a new credit-rating system for infrastructure projects, and whether India should have a 3P Institution for shepherding PPPs in the country just like the United Kingdom and Australia.

The book has a policymaker's perspective as the authors have been involved in infrastructure development in India for many years. Therefore, it should be useful for infrastructure finance professionals, private equity firms (who want an insight into government thinking on the future of infrastructure and its financing), policymakers, academicians, and teachers and students (management, infrastructure, and public policy) of infrastructure finance. To make it intelligible and interesting to its varied audience, the book illustrates its conclusions with twenty case studies, based both in India and abroad, emphasizing the universality of the themes that have been discussed.

1

The Context—The National Infrastructure Pipeline

India prepared its first National Infrastructure Pipeline (NIP) in 2020. It aims at infrastructure investment of Rs.111 lakh crore (~US$1.5 trillion) in the six-year period from financial year (FY) 2019/20 to FY 2024/25. This infrastructure investment target was drawn up by collating information about infrastructure plans from twenty-eight central infrastructure ministries/departments, all state governments, and the big private infrastructure companies. The NIP consists of over 6,800 projects, with total project cost of over Rs.100 crore each, and includes projects in both economic (energy, telecom, transport, etc.) and social (health, education, water treatment and supply, solid waste management, etc.) infrastructure. The NIP is technically feasible as infrastructure investments were Rs.51 lakh crore in the previous six years (FY 2013/14 to FY 2018/19) and were growing at a compound annual growth rate (CAGR) of 11 per cent in nominal terms during this period. However, for the NIP to actually be realized, a number of policy changes, infrastructure reforms, new financial instruments and institutions would be required.

Infrastructure investment is crucial for faster, sustainable, and inclusive economic growth. India has been at the forefront in the world in infrastructure spending and has spent an estimated $1.1 trillion on infrastructure in the decade from 2008 to 2017. The actual infrastructure investment in the six-year period from FY[1] 2014 to FY 2019 has been

---

[1] The Indian financial year is from 1 April to 31 March.

Infrastructure Financing in India. Kumar V Pratap and Manshi Gupta, Oxford University Press.
© Kumar V Pratap and Manshi Gupta 2024. DOI: 10.1093/oso/9780198884934.003.0002

estimated at Rs.51 lakh crore[2] (at an average rate of 5.8 per cent of GDP per annum).

Given the close link between infrastructure and growth, to showcase priority projects to be able to attract funding, and to throw light on the coming infrastructure reforms, countries like the United Kingdom (Box 1.1) and Australia (Box 1.2) have crafted national infrastructure plans spread over a number of years. India needed to have a similar national infrastructure plan so that infrastructure did not become a binding constraint to the growth of the Indian economy.

To address this need, the Indian NIP was announced in April 2020. The NIP is the infrastructure plan of India for the six years from FY 2020 to FY 2025, and has been collated for the first time in India. The NIP is whole-of-government exercise to provide world-class infrastructure across the country and improve the quality of life for all citizens. The NIP will improve project preparation, attract investments (both domestic and foreign) into infrastructure, and will be crucial for attaining the target of India becoming a US$5 trillion economy by FY 2025. The NIP will also help India maintain her position as the fastest-growing large economy in the world.

The Indian NIP includes both economic and social infrastructure projects covered in the updated Harmonized Master List of Infrastructure Subsectors (HML) (Box 1.3). Based on infrastructure characteristics like natural monopoly, large capital investment, sunk costs, significant externalities, impossibility of price exclusion, and non-tradability of infrastructure services, India defines infrastructure to include the sectors stated in the HML. There is a defined institutional mechanism to regularly update this list of infrastructure sectors. Inclusion in this list enables the projects in these sectors to obtain priority financing. There is close correspondence of these sectors with the infrastructure sectors covered under the Private Participation in Infrastructure (PPI) database of the World Bank (ppi.worldbank.org), giving legitimacy to the Indian definition of infrastructure.

The NIP has 6,847 projects, with central ministries/departments and entities under them accounting for 4,600 projects while state

---

[2] 'lakh' and 'crore' are Indian measurement units and stand for 100,000 and 100,00,000 respectively. Thus, a crore is equivalent to 100 lakh.

Box 1.1 National Infrastructure Delivery Plan (2016–2021) of the United Kingdom

The publication of the first-ever National Infrastructure Plan (NIP) in October 2010, and subsequent updates, provided an integrated strategy for how the government would plan, prioritize, finance, and deliver critical projects and programmes in key economic and social infrastructure sectors: transport, energy, communications, flood defence, water and waste, and science.[a] In total, more than £0.25 trillion has been invested in UK infrastructure since 2010 (contrast this with India, where US$1.1 trillion has been spent on infrastructure in the decade since 2008, underlining the fact that in developed countries, infrastructure has already been built, while large developing countries like India present unprecedented infrastructure investment opportunities for business). This investment has translated into substantial activity on the ground. Around three thousand individual projects have been completed across the country, including dozens of major road and local transport schemes, improvements to hundreds of rail stations and more than 20 GW of new electricity-generation capacity. Over 3.5 million premises have access to superfast broadband for the first time and over 1,75,000 homes are better protected from floods. Transformational projects such as Crossrail and the Mersey Gateway Bridge are well into construction.

The National Infrastructure Delivery Plan (NIDP), 2016–21 updates and replaces the previous NIP, outlining details of £483 billion of investment in over six hundred infrastructure projects and programmes in all sectors and spread across the United Kingdom (of which £57.6 billion is in social infrastructure), to 2020/21 and beyond. The NIDP sets out what will be built and where, focussing specifically on nearly £300 billion of the pipeline that will be delivered over the five years to 2020/21 (Figure 1.1). The pipeline contains both individual projects over £50 million and programmes over £50 million containing multiple individual projects. This includes over four thousand individual projects when including those grouped within active programmes. The UK government is committed to invest over £100

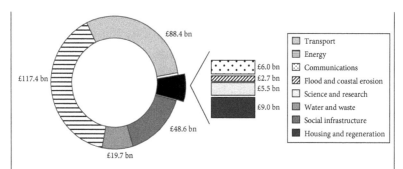

Figure 1.1 UK infrastructure investment by sector, spend from 2016/17 to 2020/21

Source: Infrastructure and Projects Authority, United Kingdom. March 2016. National Infrastructure Delivery Plan.

billion by 2020/21, alongside significant ongoing private-sector investment in UK infrastructure.

The Infrastructure and Projects Authority (IPA) provides annual updates on progress against the NIDP, starting in 2017.

[a]Infrastructure and Projects Authority, United Kingdom. March 2016. *National Infrastructure Delivery Plan* (https://assets.publishing.service.gov.uk/government/uploads/system/uploads/attachment_data/file/520086/2904569_nidp_deliveryplan.pdf)

governments account for the balance of 2,247 projects. The projects to be implemented by the centre and the states include public–private partnership (PPP) projects. The sector-wise breakup of projects (including schemes) in the NIP is at Table 1.1 below.

Stage of implementation: Out of the total expected capital expenditure of Rs.111 lakh crore, projects worth Rs.44 lakh crore (40 per cent of NIP) are under implementation, projects worth Rs.33 lakh crore (30 per cent) are at the concept stage, projects worth Rs.22 lakh crore (20 per cent) are under development (project identified and DPR prepared, but yet to achieve financial closure), and the balance projects worth Rs.11 lakh crore (10 per cent) are uncategorized (Figure 1.2).

The NIP has been hosted on a digital platform (India Investment Grid, IIG). This has provided greater visibility to the NIP and would help in its financing with prospective investors, both domestic and foreign, able to access updated project level information.

Box 1.2 Australian Infrastructure Plan (2016–2031)

Infrastructure Australia has been given the responsibility to develop fifteen-year rolling infrastructure plans. The 2016–31 Plan[a] lays out a comprehensive *package of reforms* focussed on improving the way Australia invests in, delivers, and uses its infrastructure. The reforms in the Plan are guided by four headline aspirations: productive cities, productive regions; efficient infrastructure markets; sustainable and equitable infrastructure; and better decisions and better delivery. The result is a long-term strategy that lays the foundation for a more productive Australia over the coming fifteen years and beyond.

Building and enhancing Australian infrastructure to meet the challenges of growth over the next fifteen years will require more funding, from both taxpayers and users. The balance between what users and taxpayers pay will also need to be fairer, recognizing that those who benefit the most—the users of infrastructure—should make a greater contribution (we discuss this issue in Chapter 3 in the Indian context). In most cases, including public transport, users should fund the greatest possible proportion of costs, freeing up taxpayer dollars to invest in other priorities like social services, health, and education. Government should also routinely consider land value capture (we discuss this issue in Chapter 6 in the Indian context) in public infrastructure investments.

While the benefits of reform will be experienced by all Australians, most changes will be required at the state, territory, and local government levels. The Australian Government should show the way by leveraging its investment in infrastructure to drive the delivery of the reforms and priorities in the Australian Infrastructure Plan.

The Plan has been updated to 2021–2036 with the same theme as the 2016–2031 Plan, after taking into account new realities. The 2021 Australian Infrastructure Plan is a practical and actionable roadmap for infrastructure reform. It is intended to deliver infrastructure for a stronger Australia, and support national recovery from the still-unfolding Covid-19 pandemic, as well as the bushfires, drought, floods, and cyber-attacks that have tested infrastructure resilience in recent years.

Source: Infrastructure Australia, Government of Australia[b] (2016 and 2021)

[a]Infrastructure Australia, Government of Australia. February 2016. *Australian Infrastructure Plan* (https://www.infrastructureaustralia.gov.au/sites/default/files/2019-06/Australian_Infrastructure_Plan.pdf).

[b]Infrastructure Australia, Government of Australia. February 2016. *Australian Infrastructure Plan* (https://www.infrastructureaustralia.gov.au/sites/default/files/2019-06/Australian_Infrastructure_Plan.pdf); Infrastructure Australia. August 2021. *Reforms to Meet Australia's Future Infrastructure Needs—2021 Australian Infrastructure Plan* (https://www.infrastructureaustralia.gov.au/sites/default/files/2021-09/Exec%20Summary%20%28standalone%29.pdf).

Box 1.3 Updated Harmonized Master List of Infrastructure Subsectors

Sl.No.	Category	Infrastructure subsectors
1.	Transport and logistics	• Roads and bridges • Ports • Shipyards • Inland waterways • Airports • Railway track including electrical and signalling system, tunnels, viaducts, bridges • Railway rolling stock along with workshop and associated maintenance facilities • Railway terminal infrastructure including stations and adjoining commercial infrastructure • Urban public transport (except rolling stock in the case of urban road transport) • Logistics infrastructure • Bulk material transportation pipelines

Sl.No.	Category	Infrastructure subsectors
2.	Energy	• Electricity generation • Electricity transmission • Electricity distribution • Oil/Gas/Liquefied natural gas (LNG) storage facility • Energy Storage Systems (ESS)*
3.	Water and sanitation	• Solid waste management • Water treatment plants • Sewage collection, treatment, and disposal system • Irrigation (dams, channels, embankments, etc.) • Storm-water drainage system
4.	Communication	• Telecommunication (fixed network) • Telecommunication towers • Telecommunication and telecom services • Data centres*
5.	Social and commercial infrastructure	• Education institutions (capital stock) • Sports infrastructure • Hospitals (capital stock) • Tourism infrastructure viz., (i) three-star or higher category classified hotels located outside cities with a population of more than 1 million (ii) ropeways and cable cars • Common infrastructure for industrial parks and other parks with industrial activity such as food parks, textile parks, special economic zones, tourism facilities, and agriculture markets • Post-harvest storage infrastructure for agriculture and horticultural produce including cold storage

Sl.No. Category	Infrastructure subsectors
	• Terminal markets
	• Soil-testing laboratories
	• Cold chain
	• Affordable housing
	• Affordable rental housing complex
	• Exhibition-cum-Convention centre

Note: *added via official notification dated 11 October 2022.

Source: Ministry of Finance. 2021. *Updated Harmonized Master List of Infrastructure Subsectors.*[a]

[a]*Ministry* of Finance. 2021. *Updated Harmonized Master List of Infrastructure Subsectors* (https://dea.gov.in/sites/default/files/updated%20%20Harmonized%20Master%20%20L ist%20%20of%20%20Infrastructure%20%20Sub-sectors%20dated%2024-8-2020_1.pdf)

Financing the NIP

The indicative financing plan of the NIP is shown in Tables 1.2 and 1.3.

Tables 1.2 and 1.3 show the range of financing by various sources, given the available fiscal space, and the past trends in the growth of these sources. By the very nature of the exercise, the financing, by source, has been shown in terms of interval estimates. Tables 1.2 and 1.3 also show that, as per estimates, there would be a shortfall in financing the NIP to the extent of 8–10 per cent of Rs.111 lakh crore over the period FY 2020–FY 2025. This shortfall will have to be met from new and innovative financial instruments, and other methods for which a separate Inter-Ministerial Steering Committee (IMSC) on Financing of NIP, seated in DEA, has been set up.

Figure 1.3 shows the breakup of contribution from centre, states, and the private sector in financing NIP projects. About 79 per cent of the NIP would be financed by the centre and states (and their public-sector enterprise (PSEs)), while the balance of 21 per cent would be financed by the private sector. The percentage contribution of the private sector to infrastructure financing has come down, partly reflecting the increased risky environment because of Covid-19.

Table 1.1 Sector-wise breakup of the National Infrastructure Pipeline

Ministry/Department	Number of projects	FY 2020–2025 (amount in Rs. crore)
Power	189	14,10,428
Renewable energy	4	9,29,500
Atomic energy	7	1,55,503
Petroleum and natural gas	166	1,94,572
Total energy	366	26,90,003
Roads	2,478	20,33,823
Railways	732	13,67,563
Ports	110	1,21,194
Airports	83	1,43,448
Total transport	3,403	36,66,028
Water and sanitation	10	3,62,960
Irrigation	556	8,94,473
Rural infrastructure	2	4,10,955
Total water and rural infrastructure	568	16,68,388
Agriculture infrastructure	74	1,62,472
Food processing industries	16	1,255
Food and public distribution		5,000
Total agriculture and food processing infrastructure	90	1,68,727
Urban	1,688	19,19,267
Higher education	263	1,75,729
School education		37,791
Health and family welfare	221	1,51,019
Sports	41	9,069
Tourism	34	19,777
Total social infrastructure	2,247	23,12,652
Industries and internal trade	144	3,06,732
Steel	4	8,225
Total industrial infrastructure	148	3,14,957
Digital infrastructure	25	3,09,672
Total	6,847	1,11,30,428

Source: Ministry of Finance, Government of India. 2020. *Report of the Task Force on National Infrastructure Pipeline.*

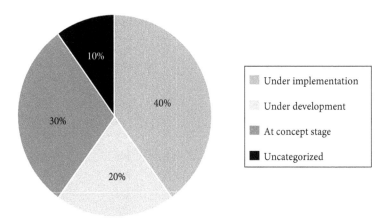

Figure 1.2 NIP by stage of implementation

Source: Ministry of Finance, Government of India (2020). *Report of the Task Force on National Infrastructure Pipeline.*

As to the mode of implementation of the NIP, a major part of the capital expenditure is expected to be implemented through the Engineering-Procurement-Construction (EPC) mode. Preponderance of EPC in the implementation mix renders realization of the NIP critically dependent on the state of government finances, which are currently stretched because of the demands of Covid-19.

Suggested Reforms

The NIP has also given recommendations on required changes to several key sectoral policies and other reform initiatives as summarized below.

General reforms

Contracting

i. *Sanctity of contracts*: As per the World Bank's 2020 *Doing Business Report*, though the country's overall rank has improved to sixty-three, India is ranked 163 out of 190 countries on enforcing contracts (the worst among the ten parameters used to rank countries).

Table 1.2 Indicative financing plan of the NIP

Total projected infrastructure investment during the period FY 2020 to FY 2025 is Rs.1,11,30,428 crore (or ~US$1.5 trillion)

Source of funds	Assumptions used in projections	Share of NIP being financed
Centre's budget	Centre's budgetary outlay on capital investments is expected to be around 1.25% of GDP	18–20%
States' budget	States' budgetary outlay on capital investments is expected to be around 1.7% of GDP	24–26%
Internal accruals of PSUs	Projected to suffice for the funding requirements of NIP	1–3%
Banks	Expected to grow at the rate of 8%	8–10%
Infrastructure NBFCs (PFC, REC, IRFC, IREDA, IIFCL, and private-sector NBFCs)	Expected to grow at an average rate of 12% for public-sector NBFCs and 15% for private-sector NBFCs	15–17%
Bond markets	Expected to grow at an average rate of 8%	6–8%
Equity	Expected to grow at an average rate of 15%, due to NIIF stepping up pace of investments	2–4%
Multilaterals/ Bilaterals	Expected to constitute half of the external aid flows	1–3%
Others		3–5%
Total		83–85%

Note: Numbers may not add up due to rounding off.

Source: Ministry of Finance, Government of India. 2020. *Report of the Task Force on National Infrastructure Pipeline.*

It is otherwise also recognized that contracts need to be honoured, and therefore, sanctity of contracts needs to be upheld by both the public and the private sectors. In case parties renege, there should be adequate safeguards for other stakeholders.

ii. *Land acquisition and other required clearances*: One of the most important causes of construction risk (risk of time and cost overrun) in projects is delays in land acquisition and key clearances like environment and forest clearance. Therefore, the NIP Task Force has recommended that at least 90 per cent of the required land should

Table 1.3 Bridging the financing gap

Particulars	Share of NIP being financed (in %)
NIP required outlay – (A)	1,11,30,428 crore
Total sources of financing– (B)	83–85
Financing gap – (C) = A–B	15–17
Bridging the gap – (D) = (a)+(b)+(c)	6–8
From new DFI – (a)	2–3
Asset monetization—centre – (b)	2–3
Asset monetization—states – (c)	1–2
Shortfall—E = (C)–(D)	8–10

Note: Numbers may not add up due to rounding off.

Source: Ministry of Finance, Government of India. 2020. *Report of the Task Force on National Infrastructure Pipeline.*

be available with the authority before bidding and all applicable clearances need to be available before project award.

iii. *Equitable risk allocation among stakeholders*: PPP contracts should have optimal risk allocation and should allocate risk to the entity best suited to manage it. In this regard, the International Federation of Consulting Engineers (FIDIC) contracts can be adapted for India.

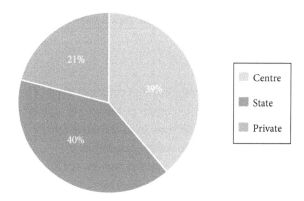

Figure 1.3 Share of centre, states, and private sector in financing NIP projects

Source: Ministry of Finance, Government of India. 2020. *Report of the Task Force on National Infrastructure Pipeline.*

Dispute resolution

i. *Improving arbitration framework*: Challenging arbitration awards should be made very selective and the approved policy of paying 75 per cent of the challenged arbitration award to the private party needs to be enforced. In case the challenged award is decided in favour of the public party, the payment of 75 per cent of the challenged arbitration award to the private party would be reversed.

ii. *Designating courts for trying infrastructure disputes*: Under the Specific Relief (Amendment) Act, 2018, there is a provision about designating courts for trying infrastructure disputes. So far twenty-two of the twenty-five high courts (HCs) in the country have operationalized designated fast-track courts to adjudicate disputes related to infrastructure contracts. Some special courts of Madhya Pradesh, Allahabad, Karnataka, and Kolkata, within the jurisdiction of the respective HCs, have even fixed special days every week for exclusive handling of relief matters pertaining to infrastructure project contracts. The balance HCs should also designate courts for trying infrastructure disputes.

Improving infrastructure financing

i. *Bond financing*: There is a need to move at least some debt financing of infrastructure from banks to the capital markets. One suggested initiative in this regard is the setting up of a dedicated credit enhancement company to raise the credit rating of bonds floated by infrastructure companies. The investment guidelines of pension funds and insurance companies also need to be streamlined to enable infrastructure investment through project bonds and infrastructure investment trusts (InvITs).

ii. *Asset monetization*: New and innovative financial instruments have been launched in India in the last few years like InvITs, real estate investment trusts (REITs) as well as models like Toll-Operate-Transfer (TOT) as part of the brownfield asset monetization strategy for augmenting infrastructure investment. India has had a fair bit of success in brownfield asset monetization with fifteen InvITs and three REITs having already been launched in the country, and six TOT transactions being carried out. The cumulative resources garnered through these instruments and models is about Rs.1,67,000 crore. There is a need to replicate the success of these models across infrastructure sectors like roads, ports, airports, power transmission, gas and oil pipelines, renewable energy, and so on to add to infrastructure financing resources.

iii. *Value capture finance (VCF)*: VCF is aimed at internalizing the externalities generated by large public projects for increased infrastructure financing. For example, for metro-rail projects, there is a need to claw back some of the unearned gains to property owners after the project has been implemented, through sharing mechanism between the project sponsors and the urban local bodies (who benefit from increased property taxes). This will improve the financial viability of such projects.

Governance structure

The NIP also suggests establishment of a robust project governance structure to ensure faster decision-making, improved procurement processes, strengthened contract management, and quick resolution of issues, to ensure timely and within-cost project implementation.

Implementing the NIP

The NIP is a six year (FY2020–FY2025) infrastructure investment plan of Rs.111 lakh crore. India spent about Rs.51 lakh crore on infrastructure in the previous six years (FY2014 –FY2019) at a nominal rate of growth 11 per cent per annum. If this rate of growth is projected over the NIP period, we would arrive at about the same shortfall in resources (8–10 per cent of NIP) as projected in Table 1.3 for implementing the NIP.

The NIP has many transformational projects (see Box 1.4 for one such project). India, in the past, has implemented many transformational initiatives like the Golden Quadrilateral project (Box 1.5) and telecom reforms (Box 1.6), which led to a temporary rise in the debt to GDP ratio, but both the growth rate and the debt to GDP ratio normalized a few years later. It is felt that implementation of the NIP in India would have a similar upsurge in the growth rate of the Indian economy. This is in

Box 1.4 Case Study: Indian Railways—dedicated freight corridors

Indian Railways through a special purpose vehicle—Dedicated Freight Corridor Corporation of India Limited-has sanctioned two dedicated freight corridors (DFCs), namely the Western DFC from Jawaharlal Nehru Port Trust to Rewari (1,504 km) and the Eastern DFC from Ludhiana to Sonnagar (1,318 km) at an estimated cost of Rs.1.24 trillion. The corridors are expected to be commissioned by 2023 (EDFC) and 2024 (WDFC) after missing five completion deadlines owing to land acquisition and contract-awarding lags. So far, 1,010 km of the proposed 2,822 km has been commissioned. Once built, the corridors are expected to help the railways regain market share of freight transport by creating additional capacity and guaranteeing efficient, reliable, and cheap freight transport to consumers. The running of the planned double-stack container trains and heavy-haul trains will further augment the carrying capacity and help reduce the unit cost of freight transportation in particular and logistics costs in general. It will also support industrial zones along the route, free up existing tracks for passenger trains, and move the country onto a greener growth path.

The electrified railway line will allow freight trains to travel about three times faster (from 25 km to 70 km per hour) while pulling heavier loads. The quicker, cheaper, and more reliable movement of goods will contribute to reducing India's inordinately high logistics costs (from about 14 per cent of GDP to the target of 8 per cent, bringing it more in line with global standards) and help bind the country into a single market. The corridor will also drive the establishment of industrial zones at junction points along the way, breathing new energy into one of India's poorest, most densely populated, and least industrialized regions. At the same time, moving freight onto a different track will free up existing railway lines, improving the speed and reliability of passenger trains on high-demand routes. This pioneering initiative will be a game changer for India's transport sector, moving India onto a greener growth path (moving freight by rail is far quicker, cheaper, and greener than sending it by road; moving from diesel-operated trucks to electrified rail, together with the shift from older railway lines to the energy-efficient corridor, will reduce India's fossil-fuel consumption and lower its carbon footprint). With state-of-the-art technology, DFCs have the potential to make India a front-runner in rail freight operations, boosting the competitive edge of its manufacturers and producers.[a]

A section of EDFC from Sonnagar to Dankuni (538 km) is to be implemented through the public–private partnership (PPP) mode at an estimated cost of Rs.19,200 crore. Indian Railways is also planning to undertake four other DFCs: East–West corridor between Mumbai and Kolkata (2,230 km), North–South corridor between Delhi and Chennai (2,343 km), East Coast corridor between Kharagpur and Vijayawada (1,100 km), and South corridor between Chennai and Goa (899 km) at an aggregate estimated cost of Rs.3 lakh crore by FY2030.

A cumulative amount of Rs.1.7 lakh crore is expected to be spent over FY2020 to FY2025 for commissioning the EDFC and WDFC and starting construction on East–West, North–South, East Coast, and South corridors.

[a]World Bank. 2021. *India Takes a Quantum Leap in Building New Freight Corridors.* (https://www.worldbank.org/en/news/feature/2021/01/12/india-takes-a-quantum-leap-in-building-new-freight-corridors?cid=SHR_SitesShareLI_EN_EXT).

consonance with the findings of Walsh et al.[3] that there is no empirical evidence that rapid infrastructure growth would undermine contemporary macroeconomic performance, implying that room is created to accommodate infrastructure booms without compromising fiscal and external sustainability.

Debt-financed Infrastructure, Fiscal Sustainability, and Growth Rate

We find that GDP growth rates in India have been higher than the prevailing interest rates over the last two and a half decades.[4] This has

---

[3] James P. Walsh, Chanho Park, and Jiangyan Yu. 2011. *Financing Infrastructure in India: Macroeconomic Lessons and Emerging Market Case Studies.*

[4] Ministry of Finance, Government of India. 2021. *Economic Survey 2020–21.*

resulted in a negative interest rate–growth differential (IRGD) in India. As advocated by Blanchard,[5] 'If the interest rate paid by the government is less than the growth rate, then the intertemporal budget constraint facing the government no longer binds.' Hence, a negative IRGD (not due to lower interest rates but much higher growth rates) has kept Indian public debt at a sustainable level. Since the fiscal multipliers are more effective during recession, there is the rationale for undertaking debt-financed public expenditure for subsequent higher growth.

India witnessed a low-growth phase during 2000–2001 (Figure 1.4). However, an expansionary fiscal policy that focussed on infrastructure spending (especially the infra push of Golden Quadrilateral project, Box 1.5), reforms (including telecom reforms, Box 1.6), Bharatmala Pariyojana (umbrella programme for the highways sector that envisages

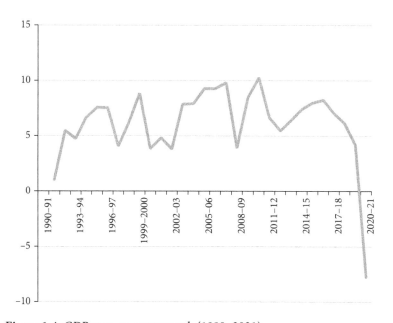

Figure 1.4 GDP year-on-year growth (1990–2021)
Source: Government of India, Ministry of Finance. Economic Survey (various years).

[5] Olivier Blanchard. 2019. *Public Debt and Low Interest Rates.* (https://www.piie.com/commentary/speeches-papers/public-debt-and-low-interest-rates).

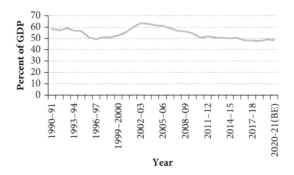

Figure 1.5 Central government's outstanding liabilities (as % of GDP)
Source: Government of India, Ministry of Finance. *Economic Survey* (various years).

Box 1.5 The Golden Quadrilateral project

Roads are the generally preferred mode of transport in India with about 90 per cent share of the total passenger traffic and 67 per cent of freight traffic. The National Highways Authority of India (NHAI), constituted in 1988, has responsibility for developing national highways in the country including the Golden Quadrilateral (GQ) project. GQ, Phase I of the National Highways Development Program (NHDP), involved connecting four major metropolitan cities, namely, Delhi–Mumbai–Chennai–Kolkata with four- and six-lane highways, totalling 5,846 km of road at a cost of Rs.25,055 crore (at 2000 prices). GQ was planned in 1999, launched in 2001, and was largely completed by 2013.

GQ's prime focus[a] is on developing international standard roads with facilities for uninterrupted flow of traffic with enhanced safety features, better riding surface, better road geometry, better traffic management and noticeable signage, divided carriageways and service roads, grade separators, over bridges, underpasses, and bypasses, and wayside amenities.

The advantages of having a well-developed network of world class highways, for a nation like India, poised to surge ahead, are: savings in vehicle operating costs, faster and comfortable journeys, reduced fuel consumption and maintenance costs leading to lower logistic costs, safer travel, benefits to trade especially in the movement of perishable material, impetus to industrial growth and employment in smaller towns, creating demand for other related sectors like cement, steel, and other construction materials through backward and forward linkages, and all-round development of areas.

Ghani et al. (2012)[b] point out the positive impact of the GQ project on the organized manufacturing sector, stating that: 'Districts that lie zero to 10 km from the GQ network experienced substantial increases in entry levels and higher productivity ... For instance, Surat in Gujarat or Srikakulam in Andhra Pradesh, which lie on the GQ, registered more than 100 per cent increase in new output and new establishment counts after GQ upgrades.' In fact, GQ resulted in very large private investments in highways, which was instrumental in lifting the economy out of recession from 2003/04 onwards.[c]

[a]Press Information Bureau, 28 November 2001, *Golden Quadrilateral Project.*

[b]Ejaz Ghani, Arti Grover Goswami, and William R. Kerr. November 2012. *Highway to Success: The Impact of the Golden Quadrilateral Project for the Location and Performance of Indian Manufacturing* (https://academic.oup.com/ej/article/126/591/317/5077429).

[c]Sebastian Morris. 2019. *The Problem of Financing Private Infrastructure in India Today.*

building more than 80,000 km of roads, bridges, highways, and greenfield expressways), Sagarmala programme (port modernization and new port development, port-linked industrialization, port connectivity enhancement, and coastal community development), and multi-modal logistics parks (hubs for freight movement enabling freight aggregation, distribution, and multi-modal transportation) led to higher growth in subsequent years (Figure 1.4) leading to lower debt to GDP ratio (Figure 1.5). Therefore, public debt, effectively utilized, can result in a higher growth trajectory, which ensures debt sustainability.

Implementation of the NIP in the First Three Years (until 2022)

The NIP was launched with 6,847 projects and has expanded to include over 9,300 projects across thirty-five subsectors with commensurate increase in the total project cost (Rs.142 trillion). Out of this, 795 projects

Box 1.6 Telecom reforms in India

The Indian telecom reform process[a] began with the entry in 1984 of private players in manufacturing of customer premise equipment and corporatization of domestic telecom operations in two metros: Delhi and Mumbai—through Mahanagar Telecom Nigam Limited, followed by the establishment of a corporation for international services in 1986 (Videsh Sanchar Nigam Limited, VSNL) and of the Telecom Commission with full government powers in 1989.

National Telecom Policy (NTP), 1994, for the first time, allowed private companies registered in India to participate in provision of basic telephone services, establishing a duopoly regime providing for two operators each in the four metros and the eighteen telecom circles. The duopoly regime that it established implied continued dominance of the market by the incumbent government operator, which inhibited growth of a competitive environment.

Subsequently, there was gradual liberalization of the telecom regime.[b] The period between 1994 and 2000 was marked by supply constraint, emanating from the duopolistic market with technology (GSM) defined by the regulator. There was huge demand for telecom services during this period with a long waiting list. NTP (1999) further liberalized the scope of cellular mobile services, fixed service and cable service. The policy unequivocally asserted that interconnection will be permitted between service providers in the mobile and basic service segments. Free entry into basic telecommunications replaced duopoly. The NTP (1999) also sought convergence of markets and technologies and permitted foreign ownership of up to 49 per cent in a telecom venture. Post-NTP (1999), the sector moved from the fixed license fee model to a revenue share model, boosting private participation in the sector. The period from 2001 to 2007 saw the result of a forward looking NTP (1999) where competition opened up with entry of new players and there was a dramatic decline in tariffs leading to significant rise in mobile subscribers. As Indian telecom transitioned from duopoly to multi-player competition and mobile penetration increased, the tariffs kept declining and handsets including feature phones and smart phones became cheaper and affordable.

Tariff trends:[c] Declining tariffs over the years has been the key enabler for the rapid and widespread adoption of voice services. In 1997, per minute call charges for local calls were Rs.16.80, which came down to nil post-2016. A number of significant developments contributed to the declining tariffs over the years—forbearance from regulating tariffs for cellular mobile services announced in 2002; Interconnection Usage Charge (IUC) regulations and introduction of the Calling Party Pays (CPP) regime during 2004; introduction of Unified Access Licensing regime in 2005; and introduction of lifetime schemes in 2006. An ITU report in 2013 found that telecom tariffs in India are the lowest in the world, with subscribers paying less than users in the US, Australia, and China.

Trends in internet services:[d] The internet services landscape in India has witnessed tremendous changes since 1995 when internet services were first launched in the country. In 1995, the public sector VSNL became the first commercial internet service provider (ISP) offering public internet services in India. In 1998, the Government opened up the sector to private participants, ending the monopoly that was enjoyed by public-sector companies in this segment. There was substantial decline in data tariffs, which enabled a corresponding increase in internet data usage. For GSM service, while the data tariffs went down from Rs.0.29 per MB to Rs.0.16 per MB from December 2013 to 2016, the monthly data usage per subscriber during the same period increased from 50 MB to 884 MB. The huge jump in data usage from June 2016 onwards was mainly on account of the entry of a new player (Reliance Jio India Limited, RJIL), which disrupted the telecom market with ultra-low tariffs, both for voice and data. The liberalization of the ISP regime in 1998, with no license fee, no entry fee, liberal roll-out obligations and no cap on the number of ISPs in a license area, enabled this transition, finally culminating in the disruption of the telecom market by RJIL.

Market disrupter—Reliance Jio: 'Disruption' is a process whereby a new company (entrant) is able to successfully challenge established incumbent businesses. Christensen's theory of 'disruptive innovation,'[e] propounds that the entrant targets the unmet needs of the market segment not catered to by established businesses. The entrant also provides associated benefits like simpler and cheaper products. Therefore, disruptive innovation dramatically alters the industry structure. In the case of India, this is exemplified by RJIL which introduced its services in 2016. The company targeted the young population with maximum usage of mobile services and highly price-elastic demand. It focussed on process innovation, product and service innovation, and business model innovation that has shifted from voice to data and provided cheap unlimited data and free voice calls initially. This unleashed a tariff war in the country and shrank the telecom space from a dozen players to three private-sector operators as others exited, merged, or went bankrupt. This aggressive pricing strategy followed by RJIL has altered market shares considerably. In the wireless service market, RJIL's share has increased from 9 per cent (as of 31 March 2017) to 33 per cent (as of 31 March 2020). Corresponding figures for Vodafone and Idea (merged) are 35 per cent and 28 per cent, respectively. Airtel has, however, witnessed a slight increase in market share from 23 per cent to 28 per cent over this period mainly due to merger (Telenor merged with Bharti Airtel on 14 May 2018).[f] Data usage has also increased unprecedently. Average wireless data usage per wireless data subscriber per month has increased to 11 GB (as of 31 March 2020) with a significant decline in data tariffs. The average data tariff reduced to Rs.11.23 per GB as of 31 March 2020.[g] Hence, the entry of Reliance Jio in the Indian telecom market immensely benefitted consumers.

[a]R. U. S. Prasad. 2008. *The Impact of Policy and Regulatory Decisions on Telecom Growth in India.*

[b]India Infoline. 2016. *Impact of the Telecom Sector in the Year 2015 and the Year ahead* (https://www.indiainfoline.com/article/news-top-story/impact-of-the-telecom-sector-in-the-year-2015-and-the-year-ahead-116010400208_1.html).

[c]Telecom Regulatory Authority of India (TRAI). 2017. *A Twenty Year Odyssey 1997–2017* (https://trai.gov.in/sites/default/files/A_TwentyYear_Odyssey_1997_2017.pdf).

[d]Telecom Regulatory Authority of India (TRAI). 2017. *A Twenty Year Odyssey 1997–2017* (https://trai.gov.in/sites/default/files/A_TwentyYear_Odyssey_1997_2017.pdf).

[e]Clayton M. Christensen, Michael E. Raynor and Rory McDonald. 2015. *What Is Disruptive Innovation?* (https://hbr.org/2015/12/what-is-disruptive-innovation).

[f]Telecom Regulatory Authority of India (TRAI). *Annual Report* (various years).

[g]Department of Telecommunications, Government of India. 2020. *Annual Report 2019–20.*

Table 1.4 Sectoral breakup of NIP and completed projects

Sector	No. of projects	Total project cost (Rs. crore)	Projects Completed	Cost of completed projects (Rs. crore)
Commercial infrastructure	609	6,14,699	76	10,902
Communication	30	1,11,232	1	62,173
Energy	685	29,73,639	104	1,93,866
Logistics	154	3,66,560	15	28,835
Social infrastructure	1,728	20,08,812	128	8,927
Transport	4,661	59,81,169	339	1,66,453
Water and sanitation	1,482	21,80,637	132	69,204
Total	9,349	1,42,36,748	795	5,40,360

Source: India Investment Grid (IIG). (https://indiainvestmentgrid.gov.in/opportunities/nip-projects) (viewed 6 July 2022).

worth Rs.5.4 trillion have been completed. The sectoral breakup of the current version of NIP and completed projects is given in Table 1.4.

Analysis of IIG data shows that an abysmal 8.5 per cent of the total number of NIP projects had been completed by the end of June 2022, representing about 3.8 per cent of the NIP total project cost. Approximately 40 per cent of the projects are in either the planning stage or yet to be awarded. While part of the reason for this low percentage of projects being completed is the several Covid-19 waves that have buffeted the country, this also points towards the need for more efforts in project preparation, arranging the finances, and timely implementation of projects. It also shows that with over half of the NIP period (FY2020 to FY2025) already over, NIP targets may not be attained even with increased efforts at project implementation.

However, two institutional initiatives have been taken recently that may help faster implementation of the NIP: the National Bank for Financing Infrastructure and Development has been set up (details in Chapter 12); and the National Monetization Pipeline was announced in 2021 (details in Chapter 6).

2

Sources of Infrastructure Finance

There are four main sources of infrastructure finance, namely gross budgetary support (GBS, direct budgetary support, dedicated funds), internal and extra budgetary resources (IEBR, retained earnings, bank credit, and bonds) of the public sector, multilateral and bilateral loans, and private investment (sponsor equity, bank credit, bonds, etc.). Many of these sources are especially constrained in the current times because of the high-priority demands of the Covid-19 pandemic (e.g., high fiscal deficit is preventing high levels of gross budgetary support to infrastructure). Traditionally, retained earnings of the public sector have also been limited because of agency problems as well as the constant pressure from the government (as the primary shareholder) to provide dividends. Therefore, there is increased reliance on the private sector for infrastructure provisioning. Given that private investment contributed about a third to infrastructure investments in the last decade, it is expected that it will contribute a high proportion to total infrastructure investment in the years ahead. To enable this, the Government of India is opening up new sectors to private investment, mainly railways (railway stations, passenger trains), social infrastructure (health, education, solid waste management, water and waste-water treatment and supply), and even strategic sectors (medical and industrial use of radio isotopes).

Infrastructure is capital-intensive, complicated, time-consuming to develop, involves multiple stakeholders and has challenging environmental, social, and governance (ESG) issues that need to be addressed. But, infrastructure needs to be provided for growth and making this growth inclusive, leading to development. The utility of infrastructure investment is well established for growing out of crises (like the one engendered by the current Covid-19 pandemic) for economic recovery, job creation, poverty reduction, and for stimulating productive investment.

Infrastructure Financing in India. Kumar V Pratap and Manshi Gupta, Oxford University Press.
© Kumar V Pratap and Manshi Gupta 2024. DOI: 10.1093/oso/9780198884934.003.0003

How Much Should India Be Spending on Infrastructure?

There is one estimate of how much India should be spending on infrastructure that we saw in Chapter 1, emanating from the National Infrastructure Pipeline (NIP). As per this estimate, India should be spending about US$1.5 trillion (Rs.111 trillion) on infrastructure in the six-year period up to 2024/25, or an average of US$250 billion per annum. With a GDP of about US$2.8 trillion in financial year (FY) 2019/20, this comes to over 8 per cent of GDP to be spent on infrastructure per annum. The Growth Report of the World Bank finds that fast-growing countries of East Asia in their fast-growing phases have spent about 7–8 per cent of their GDP on infrastructure.[1] The report also says that history suggests this is the right order of magnitude for high and sustained growth, although it is difficult to be precise. The third estimate of how much India should be spending on infrastructure is presented below (McKinsey, 6.3 per cent of GDP), taking into account both the need and the efficiency of infrastructure investments. All three estimates suggest that India should be spending more on infrastructure than it is spending at present, which is about Rs.10 trillion (or about US$135 billion or about 5 per cent of GDP) per annum.

As per McKinsey, infrastructure spending (using the broadest definition that includes real estate, oil and gas, and mining) totalled US$9.5 trillion in 2015, or 14 per cent of global GDP (see Figure 2.1 for the breakup).

Using the same broad definition, China was the world's largest infrastructure market in 2015 with 38 per cent of global spending, followed by North America (21 per cent) and Western Europe (17 per cent). It may be significant to note that infrastructure spending in China in 2015 equalled that of North America and Western Europe (or the entire developed world) combined. Over the past five years, the fastest-growing markets for infrastructure spending have been India with compound annual growth in real terms of 10 per cent, China (7 per cent), and North America (3 per cent).

---

[1] World Bank. 2008. *The Growth Report: Strategies for Sustained Growth and Inclusive Development*, p. 35.

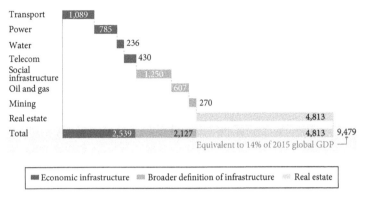

Figure 2.1 Infrastructure spending by asset class, nominal investment in infrastructure, 2015 ($ billion)

Notes: Figures may not sum because of rounding. The World Bank's definition of infrastructure includes utilities (gas and electricity, water supply, telecommunications, sewerage, and waste collection and disposal), public works (roads and major dam and canal works for irrigation and drainage), and other transport sectors (railways, ports, waterways, and airports); OECD includes public works in a country, state, or region, including roads, utility lines, and public buildings. Lower water capex due to changes in the exact category definitions applied and updates to estimates by Global Water Intelligence.

Source: Euroconstruct; IHS; IMF; OECD; World Bank; McKinsey Global Institute analysis.

However, there is a large infrastructure investment gap the world over. As per McKinsey, the current level of infrastructure investment (narrow definition) is not enough: US$3.7 trillion of investment (in constant 2017 US$, or 4.1 per cent of global GDP) in economic infrastructure alone is needed every year from now until 2035 to keep pace with projected GDP growth, of which power and roads constitutes US$1.1 trillion and US$0.9 trillion respectively. This need could increase further by up to US$1 trillion annually in order to meet the United Nations' Sustainable Development Goals (SDGs).

Fifty-four per cent of the world's need will be in Asia, the bulk of this in the world's two fastest-growing and most populous countries. China will account for 34 per cent of global need and India 8 per cent of US$69.4 trillion (or US$5.55 trillion) by 2035, compared to 3 per cent of US$29.8 trillion in the period 2000–2015. Investment will continue to shift to emerging markets—nearly two-thirds of global infrastructure investment in the period to 2035 is required in emerging economies.

There is a US$5.5 trillion spending gap globally between now and 2035 between need and expected actuals, with regional variations. India spent 5.6 per cent of GDP on infrastructure on economic infrastructure in the period 2010–2015, and the gap is 0.7 per cent of GDP for the period 2017–2035. Australia, China, and Japan have invested sufficiently to exceed their forecast infrastructure requirement, and will arguably need to spend less as a share of GDP than they have in the past. In contrast, countries including Germany, the United Kingdom, and the United States have significant gaps between their current spending commitments and estimated need. Reflecting the fact that the most demand for infrastructure is in emerging economies, some of the biggest spending gaps are in Brazil (1.1 per cent of GDP), Indonesia (1.2 per cent), and Mexico (1.3 per cent).

There is significant room to improve the effectiveness and efficiency of infrastructure investments. Up to 38 per cent of global infrastructure investment is not spent effectively because of bottlenecks, lack of innovation, and market failures. Fact-based project selection, streamlined delivery, and the optimization of operations and maintenance of existing infrastructure can close this gap, reducing spending by more than US$1 trillion a year for the same amount of economic infrastructure delivered.[2]

Given the fiscal stress of countries, exacerbated by the ongoing Covid-19 pandemic,[3] most of the resources for filling up the investment gap would have to come from the private sector. This would require better project preparation to be able to generate interest from the private sector.

---

[2] McKinsey Global Institute. 2017. *Bridging Infrastructure Gaps: Has the World Made Progress?* (https://www.mckinsey.com/business-functions/operations/our-insights/bridging-infrastructure-gaps-has-the-world-made-progress).

[3] In April 2021, public debt levels across all G20 economies were 50–100 per cent higher than they were following the Global Financial Crisis (2009). Many developing countries face major financial shortfalls due to weak fiscal and external balance sheets and elevated debt. For example, across Africa, current account deficits have been widening since 2017. But with the impact of the recent Covid-19 crisis, the average fiscal deficit is estimated to have climbed to 10.7 per cent in 2020 from 4.9 per cent in 2019 (much like India). *The Economist* (26 November 2021) reports that governments have spent US$17 trillion on the pandemic, including loans and guarantees, for a combined total of 16 per cent of global GDP. At these spending and deficit levels, most governments have limited ability to stimulate their economies solely through public investment (Marie Lam-Frendo and Morgan Landy. 23 September 2021. If You Issue It, They Will Come: Lessons from Recent Infrastructure Bonds, https://blogs.worldbank.org/ppps/if-you-issue-it-they-will-come-lessons-recent-infrastructure-bonds?CID=WBW_AL_BlogNotification_EN_EXT).

The project preparation phase is also the best time to address issues relating to ESG, climate change, value for money, fiscal impact, and debt sustainability—to avoid common pitfalls and missed opportunities. With more emphasis on these issues, we can secure more financing and come closer to getting infrastructure development right.[4]

Trends in Infrastructure Investment in India

The time series of infrastructure investment in India is shown in Figure 2.2. As can be seen, the percentage of GDP invested in infrastructure has remained in the range of 5–7 per cent in recent years (since the 1990s). The slope of the trendline is also positive, showing increasing infrastructure investment (as a per cent of GDP) over the years.

As mentioned earlier, the Growth Report of the World Bank finds that fast-growing countries of East Asia in their fast-growing phases have spent about 7–8 per cent of their GDP on infrastructure. A look at Figure 2.2 shows that infrastructure investment in India was in this range in the 11th Plan period (2008–2012) and has come down more recently.

In the last decade (2008–2017), India has spent US$1.1 trillion on infrastructure, or an average of US$110 billion per annum. Taking the benchmark of the World Bank's Growth Report (7–8 per cent of GDP) and the NIP (US$250 billion per annum), we find that India has spent much less than the required rate on infrastructure. This underinvestment in infrastructure is manifested in India's over-crowded roads and airports, slow average speeds of trains, both passenger and freight, high turnaround time of ships, and so on, which is impacting India's overall competitiveness. As per the World Economic Forum's Global Competitiveness Report 2019, India ranks 70th out of 141 countries on infrastructure. Since the overall ranking of India is 68 as per the same Report, infrastructure, which is one of the twelve pillars on which this ranking is based, is acting as a drag on India's overall competitiveness.[5]

---

[4] Jason Zhengrong Lu. 2020. A Simple Way to Close the Multi-trillion-dollar Infrastructure Financing Gap (https://blogs.worldbank.org/ppps/simple-way-close-multi-trillion-dollar-infrastructure-financing-gap).

[5] World Economic Forum. 2019. *The Global Competitiveness Report 2019* (https://www3.weforum.org/docs/WEF_TheGlobalCompetitivenessReport2019.pdf).

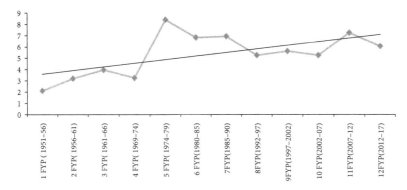

Figure 2.2 Trends in infrastructure investment in India (infrastructure investment as % of GDP at market prices)

Source: Planning Commission, Government of India. *Various Five Year Plan Documents; Report of the Task Force on National Infrastructure Pipeline.*

Sources of Infrastructure Finance

Infrastructure investment in India during 2008 to 2017 was Rs.60 trillion (lakh crore) and that in the Twelfth Five Year Plan (2013 to 2017) amounted to Rs.36 trillion at current prices.[6, 7] However, infrastructure investment in GDP terms fell to around 5.8 per cent during the Twelfth Five Year Plan (2013 to 2017) from over 7 per cent during the Eleventh Five Year Plan (2008 to 2012). As per estimates, India's infrastructure investment for FYs 2018 and 2019 are about Rs.10.2 trillion and Rs.10 trillion respectively. Infrastructure investment has been predominantly undertaken by the public sector [i.e. centre and state governments and their public-sector undertakings (PSUs) have a share of about two-thirds], while the share of private sector was the balance third. This is in consonance with the split of infrastructure investment between public and private sectors across the world. Power, roads and bridges, urban, digital infrastructure, and railway sectors together constituted about 85 per cent of the total infrastructure investment in India during FY 2013

---

[6] An earlier version of this section appeared in Kumar V. Pratap and Rajesh Chakravarti. 2018. *Public Private Partnerships in Infrastructure—Managing the Challenges.*

[7] Ministry of Finance. 2020. *National Infrastructure Pipeline: Volume 1*, p. 26.

to 2019. The centre and states were the major funding sources for sectors such as power and roads and bridges, with moderate participation from the private sector. Digital infrastructure was largely driven by the private sector while investments in the irrigation sector were predominantly made by the state governments.

As we have seen, there are four main sources of infrastructure finance, namely gross budgetary support (GBS, direct budgetary support and dedicated funds), internal and extra budgetary resources (IEBR, retained earnings, bank credit, and bonds) of the public sector, international funding (multilateral and bilateral loans, commercial finance), and private investment (sponsor equity, bank credit, bonds, etc.). We discuss each of these sources below.

Gross budgetary support

Despite the important role played by private investment in recent times, gross budgetary support continues to be a key source of infrastructure finance. This is because of the inherent characteristics of infrastructure: market failure in certain infrastructure industries due to externalities, public-good characteristics, natural monopoly characteristics, huge sunk costs, and many infrastructure sectors being merit goods (e.g. water supply and education). Given the visibility of large infrastructure projects (e.g., the Mumbai-Ahmedabad bullet train), public sector funding for infrastructure investment is also politically salient—efficiently constructed and managed projects stand out as monuments of governance, while leaving long-standing demands from constituents unmet gives fodder to the opposition.

Gross budgetary support comes in the form of direct budgetary support or dedicated funds. For example, about Rs.3.8 trillion (lakh crore) has been allocated as capital outlay for various infrastructure projects in the Union Budget 2021/22. Governments generally provide direct budgetary support to implement priority infrastructure augmentation programmes. Consider, for instance, the Jal Jeevan Mission (Urban) of the Government of India, that aims at universal piped water supply in all 4,378 urban local bodies with 28.6 million household tap connections, as well as liquid waste management in 500 Atal Mission for Rejuvenation and Urban Transformation (AMRUT) cities, envisaging an outlay of Rs.2.87 trillion over the period 2021–2026. Similarly, Urban Swachh Bharat Mission 2.0 that has a large infrastructure component will be implemented with a total financial allocation of Rs. 1.42 trillion over the five-year period, 2021–26.

Fiscal resource crunch constrains government's ability to fund infrastructure directly. Government of India's (federal) fiscal deficit in 2019/20 was 4.6 per cent of GDP, reversing a declining trend since 2011/12 (Figure 2.3), while the fiscal deficit in the Covid-19-affected 2020/21 is estimated to be 9.2 per cent of GDP and the fiscal deficit for 2021/22 is 6.7 per cent of GDP. Add to this, the deficit of the state governments of about 4 per cent of GDP and the total government deficit was over the dangerous level of about 13 per cent of GDP in 2020/21. The federal fiscal deficit trend is shown in Figure 2.3, the positive slope of which implies the reduced ability of the government to fund infrastructure through gross budgetary support.

Gross budgetary support to infrastructure may also be in the form of dedicated funds. For instance, the Central Road and Infrastructure Fund (CRIF) is a dedicated fund created out of the cess levied on high-speed diesel (HSD) and petrol, the proceeds of which are earmarked for various infrastructure sectors such as transport, including roads and bridges, and railways. In 2018/19, the total funds collected under CRIF

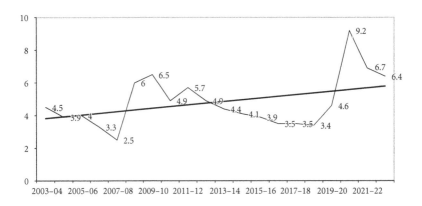

Figure 2.3 Fiscal deficit (federal) trend in India (% of GDP)
Source: Authors' compilation from budget documents.

was Rs.1,13,000 crore. The key argument for creating the CRIF dedicated fund is better *targeting* in the sense that current road users pay for road development. It also lowers the need for direct budgetary support and is environment-friendly in that it makes fossil-fuel consumption more expensive and thus promotes energy conservation. A disadvantage is the reduction in budgetary flexibility as the cess proceeds can only be used for defined purposes including road development. Besides, one can argue that it also leads to inter-generational inequity as the current road users pay for an asset that is going to last for thirty years or more, thus also benefitting future generations.

Internal and extra-budgetary resources of PSUs

Another important source of infrastructure finance is internal and extra-budgetary resources of PSUs. In India, internal resource generation (retained earnings) for infrastructure investment in the public sector is relatively low because of the low profitability of PSUs and the desire of the government (the majority shareholder) for increased dividends. There were 348 central sector PSUs as of the end of March 2019, of which 249 are in operation. Of these, 178 PSUs showed profits during 2018/19 with total profits of Rs.1,74,587 crore and seventy PSUs incurred losses of Rs.31,635 crore during the year. The overall net profit of the 249 operating PSUs went up by 15.5 per cent to 1,42,952 crore in 2018/19 from 1,23,751 crore in 2017/18.[8]

A key source of infrastructure finance that augments internal funds is tolls (user fees) on road projects. Tolls are an example of user fees for economic infrastructure (a counterpart for social infrastructure would be tuitions; we discuss reasonable user charges as a source of sustainable infrastructure financing in Chapter 3). Tolls add to investment in that a new revenue stream is created where none existed earlier. Indian toll roads collected as much as Rs.26,851 crore[9] in 2019/20 and Rs.28,548 crore in 2020/21. The design of tolls in the road sector in

---

[8] Ministry of Heavy Industries and Public Enterprises. 2020. *Annual Report 2019–20*, p. 107.
[9] NHAI. *Toll Information System* (accessed on 28 July 2021) https://tis.nhai.gov.in/faq.aspx?language=en.

India provide for uniform toll rates for publicly funded as well as PPP projects, partial indexation of toll rates to inflation, and partial exemption for local users.

Tolls and user fees can be an elegant solution if rates are set on the basis of objective principles like wear and tear caused to the road surface, saving in vehicle operating costs, acceptability and willingness of users to pay, and differentiating among user classes like trucks being charged more than cars. User charges can also have environmentally benign effects as pricing a hitherto free service (road travel) would discourage travel, saving on fossil-fuel usage. User fees on toll roads are not just about raising revenue—they also reduce congestion by affecting both the supply and demand of road space. The conventional solution to excess demand is to keep expanding an infrastructure asset as it reaches capacity limits. However, some demand management can be done without erosion of user benefits (at least not to the same extent) using variable pricing through tolls. Variable tolling, for instance, can incentivize driving at off-peak times. Similarly chaining trips (combining multiple tasks on a single trip), moving to public transport, telecommuting, or carpooling are other desirable outcomes that can be promoted through tolls. However, it is difficult to introduce tolls on an existing facility that commuters feel has already been paid for through taxes, when it is in a poor state or is not managed well. People used to free infrastructure services (like water, power, and roads) may resort to direct action (preventing providers from charging tolls, as in the Delhi-Noida Toll Bridge), adding to political risks faced by private infrastructure projects. The dismantling of toll booths in India (on the Delhi–Gurgaon NH8, for instance) has increased the political risks in PPPs. Such political risks includes expropriation, non-convertibility, and non-transferability. Not allowing concessionaires (the private party building and operating the road) to charge agreed-upon user fees effectively amounts to expropriation of assets. Regulators may also be setting user fees below costs, as in the Indian power distribution sector, owing to political, social, and affordability concerns. These political and regulatory risks would be reflected in a higher risk premium charged by the investors, thereby increasing costs and required returns from investment projects. Three critical enablers for improving usage of user fees are public education and consultation, effective enforcement, and addressing concerns about access and equity.

The IEBR of select infrastructure PSUs in FY 2020/21 and FY 2021/22 is given in Table 2.1 and Table 2.2. From the numbers, it is apparent that out of the roughly Rs.10 trillion annual infrastructure investment that India has been making in recent years, about 20 per cent has been contributed by IEBR.

International finance—donors, multilaterals, and commercial

International sources have played a critical role in funding developing country infrastructure in the past and continues to do so. Net official development assistance from organizations like the World Bank Group to developing countries around the world amounted to about US$167.8 billion up to 2019.[10] In countries like Mongolia and Mali, funds for infrastructure from donors and multilaterals are very significant (in Mali, for example, such funds could account for 80 per cent of infrastructure investment). In India, by contrast, donors/multilateral finance as a proportion of total infrastructure investment is relatively low. However, compared to a low proportion of donor and multilateral finance, India receives a sizeable amount of international commercial finance in the form of foreign direct investment and foreign institutional investment (FDI and FII) in infrastructure. Nevertheless, loans from multilateral and bilateral development banks (e.g. World Bank and Japan International Cooperation Agency (JICA)) are a major component of financing for specific projects like the dedicated freight corridors (DFCs) and metro rails in India. For example, the two existing DFCs (Eastern and Western DFCs) in India, under implementation with a project cost of Rs.1.24 trillion, are being funded through a mix of equity and debt with 36 per cent equity contribution from the Ministry of Railways (MoR), 47 per cent from JICA loans, and 17 per cent from World Bank loans.

Besides direct financing, multilaterals also improve the creditworthiness of projects through endorsement—providing comfort for other providers of long-term finance, investors, and contractors, particularly with

[10] World Bank Indicators: Net Official Development Assistance Received (https://data.worldb ank.org/indicator/DT.ODA.ODAT.CD).

Table 2.1 Internal and extra budgetary resources for FY 2020/21 (revised estimates)—select infrastructure PSUs

Name of PSU	Revised Estimates 2020/21 (Rs. crore)					
	Internal resources	EBR	Bonds/ Debentures	ECB/ Suppliers credit	Others	Total
1 Nuclear Power Corporation of India Limited	3,422	5,873	5,842	-	31	9,295
2 Airports Authority of India	2,549	2,241	-	-	2,241	4,790
3 Bharat Broadband Network Limited	200	8,500	-	-	8,500	8,700
4 Solar Energy Corporation of India Limited	593	-	-	-	-	593
5 Gas Authority of India Limited	1,742	3,900	-	-	3,900	5,642
6 Jawaharlal Nehru Port Trust	1,115	-	-	-	-	1,115
7 National Hydro Electric Power Corporation Limited	1,762	3,468	3,468	-	-	5,231
8 National Thermal Power Corporation Limited	6,566	14,434	8,787	5,648	-	21,000
9 Power Grid Corporation of India Limited	3,031	7,469	5,945	1,370	154	10,500
10 Dedicated Freight Corridor Corporation of India Ltd	3,900	-	-	-	-	3,900
11 Indian Railway Finance Corporation	1,13,567	-	-	-	-	1,13,567
12 Indian Railways	3,875	-	-	-	-	3,875
Other CPSUs	3,823	11,932	1,150	186	10,596	15,755
Total	1,46,144	57,818	25,192	7,204	25,422	2,03,962

Source: Ministry of Finance (Government of India). 2021. *Union Budget 2021/22: Expenditure Profile 2021/22*, p. 248. Available at https://www.indiabudget.gov.in/doc/eb/vol1.pdf.

Table 2.2 Internal and extra budgetary resources for FY 2021/22 (Budget Estimates)—select infrastructure PSUs

	Name of PSU	Budget Estimates 2021/22 (Rs. crore)					
		Internal resources	EBR	Bonds/ Debentures	ECB/ Suppliers credit	Others	Total
1	Nuclear Power Corporation of India Limited	3,285	7,328	7,265	-	63	10,613
2	Airports Authority of India	2,278	2,862	-	-	2,862	5,140
3	Bharat Broadband Network Limited	200	9,000	-	-	9,000	9,200
4	Solar Energy Corporation of India Limited	760	-		-	-	760
5	Gas Authority of India Limited	1,361	4,500		-	4,500	5,861
6	Jawaharlal Nehru Port Trust	2,197			-	-	2,197
7	National Hydro Electric Power Corporation Limited	2,545	5,512	5,512	-	-	8,057
8	National Thermal Power Corporation Limited	9,142	14,594	8,947	5,648	-	23,736
9	Power Grid Corporation of India Limited	1,801	5,699	5,667	27	5	7,500
10	Dedicated Freight Corridor Corporation of India Ltd	3,483	-	-	-	-	3,483
11	Indian Railway Finance Corporation	65,258	-	-	-	-	65,258
12	Indian Railways	7,500	-	-	-	-	7,500
	Other CPSUs	5,753	10,992	1,500	322	9,169	16,745
	Total	**1,05,564**	**60,487**	**28,891**	**5,997**	**25,599**	**1,66,051**

Source: Ministry of Finance (Government of India). 2021. *Union Budget 2021–22: Expenditure Profile 2021–22*, p. 248. Available at https://www.indiabudget.gov.in/doc/eb/vol1.pdf.

regard to perceived political risks, especially projects involving multiple countries. Involvement of multilaterals helps make the deals credible, especially for countries that have poor creditworthiness. They also play an important role in making projects adhere to internationally accepted standards by providing technical expertise.

Consider the Energy Efficiency Scale-up Program Project for India[11] which envisages strengthening Energy Efficiency Services Limited's (EESL) institutional capacity, enhancing its access to commercial financing and scaling up energy savings in residential and public sectors. The total project cost (TPC) is US$1.35 billion. Its financing plan involves US$220 million loan from the World Bank, US$80 million guarantee agreement with the World Bank, and US$380 million from bilateral funding agencies. The guarantee has helped EESL leverage an additional US$200 million from foreign private commercial sources and diversify its investor base. EESL will invest US$548 million.

Most multilaterals are also able to provide specific political risk insurance and partial-risk guarantees. Risk mitigation instruments usually depend on full or partial coverage of a potential loss for the lender or investor—covering credit risk issues to support debt funding, or covering investment risk issues to back equity funding. Risk cover would also depend on the nature of the risk—political (or other non-project-related) or project risks. Box 2.1 explains the type of risk mitigation instruments used in infrastructure projects.

Private investment

India has invested US$1.1 trillion on infrastructure in the last decade (2008–2017), of which a little over a third has come from the private sector. Boston Consulting Group[12] estimates that two-thirds of the investment of US$2.7 trillion that is being made on infrastructure the world over (as against a demand for US$4 trillion annually), comes from

---

[11] World Bank. *What Do We Do? Projects and Operations: India Energy Efficiency Scale-up Program* (https://projects.worldbank.org/en/projects operations/project-detail/P162849).
[12] Boston Consulting Group. 2013. *Bridging the Gap—Meeting the Infrastructure Challenge with Public–Private Partnerships.*

Box 2.1   Risk mitigation instruments in infrastructure projects

The types of risk mitigation instruments used in infrastructure financing are as follows:

- *Partial-credit guarantees*: These increase the borrower's access to long-term credit markets by sharing the credit risk between lenders and the guarantee provider. Multilaterals usually issue these guarantees, particularly to cover the 'tail-end' repayments of a long-term project-finance loan. This helps private-sector banks do project lending, even if they desire a shorter maturity.
- *Full-creditor 'wrap' guarantees*: The entire project debt can be guaranteed by another entity. Then, the lender cares primarily about the credit risk of the guarantor and no longer that of the project itself. Before the global financial crisis of 2008–2009, large private insurance companies called monocline insurers provided such guarantees. Such covers enable non-conventional funders like pension funds support projects. Here the lending instrument is usually a bond that investors can hold or sell to one another, rather than a direct bank loan.
- *Export credit agencies*: Export credit agencies provide a more common credit risk cover. Expanding from originally covering political risk only, they now cover commercial risks as well. These are usually export-promoting government entities, covering long-term loans used to finance the purchase of their exports. Consequently, such cover is often, 'tied' to the value and nationality of the exports for the project or the lender involved. It can be up to 100 per cent of the political and commercial risk associated with the underlying project cost being financed. Apart from the risk cover, these entities may also help with competitive long-term interest rates.
- *Debt underpinning*: The public authority itself may guarantee repayment of a portion of the project debt even if the cause of the potential default lies with the private-sector partner. Clearly this approach only works if the long-term creditworthiness of the

public authority is good enough for the lenders. Here it is important that the unguaranteed portion of the debt is enough to ensure that the lenders will have enough funds at risk to be concerned with the performance of the project.

- *Political risk guarantees*: As the name implies, political risk guarantees or insurance protect lenders and investors against losses due to defined political events, such as currency non-convertibility or transfer risks, expropriation, or war, as distinct from the commercial risks of the project itself. Multilateral or bilateral institutions or private insurance companies provide such cover.

Source: Adapted from Farquharson et al. (2011).[a]

[a]Edward Farquharson, Clemencia Torres de Mastle, and E. R. Yescombe with Javier Encinas. 2011. *How to Engage with the Private Sector in Public–Private Partnerships in Emerging Markets.*.

---

the public sector. In that sense, India's split between public- and private-sector shares of investment, is in sync with rest of the world. Box 2.2 expands on the role of private infrastructure investment in developing countries.

In India, the 11th Plan period (2008–2012) saw average infrastructure investment rise to over 7 per cent of GDP per annum from about 5 per cent in the previous five years (2003–2007, 10th Plan period). The share of the private sector went up from 1.1 per cent of GDP (2003–2007) to 2.7 per cent of GDP in the period 2008–2012. In recent years, on average, the public sector (GBS and IEBR) has been spending just above 4 per cent of GDP on infrastructure. So, the entire upsurge in infrastructure investment to GDP ratio seen in the 11th Plan period (2008–2012) can be explained in terms of the upsurge in private investment.[13] More recently, in the 12th Plan period (2013–2017), the infrastructure investment to GDP ratio has fallen to about 5.8 per cent because of the stressed balance sheets

---

[13] Kumar V. Pratap and Mira Sethi. 2018. Infrastructure Financing in India—Trends, Challenges, and Way Forward.

Box 2.2 Role of private infrastructure investment in developing countries

The overall trend in private participation in infrastructure (PPI) is not uniform but varies with the general economic trends. Figure 2.4 presents the trend of private participation in various infrastructure sectors in developing countries over the years. While private investment in infrastructure projects was less than US$20 billion in 1990, it rapidly increased to peak at US$81 billion in 1997. Investment in East Asian power projects and privatization of Latin American telecommunications and electricity utilities drove this rise. The East Asian Financial Crisis (1997) started the decline in investment, affecting many of the independent power projects already underway. Continued crises in Russia and Latin America culminated in a fall as sharp as the earlier rise. After a period with no real discernible trends, investment levels have increased sharply since 2004, peaking in 2012 at US$158 billion. Investment in infrastructure declined again in response to eurozone crises in 2013, OPEC oil production cuts and consequent price hike and Chinese stock market crash in 2016, and Covid-19 pandemic in 2020.

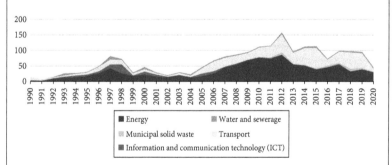

Figure 2.4 Trends in private participation in infrastructure in developing countries (US$ billion)

Source: Data sourced from Private Participation in Infrastructure database of the World Bank (http://ppi.worldbank.org).

If we look at the composition of PPI, we find that the leading sectors are energy (53 per cent of total private infrastructure investment in developing countries) and transport (35 per cent of total). However, investment in social sectors like water and sewerage and municipal solid waste (MSW) is quite limited at less than 7 per cent of the total private infrastructure investment in developing countries, reflecting the difficult political economy issues is these sectors where there is a reluctance to increase water tariffs and MSW charges.

The above pattern is also reflected in the number of projects (Table 2.3). The maximum number of projects are in the energy sector (further breakup of the energy sector reveals that the maximum number of projects are in electricity generation, where the political economy issues are lower than in electricity distribution). The minimum number of projects is in the municipal solid waste sector.

Table 2.3 Private participation in infrastructure, by sector (1990–2020) in developing countries

	Number of Projects	Investments ($ billion)
Energy	4,262	1,048
Transport	2,018	695
Information and communication technology	525	119
Water and sewerage	1,117	93
Municipal solid waste	393	38
Total	8,315	1,994

Source: Private Participation in Infrastructure database of the World Bank (ppi.worldbank.org) (accessed 5 September 2021).

As per the Private Participation in Infrastructure (PPI) database of the World Bank, India is second in the developing world, both by the number of PPP projects as well as the associated investments (see Table 2.4). In terms of number of projects, India is second to China, while in terms of investments, it is second to Brazil.

Table 2.4 Top ten countries by private participation in infrastructure in the developing world (1990–2020), ranked by investment

Rank	Country	Investments ($ billion)	Number of projects
1	Brazil	426	1,031
2	India	279	1,108
3	China	241	1,872
4	Turkey	146	250
5	Mexico	95	350
6	Russian Federation	80	373
7	Indonesia	67	140
8	Argentina	59	252
9	Philippines	57	167
10	Malaysia	52	124

Source: Private Participation in Infrastructure database of the World Bank (ppi.worldbank. org) (accessed on 8 December 2020).

of the banks and private companies (the twin balance-sheet problem), delays in land acquisition, environment and forest clearance of projects, poor performance of some contractors, delays in resolution of disputes and claims, leading to time and cost overruns of projects, and inadequate project preparation by the public sector.

As can be seen from Table 2.4, India has 1,108 PPP projects accounting for an investment of US$279 billion. The sectoral breakup of projects and infrastructure investment in India may be seen in Table 2.5.

As apparent from Table 2.5, most private infrastructure investment in India has flowed into the energy sector (mainly electricity generation) at US$152 billion, while the highest number of projects have come up in the transport sector (559 projects, and within transport, in the road sector, 488 projects).

Some of the highlights of the prominent role played by the private sector in Indian infrastructure are:

- The PPP airports at Delhi and Mumbai, from being among the worst airports in the world prior to privatization, now figure among the

Table 2.5 Private participation in infrastructure in India (1990–2020)

Sector	Investment ($ billion)	Number of projects
Energy	152	455
Electricity generation	141	416
Electricity transmission	9	26
Electricity distribution	2	13
Information and communication technology (ICT)	3	25
Transport	121	559
Roads	90	488
Ports	10	44
Airports	13	17
Railways	8	10
Water and sewerage	3	69
Total	279	1,108

Source: Private Participation in Infrastructure database of the World Bank (ppi.worldbank.org) (accessed 8 December 2020).

best[14] (Airports Council International, 2020). In addition, the revenue share from Delhi and Mumbai airports to Airports Authority of India (AAI), at Rs.3,040 crore in FY 2019, is more than the profit after tax (PAT) of AAI for that year (Rs.2,271 crore).[15] The inference is that, but for the revenue-share from Delhi and Mumbai airports, AAI would be a loss-making entity.

- *Roads*: India runs the largest PPP programme in the world in the road sector with 488 projects accounting for an investment of about US$90 billion as per the Private Participation in Infrastructure database of the World Bank.

- *Telecom*: There are about 1.15 billion mobile phones in the country, with the share of the private sector being 89.5 per cent (as on 30 November 2019).[16] From being among the most expensive telecom services in the world in the early 1990s, the price for both voice and data services has come down to become among the least expensive.

---

[14] Airports Council International. 2020. *Best Airport by Size and Region* (https://aci.aero/programs-and-services/asq/asq-awards-and-recognition/).
[15] Airports Authority of India. 2020. *Annual Report 2019–20*.
[16] Department of Telecommunications, Government of India. 2020. *Annual Report 2019–20*.

With a share of about a third in the last decade, private investment has emerged as a major source of financing infrastructure in India in recent times. The major sources of private infrastructure finance are internal accruals ploughed back (retained earnings), equity—both domestic and foreign—tolls on PPP roads and other infrastructure projects, and borrowings from multilaterals and the domestic market (both bank credit and bonds). As India seeks to accelerate infrastructure investments for getting out of the Covid-19-induced recession and restoring its usual growth rate, borrowings by private players would play a major role in financing their share of infrastructure investments. The main mode of private infrastructure investment is project finance (dealt with at length in Chapter 5), with a highly leveraged financial structure based on borrowings.

Top Private Infrastructure Project Sponsors of India

The top ten PPP infrastructure sponsors in India account for 32 per cent of total PPP investments (Figure 2.5). All of them are local companies, implying that the PPI programme in India is mainly domestic. One of the reasons for this could be the high foreign exchange risk in infrastructure sectors, with revenues generally in local currency (other than port and airport sectors where a reasonable proportion of revenues are in foreign currency), while foreign investment would generally mean the use of foreign-currency financing, thus giving rise to currency mismatch and foreign-exchange risk. Domestic investment is also subject to lower political sensitivity. Another characteristic of PPI sponsor information is the heavy presence of energy and transport firms in consonance with the rest of the world and the sectoral spread of private infrastructure investment (Table 2.5).

PPP Trends

PPP trends in India, both by number of projects and investments, are shown in Figure 2.6. While the overall trend is positive, PPPs experienced

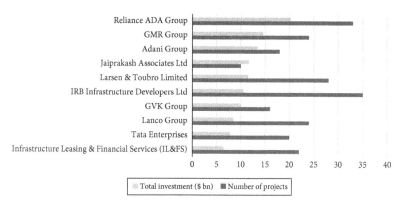

Figure 2.5 Top ten PPP sponsors in India (1990–2021)

Source: Private Participation in Infrastructure database of the World Bank (http://ppi.worldb ank.org) (viewed on 21 January 2023).

an upsurge in the 11th Plan period (2008–2012), when they contributed to more than a third of the total infrastructure investment of about US$500 billion. This was also commensurately reflected in the number of PPP projects. Given that there is a gestation period of a few years between financial closure of a project and its commercial operations, the figure also implies an increasing number of projects are in operation. The figure also shows that there was little impact of the Global Financial Crisis of 2008 on the pace of PPP investments, both because of the limited role

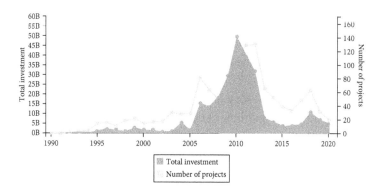

Figure 2.6 Private participation in infrastructure in India, by years

Source: Private Participation in Infrastructure database of the World Bank (http://ppi.worldb ank.org)] (viewed on 5 September 2021).

of foreign investment in Indian infrastructure and because of the pro-active measures taken by the government and the Reserve Bank of India to contain its impact. Another trend that is discernible is that since 2012, there has been a sharp deceleration in both the number and investment in PPPs.

Recent Slowdown in Infrastructure Investments

There has been a slowdown recently in private participation in infra-structure, both by the number of projects and the associated invest-ments (Figure 2.6). Private investment in Indian infrastructure that was over US$50 billion in 2010 (highest ever for India for a single year), has come down to about US$5.3 billion in 2020. Similarly, the number of pri-vate projects that achieved financial closure was as high as 129 in 2012 (highest ever for India for a single year) and has come down to twenty-one in 2020. The recent slowdown in infrastructure is attributed, inter alia, to the twin balance-sheet problem (over-stretched balance sheets of the infrastructure project sponsors combined with the non-performing assets of the banking sector),[17] making finance scarce for infrastructure. The other causes of the slowdown are issues in land acquisition and envir-onment and forest clearance of projects, aggressive bidding by the private sector, and so on. But, even after this slowdown, India continues to imple-ment one of the largest infrastructure programmes in the world, with an estimated infrastructure investment of about US$130 billion in FY 2019 (both public and private infrastructure investment), and occupies the second position in the developing world both by the number of PPP pro-jects as well as the associated investments (Table 2.4).

The on-going Covid-19 pandemic has accentuated the slowdown in infrastructure. In April–May 2020, the Covid-19 pandemic slowed down the infrastructure programme of the country, both from the demand and the supply side. Passenger traffic on roads, railways, and by air was under lockdown, and in the power sector, there was a major demand slowdown with most industrial and commercial activity locked up. On the supply

---

[17] Arvind Subramanian. 2018. *Of Counsel—The Challenges of the Modi-Jaitley Economy.*

side, supply chains and the construction labour force were dislocated because of the pandemic.

The more recent infrastructure numbers, however, are encouraging and suggest that, barring the onset of a new Covid-19 wave, the worst is behind us. Power consumption, freight traffic by railways, fuel consumption, and GST collections are all increasing to more normal levels. This resilience is reflected in the infrastructure green shoots that have appeared recently (see Chapter 11 for a detailed discussion of the impact of Covid-19 on infrastructure).

In addition, to enable higher private investment and to improve service delivery, the following sectors have recently been opened up to private participation.

Sectors recently opened to private participation

Social sectors

As per the Private Participation in Infrastructure database of the World Bank (ppi.worldbank.org), India is second in the developing world, both in terms of the number of PPP projects as well as the associated investments (Table 2.4 shows 1,108 PPP projects, accounting for an investment of US$279 billion since 1990). The Indian success in PPPs is built on a robust policy framework, the financial incentive [viability gap funding (VGF)] scheme, and the standardization of procurement (Request for Qualification (RfQ) and Request for Proposal (RfP)) and substantive (Model Concession Agreements across infrastructure sectors) documents.

However, if we see the sectoral breakup of PPP projects, we find that almost all projects have come up in economic infrastructure (power, transport, and telecom) compared to social infrastructure. The sector where there is tremendous infrastructure deficit and could gain immensely from private investment is the water and sewerage sector. Social infrastructure (like water supply, solid waste management, health, and education) have low cost-recovery and, consequently, face even operational losses and a massive resource-crunch (see Chapter 4 for details). So, it is timely that the Government of India recently raised the VGF limit to 30 per cent of the TPC for some social infrastructure sectors (and 40 per cent of the TPC for health and education sectors) compared to 20 per cent for economic infrastructure. There are examples across the world where PPPs have brought about sanguine results in social infrastructure, for example, Manila Water Supply PPP and health and education PPPs in developed countries like the United Kingdom and Australia. By increasing the VGF limit to 30 per cent of TPC (and 40 per cent for health and education sectors), which can be matched by a further 30 per cent (40 per cent) of TPC by the project authorities, a total of 60 per cent (80 per cent) of the TPC can theoretically be funded by grants, which would address the non-commercial aspects of social infrastructure. Accordingly, out of the total budget of Rs.1,41,600 crore, 16,730 crore is expected from the private sector in solid waste management (collection and transportation), waste-water treatment plants, and so on, under Swachh Bharat Mission (Urban) 2 (or Clean India Mission). Under Jal Jeevan Mission (aimed at providing piped-water supply to all households), private participation in the implementation of 10 per cent worth of projects will be mandated. With these initiatives, it is expected that the success of PPPs in economic infrastructure in India (in terms of augmenting resources and improving service delivery) will also be replicated in social infrastructure.[18]

Railway stations

In major developed countries like the United Kingdom, Japan, and the United States, railway stations are considered stand-alone individual business units and hence implemented as separate project-financed entities in a variety of ways as can be seen from examples below:

- *St. Pancras Rail Station, United Kingdom*: Redevelopment was undertaken in 2001 by London and Continental Railways (LCR) at a project cost of US$1.33 billion. LCR was a private property development company at that time (but was nationalized later) and had ownership of the station. Financing was primarily by LCR, with only US$73 million from the UK Department of Transport. Project scope also included construction of platforms and terminals, multi-modal

---

[18] Kumar V. Pratap. 12 June 2020. Renewing Faith in Public–Private Partnerships. *Financial Express* (https://www.financialexpress.com/opinion/renewing-faith-in-public-private-partnerships/1988892/).

integration, a shopping centre, and mixed-use development including a hotel. Revenue was also generated from 9,000 square meters of retail space.

- *Shinjuku station, Japan*: This was owned and financed by Japan Railway (JR) East (privately owned regional railway entity). The project was implemented in 2012 at a cost of more than US$1 billion. Revenue generation involved a significant component of asset monetization—land and airspace of about 1,11,000 square meters of floor space.

Station redevelopment requires huge capital expenditure, which is estimated at Rs.1 trillion in the case of India. Given the resource crunch, private-sector participation (PSP) is envisaged by Indian Railways (IR) which has also adopted the strategy of treating passenger station redevelopments as standalone projects (see Box 2.3 for re-development of Habibganj station on PPP mode).

For the purpose of station redevelopment, a special purpose vehicle, Indian Railway Stations Development Corporation Limited (IRSDC), a joint venture company of Rail Land Development Authority (RLDA), a statutory authority under the MoR, and IRCON International Limited (IRCON, a PSU under MoR) was incorporated under the Companies Act, 1956 on 12 April 2012. Presently, the authorized share capital of IRSDC is Rs.250 crore and the paid-up capital has been increased to Rs.200 crore. Rail India Technical and Economic Service Limited (RITES) has recently been inducted as the third promoter with 24 per cent equity stake. The enhanced paid-up capital is held by RLDA, IRCON, and RITES in the ratio of 50:26:24.

IR has used the following 3 PPP models for station redevelopment (Table 2.6).

The commercially viable station redevelopment projects would now be implemented on the *Design-Build-Finance-Operate-Transfer* (DBFOT) model where the developer would earn revenue from fare box/user fees, non-fare box revenue, and land monetization during the concession period. The scope of the project includes both the upgrading and redevelopment of railway stations and the development of surrounding railway land (station estate), with operation and maintenance of these facilities as per the concession agreement. User fees would be charged from passengers from at least 15 per cent of the more than seven thousand railway stations in India to improve the financial viability of station redevelopment projects.

Table 2.6 Indian Railways—a comparison of current PPP models

Models→	Modified Swiss Challenge model	Single stage PPP model	New DBFOT Model
Specific examples	• 23 stations were envisioned under this model	• Habibganj station (see Box 2.3)	New Delhi (cost: Rs.6,500 crore), CSMT in Mumbai (cost: Rs.1,642 crore) and Puducherry (RLDA). • Gwalior, Amritsar, Nagpur, and Sabarmati (IRSDC)
Capital expenditure responsibility	• Private sector	• Private sector	• Private sector
Operational expenditure responsibility	• Private sector	• Private sector	• Private sector
Traffic risk	• Private sector	• Private sector	• Private sector
Concession period	• 45 years	• 5 years (station development) • 45 years (commercial/ real estate development)	• 60 years commercial real estate and station development • 99 years residential real estate
Bid parameter	• Combination of lease premium and revenue share	• Upfront lease premium	• Annual concession fee (for New Delhi) • Annual concession fee or upfront premium for IRSDC stations
Current status	• Modified Swiss Challenge method was not taken forward due to lukewarm response from private sector. Primary issues were private participants having the	• It is the only station redevelopment project successfully awarded on PPP basis. • Habibganj project is nearing completion (over 98 per cent of civil work completed as of 30 June 2020).	• RLDA is planning to develop 62 stations as part of smart city projects. • Stations like New Delhi, Puducherry, Tirupati, and Dehradun are at the bidding stage.

Table 2.6 Continued

Models→	Modified Swiss Challenge model	Single stage PPP model	New DBFOT Model
	responsibility of getting necessary approvals and land-related clearances and the concession period being relatively short, among others.		• IRSDC is developing about 60 stations under this model; 9 bidders shortlisted at the RfQ stage for CSMT. However, recently IRSDC has been shut down and the responsibility of station redevelopment given to other entities in the MoR.

Source: Ministry of Railways. 2020. *National Rail Plan—India: Draft Final Report, Volume 1.*

However, recently (September 2022), there has been a rethink on station redevelopment with PSP. The government has approved re-development of New Delhi, CST (Mumbai), and Ahmedabad railway stations at a cost of Rs.10,000 crore to be funded and implemented by government (not through PPP) and to be completed by 2026. These station redevelopment projects will be taken up on EPC mode. Accordingly, the earlier decision to levy a 'station development fee' (SDF) or user fee on the lines of airports will not be pursued. SDF of between Rs.10 and Rs.50 per passenger (depending on class of travel) had earlier been approved.

Passenger Train Operations: IR, the world's fourth largest rail net-work, runs 13,523 trains and ferries over 23 million people every day. IR handled 8.4 billion passengers in 2019, which is expected to go up to 13 billion by 2030. However, IR could not provide reservation to around 88 million passengers per annum. There are about 76 million passenger coaches (as in March 2020) in service. Out of these, none are owned by the private sector—85 per cent are financed and owned by Indian Railway Finance Corporation (IRFC) and leased to IR and the balance 15 per cent are owned by IR.

Box 2.3 Development of Habibganj railway station in PPP mode

The redevelopment and modernization of Habibganj railway station in Bhopal, Madhya Pradesh, through PPP mode was estimated to cost Rs.450 crore divided between station redevelopment (Rs.100 crore) and commercial development (Rs.350 crore). The PPP agreement was signed between IRSDC and Bansal Group. The SPV is called Bansal Pathways Habibganj Private Limited.

After IRSDC and the developer met the 'conditions precedent' the operation and maintenance of the Habibganj station was taken over by the developer on 1 March 2017. Habibganj railway station has dedicated pick-up and drop-off parking facilities for users, as in airports. Other facilities in the redeveloped 'world-class' station include environment-friendly practices like solar-energy usage, catering and food stalls, cinema, hotel, corporate office, shopping mall, hospital, public conveniences at affordable rates, and accessibility to differently abled people. It is also a part of multi-modal transportation hub. The cost of providing these facilities to railway users would largely be recovered from commercial development at the railway station. The station was inaugurated in November 2021 as Rani Kamalapati Railway Station.

In key international rail markets, most of the components of passenger rail transportation have been privatized. For example, in the United Kingdom, the rail network is owned by the government, which leases it to private train operators—Train Operating Companies (TOCs)—for a specified period of 7–10 years on payment of network access fee. Manufacturing of coaches is by the private sector, which are owned by Rolling Stock Companies (ROSCOs). They lease coaches to TOCs for a period (7–10 years) less than asset life (30–35 years). This has facilitated development of the leasing market. Maintenance of the coaches is undertaken by TOCs or ROSCOs as per the lease arrangement.

In this context and the experience of Tejas Express (two are operational on Delhi-Lucknow and Ahmedabad-Mumbai routes), which is

India's first corporate train launched in October 2019, the government has decided to introduce private trains with the following objectives: to introduce modern technology rolling stock with reduced maintenance requirements, reduced transit time (running time taken by a train shall be comparable to or faster than the fastest train of IR operating on the same route; maximum speed 160 km per hour), boost job creation, provide enhanced safety, provide a world-class travel experience to passengers (comfort, facilities, cleanliness), and also reduce the supply deficit in the passenger transportation sector.

The scope of the project includes designing, engineering, procurement, financing, operation and maintenance of passenger trains (151 trains) over 109 routes bundled into twelve clusters (O&M of the passenger trains would be governed by standards, specifications, and requirements of IR). The expected private investment is about Rs.30,000 crore (151 trains of Rs.200 crore each). The majority of trains are expected to be manufactured in India (under the Make in India initiative). The concession period would be thirty-five years. Concessionaires would have to pay fixed haulage charges for path, stations, and access to railway infrastructure, and energy charges would be based on actuals. Private operators would have to conform to key performance indicators like punctuality, reliability, upkeep of trains, and so on. Operators will have the freedom to decide on fares to be charged from passengers. Revenue will be earned from the passenger fare, on-board catering services, and non-fare revenue. The bidding parameter is revenue share to Railways. It was expected that the first private train will start operations in 2023.

There will be a two-stage bidding process. RfQ has been issued and fifteen companies (including L&T, GMR, BHEL) have submitted bids to qualify for running passenger trains, of which thirteen companies have been shortlisted. At the RfP stage, IR received bids from only two companies, the public sector, Indian Railway Catering and Tourism Corporation, and the private sector, Megha Engineering and Infrastructure Ltd, for operating twenty-nine pairs of private trains with forty rakes (two clusters in Delhi and one cluster in Mumbai) with an investment of about Rs.7,200 crore. However, this tender was scrapped by IR because of low interest from the private sector.

There are certain issues in PSP in passenger trains, some of which could have been responsible for lower eventual interest from the private sector: clarity on dispute resolution as IR would have an incentive to slow down private trains, especially as there is a capacity constraint with 150 per cent capacity utilization on trunk routes; maximum speed for private trains is 160 kmph, which may not be feasible across railways (only the Delhi-Agra section can allow for this currently). In addition, there is a demand for an independent sectoral regulator for IR to provide a level playing field to the private train operators (dealt with at length in Chapter 10). Other reasons for eventual low investor interest could be the high haulage charge and its escalation with time as provided in the bidding documents, and inflexible scheduling (not providing for seasonal adjustment, frequency, etc.). Besides, there is the issue of IR best routes being transferred to the private sector, which may lead to IR becoming sick just like Air India. The government in 2022, however, decided to scrap the private trains initiative.

Other miscellaneous sectors: In May 2020, the Indian finance minister announced the following structural reforms under AtmaNirbhar Bharat package to increase private-sector investment in strategic sectors: establish a research reactor in PPP mode for the production of medical isotopes to make the treatment of cancer and other diseases affordable; establish facilities in PPP mode to use irradiation technology to preserve food and hence assist farmers; linking start-up ecosystem and nuclear sector by setting up technology development cum incubation centres—five such centres have been set up at Mumbai, Kalpakkam, Indore, Kolkata, and Gandhinagar.

3

Reasonable User Charges for Sustainable Infrastructure Financing

Though user charges are a source of infrastructure finance and would be reflected in retained earnings, it has been given an exclusive treatment as a separate chapter to emphasize the importance of this financing source for increased infrastructure financing.[1] User charges are traditionally low and, in many cases, not even enough to recover the operation and maintenance (O&M) expenses of infrastructure assets. We find examples of this in economic (electricity distribution, metro rail, etc.) and social infrastructure (health, education, water supply, etc.). This leads to a vicious cycle of asset creation, their gradual deterioration owing to inadequate O&M, leading to a requirement for increased fresh investment to re-build the assets. Since the infrastructure sector is capital-intensive, and since it involves public utilities like electricity, metro-rail services, water supply, and so on, full cost recovery from user charges may not always be possible or desirable. Therefore, many Government of India committees (e.g. Fourteenth Finance Commission, Expenditure Management Commission) have repeatedly emphasized recovery of at least O&M costs from user charges for financial sustainability of infrastructure projects. Reasonable user charges would also promote ownership and accountability, and therefore improve governance of infrastructure assets.

Infrastructure is necessary for broad-based growth and development, as well as for achieving and maintaining the delivery of public goods (water supply, rural roads, primary education, and healthcare, etc.) and

---

[1] Substantial parts of this chapter appeared earlier in Kumar V. Pratap and Manshi Gupta. 2022. The Role of Reasonable User Charges in Financing the National Infrastructure Pipeline. *Vikalpa,* 47(3): 1–6, 2022 (https://journals.sagepub.com/doi/pdf/10.1177/02560909221117698).

Infrastructure Financing in India. Kumar V Pratap and Manshi Gupta, Oxford University Press.
© Kumar V Pratap and Manshi Gupta 2024. DOI: 10.1093/oso/9780198884934.003.0004

therefore social well-being. To give an organized thrust to infrastructure, in April 2020, the Government of India released the first-ever National Infrastructure Pipeline (NIP) with details of 6,847 projects valued at over Rs.111 trillion (or~US$1.5 trillion) to be implemented over a six-year period from financial year (FY) 2020 to FY 2025.

Infrastructure services need to be paid for, either through user charges by consumers of these services or from the budget. User charges are essential for remunerating investors in toll-based infrastructure projects. If the user charges have to be below the cost of provision of these services, the government should provide explicit subsidies (e.g. after the Delhi power distribution privatization, the tariffs for households consuming below 200 units of electricity per month is zero and those consuming between 200 and 400 units are subsidized, and the difference between the tariffs and cost of supply to these market segments is paid explicitly by the Delhi government to the private providers as a subsidy, which was Rs.3,090 crore in 2021/22).

Since many infrastructure services are merit goods (primary health and primary education, for example), full cost recovery (including both capital cost and operational cost) may not always be possible or desirable. Therefore, user charges should at least recover the O&M costs of all infrastructure assets.

Why Do We Need Reasonable User Charges?

User charges add to investment in that a new revenue stream is created where none existed earlier (e.g. toll roads collected Rs.26,851 crore in 2019/20)[2] facilitating more infrastructure investment. Reasonable user charges also help manage demand and mitigate adverse environmental and resource-use impacts. More generally, reasonable user charges help improve efficiency in the use of resources, equity, cost recovery, and alleviate undesirable environmental effects.

Since an important rationale of inducting the private sector into infrastructure is the resource crunch of governments, creation of an additional

---

[2] National Highways Authority of India (NHAI) Toll Information System. 2020. *Snapshot of tolling as on 31 March 2020 under NHAI projects* (accessed 30 December 2020).

revenue stream facilitates the creation of additional infrastructure, and thus addresses the issue of infrastructure deficit in the country. As we have seen, toll roads collected Rs.26,851 crore in 2019/20, which would help increase the retained earnings of companies operating these toll roads, which in turn would help increase funding of road assets. Then there is the environmental rationale. For example, the Central Ground Water Board imposes no charges for extraction of groundwater, which is partly responsible for the depleting groundwater levels across the country. Out of the total 6,881 assessment units (Blocks/Mandals/Talukas) in the country, 1,186 units in various states (17 per cent) have been categorized as 'over-exploited' indicating groundwater extraction exceeding the annual replenishable groundwater recharge. Only 4,310 assessment units (63 per cent) have been categorized as 'safe' where groundwater extraction is less than 70 per cent of the recharge.[3] If water is priced, less water would be extracted from the ground (as users would try to equate the marginal benefits to the marginal costs of groundwater extraction thus managing demand), and this would help mitigate adverse environmental and resource-use impacts.

Similarly, as per the Composite Water Management Index[4], there are over 20 million wells pumping water with (subsidized) power supply provided by the government. This has been depleting groundwater, while encouraging wastage of water in many states. A comparison of depth to water level of pre-monsoon 2018 with decadal mean pre-monsoon (2008–2017) level reveals that about 52 per cent of wells are showing a decline in water level. Part of the reason for the declining groundwater level is that there is no charge for groundwater extraction and the power supply is subsidized. Even when there is a charge for water, it is a flat rate for households. Volumetric water charges would make households conserve water and thus promote environmental sustainability.

Low user charges are justified in the name of the poor, that is, the poor would not be able to afford higher rates. However, because of low user charges and resultant low cost recovery, the poor may be getting

---

[3] Ministry of Jal Shakti, Department of Water Resources, River Development and Ganga Rejuvenation. 2019. *National Compilation on Dynamic Ground Water Resources of India, 2017.*

[4] Niti Aayog. 2019. *Composite Water Management Index* (https://social.niti.gov.in/uploads/sample/water_index_report2.pdf).

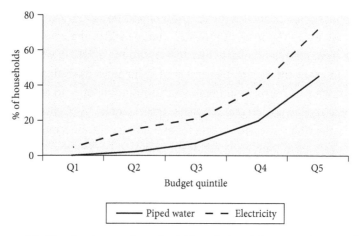

Figure 3.1 Piped water supply and grid-based electricity, access by quintile
Source: As quoted in Vivien Foster and Cecilia Briceño-Garmendia (eds). 2010. *Africa's Infrastructure—A Time for Transformation.*

rationed out of publicly provided services (Figure 3.1 shows that access to piped-water supply and grid-based electricity is quite limited in the lowest-budget quintile, Q1). For example, the Delhi Jal Board has only 2.2 million metered connections and about 0.15 million unmetered connections[5] for the over 5 million households in Delhi, implying that the vast majority of households (which invariably would be poor) are not connected to piped-water supply. These poor households may be paying high charges for water supply in private markets (water supply to poor households from tankers and standposts, see Figure 3.2). In fact, it is well established that consumption subsidies (or low user charges) should be replaced with connection subsidies for improving both efficiency and equity in provision of such services.[6]

Low user charges lead to the vicious cycle of asset creation, their steady deterioration because of inadequate O&M owing to low cost recovery, and finally re-building these assets at huge costs. Adequately maintained

---

[5] Government of NCT of Delhi. 2020. *Economic Survey of Delhi 2019–20* (http://delhiplanning.nic.in/content/economic-survey-delhi-2019-20).
[6] Kumar V. Pratap and Rajesh Chakrabarti. 2018. *Public–Private Partnerships in Infrastructure: Managing the Challenges.* (http://www.springer.com/la/book/9789811033544).

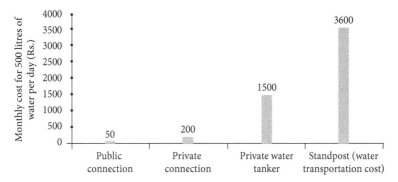

Figure 3.2 The poor end up paying much more for water than the rich

Note: Water from standposts is actually free, but it turns out to be the most expensive source as private operators collect water in containers provided by households and deliver it to their doorstep at a transportation charge, which in many cases would be Rs.6 for 25 litres.

Source: Report on Indian Urban Infrastructure and Services (2011) (https://icrier.org/pdf/Fina lReport-hpec.pdf).

assets are a much more efficient and financially prudent way of providing infrastructure services than the wasteful vicious cycle described above.

Low user charges also lead to private project failures, exemplified by the high rate of such failures in the water and sewerage sector, where 4.7 per cent of the projects have failed accounting for 17.7 per cent of investment in the sector as per the Private Participation in Infrastructure database of the World Bank,[7] both significantly higher than the overall project failure rate of infrastructure.

People who have got used to receiving infrastructure services free (say water, power, and roads) may take recourse to direct action (preventing providers from charging tolls), adding to political risks (because of de facto expropriation that such action entails) faced by private infrastructure projects. Regulators may also be setting user fees below costs, as in the power distribution sector. Section 61 of the Electricity Act (2003) states that 'The Appropriate Commission shall, subject to the provisions of this Act, specify the terms and conditions for the determination of tariff, and in doing so, shall be guided by the following ... that the tariff progressively reflects the cost of supply of electricity.' Though, recently,

[7] World Bank. Private Participation in Infrastructure database (ppi.worldbank.org) (accessed 8 December 2020).

the electricity tariffs have gone up in some states, the gap is still quite wide at Rs.0.72 per unit of electricity supplied in the country.[8] These political and regulatory risks would be reflected in a higher risk premium charged by the investors, thereby increasing costs and decreasing the cost competitiveness of the Indian economy.

The Current Scenario

Most infrastructure is under-priced in India, that is, there is inadequate cost recovery (water supply, power supply, metro fares, fees in public hospitals and educational institutions, etc.). In the railways, passenger rates are low and cross-subsidized from higher freight rates, with the result that railways are losing market share (for freight) to the road sector despite being more economically and environmentally efficient. The overall recovery rates (i.e. the cost of publicly provided services recovered from the users) on services provided by the central government was estimated by the Eighth Five-Year Plan (1992–1997) to be as low as about 35 per cent; it was even lower at about 14 per cent for the services provided by state governments.[9]

The current user charges in public utilities in India are well below those found internationally (after normalizing the user charges in US dollar terms on a purchasing-power-parity basis) (see Tables 3.1 to 3.3 for international comparisons of user charges for metro rail, drinking water, and tuition fees). These tables clearly emphasize the need for raising user charges across sectors in India.

However, because of the inefficiency of some of the government departments and corporations that provide these public utilities, the actual costs of provision of many of these services themselves are much higher than what they ought to be. To that extent, the whole of the unrecovered costs of these public utilities does not constitute a subsidy to the users of these services. Nevertheless, it would be reasonable to assume that

[8] Power Finance Corporation (2020). *Report on Performance of State Power Utilities, 2018–19* (https://www.pfcindia.com/DocumentRepository/ckfinder/files/Operations/Performance_Reports_of_State_Power_Utilities/Report%20on%20Performance%20of%20State%20Power%20Utilities%202018-19.pdf).

[9] Planning Commission, Government of India. 1992. *Eighth Five Year Plan.*

Table 3.1 Metro fares (for 1–6 km distance)

Country/City	Rates (local currency)	Rates (US$ PPP)
Tokyo	JNY 170	1.54
Singapore	SG$ 1.90	1.8
Paris	EUR 1.90	2.28
Delhi (DMRC)	INR 30	1.42

Note: PPP conversion factor have been used to convert local currency charges into US$ PPP.

Note: For DMRC, fare between Adarshnagar and Vidhan Sabha is considered (distance 6.10 km). For Singapore, fare between Clarke Quay and Potong Pasir is considered (distance 5 km).

Source: Tokyo Metro, Regular Tickets (https://www.tokyometro.jp/en/ticket/regular/index.html); Singapore MRT/LRT Fare Calculator, Travel Time and Route Guide (https://mrt.sg/fare); Paris Public Transport (https://en.parisinfo.com/practical-paris/how-to-get-to-and-around-paris/public-transport); DMRC, Journey Planner (http://www.delhimetrorail.com/metro-fares.aspx).

Table 3.2 Domestic water-use charges (per 1,000 cubic feet)

Country/City	Rates (Local currency)	Rates (US$ PPP)
Singapore	SG$ 104	99
Seattle	US$ 110.8	110.8
Boston	US$ 62	62
Maharashtra	INR 28.32	1.34
Delhi	INR 1,244	59

Note: For Singapore, total price is considered for consumption exceeding 40 m³. For Seattle, water rates for third-tier (over 36 CCF in 60 days inside Seattle) has been considered. For Boston, water rates for next 50 cubic feet per day has been taken. For Maharashtra standard rates for domestic water use for municipal corporations (Rs.0.50 per m³) has been considered. This is adjusted as per water use—twice the standard rate when quantity exceeds 140 per cent of norm-based water use (Rs.1 per m³). For Delhi, rate slab is taken for monthly consumption exceeding 30 kilolitres (Rs.43.93).

Source: PUB (Singapore's National Water Agency). 2017. Water Price Revisions (https://www.pub.gov.sg/sites/assets/PressReleaseDocuments/WPR2017-AnnexA.pdf); Seattle Government, Residential Drinking Water Rates Effective from 1 January 2020 (Residential Commodity Charges) (http://www.seattle.gov/utilities/your-services/accounts-and-payments/rates/water/residential-water-rates); Boston Water and Sewer Commission, Current Water and Sewer Rates Effective from 1 January 2020 (Residential) (https://www.bwsc.org/residential-customers/rates); Maharashtra Water Resources Regulatory Authority. Review and Revision of Bulk Water Rates for Domestic, Industrial and Agriculture Irrigation Use in Maharashtra State, Order 1/2018; Delhi Jal Board, Revised Water Tariff w.e.f 1 February 2018 (http://www.delhijalboard.nic.in/sites/default/files/All-PDF/Revised%2BWater%2BTarif%2Bwef%2B01022018_0.pdf).

Table 3.3 Tuition fees for studying law (for two terms in a year)

Country/City	Rates (local currency)	Rates (US$ PPP)
Singapore	SG$ 38,200	36,380
United States	US$ 28,264	28,264
Delhi	INR 180	8.54

Source: National University of Singapore, Tuition Fees Per Annum (Applicable for Academic Year 2020/2021) (http://www.nus.edu.sg/registrar/docs/info/administrative-policies-procedures/ugtui tioncurrent.pdf); Ilana Kowarski. 2020. *See the Price, Payoff of Law School before Enrolling* (https:// www.usnews.com/education/best-graduate-schools/top-law-schools/articles/law-school-cost-starting-salary); Delhi University (Faculty of Law), Schedule of Fees: 2020–21 (http://www.du.ac. in/du/uploads/COVID-19/pdf/adm2020/Notice_Admission%20in%20Faculty%20of%20Law. pdf).

a substantial part of these unrecovered costs of public utilities is, in fact, a subsidy to the users. This calls for some increase in the user charges of some of these public utilities aimed at recovering at least the O&M costs. At the same time, the government departments and corporations providing these utilities should be forced to become more efficient by imposing harder budget constraints on them.[10]

What Can Be Done?

However, the under-pricing and political difficulties in raising user charges does not mean that there is no room for improvement. For example, in the road sector, a common electronic toll system for the whole country would be ideal and would ensure against long lines of vehicles at toll booths and the consequent wastage of time and fuel, while also being a check against a major source of leakage and theft (prevalent when there is physical cash collection of tolls), thus increasing the realized user charges. The Government of India has already decided to implement the electronic toll collection system on a pan-India basis, and FASTags were made mandatory on vehicles from 1 January 2021.[11] There are also some successful

[10] Planning Commission, Government of India. 1992. *Eighth Five Year Plan.*
[11] Press Trust of India. 25 December 2020. User Fee Collection through FASTag Crosses Rs 80 cr per day with Record 50 lakh Transactions: NHAI. *The Economic Times*

examples of addressing political difficulties in raising user charges through a gradual increase in prices over a long period as in the case of kerosene fuel[12] (Choudhary 2020) that can be replicated across sectors.

Kerala Water Authority has recently revised water rates by notifying the current water tariff as the floor rate that is subject to 5 per cent annual increase from 1 April 2021 for all categories of consumers.[13] This is to make the state eligible for additional borrowing of 2 per cent of gross state domestic product from the centre, conditional upon reforms undertaken to boost urban local body revenues. So, incentivizing reasonable user charges in the most politically sensitive water sector can also play a part in making tariffs cost-reflective.

It is not our intention to convey that there is no space for subsidies in the quest for reasonable user charges. However, subsidies need to be well targeted through 100 per cent metering, supplemented by lifeline tariffs and volumetric pricing (with an increasing block tariff) so that those meant for the poor are not siphoned off by the rich.

This has also been reiterated by the 15th Finance Commission and finds mention in the principles of draft National Water Framework Bill, 2016:[14] water used for commercial agriculture and for industry or commerce may be priced on the basis of full economic pricing, or higher if needed and appropriate in a given case. For domestic water supply, a graded pricing system may be adopted, with full-cost-recovery pricing for high-income groups, affordable pricing for middle income, and a certain quantum of free supply to the poor to be determined by the appropriate government, or alternatively, a minimal quantum of water may be supplied free to all. Smart and pre-paid metering in power distribution would also help in improving billing and collection efficiency,

---

(https://economictimes.indiatimes.com/news/economy/infrastructure/user-fee-collection-through-fastag-crosses-rs-80-cr-per-day-with-record-50-lakh-transactions-nhai/articleshow/79955960.cms#:~:text=NEW).

[12] Sanjeev Choudhary. 13 March 2020. Kerosene Subsidy Removed via Small Price Hikes over 4 Years. *The Economic Times* (https://economictimes.indiatimes.com/industry/energy/oil-gas/kerosene-subsidy-removed-via-small-price-hikes-over-4-years/articleshow/74601660.cms?from=mdr).

[13] Kerala Water Authority. 2021. Water Tariff (accessed on 10 June 2021) (https://kwa.kerala.gov.in/water-tariff/).

[14] Ministry of Water Resources. 2016. *Draft National Water Framework Bill, 2016.* p. 20. (http://www.mowr.gov.in/sites/default/files/Water_Framework_May_2016.pdf).

with a commensurate impact on lowering aggregate technical and commercial losses. This will help meet the objectives of cost recovery, economic efficiency, equity, affordability, and the financial viability of utilities.

One of the established principles of optimal risk allocation is that risk should be allocated to the party that has more control over the risk factor. Using this principle, political risks should be assigned to the government, which should have the responsibility of upholding the rule of law and not allow goons to take over toll booths. Similarly, regulatory risk can be mitigated by making regulatory institutions truly autonomous; it is no coincidence that all infrastructure regulators in India are headed by re-tired bureaucrats too eager to tow the government line. The selection of regulators and regulatory processes needs to improve for their improved credibility and for user charges to be cost-reflective[15].

Cost-recovering user charges also need to be prioritized in view of the growing fiscal crunch during the current Covid-19-pandemic times. There is immense potential for increasing revenues from reason-able user charges. In the scheme of financing of the NIP, user charges will be reflected in higher internal accruals and retained earnings of the providing enterprises, both public and private. However, the NIP has budgeted only 1–3 per cent (roughly Rs.1–3 lakh crore) from this source, which we feel is a huge underestimate. Let's illustrate this as-sertion through an analysis of the power distribution sector. There is a revenue gap of Rs.0.72 per unit of electricity consumed in the country (Power Finance Corporation 2020). The total energy generated in the country in 2018/19 was 1,547 billion units (*Economic Survey 2019–20*),[16] of which about 22 per cent is lost in AT&C losses. So, if cost-recovering level of tariffs were to be imposed on the power sector, the additional potential revenue generation would amount to Rs.86,900 crore per annum. Since the NIP is a six-year infrastructure plan for the country, the total resource generation potential from making the power tariffs cost-reflective is Rs.5,21,400 crore, which is much more than that

---

[15] Kumar V. Pratap. 2015. *User Fees and Political and Regulatory Risks in Indian Public–Private Partnerships*. Economic and Political Weekly, L(36) (5 September) (https://www.epw.in/journal/2015/36/commentary/user-fees-and-political-and-regulatory-risks-indian-public-private).

[16] Ministry of Finance, Government of India. 2020. *Economic Survey 2019–20*.

estimated in the NIP financing plan, and that too from just one major infrastructure sector.

The NIP projects a resource gap of 8–10 per cent (roughly Rs.8–10 lakh crore) over six years. Given the rough estimate of additional resource generation potential just from the power sector calculated above, it is clear that reasonable user charges across infrastructure sectors would wipe away the entire resource gap of the NIP and more.

4

Financing Economic and Social Infrastructure

Sectoral analysis of private participation in infrastructure shows that most private investment has gone into economic infrastructure (like telecom, power, transport) as opposed to social infrastructure (like water supply, health, education). Social infrastructure in India is currently suffering from resource crunch as well as abysmal levels of efficiency. Therefore, the need for private investment may perhaps be greater in these sectors. However, the projects in social sectors tend to be small (e.g., the cost of a primary school is much less compared to a power plant), and there may be issues in imposing full-cost-recovery user fees, given that many services provided (like water supply and primary education) are merit goods. Therefore, they are much less attractive to the private sector, which could help improve the sector both in terms of resources and efficiency. The chapter focuses on challenges in financing social infrastructure and the strategies to overcome them. The Manila Water Company example for water supply, and the numerous education and health public–private partnership (PPP) projects in Australia and the United Kingdom show that private participation in social infrastructure is possible for mutual benefit to the private and public sectors. Impact investment, the importance of environmental, social, and governance (ESG) norms, social stock exchange, and so on, will also play a part in popularizing private investment in social infrastructure.

In consonance with the rest of the world, in India too, private participation in infrastructure is limited mainly to economic infrastructure (see Table 4.1). Thus, most private participation has happened in energy and transport sectors, both by the number of projects (91.5 per cent of the total

Infrastructure Financing in India. Kumar V Pratap and Manshi Gupta, Oxford University Press.
© Kumar V Pratap and Manshi Gupta 2024. DOI: 10.1093/oso/9780198884934.003.0005

Table 4.1 Private participation in infrastructure in India (1990–2020)

Sector	Number of projects	Investment (US$ billion)
Energy	455	152
ICT	25	3
Transport	559	121
Water and sewerage	69	3
Total	1,108	279

Note: ICT: Information and Communications Technology.

Source: Private Participation in Infrastructure database of the World Bank (ppi.worldbank.org) (accessed 8 December 2020).

in Table 4.1) as well as the associated investments (97.8 per cent). Water and sewerage, a typical social infrastructure sector, has sixty-nine projects (including waste collection and transport (six projects), integrated municipal solid waste (twenty-nine projects), treatment and disposal of waste (fourteen projects), and water and sewerage (twenty projects)) accounting for an investment of US$3 billion, which implies that social infrastructure projects, besides being fewer, are typically smaller compared to economic infrastructure projects (average investment per project is US$43 million in social infrastructure as compared to US$267 million in economic infrastructure).

This highlights the challenge of private investment in social infrastructure, where projects are smaller, cost recovery is low, subjecting these projects to political economy issues, which adds to their risk profile, and projects also tend to be more complex because of direct interface with retail consumers, all of which results in less private investment in social infrastructure. The private sector often finds social infrastructure projects more challenging as financial rewards are smaller and the operational demands are more complex.

The National Infrastructure Pipeline (NIP) is the focus of Government of India's effort to augment India's infrastructure through a planned investment of about Rs.111 lakh crore over financial years (FYs) 2020–2025 across 6,847 projects (see Chapter 1). Urban infrastructure is slated to see investments worth Rs.19.19 lakh crore (17.3 per cent) across 1,688 (24.7 per cent) projects while the other projects in the social infrastructure sector are expected to see an investment of Rs.3.93 lakh crore (3.5 per cent) across 559 (8.1 per cent) projects.[1]

Most investment in social infrastructure has come through the public route (including federal grants) and more recently as engineering–procurement–construction contracts, given the paucity of private investment in the sector. Easy availability of public money and the rigour of being subjected to the discipline associated with dealing with private investment have acted as impediments for a systematic approach to increasing private participation in the sector. There are many well-known recommendations for shoring up revenues of urban local bodies, who have a role in improving social infrastructure, like imposing reasonable user charges (see Chapter 3), institutionalizing value capture finance to part-fund major public investments like metro rail in cities (see Chapter 6), and encouraging development of municipal bond, pooled finance, and blended finance (see Chapter 8) markets. This chapter will concentrate on increasing the role of private finance in social infrastructure through PPPs in water supply, education, and health, social stock exchange, impact investing, and integrating ESG concerns to attract institutional investment in social infrastructure.

Leveraging Grants for Private Participation in Social Infrastructure

To enable more PPPs in social infrastructure, given the low cost recovery in such sectors and externalities generated by projects that cannot by captured by the project revenue streams, the Government of India has increased the viability gap funding (VGF) limit of the Ministry of Finance to 30 per cent of total project cost (TPC) for social infrastructure (with another 30 per cent of TPC as VGF by project authority) compared to 20 per cent each for economic infrastructure. For demonstration projects, VGF has been increased to 40 per cent of TPC (and 25 per cent operational cost in the first five years after project completion) for health and education projects by the Ministry of Finance, with another 40 per cent of TPC and 25 per cent operational cost by project authority. VGF is given

---

[1] Ministry of Finance. 2020. *National Infrastructure Pipeline*.

as a grant to competitively bid PPP projects where VGF is the bidding parameter. VGF enables leveraging of limited budgetary resources to access a larger pool of private capital. By increasing the VGF limit to 30 per cent of the TPC, which can be matched by a further 30 per cent of TPC by the project authorities (and increasing the VGF limit to 40 per cent for demonstration projects), the non-commercial aspect of social infrastructure would be addressed, and it is expected that the success of PPPs in economic infrastructure in India (in terms of augmenting resources and improving service delivery) will also be replicated in social infrastructure.[2]

Increased investment funded by both public and private sources in social infrastructure is important. By 2050, the world's population is estimated to grow to almost 10 billion from the current 8 billion, and the future is definitely urban: according to the World Bank's Demographic Trends and Urbanization report, 56 per cent of the global population already lives in urban areas, and urbanization is set to become the defining megatrend of the century with three-quarters of humanity expected to be living in cities by 2050 (the comparable numbers for India are 34.9 per cent and 52.8 per cent). Over 2018–2050, India, China, and Nigeria are together expected to contribute nearly 35 per cent to the projected global urban population growth, with India contributing 416 million urban dwellers. Indian cities are likely to accommodate almost half of the population of the country by 2040. This suggests an increased need for integrated, sustainable, technology-enabled, and inclusive design and development of physical, institutional, social, and economic infrastructure in the country. This will contribute to both increased economic growth (it is estimated that urban areas in India with one-third of the population residing in them currently contribute two-thirds to the GDP) and improved quality of life.

PPPs have been leveraged in developed countries like the United Kingdom, Australia, and Canada (and some developing countries like the Philippines where the Manila Water Company is the most celebrated

---

[2] In a series of research reports, KPMG has found that students attending classes in new buildings that were procured, built, and operated under a PPP structure, achieve a faster rate of improvement in educational attainment than those that attend schools that were conventionally procured (KPMG. 2010. *Infrastructure 100*).

water sector PPP in the developing world, see Box 4.1) to provide social infrastructure with special emphasis on education and health sectors (see Boxes 4.2 and 4.3). These best practices can be replicated in India for the sustainable provision of public services like water supply, education, and health, thereby reducing the burden on state finances while also improving efficiency in the delivery of these services.

This will also help in achieving the Sustainable Development Goals (SDGs). Social infrastructure is both an explicit and implicit component of the SDGs (SDG 9 is: Build resilient infrastructure, promote inclusive and sustainable industrialization and foster innovation). Progress on Target 9.1 (Develop quality, reliable, sustainable, and resilient infrastructure to support economic development and human well-being, with a focus on affordable and equitable access for all) would require progress in access to quality education, healthcare, water, and sanitation, among other targets and indicators. It would also focus on those hardest to reach, thus enabling inclusive growth.

The main PPP models in social infrastructure are similar to those used in economic infrastructure: Build-Operate-Transfer (BOT), Design-Build-Finance-Operate-Transfer (DBFOT), and Operation and Maintenance (O&M) of assets. Since some provisioning of social infrastructure (health, education, water supply, solid waste management, etc.) would be prevalent in rural and urban areas of countries, O&M of assets has emerged as an important way to associate the private sector in public services, while also being less intrusive (and therefore, 'asset-light', reducing cost and complexity) compared to the DBFOT model.

Water and sewerage

Water is unique among infrastructure sectors in that it is essential to life.[3] One can survive without power, telecom, or transport facilities for days and weeks, but not without water. Water is also under-priced in most jurisdictions and may need an increase in user charges for its provision to be

---

[3] Drawn partly from Kumar V. Pratap and Rajesh Chakrabarti. 2018. *Public–Private Partnerships in Infrastructure—Managing the Challenges.*

commercially viable for the private sector. Because of this, private investment in the sector may be subjected to unmanageable political risks and
therefore, 85 per cent of water utilities worldwide are publicly owned and
controlled.

India is a water-stressed country as it supports about 17 per cent of the
world's population with 4 per cent of freshwater, 78 per cent of which is
consumed by agriculture.[4] Water is an inherently difficult sector for the
private sector to enter and there is a high rate of failure of PPP projects
in the sector.[5] As shown in Table 4.1, the water and sewerage sector accounts for the least private investment among all infrastructure sectors
in India. It is very difficult to get the private sector interested in the provision of water mainly because of poor cost recovery and any effort to raise
tariffs is subject to heightened political risk. If a foreign company is providing water, the risk of project cancellation increases further. However,
there are many PPP water and sewerage projects in developed countries
like Australia, Canada, and the Netherlands. One of the most celebrated
PPP water projects in developing countries is in Manila, Philippines (see
Box 4.1).

Water sector issues

Political and regulatory risk in water sector: There may be opposition from
consumers to pay for water when they are used to getting it free. This
may cause them to force removal of water charges by dismantling water
meters, and so on. This would amount to defacto expropriation and increase the political risks to water projects.

The main regulatory risk in the water sector is tariff risk, which is the
risk that regulators would not set the tariffs at cost-recovery levels. Thus,
on average, the cost recovery in the water sector could be as low as 10–
20 per cent of even the O&M expenditures. However, the water sector
in India has few independent regulators and the regulatory role is performed mostly by the public authority or contracts.

---

[4] *Times of India*. 20 June 2022. Follow the Clouds.
[5] Clive Harris and Kumar V. Pratap. 2009. *What Drives Private Sector Exit from Infrastructure—
Economic Crises and Other Factors in the Cancellation of Private Infrastructure Projects in
Developing Countries* (https://openknowledge.worldbank.org/bitstream/handle/10986/10569/
478840BRI0Grid10Box338868B01PUBLIC1.pdf?sequence=1&isAllowed=y).

Box 4.1 Case study: Manila Water Company, Philippines

The government corporation that owned the water utility and its assets, before privatization, was Metropolitan Waterworks and Sewerage System (MWSS). Just before privatization, water rates were increased by 38 per cent and employment was decreased by 30 per cent to make the water utility attractive to the private sector. Private concessionaires were chosen through competitive bidding, with the bidding parameter being lowest initial tariffs. The concession period was twenty-five years. There were targets for improvement in service coverage, water quality, service quality and reduction in non-revenue water (NRW)[a] specified in the concession contract.

The bids received and winning bids are shown in Table 4.2. As is apparent from the table, the bids received were much lower than the pre-privatization rate.

Table 4.2 Bids received and winning bids (in Philippine peso per cubic meter)

	Bid
Pre-privatization rate	8.56
East zone	
Ayala-International Water (Manila Water Co. Inc.)	2.32 (winning bid)
Aboitiz-Compagnie Generale des Eaux	5.52
Metro-Pacific-Anglian Water International	5.66
Benpres-Lyonnaise des Eaux (Suez)	6.13
West zone	
Ayala-International Water	2.51
Benpres-Lyonnaise des Eaux (Maynilad Water Services Inc.)	4.96 (winning bid)
Aboitiz-Compagnie Generale des Eaux	4.99
Metro-Pacific-Anglian Water International	5.87

Source: XunWu and Malaluan A. Nepomuceno. 2008. *A Tale of Two Concessionaires: A Natural Experiment of Water Privatisation in Metro Manila.*

Concessionaire Selection

On the basis of the bids received and shown in Table 4.2, concession contracts were awarded in 1997 to Manila Water Co. Inc. (MWCI) (east zone of Manila) and Maynilad Water Services Inc. (MWSI) (west zone) though the same bidder was the lowest bidder for both the zones. This was done to:

- Give public authority/regulators more leverage in their negotiation with concessionaires;
- Provide opportunities for competitive benchmarking between the two zones (competition in the market—also known as yardstick competition—involves splitting the market into service areas covered by operators that do not compete directly but that can be compared by a regulator. Yardstick competition is often used to deal with the problem of information asymmetry and to ascertain cost information);
- This arrangement served as a safety valve, such that if one concessionaire got into financial trouble, the other concessionaire could take over.

Concession Agreement

The concession agreement had provision for adjusting the tariff annually for inflation and for unforeseen developments like a large change in the exchange rate (called Extraordinary Price Adjustment). The concession agreement also stipulated that tariffs will be re-based every five years to ensure that the concessionaire can recover all prudent and efficient expenditures at an appropriate discount rate (ADR). This provided a strong incentive to bidders to submit very low tariff bids initially, which led to lower cash flows and reduced capital expenditures initially. This prognosis is brought out in Table 4.3, which shows that the base tariff for Manila Water went up 6.4 times and Maynilad Water by 4.3 times in the near ten-year period since privatization.

Capital expenditures of MWCI were at a low level until its tariffs were rebased in 2003. After 2003, the capital expenditures that were financed by the improved cash flows and greater access to debt financing were used to carry out a successful NRW reduction

Table 4.3 History of tariff rates before and after privatization (Philippine peso per cubic metre)

	Average base tariff		Average all-intariff[a]	
	Manila Water	Maynilad	Manila Water	Maynilad
Pre-privatization	8.56		8.78	
Post-privatization				
1997/98	2.32	4.96	4.02	7.21
1999	2.61	5.80	4.37	8.23
2000	2.76	6.13	4.55	8.63
2001	2.95	6.58	4.78	9.17
2002	4.51	11.39	9.37	19.92
2003	10.06	11.39	13.38	19.92
2004	10.40	11.39	14.00	19.92
2005	13.95	19.72	18.55	30.19
2006	14.94	21.12	19.73	32.34

[a]All-in tariff = base tariff + CERA (currency exchange rate adjustment) + FCDA (foreign currency differential adjustment) + EC (environmental charge) + VAT (value added tax).
Source: Xun Wu and Nepomuceno A. Malaluan. 2008. *A Tale of Two Concessionaires: A Natural Experiment of Water Privatisation in Metro Manila*.

programme as well as additional investments in distribution. This resulted in more revenues and profits, which, in turn, gave the company even more access to equity (through an Initial Public Offer (IPO)) and debt financing making it a virtuous circle. Capital expenditures peaked in 2006 at 4.8 billion pesos (see Figure 4.1), as the NRW reduction programme brought the NRW level to economically efficient levels.

Political Economy of Water Tariffs

The basic water tariff more than quadrupled after the tariffs were rebased in 2003 and 2008 for both the concessonaires. However, the 'Water for the Community' programme helped Manila Water build legitimacy whereby the company has been able to provide water services to poor communities that the public water utility had failed to reach. This also made business sense for the company as it reduced NRW by minimizing illegal connections. Nearly two million people from marginalized communities have been given access to clean and affordable

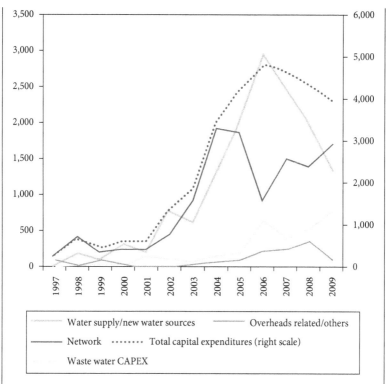

Figure 4.1 Manila Water Co.—Capital Expenditure (million peso)
Source: Manila Water Company.

water through the company's flagship 'Water for the Community' programme. Manila Water mobilized unserved communities to overcome resistance to tariff increases—in the public hearings on the tariff increases, people who represented NGOs and groups that were against the tariff increases were often outnumbered by representatives of unserved communities that had been programmed for connection in the business plan justifying the tariff increases. In this way, MWCI aligned its social (connecting the unconnected to piped water supply), economic, and financial (higher revenues and profits) objectives. The success of the 'Water for the Community' programme suggests that public benefits and private-sector profit motives may not be inherently incompatible in water privatization.

Contrasting Outcomes—Manila and Maynilad

Maynilad never made a profit during its eight years of operation because NRW remained persistently high. In 2005, Maynilad was turned over to MWSS under a so-called debt-for-equity exchange (PPP project cancellation). In contrast, Manila Water had begun to make a profit by 1999 as a result of rapid decrease in NRW (63 per cent in 1997 to 35 per cent in 2005). In 2005, Manila Water was listed on the Philippine Stock Exchange through an IPO.

Today, Manila Water Company, Inc. is a publicly listed company with extensive experience in the Philippine Water Sector from water treatment and distribution to wastewater management and sanitation services. The Company delivers water supply, wastewater, and sanitation services in the East Zone concession in Metro Manila and the province of Rizal, serving a population of over 7.3 million with clean water and 24/7 access (from 26 per cent to near 100 per cent access now). It has reduced NRW from 63 per cent in 1997 to an average of 13 per cent now. The success of Manila Water in its Manila concession is now being replicated in other Philippines' top metropolitan cities like Laguna, Boracay, Clark, Davao, among others. The company now has international business operations in Vietnam, Thailand, Indonesia, and the Kingdom of Saudi Arabia. In 2022, Manila Water became the first water company from the Philippines and from any developing country, to be given the distinction as Water Company of the Year in the highly coveted 2022 Global Water Awards.[b]

[a] Non-revenue water (NRW) refers to water that is not billed because of leakage through holes in the pipes, illegal connections, or measurement problems due to faulty meters.

[b] Manila Water Press Release. 2022. Manila Water in Historic Win as First Philippine Company to Be Named 'Water Company of the Year' at the 2022 Global Water Awards (https://www.manilawater.com/corporate/sustainability/agos/2022-05-20/manila-water-in-historic-win-as-first-philippine-company-to-be-named--water-company-of-the-year--at-the-2022-global-water-awards).

The water sector is subject to high non-revenue water losses: The volume of water entering the distribution system minus the volume billed to customers is termed non-revenue water (NRW). It has three major components: physical water loss, commercial loss (theft), and unbilled authorized consumption (free water). In India, about half of the water supply is lost to NRW, the major constituent of which is water theft.

Some solutions

- Uncertainty about the condition of assets (water pipelines, etc.) as they are mostly underground and may have been there for decades. This adds to risks and may increase project costs. One way to reduce uncertainty arising from the condition of assets is to allow an enhanced monitoring period (EMP) during which the private sector may monitor the system after contract award, in the process of which it may get to know more about the condition of assets. If the condition of the assets is worse than assumed, the private sector may be given the liberty to ask for a re-calibration of tariffs. However, this is politically sensitive and the public sector may be subjected to the charge of changing the rules of the game after contract award.

- In common with the majority of brownfield projects, employee resistance could be another challenge for PPP in the water sector. One way to handle this challenge would be to allow those employees who do not want to join the PPP to be deployed elsewhere. In addition, a monetary incentive can also be considered and the conditions of service of employees not allowed to worsen after the project has been contracted out to the private sector.

- Opportunity provided by a high level of NRW: The high level of NRW seen in the developing world could also be an opportunity as decrease in NRW could be a win–win solution for most stakeholders. Decrease in NRW would mean extra revenues for the utility, which should reduce the need for tariff increases that may be required for financially sustainable and qualitatively improved private operations. Making the reduction of NRW part of a comprehensive reform programme, including increasing water access to those unconnected to piped water supply, often yields good outcomes. Reducing technical losses in water can cost less than 3 per cent of the cost of adding capacity and can be attained much faster.

- User charges should at least cover O&M costs: Keeping user charges low to benefit the poor is a false premise (see Figures 3.1 and 3.2 in Chapter 3). The poorest households are generally not connected to public services (the coverage of piped water supply is less than 20 per cent in the lowest-budget quintile in many jurisdictions). So, these households cannot benefit from low unit charges made possible through consumption subsidies, typically associated with these public services. The primary beneficiaries of consumption subsidies are the richer households that are connected to these public services. In other words, the poor do not benefit from low user charges and end up paying much more to water vendors. Connection subsidies (connecting the poor households to piped water supply) may be more desirable than consumption subsidies (low-per-unit cost of water) on both efficiency and equity considerations. So operational cost recovery of public services should be a feasible objective. But any such move would have political resistance. Necessary user charge revisions must have perceptible service delivery improvements to make the hike palatable to users. Improvement in service coverage would also help in building political support for necessary increases in user charges (as was done in the case of Manila Water Company through its 'Water for the Community' programme, see Box 4.1).

Education

PPPs in education are common in many developed countries like the United Kingdom, Australia, and Canada. The United Kingdom is home to the world's largest and most sophisticated PPP schools programme based on the DBFOT model. Under this model, while the government continues to provide core services (teaching), the private sector invests in the school infrastructure and provides related non-core services (school transport, food services, cleaning, etc.) under contract. Thus, PPPs enable the government to concentrate on the core teaching function while non-core activities are provided by the private sector. The United Kingdom has signed nearly one hundred education Private Finance Initiative (PFI) deals valued at £3.5 billion. There is increasing investor interest in education PPPs in Australia, with projects valued at US$3.7 billion in the pipeline.

Challenges in education PPPs: Budgeting is a challenge because of high procurement costs for small projects and the uncertainty of revenue streams. User fees (tuitions) may be too high, not taking into account externalities (positive externalities in primary education may be more than tertiary education; positive externalities in girls' education may be more than that for boys). Future demographic and policy changes also make rigid, long-term contracts less suitable for schools. One way to address the issue of the small size of projects with associated high transaction costs in the education sector is bundling, in which the concessionaire would be handed over the responsibility of a number of schools. In education, the financial viability of a PPP increases with the number of schools covered by the contract, especially for primary schools, where projects are limited in both size and scope.

Scheme for PPP in School Education in India: India has introduced a scheme for setting up of 2,500 Model Schools under the PPP mode, with every block having at least one such school. School infrastructure will be provided by the private entity like in the United Kingdom. The PPP will be governed by an initial ten-year contract, extendable on mutual agreement, and have classes from Grade VI to Grade XII. In these schools, the government would pay for the students it sponsors. In addition, the school management can admit fee-paying students as appropriate without exceeding the cap on total students of 2,500. Government-sponsored students study free till class VIII, and after that at a nominal monthly charge of Rs.50, further halved for students from deprived sections of society. The non-government-sponsored students would pay regular fees.[6] For a single private entity, there is a ceiling of twenty schools per state and fifty schools overall in the country. The private partner will enter into a concession agreement with central government. Since payment to the private entity will be based on output parameters, close monitoring would be enforced as per the concession agreement. The pilot phase for fifty schools has been launched. Sixty-five potential bidders have been shortlisted on the basis of Request for Qualification.

Another initiative to augment funding of education in India is the setting up of the Higher Education Funding Agency in 2017 as a non-profit NBFC (Non-Banking Finance Company) to mobilize extra-budgetary resources to build crucial education infrastructure.

---

[6] Model School under Public–Private Partnership (PPP) Mode (http://pibmumbai.gov.in/English/PDF/E0000_H114.PDF).

Box 4.2 Case study: PPP in the education sector—New Schools Privately Financed Project, New South Wales, Australia

---

The New Schools Project was the first project delivered under the NSW Government's Working with Government initiative.[a] The project required the development of new procurement 'tools' for the acquisition of school facilities, including schools' output specification, risk analysis and allocation, and payment mechanism. A total of nine schools have opened in north-western and western Sydney, the Illawarra, and the Central Coast. Four schools opened in 2004 and five in 2005.

The private sector parties that were given the contracts are: Axiom Education Pty Limited ('the Contractor'), Hansen Yuncken Pty Limited and St Hilliers Contracting Pty Limited (the two 'Construction Contractors'), and Spotless Services Australia Limited ('the Operator'). The private sector financed this project through a special purpose vehicle (SPV). The SPV issued debt (~95 per cent) and equity (~5 per cent) to support the New School Project.

What the New School Project involved

i. Private sector design, financing, and construction of nine new public schools, in new urban release areas in north-western and western Sydney. Axiom Education will pay the Government up-front fees for these centres.

ii. Private sector cleaning, maintenance, repair, security, safety, utility, and related services for these school buildings, furniture, fittings, equipment, and grounds until 31 December 2032, when the buildings will be handed over to the public sector in return for performance-based monthly payments by the Department of Education and Training (DET) during the operational phase of the project.

Benefits from the project

i. The PFP (Privately Financed Project) schools were delivered some two years earlier, on average, than would have been possible had traditional public-sector funding been used.

ii. The New Schools Project was able to deliver better value for money as tested against the Public Sector Comparator (PSC). The risk adjusted PSC produced a range of likely costs as follows:

PSC best case	PSC most likely	PSC worst case
US$134.3 million	US$141.8 million	US$152.6 million

The risk adjusted cost of private sector delivery over the thirty-year life of the Project was US$131.4 million. The Project's savings are measured against the most likely scenario for public-sector delivery (US$141.8 million), producing an estimated saving of just over 7 per cent. The savings achieved were returned to DET, with US$7 million of capital savings retained within DET's capital programme, thus freeing up funds for use on other projects.

Innovation

The bundling of the schools, the bundling of the non-core services, and the life-cycle focus represent innovations delivered by the New Schools Project. These are discussed below.

Construction bundling: The PFP model allowed DET to bundle the construction and operation of a group of new schools. This delivered service and construction innovation. Construction economies of scale were achieved, through reduced management fees. The nature of this bundling over a thirty-year period also necessitated the interaction of builders, designers, and operators. This interaction does not easily occur under traditional delivery.

Non-core service bundling: The PFP bundled a number of school facilities management services for the first time, for example, maintenance, cleaning, pest control, and furniture porterage. These services are traditionally delivered by local school arrangements and/or contractors overseen by DET and/or Commerce. To manage the delivery of these services, the contractor was required to provide a help desk. In addition, Axiom has chosen to provide a full-time on-site manager at each school. This is a key benefit of the PFP—the single point of contact under the PFP contract. This relieves school principals or teaching staff of sometimes having to navigate or deal with different contracts, contractors, and sub-contractors and different government departments in order to address a facilities management issue.

The performance mechanism and abatement regime: The perform-ance management regime, payment mechanism, and abatement (deduction) regime provides the key link between the pro-ject objectives and the project outcomes/service delivery. The New Schools PFP requires the Contractor to prepare a monthly 'Performance and Payment Report'. The reporting requirements shift the burden of reporting and compliance monitoring from the State onto the Contractor. This is a major departure from traditional contract management and payment procedures where monitoring falls on the State. PFP provides a clear abate-ment framework and allows DET to withhold payment for ser-vice failures.

---

[a]New South Wales Treasury. 2005.*New Schools Privately Financed Project—Post Implementa-tion Review* (https://www.treasury.nsw.gov.au/sites/default/files/pdf/trp053_New_schools_privately_financed_project_-_POST_IMPLEMENTATION_REVIEW_dnd.pdf).

Health

Like a number of developing countries, approximately 45 per cent of the Indian population has to travel 100 km or more for access to quality health care. Health-care access is especially poor in rural areas. For ex-ample, India's bed density is still the lowest among the BRICS nations and about 70 per cent of the available beds are concentrated in the top twenty cities of the country. Average spending by OECD countries on health care is 9.9 per cent of GDP compared to 3.9 per cent of GDP (both public and private spending on health care) in India.

Like in economic and social infrastructure generally, the objective of PPPs in the health sector is to improve access to quality and affordable health-care facilities and address resource constraints. PPPs may be used for new infrastructure (new hospitals) or management of existing in-frastructure (primary health-care centres). Like its social infrastructure twin (education), PPPs in the health sector are quite challenging owing to the need for standardizing the risk-return framework and key perform-ance indicators through model concession agreement, and the need for a strong monitoring mechanism, especially as it has direct interface with users. User charges are also low, adding to the political sensitivity of pri-vate investment in the health sector. Public-sector capability to procure PPP health projects is also suspect in India.

In the United Kingdom, 130 PFI hospitals have been built since 1997 com-pared to twelve publicly funded hospitals. Medical services usually remain the responsibility of the public sector, while the private sector builds and op-erates the facilities. The contract term is generally thirty to thirty-five years.

PPP in health care in India: The Government of India has rolled out the National Rural Health Mission (NRHM) to address health-care gaps. PPPs are expected to play an important role under NRHM. It is esti-mated that India has eight health-care PPPs currently, with investment of Rs.1,833 crore (across all segments of healthcare). This includes super speciality hospitals and medical colleges (Punjab Institute of Medical Sciences—750 beds), diagnostics as an example of an 'asset-light' model (magnetic resonance imaging in Sawai Mansingh Hospital, Jaipur), dia-lysis centres (B Braun Dialysis Centers in Andhra Pradesh;[7] eleven centres are in operation housing 111 haemodialysis machines), and mobile med-ical units in Odisha and Uttarakhand under NRHM.

The Covid-19 pandemic has repositioned the health-care sector at the top of the government's priority list. India has been underspending on healthcare and so this focus on health is overdue. Healthcare in India is undergoing transformation, with changing demographics, increasing consumer spending, and rising lifestyle diseases driving the need to build better, accessible, and inclusive health-care infrastructure.[8] An example of PPPs in healthcare is in Box 4.3. Figure 4.2 in Box 4.3 shows the con-tractual arrangement in the health care PPP project.

---

[7] Government of Andhra Pradesh has selected Braun to establish and operate dialysis centres in eleven tertiary-care state-run hospitals on a Build—Operate-Transfer (BOT) basis for seven years. Dialysis is provided to the below-poverty-line population free of cost through the state-sponsored health insurance scheme. Government pays the private operator an agreed price for each dialysis (shadow pricing). The scheme's robust payment mechanism ensures timely pay-ment to the private operator and seamless service to the people.

[8] Ministry of Finance. 2020. *National Infrastructure Pipeline:Draft Report by Sub Group—Urban and Social Infrastructure Finance.*

Box 4.3 Case study: PPP in the health sector—West Middlesex University Hospital, Isleworth, United Kingdom

West Middlesex University Hospital NHS Trust (the Trust) in 2001 let out a Private Finance Initiative (PFI) contract (DBFM) to a private sector consortium called Bywest, comprising Bouygues UK and Ecovert. The contract is for thirty-five years and has an estimated net present value (NPV) of unitary payments of about £125 million. Bouygues UK was subcontracted construction and Ecovert, facilities management. Bywest received an annual unitary payment of £9.3 million. Bywest also carried out extensive refurbishment of newer, existing buildings, with a capital cost of some £12.2 million.

Sources of finance: Senior term debt comprised 91% of total debt funding at long term swap rate of 5.63%. It was provided by Abbey National Treasury Services Ltd. Subordinated debt and equity share was 9% and 14%. It was contributed by Charterhouse Project Equity Investments Ltd. and West Middlesex Hospital Projects Ltd.

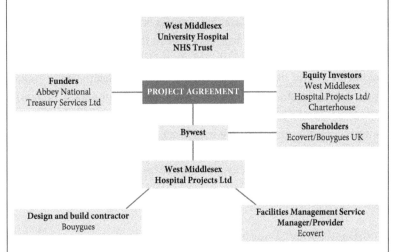

Figure 4.2 Contractual arrangement in West Middlesex University Hospital, Isleworth, United Kingdom

Source: National Audit Office. 2002. *The PFI Contract for the Redevelopment of West Middlesex University Hospital* (https://www.nao.org.uk/report/the-pfi-contract-for-the-redevelopment-of-west-middlesex-university-hospital/).

Benefits:[a] The PFI contract calculations showed a risk-adjusted saving of £5.5 million compared with a public-sector comparator (PSC), including project costs and clinical costs of £989 million over thirty-five years (net present value). The reduction in the annual unitary payment due to an increase in the contract term from thirty years to thirty-five years was £1.1 million. There is a saving from the backlog of maintenance investment of around £28 million, which is now the responsibility of the contractor and in the absence of the PFI contract would have been invested by the government.

The PFI gave greater price certainty and incentivized the contractor to complete the project on time (2003) as unitary payments commenced when the project became operational. Payment deductions are made in case quality of service as specified in the contract is compromised. Since the same contractor designed, maintained, and operated the building under one contract, it was incentivized to adopt a life-cycle approach to costing. This also ensured that the construction contractor would construct the assets to a good quality knowing that it would have to operate and maintain it over the thirty-five-year contract period.

[a]Duncan Cartlidge. 2006. *Public–Private Partnerships in Construction* (https://vdocume nts.mx/reader/full/public-private-partnerships-in-construction).

Augmenting Social Infrastructure Financing

A Social Stock Exchange (SSE), impact investment, the importance of ESG norms, and so on, will play a part in augmenting private investment in social infrastructure. The Indian Finance Minister, in her 2019 Budget speech, proposed setting up an SSE in the country, regulated by the Securities and Exchange Board of India (SEBI) in the following words: 'It is time to take our capital markets closer to the masses and meet various social welfare objectives related to inclusive growth and financial inclusion.'

Following this, a working group on the SSE was constituted by SEBI[9] to evaluate the prospect of setting up an SSE in India. The working group

[9] Security and Exchange Board of India. 2020. *Report of Working Group on Social Stock Exchange* (https://www.sebi.gov.in/reports-and-statistics/reports/jun-2020/report-of-the-work ing-group-on-social-stock-exchange_46751.html).

made several high-level recommendations, including the participation of non-profit organizations and for-profit enterprises in SSE, subject to committing to minimum reporting requirements. The SSE can be housed within the existing stock exchange such as the Bombay Stock Exchange (BSE) and/or National Stock Exchange (NSE). This would help the SSE leverage the existing infrastructure and client relationships of the exchanges to onboard investors, donors, and social enterprises (non-profit and for-profit).

What is a Social Stock Exchange

An SSE is a platform to bring together social organizations and impact investors (discussed later) whereby the latter can buy a stake in listed organizations whose mission is aligned to that of these investors. It operates like a regular stock exchange by facilitating listing, trading, and settlement of shares, bonds, and other financial instruments except that instead of solely reporting their traditional financial status (e.g. profit and loss status), the listed companies are required to also demonstrate their social and environment impact. Thus, SSE is a market-based solution to re-directing investment and capital from investors for triple purposes (financial, social, and environmental), which is in consonance with UN SDGs.

Benefits of SSE

Setting up the SSE will bridge the funding gap that social-sector players often run into, institutionalizing the measurement and reporting of social impact, and mainstreaming the social sector for a wider set of investors.[10] With over Rs.246 billion spent by companies on corporate social responsibility in FY2020, the social sector is now deep. There are over 3.1 million NGOs on the demand side. From those working to preserve the marine

---

[10] Karen Wendt.2017. *Social Stock Exchanges—Democratization of Capital Investing for Impact*. 30th Australasian Finance and Banking Conference, 2017 (https://papers.ssrn.com/sol3/papers.cfm?abstract_id=3021739).

ecosystem, to providing free midday meals, to improving education outcomes, all these are expected to benefit from the SSE:[11]

- SSEs improve market access by connecting impact companies with investors who are looking to combine financial return with desired social and environmental outcomes.
- SSEs help democratize and popularize impact investing by making it accessible to a wider set of investors. SSEs would help this as they create a liquid market and also allow the bundling of assets, creation of derivatives, and could boost market capitalization—by reducing transaction and research costs.
- By aggregating data on impact companies and organizing analyst coverage, SSEs reduce information and transaction costs while helping the accurate valuation of the listed securities and making capital markets work for society.
- Without a liquid marketplace, investors may be excessively cautious, reducing the amount of capital available to impact companies. SSEs offer an exit route for early-stage investors and make impact assets more attractive to investors in general.
- SSEs introduce market discipline and encourage competition among impact companies.
- Just like conventional stock exchanges serve an important regulatory function, SSEs would help establish the currently underdeveloped regulatory framework for social finance.
- By making impact investing more accessible and popular, SSEs would increase investment for sustainable development.

Global Models of SSE

United Kingdom—SSX: On 6 June 2013, the UK prime minister announced the launch of the SSX. The London Stock Exchange supported the launch of the world's first Social Stock Exchange, an online portal

---

[11] Amit Tandon. 21 December 2021. An Over-engineered Social Stock Exchange?*Business Standard*.

that has become the first information platform in the world to showcase publicly listed social impact businesses. SSX is not an actual trading platform. It is more accurately described as an information portal that investors can access to learn about impact-investing opportunities. Overtime it has become a strong information repository with a base of thirty-six member companies and its members have raised £400 million for, among other things, affordable housing, clean energy, and new health-care facilities.

Canada—SVX: Social Venture Connexion is backed by the Government of Ontario. It is an online platform that uses crowd funding and private placement to support capital raising by impact ventures and funds. At present, SVX has twelve social enterprise issuers and has helped mobilize US$100 million in impact capital.

Singapore—IIX: The Impact Investment Exchange is based on a crowd-funding model that allows mature social enterprises to raise capital by issuing securities on a public platform that facilitates trading in listed securities. IIX's US$20 million women's livelihood bond was the first instrument listed on IIX. The exchange has over thirty thousand partners and has helped raise impact-investment capital of around US$40 million per year.

South Africa—SASIX: The South Africa Social Investment Exchange allows ethical investors to start investing as little as Rand 50 in social businesses and claim tax benefits. It has made a significant contribution to South African development with over Rand 34.6 million invested in fifty-three social development projects.

The Challenges and the Way Forward to Setting Up SSE in India

- *Define social enterprise*: Various enterprises are involved in provision of 'social good'. So, it is imperative to clearly define contours of a social enterprise. This will help the enterprise with the desired characteristics to get listed on SSE.
- *Listing and governance requirements*: It is imperative to collect and monitor information pertaining to issuers' social integrity, which again has to be defined first.

- *Disclosure and reporting requirements*: To establish a fair, healthy, and trustworthy market for impact securities, SSEs must devise mechanisms for filling information gaps to correct asymmetries between insiders and outsiders thus reducing transaction costs, and promote the standardization of social finance. This can be achieved through a metric of impact evaluation.

- *Enforcement mechanisms*: To effectively protect both investors and beneficiaries, SSEs should regulate not only issuer conduct, but also investor conduct. SVX (Canada) does the best job in this regard since it requires issuers and investors to enter into contractual agreements with relatively robust remedy provisions.

- *Regulating investors*: Regulating investors is particularly important for an SSE to promote liquidity and their freedom to exit investments. The SVX Investor Agreement requires that investors acknowledge the possibility that their investments will yield no financial return.

- *Grievance redressal mechanism*: A key ingredient for SSE success is investor trust. This can be ensured by setting up an effective grievance redressal mechanism.

Proponents of social finance see it as a vehicle for transforming the role of business in society and harnessing market forces to better meet social challenges. Social regulations should be imposed not only on the listed businesses, but also on the investors who transact on these platforms, in order to minimize incentives to drift from the social mission.[12]

Considering the increasing and huge appetite for impact investment and the need for private finance in infrastructure in general and urban and social infrastructure in particular (see Box 4.4 on how SSE can help in channelizing funds for the NIP), setting up an SSE in India under the regulatory ambit of SEBI would be a step in the right direction.[13] As both the demand and supply of impact funds increase, the case also grows for more widely accessible investment platforms. For-profit stock exchanges

---

[12] KPMG. 2020. *Analysing the Concept of Stock Exchange in India*, p. 5 (https://assets.kpmg/content/dam/kpmg/in/pdf/2020/07/analysing-the-concept-of-social-stock-exchange-in-india.pdf).

[13] In September 2021, SEBI has cleared the proposal for setting up the social stock exchange for fundraising by social enterprises.

Box 4.4   How SSE can help in channelizing funds for the NIP

Brownfield asset recycling:[a] Asset classes which upon suitable structuring would be of interest to the target investor set in social infrastructure, in particular stadia, hospitals, and so on may be chosen for asset monetization. Social securitized products may be traded on SSE. India has introduced ESG mutual funds (currently eight in number) which invest in companies that are committed towards the environment and society. Newer financial instruments such as crowd funding, credits for participation, and philanthropic investments can also help.

Develop capital market for social bonds:[b] There is a need to target specific liquidity pools, particularly in the context of ESG investing. Dedicated desks at sectoral nodal agencies may need to proactively engage this investor class and map out eligible projects to fit into their investment criteria (primarily ESG). Renewable sector, water treatment and supply, solid waste management, rural development sector, and so on will help in targeting a new pool of liquidity from the ESG investor base. Issuance in the form of green bonds and social bonds can be explored (depending on the sector being financed) for access to a wider and deeper global investor base. Social finance will become cheaper as global funds will be interested in investing in environment and socially responsible projects backed by sound corporate governance framework. Their appetite as the anchor investor/credit enhancement provider can be leveraged meaningfully to boost the commercial investor demand. Presently investments from this investor class is less organized and low on attention/priority as compared to commercial investors.

From a municipal bond perspective, the share of municipal bonds in India in the total debt market is still insignificant—only 1 per cent of urban body financial demands are met through municipal bonds as against 10 per cent in the United States. The low credit worthiness of urban local bodies as a result of their weak finances continue to act as impediments in the growth of this market in India. Municipal bonds can also be posed to impact investors for sanguine results.

Project finance approach will give a fillip to market size for social bonds:[c] Social infra and urban infra projects such as healthcare, education, agriculture, and so on are undertaken mostly by a trust instead of a special purpose vehicle (SPV). This creates problems in security requirements which are not in line with the requirements of project finance lenders. Implementation of such projects may be promoted under SPV arrangement. This will accelerate impact finance flows into social infra projects.

[a]Ministry of Finance. 2020. *Strategic Asset Recycling Initiative (SARI): Draft Report by Sub-Group on Asset Recycling and Infrastructure Equity.*

[b]Ministry of Finance. 2020. *Recommendations of the Report of the Sub-group on Capital Markets for Financing of National Infrastructure Pipeline.*

[c]Ministry of Finance. 2020. *Report of Project Finance/Refinance Sub-Group Constituted under IMSC for Enabling Financing of Infrastructure Projects under NIP.*

are by no means protected against the tendencies often associated with financial markets, such as short-termism, excessive speculation, or questionable accounting practices. Well-developed regulation and rules of governance are thus essential for ensuring the integrity of SSEs, and by extension, the impact economy as a whole.

What is Impact Investment?

Impact investments are made in companies or organizations with the intent to contribute measurable positive social, environmental, and developmental impact, alongside a financial return. This is a new paradigm based on a three-dimensional assessment (risk, return, and impact). Far from being a niche within the wider investment industry, 'impact' is increasingly becoming a central part of mainstream finance as major investors (from private equity and venture capital to pension funds) are increasingly optimizing across the three dimensions of risk, return, and impact in their capital allocation decisions (e.g. an exchange traded fund, named 'SHE', invested in companies with women in top executive posts). Impact investors are usually willing to expect lower returns or wait for return of their capital and/or returns until after other investors have earned expected returns. Impact investing is also a powerful tool to raise awareness and address diversity, gender (equity and empowerment), and inclusion issues, enhancing social inclusion. This acknowledges the key role of business and investment to build more inclusive and sustainable economies.[14] Global and regional charitable organizations are among the growing number of impact investors.[15] Specifically, the definition encompasses three observable attributes of impact investors that can distinguish them from other investors:

- *Intent*: The investor articulates an intent to achieve a social or environmental goal by identifying outcomes that will be pursued through the investment and specifying who will benefit from these outcomes.
- *Contribution*: The investor follows a credible narrative, which describes how the investment contributes to achievement of the intended goal.
- *Measurement*: The investor has a system of measurement in place to link intent and contribution to the improvements in social and environmental outcomes delivered by the enterprise in which the investment was made. This enables the investor to assess the level of expected impact, *ex ante*, to continuously monitor progress and take corrective action when appropriate, and then finally to evaluate the achievement of impact, *ex post*. However, investors face significant hurdles in that there is a lack of standardized metrics and reporting framework for companies about impact investments.

One instrument that India has used for supporting impact investments is the VGF support to PPP investors in economic and social infrastructure sectors. VGF is a one-time financial support that private investors are eligible to receive to partially finance capital expenditures for creating impact infrastructure. VGF is a grant (as opposed to a loan or an equity contribution) given with the objective of making the impact intervention financially viable and is financed by the government's budgetary

---

[14] B20 Italy. 2021. *Finance and Infrastructure Policy Paper*.
[15] Patricia Sulser. 2021. Scaling up PPPs by Engaging Impact Investing Charities and Foundations (https://blogs.worldbank.org/ppps/scaling-ppps-engaging-impact-investing-charities-and-foundations?CID=WBW_AL_BlogNotification_EN_EXT).

resources. Under this, grant support of up to 20 per cent of the TPC is allowed for economic infrastructure projects, which can go up to 30 per cent of TPC for water and solid waste management projects, and further to 40 per cent of TPC for identified social infrastructure projects in the health and education sectors. VGF can serve as a model intervention to implement impact PPPs where projects are economically viable but cannot reach the standard thresholds of financial viability.

The Global Impact Investing Network (GIIN): The GIIN is a non-profit 501c(3) organization dedicated to increasing the scale and effectiveness of impact investing. The GIIN builds critical infrastructure and supports activities, education, and research that help accelerate the development of a coherent impact-investing industry.

Impact measurement and management is at the heart of impact investing. For this GIIN has developed IRIS+ (impact reporting and investment standards), which is the generally accepted system for measuring, managing, and optimizing impact that the majority of impact investors use to measure social, environmental, and financial success.

Findings of GIIN, 2020 Annual Impact Investor Survey:[16] Collectively, respondents to the survey manage US$404 billion of impact-investing assets, but the median investor manages only US$89 million.

The fastest-growing regions of investment were Western, Northern, and Southern Europe (WNS Europe) and East and South East Asia (SE Asia), which grew at 25 per cent and 23 per cent compound annual growth rate, respectively. Growing interest in SE Asia is also evident, as over half of the respondents (52 per cent) plan to grow allocations to SE Asia over the next five years.

Regarding how respondents set their impact performance goals, 60 per cent target both social and environmental impact in their investments. There is broad use of the SDGs with 73 per cent using this framework for at least one measurement and management purpose. Nearly three-quarters of respondents target 'decent work and economic growth' (SDG 8).

---

[16] Global Impact Investing Network. 2020. *Annual Impact Investor Survey 2020 (Executive Summary)*, pp. 5 and 7 (https://thegiin.org/assets/GIIN%20Annual%20Impact%20Investor%20 Survey%202020%20Executive%20Summary.pdf).

On average, respondents target eight different SDG-aligned impact themes, reflecting the diversity of their impact goals.

International Finance Corporation's (IFC) Operating Principles for Impact Management: Another step to promote impact investment is 'Operating Principles for Impact Management', launched in 2019 by the IFC to establish a set of best practices for impact management. Signatories to the Impact Principles are required to ensure a purposeful integration of these best practices throughout the manager's full investment cycle. These principles describe essential features of managing investment funds with the intention to contribute to the achievement of social, economic, or environmental impact alongside financial returns. The market size for the total assets of potential private impact investors was slightly above US$2 trillion in 2019.[17]

The Impact Principles are as follows: (i) define strategic impact objective(s), consistent with the investment strategy; (ii) manage strategic impact on a portfolio basis; (iii) establish the manager's contribution to the achievement of impact; (iv) assess the expected impact of each investment, based on a systematic approach; (v) assess, address, monitor, and manage potential negative impacts of each investment; (vi) monitor the progress of each investment in achieving impact against expectations and respond appropriately; (vii) conduct exits considering the effect on sustained impact; (viii) review, document, and improve decisions and processes based on the achievement of impact and lessons learned; (ix) publicly disclose alignment with the Principles and provide regular independent verification of the alignment.

As of 1 April 2020, more than ninety institutions have signed up to the Principles, which corresponds to more than a third of the 266 respondents to the latest GIIN survey of impact investors. Many development finance institutions have taken the opportunity to be early adopters of the Impact Principles. The signatories show a strong focus on investments in emerging markets, with 71 per cent of signatories in the survey investing only in emerging markets, possibly to take advantage of untapped business opportunities in geographical areas with the greatest development

---

[17] International Finance Corporation. 2020. *Growing Impact—New Insights into the Practice of Impact Investing* (https://www.ifc.org/wps/wcm/connect/8b8a0e92-6a8d-4df5-9db4-c8888 88b464e/2020-Growing-Impact.pdf?MOD=AJPERES&CVID=naZESt9).

needs. In August 2019, the Japan International Cooperation Agency adopted the Operating Principles for Impact Management. Omnivore Capital Management Advisors Private Ltd from India is also a signatory to these Principles. Combining impact investing and blended finance offers an opportunity to make more infrastructure happen in traditionally low-return sectors like water and sanitation and healthcare.

5

Project Finance

Infrastructure projects are capital intensive, for example, an ultra-mega thermal power project of 4 GW capacity would require about Rs.200 billion to be built.[1] A company could have a number of such projects and raising this amount of capital based on the balance sheet of the company would limit the number of such projects that it can finance. Therefore, it is best to create special purpose vehicles (SPVs) for implementing each of these projects with project financing being used to finance them. This is the best way of accessing infrastructure finance by the private sector as it allows companies to raise finances on the basis of the cash flows generated by the project, with no recourse to the balance sheet of the project sponsor (non-recourse financing). A ring-fenced company (SPV) is created whose only purpose is to implement the project and the interests of other stakeholders (construction company, fuel supplier, off-taker, lenders, and so on in a power plant) are protected through watertight contracts. The chapter discusses the reasons why project finance is used in financing private infrastructure projects, features of project finance, and contractual structure among stakeholders. The chapter also discusses project financing trends in India and the world.

Private investment in infrastructure projects is primarily financed by debt, mostly loans, with the average debt-equity ratio being 3:1. Figure 5.1 provides a snapshot of recent experience in private investment in infrastructure. While debt financing dominates, within debt it is the bank financing of infrastructure which is pre-eminent. However, the dominance of bank loans creates its own problems in terms of asset–liability mismatch. Therefore, efforts are ongoing to move some of this debt from

---

[1] An earlier version of this chapter appeared in Kumar V. Pratap and Rajesh Chakrabarti. 2018. *Public–Private Partnerships in Infrastructure—Managing the Challenges.*

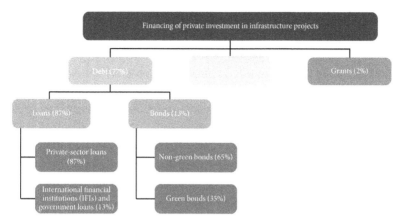

Figure 5.1 Private investment in infrastructure projects by instrument type, 2010–2020 (% of total value)

Source: Global Infrastructure Hub. 2021. *Infrastructure Monitor.*

banks to bonds and institutional sources of finance (pension, insurance, and sovereign wealth funds), but with limited success.

Most private infrastructure projects are project financed. This is also a mode of financing that is by and large special to this sector. Hence, we must understand the nature, benefits, and limitations of project financing.

Project finance involves the financing of one specific project by an entity that is created with the sole purpose to design, build, and operate that specific infrastructure (SPV). On the contrary, in traditional corporate finance, one company typically carries out multiple simultaneous initiatives that get financed as a portfolio of projects. In project finance, project company's obligations are ring-fenced from those of the equity investors and thus facilitate off-balance-sheet financing. In project finance, therefore, lenders and investors rely either exclusively ('non-recourse' financing) or mainly ('limited recourse' financing) on the cash flows generated by the project to repay their loans and earn a return on their investments. 'Recourse' refers to access to other, that is, non-project, assets of the company promoting the project as collateral for the loan in question. In non-recourse financing, debt repayment comes exclusively from the project company (the SPV set up only for the lifetime of the project with the mandate to exclusively undertake the project), rather than from any other source.

In limited recourse debt, debt servicing carries a repayment guarantee by the promoter up to a time, a fraction of the principal or until a milestone is reached. The distinguishing feature of project financing is that at least some portion of the debt eventually becomes non-recourse. This is unlike corporate lending where the strength of the borrower's balance sheet protects lenders. Since senior lenders (debt A is 'senior' to debt B if A needs to get repaid before B) do not have access to sponsors' financial resources in project-financed transactions, cash flow and adequate debt service coverage are critical and this needs to be secured through watertight contracts.

Unlike in normal bank lending, collaterals, sponsor guarantees and covenants do not work in capital-intensive infrastructure projects where such security/guarantees would not be able to cover the large quantum of project debt. The principal security for debt here, therefore, is the revenue streams of such projects, and the banks lend primarily on the strength of such security. This is true for Indian private infrastructure projects as well.

What Makes Infrastructure Suitable for Project Finance?

Infrastructure is characterized by stable, predictable operating cash flows over a long period making it amenable to project finance. Stable and predictable operating cash flows occur because infrastructure is characterized by long-term assets with a long economic life; stable technology and therefore low technological risk; provision of key public services like power and water supply, which have strong non-elastic demand; high entry barriers—natural monopoly or quasi-monopoly markets; frequently user charges are hedged against inflation; and low correlation with traditional asset classes and overall macroeconomic performance.

Project Finance Contractual Structure

A typical project finance contractual structure (with particular reference to a power generation project) is shown in Figure 5.2.

SPVs to implement public–private partnerships (PPPs) in infrastructure are associated with a complex set of contracts because of the presence

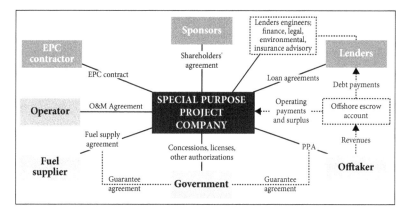

Figure 5.2 Project finance contractual structure

Source: Taylor DeJongh. 2009. *Assessing the Impact of Recent Credit Constraints on Energy Sector Investment Requirements in Bangladesh*, a study commissioned by the World Bank.

of different actors with different goals, objective functions and interests, the need to reconcile or harmonize these varying objectives to meet a particular infrastructure goal, the presence of many risks affecting PPP projects, and the need for agreement on risk allocation and management. To protect the interests of all stakeholders, there have to be watertight contracts with all of them. In fact, large deals involve highly complicated contractual bundles with hundreds of documents. For example, when the $3.6 billion Baku-Tbilisi-Ceyhan pipeline project closed in 2002, it involved more than two hundred documents with seventeen thousand signatures from seventy-eight different parties.

Typically, a SPV company is created for the sole purpose of implementing the project (Figure 5.2). It is responsible for the evolution, implementation, and operation of the project in a financially viable manner. This company would have a shareholders' agreement with the project sponsors. The promoters or project sponsors set up the SPV, undertake equity investments in it, and mobilize resources for it like debt, and decide on the management of the SPV. Thus, Coastal Gujarat Power Limited, a subsidiary of Tata Power, is the SPV created for implementing the 4,000 MW ultra-mega power project in Mundra in Gujarat, India. The sponsors (Tata Power) would have the shareholders' agreement with the SPV. The SPV would typically enter into an engineering–procurement–construction (EPC) contract with specialized construction companies and transfer the construction risk to the specialized EPC companies. The EPC company would be responsible for designing, constructing, and finally commissioning the project on a 'fixed-time and fixed-price' basis (so as to transfer the construction risk of time and cost overrun to the EPC company). The SPV would enter into an operation and maintenance (O&M) contract with a specialized O&M company, thus transferring the O&M risk to the specialized O&M company. The O&M company is expected to operate and maintain the project according to the performance parameters defined in the O&M contract.

In the case of a power generation project, there would be a fuel-supply agreement with the fuel (say, coal) supplier like Coal India Limited (CIL) thus transferring the fuel-supply risk to CIL. The government or public-sector agency gives a concession (or contract or license) to the SPV for constructing and operating the project for the duration of the concession period. Thus, Delhi International Airport Limited, the SPV for the rehabilitation and operation of Delhi Airport, has been given the concession for thirty years (plus another thirty years) to operate Delhi Airport by the public sector agency, Airports Authority of India. Given that infrastructure services often have a single purchaser or few buyers, there is often significant demand risk associated with the project. To address the demand risk for a power project for instance, there may be a power purchase agreement (PPA) with the off-taker (or buyer, typically a power distribution company). Thus, power generation projects (e.g., Coastal Gujarat Power Limited) generally have PPAs with off-takers (power distribution companies of Punjab, Haryana, Rajasthan, Gujarat, and Maharashtra) to buy the power generated by the project, thus mitigating demand risk.

Since lenders (they provide debt finance for project construction and are typically a consortium or syndicate of banks for large projects) have to depend on revenue streams of just the project (non-recourse financing, typical in a PPP project), rather than the credibility of the project sponsors, they may insist on all revenues of the project to be put in an escrow account on which the lenders would have the first charge. The payments typically follow a 'waterfall mechanism' whereby revenues of the project first meet operating expenses, administration costs, payment on senior debt, payment on subordinated debt, followed by the debt service reserve account and the maintenance reserve account and finally, distribution to equity holders. In addition, lenders may want the following defined in a watertight contract (concession agreement): source of revenue like user fees or budgetary payments, indexation of user fees to inflation, incentives and penalties related to performance, termination payments, and so on.

The various contracts associated with a project finance contractual structure seek to transfer risk from the SPV to entities who have more control over the risk factor.

Features of Project Finance

There is a wide variety of project finance structures. But there are certain common features underlying the project finance approach:

- A 'ring-fenced' project implemented through a SPV whose only business is the project;
- Usually associated with a new project rather than an established project;
- High debt–equity ratio (leverage or gearing)—debt may constitute 70–90 per cent of project cost. Project losses are borne first by the equity investors, with lenders suffering only after the loss of the equity investment. Equity investors, therefore, accept a higher risk and need a higher return on their investment. Minimizing the cost of finance is the primary aim of financial structuring for the project. Given the higher cost of equity, higher leverage helps in optimizing the cost of finance;
- No guarantees from sponsors in the SPV (non-recourse financing) or limited guarantee (limited recourse financing) for project finance debt—lenders rely on future cash flows to be generated by the project (only or mainly) for debt service;
- Main security for lenders is the project company's contracts, licenses, or ownership rights to natural resources, which are much more valuable than the physical assets of the project, which, in any case, may be worthless given the highly specific nature of these assets (sunk costs);
- Project has a finite life, based on such factors as length of the contract or license; therefore, project finance debt must be fully repaid by end of project life;

- Project finance differs from corporate finance, where loans are against balance sheet of an existing diversified business and projections from past cash flows and profit record can be made; corporate finance also assumes that the company will remain in business indefinitely as compared to finite life of project-financed projects;
- Whether or not ownership of the project is transferred to the public sector at the end of the concession period (as in Build–Operate–Transfer (BOT), Build–Own–Operate–Transfer (BOOT) project), or remains indefinitely with the private sector (as in Build–Own–Operate, BOO), makes little difference from the project finance point of view. This is because the lenders rely on cash flows generated from the project and the discounted value of such cash flows becomes quite small after the concession period of thirty years or more. However, any long-term residual value of the project (as there may be in a BOO) may be of relevance to the investors in assessing their likely return.

Why Use Project Finance?—Investors

There are several reasons why investors would prefer project finance.

- Project finance is associated with higher leverage. High leverage improves investor returns as debt is cheaper than equity. Since interest is also tax deductible, the advantage of lower cost of debt persists at the profit-after-tax stage as well.
- Table 5.1 shows an example of the benefits of leverage on investor returns. Both low-leverage (20 per cent debt) and high-leverage (75 per cent debt, typical level of debt for project finance) columns relate to the same investment of Rs.100 which produces revenue of Rs.10 per annum. The low-leverage column shows the return on equity at 11.5 per cent while the high-leverage column shows the return on equity at 22 per cent, despite an increase in the cost of debt from 4 per cent to 6 per cent reflecting the higher risk for lenders in the highly leveraged project.
- Interest is also tax deductible and therefore the advantage of lower cost of debt persists at the profit-after-tax stage as well. If the tax rate is 30 per cent, the after-tax profit in the low-leverage case is 6.44 (9.2

Table 5.1 Benefit of project financing to investors

	Low leverage	High leverage
Project cost	100	100
(a) Debt	20	75
(b) Equity	80	25
(c) Revenue from project	10	10
(d) Interest rate on debt (per annum) (%)	4	6
(e) Interest payable ((a)*(d))	0.8	4.5
(f) Profit ((c)−(e))	9.2	5.5
(g) Return on equity ((f)/(b))(%)	11.5	22

Source: Adapted from E R Yescombe. 2002. *Principles of Project Finance.*

* 70 per cent), which translates into an after-tax return on equity of 8.05 per cent, whereas in high-leverage case, it is 3.85 (5.5 * 70 per cent), or an after-tax return on equity of 15.4 per cent.

- Off-balance-sheet financing: A major characteristic of project finance is non-recourse financing, which increases an investor's borrowing capacity, enabling the investor to undertake several major projects simultaneously. Project finance structure may allow the investor to keep debt off the investor's balance sheet as the debt would belong to the SPV. This would be beneficial to a company's position in the financial markets. However, a company's shareholders and lenders should consider the risks of off-balance-sheet activity, which appear in notes to the published accounts. So, project finance should not usually be undertaken purely to eliminate debt from the investor's balance sheet.

- Risk limitation and spreading across stakeholders: In project finance, the sponsor's risk is limited to the amount of equity investment in the SPV. This preserves the credit rating of the sponsor. In addition, projects using project finance may be too large for one investor (e.g. the Coastal Gujarat Power Limited project is a Rs.20,000 crore project). SPV may have an O&M operator, EPC contractor, and off-taker to share risk, thereby making it possible to implement the large infrastructure project with limited risk to the sponsor.

- Long-term finance: Project finance loans typically are of longer maturity than corporate finance. It is the result of high-capital-cost assets, like infrastructure, that cannot be recovered over a short term without pushing up the user charges for the project's end product or service to infeasible levels. Mexico was on a massive road-building spree in the 1990s. However, the bidding parameter that was used was the length of the concession period, with the result that some of the winning bids had a concession period of 3.5 years for an asset (roads) that was going to last for thirty years or more which resulted in very high and therefore, unsustainable user charges. The rule of thumb is that the term of the loan should be equal to the life of PPP projects to keep the user charges reasonable. Many of these Mexican projects failed, partly because of the short length of the concession period and consequent short-term financing, which raised user charges to unsustainable levels.
- Enhanced credit: If the off-taker has a better credit standing than the project sponsor, debt may be raised on better terms. In the Indian road sector, for example, there are annuity-based road projects for which payments are made by the public authority (NHAI) based on availability of the road. Since the credit rating of NHAI is AAA, companies like GMR Infrastructure that have much lower credit rating, can raise debt on much better terms for its annuity-based project-financed road projects.

Why Use Project Finance?—Third Parties

Third parties also benefit by using project finance. For example, project finance facilitates lower cost of product or service by using a high level of debt (see Table 5.2).

- *Lower cost of services*: Suppose the required return is 15 per cent, then as Table 5.2 shows, a revenue of 12.8 is needed using low-leverage corporate finance, but only 8.25 using high-leverage project finance, reducing the cost to the off-taker or end user. Hence the preference for the latter (high leverage) by the off-taker or end user. Many of the infrastructure sectors are under-priced (exemplified by

Table 5.2 Benefit of project financing to third parties

	Low leverage	High leverage
Project cost	100	100
(a) Debt	20	75
(b)Equity	80	25
(c)Required return on equity ((b)*15%)	12	3.75
(d)Interest rate on debt (pa)(%)	4	6
(e)Interest payable ((a)*(d))	0.8	4.5
(f)Revenue required ((c)+(e))	12.8	8.25

Source: Adapted from E R Yescombe. 2002. Principles of Project Finance.

low cost recovery in power and water sectors in developing countries, including India). The lower cost of services associated with project finance financial structure may be the crucial difference between providing these services and not providing them at all in these countries.

- Additional investment in public infrastructure and crowding-in of private investment: Project finance facilitates additional investment in public infrastructure as typical debt–equity ratio in such projects is 70:30. So, the total investment would be higher with the same level of equity. Investment in power, telecom, roads, and ports also crowds-in private investment thus raising the investment rate and consequently the growth rate.

- Risk transfer, especially cost overrun: Public-sector project implementation is notorious for cost overruns. When the public sector has a fixed price contract with the private sector with liquidated damages, the risk of cost overrun is effectively transferred to the private sector. It has also been found that even if there is cost overrun in private implementation of public projects, private-sector companies with strong balance sheets and reputations would absorb this, thus effectively shielding the public sector from the risk of cost overruns.

- Transparency and third-party due diligence: Many large infrastructure projects may be implemented for political rather than financial/economic reasons. However, if the private sector is implementing the project, the analysis would be more transparent in that it is a ring-fenced project being implemented by a SPV and there is likely to be third-party due diligence (by lenders, for example, who would be providing for most of the project costs and would be depending on the cash flows generated by the project and not on the balance sheet and profit and loss of a diversified company as in corporate finance). Therefore, project selection in a project financed project may be more objective.

Project Finance: Global Market Trends

After the onslaught of the first wave of Covid-19 in March 2020, project finance appeared to have recovered in H2 2020. Global project finance value stood at US$214 billion in the second half of 2020 (Figure 5.3) and a number of high-value deals reached financial closure in this period (Figure 5.4). Both transaction value (33 per cent) and count (58 per cent) were driven by renewables as more and more investors and lenders are becoming environmentally conscious and applying ESG criteria in project finance.

Commercial loans were the main source of infrastructure project finance with the quantum reaching US$221 billion in 2020 (Figure 5.5). The low equity percentage in project finance reflects the high leverage in such transactions. While countries want to move debt financing from

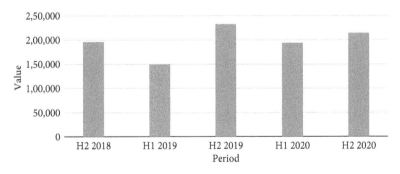

Figure 5.3 Global project finance by transaction value H2 2018–H2 2020 (US$ million)

Source: IJ Global Project Finance League Report full year 2020 and PF charts https://ijglobal.com/reports (viewed on 7 June 2021).

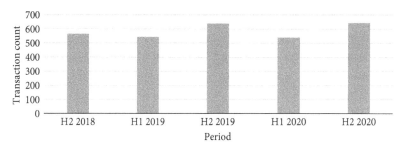

Figure 5.4 Global project finance by transaction volume H2 2018–H2 2020

Source: IJ Global Project Finance League Report full year 2020 and PF charts https://ijglobal. com/reports (viewed on 7 June 2021).

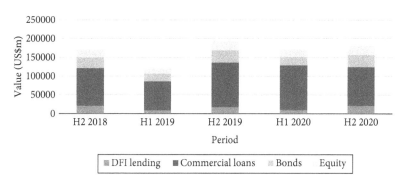

Figure 5.5 Global project finance value by sources of funding H2 2018– H2 2020

Source: IJ Global Project Finance League Report full year 2020 and PF charts. (https://ijglobal. com/reports) (viewed on 7 June 2021).

banks to the capital market, the percentage of funds garnered through bonds in project finance transactions is quite limited.

The Current State of Project Financing in India

The main source of debt finance: bank finance

Banks and sector-specific non-banking financial companies (NBFCs) provide much of the greenfield infrastructure financing in India (see

Chapter 12 for a list of sector-specific NBFCs in India).[2] The total outstanding credit to the infrastructure sector, as a percentage of gross non-food credit, by banks was around 15 per cent until fiscal 2016. However, declining asset quality of infrastructure assets, asset–liability mismatch (bank liabilities or deposits are short term, while infrastructure assets are long term), group concentration limits, concentration risk, and capital constraints have resulted in banks taking a cautious approach to financing infrastructure projects. The share of outstanding credit to the infrastructure sector, as a percentage of gross non-food credit, has declined to 11.38 per cent in financial year (FY) 2021. This is largely attributed to degrowth in the infrastructure loan portfolio of banks in FYs 2017, 2018, and 2020. The compound annual growth rate (CAGR) of outstanding gross bank credit to infrastructure has declined from about 15 per cent over FYs 2011–2015[3] to about 3 per cent over FYs 2016–2021.[4] Stressed advances ratio as a percentage of total advances for the infrastructure sector reached 22.6 per cent as of March 2018.[5] Figure 5.6 shows the trend in the share of infrastructure in the total lending portfolio of scheduled commercial banks.[6]

Figure 5.7 elaborates further on bank financing of infrastructure in recent years. In FY 2019 the incremental bank credit to infrastructure was Rs.1.7 lakh crore after two years of negative growth (or degrowth). In the succeeding year, the incremental bank credit to infrastructure was negative again followed by a Rs.0.5 lakh crore increase in FY 2021. The low contribution of bank finance to infrastructure in recent years would make it difficult to achieve the targets envisaged in the NIP as banks

[2] Ministry of Finance, Government of India. 2020. *Draft Report of Sub-Group on 'Expanding Institutional Finance for Infrastructure' constituted under IMSC for Enabling Financing of Infrastructure Projects under NIP.*

[3] In fact, the growth rate of bank financing to infrastructure was even higher earlier—the outstanding bank credit to the infrastructure sector, which stood at Rs.95 billion in March 2001, increased to Rs.9,648 billion in March 2016, a compound annual growth rate (CAGR) of 39 per cent in the first fifteen years of this millennium (N. S. Viswanathan. 2016. *Issues in Infrastructure Financing in India*).

[4] Reserve Bank of India. 2018 and 2021. *Handbook of Statistics on Indian Economy.*

[5] Reserve Bank of India. 2018. *Financial Stability Report.*

[6] Ministry of Finance, Government of India. 2020. *Report of Project Finance/Refinance Sub-Group Constituted under IMSC for Enabling Financing of Infrastructure Projects under National Infrastructure Pipeline.*

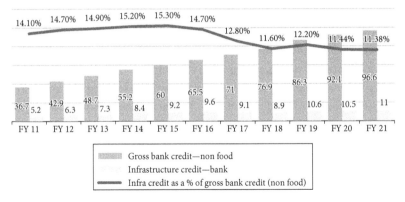

Figure 5.6 Overall bank financing and bank financing of infrastructure (Rs. trillion (lakh crore))
Source: Reserve Bank of India.

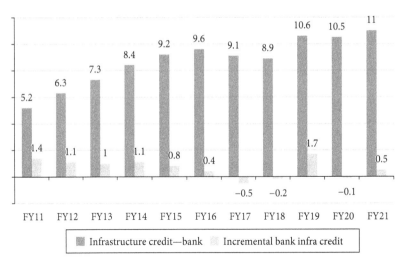

Figure 5.7 Bank financing of infrastructure (Rs. trillion (lakh crore))
Source: Reserve Bank of India.

were expected to contribute about Rs.1.5 lakh crore annually towards financing infrastructure projects.

As already stated, bank financing of infrastructure suffers from asset–liability mismatch (ALM) as bank liabilities are relatively short term compared to infrastructure assets that have a life of thirty years or more. The ALM also exposes prospective bidders to interest-rate risk, which would prevent them from bidding effectively for an infrastructure project.[7] In this sense, banks are not the ideal institutions for funding infrastructure. It has also been alleged that there was reckless lending by the banks in the period before 2016 (e.g. information relating to some individual projects suggests that in several cases, the banks have been lending far in excess of the duly approved total project cost. This is leading to a situation where the concessionaires may not only be spending beyond reasonable costs, but also siphoning out funds at public expense.[8]The stench of crony capitalism permeates discussions of the twin balance-sheet problem where over-leveraged corporates contributed to the non-performing assets (NPAs) of banks.[9] Lack of autonomy in the banking system resulted in failure of accountability for dud loans).[10] The CAGR of bank lending to infrastructure was 39 per cent per annum over the period from 2001 to 2016, which contributed to the NPA problem, which the banking sector is still grappling with. As a result, the CAGR of bank credit to infrastructure in the subsequent five years (2016–2021) came down to a measly 3 per cent, including three years of negative growth (Reserve Bank of India 2013 and 2021).[11]

NBFC finance for infrastructure

NBFCs play a major role in financing infrastructure as shown in Figure 5.8. In fact, in FY 2016 NBFCs overtook banks as the most important source of debt financing of infrastructure and continue to retain that position today.

Sector-specific NBFC-IFCs in the infrastructure space play a dominant role in financing power and railway projects. Around 50 per cent of the sectoral investment in power (from PFC, REC) and 40 per cent

---

[7] Sebastian Morris. 2019. *The Problem of Financing Private Infrastructure in India Today*.

[8] Gajendra Haldea. 2010. *Sub-prime Highways—An Issues Paper* (gajendrahaldea.in/download/Sub-prime_Highways-An_Issues_Paper.pdf).

[9] Arvind Subramanian. 2018. *Of Counsel—The Challenges of the Modi-Jaitley Economy*.

[10] Sebastian Morris. 2019. *The Problem of Financing Private Infrastructure in India Today*.

[11] Reserve Bank of India. 16 September 2013 and 15 September 2021. *Handbook of Statistics on Indian Economy* (Industry-wise deployment of gross bank credit) (https://www.rbi.org.in/scripts/AnnualPublications.aspx?head=Handbook%20of%20Statistics%20on%20Indian%20Economy).

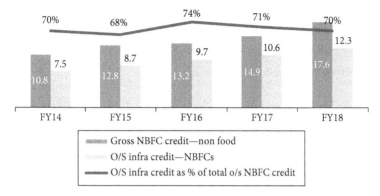

Figure 5.8 NBFC financing of Infrastructure (Rs. trillion (lakh crore))
Source: Reserve Bank of India.

of sectoral investment in the railways (from IRFC) has been financed by NBFC-IFCs. Sector-specific NBFC-IFCs that have the domain expertise to appraise and lend to under-construction projects complement the role of banks in financing greenfield projects in such sectors.

The gross disbursement of NBFC-IFCs in FY 2019 was Rs.3.6 lakh crore, out of which the gross disbursement of NBFC's dedicated for power and railways was 1.56 lakh crore and 0.52 lakh crore respectively. Given the integral role played by government-owned power NBFCs in supporting the working-capital cycle of DISCOMs, only part of the gross disbursement of the power NBFCs is channelized for greenfield asset creation. For example, out of PFCs' disbursement in the past five years, only around 47 per cent were disbursed for greenfield project finance.

India does not have dedicated institutions for financing projects in roads and renewable energy sectors, which has largely been financed by banks and sector agnostic NBFCs. The annual funding envisaged from NBFC-IFC ranges from Rs.2.3 to 3.6 lakh crore in the NIP (as compared to Rs.1.7 lakh crore in FY 2019). Hence, apart from power and railways, other infra NBFCs need to significantly scale up to support the lending envisaged in the NIP.

As is evident from above, the NIP assumption around financing from banks and NBFCs and its comparison against the reality on the ground would call for a large step-up in these sources. Given the negative growth in lending to infrastructure by banks in some years and limited lending by NBFCs to greenfield infrastructure assets, the expectation of 25 per cent of NIP financing by banks and NBFCs appears to be a very optimistic proposition for the following reasons:

- Decline in three out of the last five years in infrastructure finance from banks;
- Exits by Axis Bank, IDFC First, Yes Bank amongst banks, by Aditya Birla Finance Limited (ABFL) and others in NBFCs from infrastructure financing;
- Covid-19's impact on bank balance sheets, project execution, and viability of projects;
- Amongst NBFCs, PFC and REC, which have been major contributors, will be focussed on financing DISCOM dues and they are likely to contribute limited amounts for financing new asset creation.[12]

Given these constraints to financing infrastructure by banks and NBFCs, the following steps may help in boosting their contribution to infrastructure:

- *Realistic project appraisal and structuring*: The projects need to be appraised properly, ensuring that all risks are identified and the project schedule is reasonable. Financiers of infrastructure projects should have the right risk appetite and also the ability to assess the fundamentals of a project, the appropriateness of its design and the reliability of the projections. A proper mix of financing instruments and sources, and the right levels of leverage must be ensured. Repayment schedule should be properly drawn up and aligned with expected cash flows. Pricing of the loans should be commensurate with risk and provide for flexible financing that recognizes changes in the risk profile of the infrastructure asset.[13]

---

[12] Ministry of Finance, Government of India. 2020. *Draft Report of Sub-Group on 'Expanding Institutional Finance for Infrastructure' Constituted under IMSC for Enabling Financing of Infrastructure Projects under NIP.*

[13] N. S. Viswanathan. 2016. *Issues in Infrastructure Financing in India.*

- *Capital infusion in banks and NBFCs to maintain the statutory capital ratios*: Banks and infrastructure-lending NBFCs (such as IIFCL, PFC, REC, IRFC, L&T Finance, IREDA, HUDCO, etc.) should be adequately capitalized to absorb the increased provisioning requirements due to the possible deterioration in the profile of underlying infra projects to meet regulatory requirements and avoid rating downgrades, fund cost overruns of existing infra projects, and continue with the business of extending financial assistance to new infra projects. Additionally, increased CRAR requirement (post-September 2020, banks are required to maintain 9.5 per cent Tier I capital, the minimum required capital as per Basel III norms) will pose a further challenge to the lending ability of the banks and NBFCs, further inhibiting their ability to finance projects. The capital infusion requirement in public-sector banks alone is envisaged at about Rs.1 lakh crore.

- *The 5/25 Scheme may be restored*: The 5/25 Scheme was announced in the Union Budget 2014/15 to encourage banks to extend long-term loans to the infrastructure sector. The announcement read as follows: 'Long-term financing for infrastructure has been a major constraint in encouraging larger private sector participation in this sector. On the asset side, banks will be encouraged to extend long-term loans to infrastructure sector with flexible structuring to absorb potential adverse contingencies, sometimes known as the 5/25 structure.' A 5/25 structure allows banks to lend to a project for twenty-five years, with an option of rewriting the terms of the loan (called reset in banking parlance) or transferring it to another bank or financial institution after five years. It is structured thus to allow the tenure of the loan to match the life cycle of the underlying asset. It aims to improve debt servicing capacity and viability of projects. However, the Scheme was withdrawn in 2018, but it may be restored for enabling long-term bank financing to infrastructure.

- *Credit enhanced infrastructure asset securitization*: Securitization can be an effective option to lenders to monetize infrastructure assets and raise resources for incremental lending. However, securitization for infrastructure as an asset class is yet to take off in India. Credit enhancement along with credit tranching of asset portfolio can provide the necessary impetus in developing the securitization market for infrastructure assets in India. The funds unlocked through securitization can be recycled by banks and NBFC-IFCs towards incremental greenfield asset financing. However, unlike housing loans, retail loans, or car loans portfolio where there is a standard template of a loan agreement, infrastructure loans are individually negotiated since project and sectoral characteristics are fundamentally dissimilar. The lending clauses may also be conflicting. Standardization of loan documentation would help in avoiding potential conflict in this regard.

- *Expanding the scope of take-out financing and stimulating refinancing of operational assets*: There is a need to broaden the scope of take-out financing for it to play a meaningful role in churning the resources for greenfield asset financing. For take-out to be effective, the entire exposure of the existing lender to an infrastructure project needs to be taken out. The current take-out financing scheme of IIFCL permits take-out of a maximum of 51 per cent of the total outstanding project loan, resulting in a suboptimal outcome as both residual capital and management bandwidth in monitoring the asset remains blocked for the taken-out institution. For true take-out, it is recommended that 100 per cent of exposure of the institution financing the construction should be taken out. This would free up the headroom as well as the management and monitoring bandwidth of existing specialized greenfield financiers to take up more greenfield projects.

- *Bond and institutional financing may be encouraged, especially after project risks have come down post-construction*: The Infrastructure Debt Funds (IDFs) and credit enhancement would play a part in encouraging bond financing of infrastructure (dealt with at length in Chapter 7). Given the mainstreaming of environmental concerns because of climate change, green bonds present a useful avenue for raising finance, especially for renewable energy projects. Similarly, institutional investment into infrastructure (from pension, insurance, and sovereign wealth funds) would enable infrastructure financing without the asset–liability mismatch usually associated with bank financing of infrastructure. Increasing use of bonds would free up bank balance sheets for undertaking more greenfield infrastructure financing.

Generic Issues with Project Finance

The non-recourse or limited recourse financing nature of infrastructure projects adds to their financing challenge. Investment protection is through concession agreements providing for user fees, indexation, termination payments, and dispute resolution, as well as autonomous regulatory institutions. In this context, Model Concession Agreements (MCAs) have also been developed across infrastructure sectors in India.

Infrastructure projects are characterized by a long gestation period, subjecting them to numerous risks over the project lifecycle. Appropriate risk assessment is necessary as well as risk allocation through contracts (see Figure 5.2), which is at the heart of structuring a PPP project. Risk-management strategy would reduce the cost of funding (efficient) and induce optimal behaviour in stakeholders (effective). Risk should be allocated to the party that can bear it at least cost (efficiency) and which has the greatest impact on its outcome (effectiveness). For instance, construction risk may be allocated to the EPC contractor through a fixed-price and fixed-time contract with liquidated damages. Counterparty contracts should be well written and enforceable to allocate the risks to these parties.[14]

Foreign-exchange risk mitigation may be achieved by increasing local currency financing as project revenues are generated in local currency in most infrastructure projects (recently Noida International Airport Limited sourced its entire debt capital (Rs.3,725 crore) from the State Bank of India in local currency, though the entire equity (Rs.2,005 crore) would come from Zurich AG, Switzerland, the promoter of the project). But risk mitigation in other areas may not be as straightforward. For example, fuel price and availability risk was borne by the private sector in the old standard bidding documents (SBDs) of the Ministry of Power for power generation projects. But the private sector had represented that

[14] Vikas Srivastava and V. Rajaraman. 2018. *Project and Infrastructure Finance-Corporate Banking Perspective.*

it cannot manage this risk—higher imported coal prices had made the Tata Mundra UMPP unviable. However, the new SBDs of the Ministry of Power in which fuel price is a pass through are also problematic. This is because when retail tariffs are *politically* capped, any increase in (pass-through) input costs would only be reflected in increased losses of distribution companies, which are predominantly in the public sector.

There are other issues which are important for sustainable infrastructure financing like imposing reasonable user charges, maintaining sanctity of contracts, and the autonomous regulation of infrastructure. These are dealt with in Chapter 3 (reasonable user charges) and Chapter 10 (maintaining sanctity of contracts and autonomous regulation of infrastructure).

6

Augmenting Infrastructure Financing— Brownfield Asset Monetization and Value Capture Finance

This chapter discusses some new initiatives on augmenting infrastructure financing. One of them is brownfield asset monetization (BAM) to be able to fund more greenfield infrastructure. Some of the vehicles used for BAM are Toll-Operate-Transfer (TOT) model and Infrastructure Investment Trusts (InvITs). The risks faced by infrastructure projects are considerably reduced over the project lifecycle from construction to operation stage, as issues related to land acquisition and environment and forest clearances are addressed at the construction stage. Therefore, operational projects (brownfield infrastructure) may be able to attract finance from institutional investors consisting of pension, insurance, and sovereign wealth funds. The chapter also includes a case study of IndiGrid, which is India's first power transmission InvIT.

This chapter also discusses another infrastructure financing vehicle, Value Capture Finance (VCF). This is associated with internalizing the externalities generated by large public investments like in metro rail to improve the financial viability of these projects. This part of the chapter also discusses metro-rail financing in India and lessons that can be learnt from Hong Kong metro for sustainable financing of metro-rail projects.

The ongoing Covid-19 pandemic has stretched the finances of the government when there is a need for increased infrastructure investment, both for coming out of the pandemic-induced recession as well as for laying the foundation for broad-based growth. In this context, BAM and VCF are non-traditional means for augmenting infrastructure financing, without increasing government debt or taxes.

Infrastructure Financing in India. Kumar V Pratap and Manshi Gupta, Oxford University Press.
© Kumar V Pratap and Manshi Gupta 2024. DOI: 10.1093/oso/9780198884934.003.0007

BAM or Asset Recycling

Project risks come down as projects move from construction stage to operation stage as issues related to land acquisition and environment and forest clearances are addressed at the construction stage. Therefore, operational projects become amenable to investment by institutional investors like pension, insurance, and sovereign wealth funds as these investors have a preference for low-risk long-term steady returns, which are characteristics of operational infrastructure projects. Even in the current Covid-19-pandemic times, there is considerable interest among institutional investors for infrastructure as an asset class in emerging markets, primarily for two reasons—low yields in the developed world and the fact that infrastructure is functioning and is producing yields despite the pandemic, that is, power, telecom, transport, water and sewerage projects, and so on, are still operational.

The Roadmap to Infrastructure as an Asset Class endorsed by the G20 countries acknowledges that financial vehicles need to be developed to tap into the changing risk profile of infrastructure projects over their lifecycle. The basic idea of BAM is to augment infrastructure resources through brownfield asset recycling for accelerated greenfield infrastructure project financing by freeing up funds tied up in de-risked brownfield public-sector assets such as telecom towers, roads, power transmission lines, gas and oil pipelines, power plants, airports, railway tracks, and so on, by transferring these infrastructure assets to a trust (InvITs) or a corporate structure (TOT), which receive investment from institutional investors like pension and insurance funds, and high-net-worth individuals, against a capital consideration which captures the value of future cash flows from these underlying assets. In such transactions, the capital value realized is often more than the sum total of discounted cash flows as such arrangements also unlock efficiencies. This is done either through the transfer of the operational control of underlying assets (as in the case of TOT), or even without the transfer of such control over underlying assets (as in the case of InvITs) to the private sector. Many countries including India, Australia, and the United States are working towards expanding the role of BAM (see Box 6.1).

It is critical to clarify what would not constitute asset recycling. Asset recycling should generally not include instances such as seeking

Box 6.1 International experience with asset monetization

- In 2005–2006, Indiana East West Toll Road (157 miles) connecting the Chicago Skyway to the Ohio Turnpike was monetized with a view to fund a ten-year plan for building and fixing roads throughout the state of Indiana, United States. The project was structured as a seventy-five-year concession for managing and operating the road and collecting tolls from motorists for an upfront consideration, while the road continued to be owned by the state. On 29 June 2006 the Indiana Toll Road Concession Company—a joint venture between Cintra, a Spanish construction firm and Macquarie Atlas Roads, an Australian road company—was awarded the right to operate the road for seventy-five years. The consortium won the contract with a winning bid of US$ 3.8 billion upfront payment. The concession helped in financing Indiana state's entire road-asset management plan for a period of ten years. During 2014, the concessionaire, Indiana Toll Road Concession Company filed for bankruptcy and subsequently a new investor and management was inducted, while allowing the creditors' dues to be settled through the bankruptcy process. The toll road is since being operated by Australia's IFM Investors for the next sixty-six years.

- The Australian Asset Recycling Initiative (ARI), launched in 2014, was aimed at encouraging states to recycle assets and utilize the sale proceeds for new productivity enhancing infrastructure by encouraging private companies to fund and run public infrastructure. Overall, three of Australia's eight states and territories participated in the scheme. By 2018, twelve major public assets were rolled out under ARI across New South Wales, Victoria, the Northern Territory, South Australia, and the Australian Capital Territory. One of the factors for the success of ARI was a 15 per cent bonus payment by central government for any asset monetization at the state level, if the proceeds are reinvested in new infrastructure. Approximately, AUD 3 billion in incentive payments were paid to participating states and territories over the life of the scheme. The initiative helped to enhance investments in new transportation infrastructure by states through sale or lease of assets such as ports, electricity generation, transmission and distribution, and roads. New South Wales, Australia leased three electricity transmission and distribution assets for ninety-nine years and raised US$26.34 billion. The private consortia, which won the bids were led by local pension funds. Safeguards, taking into account national security considerations, were added to the transaction citing Transgrid as critical infrastructure, including the following: Transgrid's operation and control be undertaken solely from Australia and that foreign consortium members retain an interest of no more than 50 per cent; half of Transgrid's board, including an independent chair and director, must be Australian citizens and residents. However, it is important that there is adequate regulatory oversight over pricing also, as electricity prices doubled in five years after monetization and the government had to step in with an energy affordability package to lower the burden on consumers.[a]

- There are a number of other innovative models being used in developing countries, including the Limited Concession Scheme (LCS) in Indonesia as an alternative to the existing PPP scheme. Under the LCS scheme, the private sector is invited to operate, maintain, and expand existing assets in return for the private sector paying the government an upfront concession fee or instituting ongoing revenue share schemes with the government. The existing infrastructure assets consist of transportation (seaports, airports, railways, and bus terminals), toll roads, water resources, sewerage and waste management systems, telecommunications, power plants, renewable energy, and oil and gas (LCS Assets). To qualify as LCS Assets, infrastructure should have been in operation for at least two years, and the remaining life of the assets must be at least ten years. The additional revenues aim to enable the government to complete its massive infrastructure programme, in particular to fund economically important, but sub-financial projects, such as the Trans Sumatra Highway, as well as social infrastructure projects in less-developed regions of Indonesia. India is using TOT and InvITs (discussed later), and Mexico and Uruguay are using revenue securitization models for BAM.

- The business trust model has been used in the United States, the United Kingdom, Singapore, and Hong Kong, which have a well-developed Real Estate Investment Trust (REIT) structure. The United States is the largest and the oldest REIT market (originating in the 1960s). It is estimated that there are more than 1,100 REITs in the United States, out of which 225 REITs are public (REITs registered with the Securities and Exchange Commission (SEC)). As of December 2019, REITs in the United States owned more than US$3.5 trillion of gross real estate assets and 5.16 lakh properties. REITs may be categorized as public REIT (in case of shares registered with SEC) or private REITs. Today, about forty countries and regions around the world have a REIT regime in place. Globally, fifteen of the thirty largest listed real estate companies in the world are REITs, which includes thirteen US REITs. The market capitalization of the United Kingdom's REITs are estimated at US$3.4 trillion, while that of Singapore's REITs are estimated at US$76 billion.

REITs invest in a wide variety of real estate property types, including offices, apartment buildings, distribution centres, warehouses, retail centres, medical facilities, data centres, cell towers, and hotels. Distribution centres and warehouses, which are collectively referred to as "logistics" real estate are some of the biggest industrial REITs listed on NYSE. Given the growth in e-commerce industry over the past few years, one of the biggest beneficiaries of the growth in investment and capital deployment of industrial REITs have been warehousing facilities, distribution and other storage facilities, where investors are guaranteed of off-take and income from investments, thereby ensuring the attractiveness of industrial REITs.

Most REITs operate on a straightforward business model, that is by leasing space and earning rental/leasing income on the underlying real estate, which is then paid out to shareholders in the form of dividends. REITs typically must pay out at least 90 per cent of their taxable income to shareholders. The key value proposition of REITs is that they provide investors the chance to own valuable real estate, with an opportunity to access dividend-based income and returns, without actually having to go out and buy, manage or finance property.[b]

[a]Andy Mukherjee. 2021.AustraliaHas Lessons for India's Asset Recycling Plan. *Business Standard.*

[b]NITI Aayog, Government of India. 2021. *National Monetization Pipeline, Volume 1: Monetization Guidebook* (https://www.niti.gov.in/sites/default/files/2021-08/Vol_I_NATIONAL_MONETISATION_PIPELINE_23_Aug_2021.pdf).

private management of operations under contractual arrangements, for example, operation and maintenance (O&M) for airports, distribution franchisee for power distribution companies (DISCOMs), EPC contracts, and so on, as they do not attract much value or investment from commercial investors. Such arrangements are therefore not considered BAM.[1]

Basic Features of BAM

- The focus of BAM is on profit-making core public-sector assets such as transmission lines, operational roads, oil and gas pipelines and so on, which would potentially lead to public-sector enterprises (PSEs) receiving a premium on the transfer of operational rights of these assets. They would be able to receive a premium because these assets are considerably de-risked as they are in operation (as opposed to being under construction, when they are subject to many risks including land acquisition and environment and forest clearance).
- Under BAM, the ownership of the underlying assets could remain with the government/PSE and in many cases, the assets can even continue to be operated by these PSEs (as in the case of InvITs). Moreover, the transfer of operation of assets (as under the TOT model) is only for a limited period, that is, the concession period, after which the operation of the assets would revert to the PSEs/public authority. However, BAM transactions can also include full sale and 100 per cent divestment of assets.

---

[1] Ministry of Finance, Government of India. 2020. *Strategic Asset Recycling Initiative: Draft Report by Sub-Group of Inter-Ministerial Steering Committee on Asset Recycling and Infrastructure Equity.*

- Ring-fencing of monetization proceeds: The funds generated from BAM may be transferred to PSEs whose assets have been taken up for monetization, and not as disinvestment proceeds, which get credited to the Consolidated Fund of India and used for meeting general government expenditure, whether revenue or capital. This would incentivize these PSEs to go in for BAM as they would be the recipient of the financial resources garnered through BAM for their, in many cases, best assets. An additional requirement of reinvestment into greenfield assets by the PSEs that get the BAM financial resources would close the loop of BAM leading to more greenfield infrastructure investment.

Advantages of BAM

- BAM seeks to optimize the mix of public and private financing through the life cycle of infrastructure assets. Government builds the project as it can absorb the project development risk better. After the project is built and enters the operation stage, BAM takes advantage of investor appetite for operational infrastructure assets, which are low risk and typically have long-lived, and relatively stable cash flows, which match the risk appetite of risk-averse institutional investors.
- BAM could lead to improvement in operational efficiency and service quality that may arise from transferring management responsibility to a specialized third-party asset operator. However, adequate institutional and regulatory framework for asset monetization (including contract management) is necessary, as private-sector goals of profit maximization and public-sector goals of welfare maximization might imply diverging interests just like the Australian case related in Box 6.1 where the electricity prices doubled following BAM.
- BAM helps in generating extra resources for infrastructure development, without the government incurring higher debt or levying additional taxes and thus, building and managing infrastructure in a fiscally sustainable manner.
- Unlocking the value of investment for the Government and generating optimal returns on them.

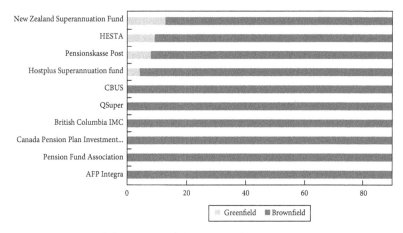

Figure 6.1 Greenfield vs brownfield pension fund investment (select pension funds)

Source: Ministry of Finance, Government of India. 2020. *Strategic Asset Recycling Initiative: Draft Report by Sub- Group of Inter- Ministerial Steering Committee on Asset Recycling and Infrastructure Equity.*

- Suitable for institutional investors meeting their preference for de- risked post-construction brownfield assets with an established revenue profile and stable returns accruing over a long period. Figure 6.1 shows a clear preference of pension funds for investment in brownfield operational assets.
- Enabling institutional investment into infrastructure causes such financing without the asset–liability mismatch, typically associated with bank financing of infrastructure. Banks can redeploy the freed resources (because of BAM) into fresh greenfield investment.
- Citizens benefit twice, as users of more efficient infrastructure services and as investors through their retirement savings portfolio (institutional investment) being directed towards infrastructure with relatively high and long-term stable returns.

BAM or Asset Recycling Process

The public-sector enterprise selects those infrastructure assets that can be monetized (e.g. existing infrastructure (A1)—see Figure 6.2). These assets would very often be operational, profit-making, and cash-generating,

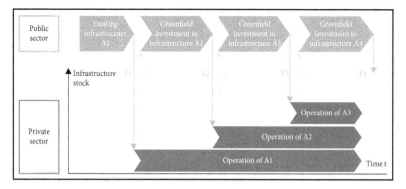

Figure 6.2 Brownfield asset monetization (BAM) or asset recycling process

Source: Ministry of Finance, *Government of India. 2020. Strategic Asset Recycling Initiative: Draft Report by Sub- Group of Inter- Ministerial Steering Committee on Asset Recycling and Infrastructure Equity.*

but can also be loss-making provided the private sector perceives that the loss-making assets can be turned around with increased efficiency. The operation of this infrastructure is then transferred to private-sector investors (transfer T1). In return, the public sector receives a monetary transfer (M1) from the private sector, all (or some) of which, may be ring-fenced, to ensure that the funds do not go into the government's consolidated revenue fund, but are rather conserved for infrastructure investment. The fund could, for instance, be a special earmarked government account, or a fund vehicle or company dedicated to infrastructure investment, or go to the same company that made its assets available for BAM for incentivizing such transactions.

Funds M1 are then directed to greenfield infrastructure asset construction (i.e. greenfield investment in infrastructure asset (A2)). After completion of the construction phase, infrastructure asset (A2) is transferred to the private sector for operation (transfer T2). The public sector in return receives a payment from the private sector (monetary transfer, M2). In this way, the cycle of BAM can be combined with greenfield infrastructure investment for infrastructure augmentation in a country.

Creating a Viable Monetization Structure

Structuring of the long-term concession and the risk-reward framework (or the transfer of operations to the private sector through TOT or

InvIT vehicles) is critical to achieve scale and realize the right monetary value for the identified assets. Guiding principles which could be suitably adapted and contextualized across sectors and assets are presented below:

- Creating positive public perception: Communication on the importance and purpose of asset monetization is critical for successful transactions. The stakeholders need to be engaged at an early stage. Since institutional investors are expected to participate in the transactions, environmental, social, and governance issues need to be addressed upfront. Key to creating buy-in of consumers to monetization would be enhanced with efficient delivery of services at reasonable tariffs, which needs to be suitably stated in the concession agreement with associated penalties in case of non-realization.
- Operating assets generating stable cash flows should be chosen for monetization as they are considerably de-risked (past land acquisition and environment and forest clearance stages).
- Cash flows need to be predictable, monitorable, and transparent. This would be helped, for example, through electronic tolling of traffic (Government of India has mandated FASTag on motor vehicles, with effect from 1 January 2021, to promote digital payments and reduce waiting time and fuel consumption at toll booths; all 722 toll plazas on national highways and another 196 toll plazas on state highways collect user fees only through FASTags; toll collection through FASTags reached the all-time high of Rs.1.22 billion on 30 October 2021)[2], metered electricity flows through power transmission lines, and metered flow of gas and oil through pipelines.
- There should be reliable and credible regulatory structure for determining tariffs (which may be either through contract or independent sectoral regulator).
- Size of package: Financial investors may not be interested in anything less than US$200 million. So, the assets may need to be bundled as NHAI is doing (more than five road assets in TOT

---

[2] *Times of India*. 1 November 2021. Record FASTag Collection Points to Recovery Road.

transactions) to have the desired minimum size of the bundle to be able to attract large institutional investors with long-term investment horizons.

- Term of Concession: Assets which are fully built and have small operational expenditure requirement, such as highways, port terminals, rail lines, transmission lines may have a concession period of twenty-five to thirty years. Assets with ongoing capital expenditure phases linked to usage growth, such as airports may have longer concession periods, say fifty to sixty years, given the need to recover capital investment while keeping the tariffs reasonable.

- Need for Model Concession Agreements across sectors with clearly defined risk-return framework: concession agreements should be crafted with clauses that protect the service levels for users and investor returns through key performance indicators (KPIs) and safeguards, operations and maintenance standards, asset capacity upgrades, and agreement on pricing levels and indices.[3]

- Incentive structures would need to be defined upfront. This may include retention of cash generated from asset monetization transactions by the entity (e.g. PSE or state government) that makes its assets available for such transactions.

- Use of resources garnered through BAM: It needs to be clarified upfront that BAM resources would go to the same agency making its assets available for BAM. In addition, these resources can only be used for increasing the agency's infrastructure investment or reducing its debt (e.g., NHAI).

- Top level political commitment and support is necessary to make asset monetization a viable tool for financing infrastructure. Resistance to asset monetization may happen at the employee level, for example, or more generally, which would have to be addressed and political support for the initiative would be crucial. The creation of a ring-fenced infrastructure fund (where the BAM resources are stored) and an independent agency to take the process forward (like

---

[3] World Economic Forum. 2017. *Recycling our Infrastructure for Future Generations* (http://www3.weforum.org/docs/WEF_Recycling_our_Infrastructure_for_Future_Generations_report_2017.pdf).

3P India, discussed in Chapter 12) will also demonstrate the political commitment to the initiative.

Models of BAM in India

Various forms of private participation may be used for asset monetization depending on the type of assets and the market structure:

- Outright sale or divestment may be considered for assets in sectors which have ample competition from private players like power generation, logistics, and telecom towers.
- Monetization through PPP or privatization with economic regulation may be considered for assets that have monopolistic characteristics like roads (through TOT), power transmission and distribution, ports, and airports (through an operation, management, and development agreement (OMDA)).
- Monetization via InvITs (described later) with the PSEs as sponsors may be considered for assets that are strategic in nature and there is a need for continued government oversight over existing assets in strategically important PSEs such as Nuclear Power Corporation of India Limited, and Indian Strategic Petroleum Reserves Limited, ISPRL.
- For large land banks held by strategically important PSEs/government/railways/municipalities, an outright sale of land may be considered, combined with monetization via PPPs for connected assets such as railway station development.

In asset recycling, the most popular option for divesting assets is through a lease and concession agreement. This allows governments or public-sector enterprises and the private sector to agree on a concession agreement with safeguard clauses to protect service levels, and allows government to get the full ownership of the asset after the concession period. Meanwhile, the private party takes full responsibility for operating the asset for the concession period, assuming all or most commercial risks, and guaranteeing a level of service for the right to collect user fees.

The three main models for BAM in India are described next.

Toll-Operate-Transfer (TOT)

Ministry of Road Transport and Highways (MoRTH) introduced the TOT concession framework (akin to Operate-Maintain-Transfer[4] model) in 2016 for monetization of the road assets portfolio of NHAI to long-term investors. Under the TOT model, O&M obligations and the right to collect user fees for operational infrastructure assets are transferred from the public-sector operator to the highest private bidder for the concession period (thirty years) in return for an upfront fee paid to the public-sector entity (like NHAI). The TOT model effectively entails securitization of the toll receivables by collecting an upfront concession fee from the selected bidder and is determined through a transparent competitive bidding mechanism. However, even though the function of operating the asset is transferred to the private sector, the ownership of the asset remains with the public sector.

Key recent reform initiatives for TOT transactions include:

- Flexibility in the concession period: the concession period of toll projects may now be between fifteen and thirty years as against the fixed term of thirty years earlier. This is expected to increase participation from Indian developers in addition to large pension funds, insurance companies, and sovereign wealth funds;
- Reduced minimum operating history requirement: minimum operating history of one year allowed compared to two years of operations post-commencement of tolling earlier. This is expected to expand the eligible universe of operating toll roads to be considered for the TOT package.

Five rounds of TOT transactions have been undertaken till 2022, covering a stretch of 2,395 km, out of which three rounds have been completed: Bundle 1, Bundle 3, and Bundle 5. NHAI has raised Rs.16,954 crore across these three rounds of TOT entailing toll road assets of 1408 km (See Table 6.1).

The first (TOT-1) bundle of nine highway projects (682 km) was awarded by NHAI for Rs.9,681 crore in 2018 for a concession period of thirty years.

---

[4] Between 2009/10 and 2014/15, NHAI has awarded a total of around 2,400 km of National Highways on an OMT basis.

Table 6.1 TOT bundles bid out by NHAI till 2022

	Bundle	Date	Length (km)	Value (Rs. crore)
1	TOT Bundle 1	Aug 2018	682	9,681
2	TOT Bundle 2	Feb 2019	586	Bid cancelled
3	TOT Bundle 3	Nov 2019	566	5,011
4	TOT Bundle 4	Sep 2020	401	Bid cancelled
5	TOT Bundle 5A-1	Jan 2021	54	1,011
6	TOT Bundle 5A-2	Jan 2021	106	1,251

Source: NITI Aayog, Government of India. 2021. *National Monetization Pipeline, Volume 1: Monetization Guidebook* (https://www.niti.gov.in/sites/default/files/2021-08/Vol_I_NATIONAL_MONETISATION_PIPELINE_23_Aug_2021.pdf).

Six of these projects were in Andhra Pradesh and are part of the NH-5 of the Golden Quadrilateral connecting Kolkata and Chennai. They have a strong traffic potential given the presence of ports, industrial clusters, and consumption centres in the project vicinity. The premium in this transaction was Rs.3,423 crore (55 per cent, or about Rs.5 crore per km of road), which is calculated as the difference between the amount that would have accrued to NHAI under business-as-usual (Rs.6,258 crore)[5] and the winning bid. This premium emanates from the unlocking of efficiencies from transferring the operations of the road assets to a specialist private-sector operator. The winning bidder was a consortium of Macquarie (an Australian multinational investment bank and financial services company) and Ashoka Buildcon (a leading highway developer of India).

TOT-3 Bundle (nine road projects, 566 km) was awarded to Cube Highways and Infrastructure Pvt Ltd., a road developer backed by global infrastructure fund, I-Squared Capital and the International Finance Corporation (IFC), which placed the winning bid of Rs.5,011 crore against a reserve price/initial estimated concession value of Rs.4,995 crore, which is the value of these road projects under business-as-usual.

NHAI has also raised Rs.6,267 crore from monetization of the Eastern Peripheral Expressway, half of the new ring road around the National

---

[5] Aggregate toll revenue was Rs.664 crore in FY 2019 as against Rs.513 crore in FY 2018 showing a growth of 29 per cent.

Capital Region. Indian Highway Concession Trust, a joint venture of Maple Highways, a private company incorporated in Singapore, and CDPQ, a Canadian Pension Fund, has bagged the project under the TOT model (November 2022).

Certain state government entities have also adopted the TOT model for monetizing state toll roads. In June 2020, Maharashtra State Road Development Corporation (MSRDC) awarded the tolling rights of Mumbai Pune Expressway and the old Mumbai-Pune corridor (NH-48) for thirty years to IRB Infrastructure Developers for a total consideration of Rs.8,262 crore comprising an upfront payment of Rs.6,500 crore and the balance in staggered instalments over a period of three years.

The TOT model in the road sector can be adopted in the power and energy sectors for monetizing power transmission lines and oil and gas pipelines.

Infrastructure Investment Trusts (InvITs)

InvITs are trust-based structures which pool operating infrastructure assets and source funds from long-term institutional investors to invest in these assets. InvITs are securitization vehicles that own, operate, and maintain income-generating infrastructure assets.[6] At least 90 per cent of the profits generated by these assets need to be distributed to unit-holders as dividends as per SEBI regulations. InvITs are like mutual funds; however, instead of owning financial securities, InvITs own and manage real infrastructure assets. InvITs pool resources from domestic institutional investors,[7] foreign institutional investors, and high-net-worth individuals to invest in operational (and therefore de-risked) infrastructure assets against pay-out of cash flow generated by the assets on a periodic basis. InvITs are pass-through entities and are income-tax exempt at the InvIT level. With no construction risk, InvITs can give superior risk-adjusted

---

[6] The projects' ownership and operation can also remain with the current operator (in this case, the PSEs) and investors would have a claim on dedicated revenue stream generated by mainly these operating assets.

[7] For example, the Pension Fund Regulatory and Development Authority (PFRDA) issued a notification in 2015 allowing investments up to 5 per cent in InvITs by pension funds.

returns with little volatility in these returns while listing gives an exit option to unit-holders. Improved yields for unit-holders can be ensured by adding revenue-generating projects and expanding the InvIT portfolio.

Under an InvIT transaction, infrastructure asset owners transfer multiple revenue-generating asset SPVs through holdco or otherwise to a trust which then issues units to investors for raising money. The minimum value of assets under InvIT should be Rs.500 crore (initial offer size should be at least Rs.250 crore). The minimum number of investors is twenty; if the number of investors is more than a thousand, then there needs to be a public issue.

InvITs allow companies to unlock tied capital (sponsor's and lender's capital) in completed projects; monetize revenue-generating infra assets and thus reduce debt; attract institutional investors, including foreign capital; and lower the cost of capital. InvITs are established as trusts under the Indian Trust Act, 1882 and regulated under the SEBI (Infrastructure Investment Trusts) Regulations,[8] 2014 (and InvIT guidelines issued in 2016), which ensures better governance and transparency, for example, the investment manager has to be a separate entity from the sponsor. The structure of an InvIT is shown in Figure 6.3.

Some recent measures to popularize InvITs are: consolidated leverage raised from 49 per cent to 70 per cent of the value of InvIT assets with certain conditions like a AAA rating of InvIT debt; banks allowed to lend to InvITs; allowing InvITs to access external commercial borrowing markets for debt finance; unlisted InvITs allowed; allowing FPIs, pension funds, and insurance funds to invest in debt securities of InvITs (Budget 2021/22 has allowed this); and minimum subscription and lot size for retail investors reduced to increase their participation in InvITs.[9]

There are fifteen (of which eleven are active) registered InvITs in the country, of which four are publicly listed (see Table 6.2). The majority of registered InvITs are private and are expected to attract investment from

---

[8] In order to generate investor confidence in subscribing to units of InvIT, it was necessary that the conflict of interest between project sponsors and InvIT unit-holders was addressed, including valuation of assets, making the units tax efficient, disclosures, and so on, which was provided by the SEBI InvIT Regulations, 2014.

[9] SEBI recently amended to InvIT/REIT regulations revising the minimum subscription and trading lot. Accordingly, for publicly issued InvITs and REITs, the revised minimum application value was brought down within the range of Rs.10,000–15,000 and the trading lot to one unit. This is expected to provide a boost to retail participation in InvITs/ REITs.

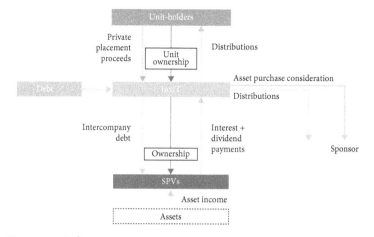

Figure 6.3 Infrastructure Investment Trust (InvIT) structure
Source: Ministry of Finance, Government of India. 2020. *Report of the Sub-group on Capital Markets for Financing of National Infrastructure Pipeline.*

large institutional investors. As shown in Table 6.2, there are two public-sector-sponsored InvITs, one sponsored by PGCIL (transmission assets) and the other by NHAI (roads), which are also public. Cumulatively, these InvITs have assets under management (AUM) of around Rs.1.4 lakh crore. The bulk of the assets are constituted by toll roads (Rs. 55,600 crore), followed by telecom (Rs. 42,000 crore), power transmission (Rs. 22,800 crore), and gas pipeline (Rs. 14,500 crore). Renewable energy is the emerging sector for InvITs with considerable potential. Virescent InvIT, as of the end of 2021, manages thirteen operating renewable energy assets across seven states of India. The case study of one of the earliest Indian InvITs (IndiGrid) is at Box 6.2.

Real Estate Investment Trusts (REITs)

Real estate assets are capital intensive and require substantial upfront investment by the developer. While the land and building-based debt products have been available, they do not provide for effective risk-sharing and cost-effective financing for the developer. In this context, REITs have been developed and are similar in structure to InvITs. As against an InvIT which is unique to the Indian context, REIT structures have seen traction

Table 6.2 InvITs in India

	InvIT—promoter and main investors	Sector	Public/ Private	Listing month	Assets under management (Rs. crore)
1	IRB InvIT Fund—IRB Infrastructure Development Ltd	Toll roads	Public	May 2017	6,500
2	India Grid Trust—Sterlite Power Grid Ventures Limited, KKR, GIC	Power transmission	Public	June 2017	15,000
3	IndInfravit[a] Trust—L&T IDPL, CPPIB, Allianz, Omers	Toll roads	Private	June 2018	10,500
4	India Infrastructure Trust— Reliance, Brookfield	Gas pipeline	Private	March 2019	14,500
5	Oriental Infra Trust— Oriental Structural Engineering Pvt. Ltd, IFC, AIIB, DEG	Toll roads	Private	June 2019	11,000
6	IRB Infrastructure Trust— IRB Infrastructure, GIC	Toll roads	Private	Feb 2020	22,500
7	Tower infrastructure Trust— Reliance & Brookfield[b]	Telecom towers	Private	Sep 2020	42,000
8	Digital Fibre Infrastructure Trust—Reliance	Fibre optic	Private	Oct 2020	1,500
9	National Highway Infra Trust—NHAI	Toll roads	Public	October 2020	5,100
10	Powergrid InvIT—Powergrid	Power transmission	Public	May 2021	7,800
11	Virescent Renewable Energy Trust (VRET)—KKR	Renewable energy	Private	February 2021	460

[a]IndInfravit has five road-sector assets, and has added eight more road assets from Sadbhav Infrastructure Project Ltd. for Rs.6,300 crore.

[b]Brookfield Infrastructure has acquired a high-quality portfolio of approximately 1,35,000 recently constructed communication towers that form the infrastructure backbone of Reliance Jio's telecom business. This portfolio provides a well-placed platform to capitalize on the rollout of 5G across the country, as the towers are largely connected by fibre backhaul.

Source: Authors' compilation from SEBI (2020) *Registered Infrastructure Investment Trusts* (https:// www.sebi.gov.in/sebiweb/other/OtherAction.do?doRecognisedFpi=yes&intmId=20);Ministry of Finance, Government of India. 2020. *Report of the Sub-group on Capital Markets for financing of National Infrastructure Pipeline*; NITI Aayog, Government of India. 2021. *National Monetization Pipeline, Volume 1: Monetization Guidebook* (https://www.niti.gov.in/sites/default/files/2021-08/Vol_ I_NATIONAL_MONETISATION_PIPELINE_23_Aug_2021.pdf); and KKR-Sponsored Virescent Infrastructure Raises INR4.6 Billion in India's First Renewable Energy InvIT from AIMCo and Other Investors (https://www.businesswire.com/news/home/20210928006194/en/).

Box 6.2   Case study: IndiGrid—India's first power transmission InvIT

IndiGrid is the Indian power sector's first InvIT, and owns transmission assets.[a] Its sponsor is Sterlite Power Grid Ventures. IndiGrid owns two assets of Sterlite—Jabalpur Transmission Company and Bhopal Dhule Transmission Company. In total, now, it has thirty-two transmission-line assets across sixteen states with 6,600 circuit km length and ten substations with 14,995 MVA transformation capacity.

As per SEBI InvIT Regulations, 2014, the InvIT should have the following actors:[b]

- *Sponsor*: The sponsor sets up the InvIT, appoints the trustees of the InvIT and is the infrastructure developer of the SPVs included in the InvIT. It should have a net worth of not less than Rs.100 crore if it is a body corporate/ company and should have a track record of five years, and in case of a developer, should at least have two projects in infrastructure development or fund management in the infrastructure sector. The sponsor shall transfer or undertake to transfer to the InvIT its entire interest in the SPV or ownership of the infrastructure projects before allotment of units of the InvIT. It is required to hold at least 15 per cent of the total units of the InvIT if the project manager (PM) is an associate of the sponsor. In all other scenarios, the requirement is to have a minimum of 25 per cent holding for three years in InvITs.
- *Investment manager (IM)*: The IM is responsible for investment decisions concerning the underlying assets or projects following the investment strategy of the InvIT. The IM will have to enter into an investment agreement with a registered independent trustee and should appoint and oversee the activities of the PM in terms of the project implementation/management agreement. The IM, in consultation with the trustee, will appoint the valuer(s), auditor, registrar, transfer agent, merchant banker, custodian, and any other intermediary as may be applicable concerning the activities of the InvIT. The IM would also ensure that all the activities of the intermediaries are as per SEBI regulations.

- *Trustee*: The trustee is responsible for holding the InvIT assets in the name of the InvIT for the benefit of the unit-holders, following the Trust deed and the SEBI regulations. The trustee shall oversee the actions of the IM and the PM to ensure that they comply with the regulations/ project management agreement, including compliance with any reporting and disclosure requirements. It shall also review transactions between the IM and its associates to ensure that they are at arms' length.
- *PM*: The PM is responsible for the O&M of the InvIT assets, including making arrangements for the appropriate maintenance required under any project agreement or concession agreement in the case of the PPP project. For under-construction projects, the PM shall oversee the progress of development up to its completion.

In the case of IndiGrid, Sterlite Power Grid Ventures is the sponsor (holding 15 per cent of the InvIT in 2019) and PM, while Sterlite Investment Managers Limited is the IM and Axis Bank is the trustee.

The units of IndiGrid were listed on 6 June 2017. IndiGrid assets are low risk as they are in operation stage and fetch returns based on annuity payments, and thus not subject to revenue risks associated with some other infrastructure assets like toll roads. In addition, there is a credible counterparty—PGCIL. As a result, the IndiGrid units *beta* (β) is low (0.09 as compared to 0.05 for government security (G Sec) bonds). Reflecting these financial features, the credit rating of IndiGrid is the highest possible at AAA by the three major credit-rating agencies in India (CRISIL, India Ratings, and ICRA). The annuity returns of the InvIT are to be distributed to the unit-holders of the InvIT to the minimum extent of 90 per cent to qualify as a tax-free entity.

InvITs are allowed to invest in assets directly or through SPVs, which need to be owned at least 51 per cent by the InvIT. The AUM of IndiGrid were Rs.5,300 crore in September 2018, and Rs.15,000 crore in Q3 financial year (FY) 2021, which the InvIT expects to increase to Rs.30,000 crore by 2022. KKR (now a sponsor holding 22 per cent of the InvIT), GIC (20 per cent), and several other well-known investment firms have invested over Rs.2,500 crore in

IndiGrid. This has improved the management and governance of the InvIT.

IndiGrid had many firsts to its credit. IndiGrid was the first Indian power transmission InvIT, the first transmission InvIT to get listed after a successful public offering (June 2017), the first InvIT to acquire third-party assets (Patran Transmission Company Limited in September 2018), the first InvIT to issue debt securities at the trust level, and the first InvIT to do a follow-on capital issue.

[a]Indian Institute of Management, Ahmedabad. 2020. *IndiGrid: Creating India's First Power Transmission InvIT*.

[b]In addition, there are the unit-holders. The unit-holders are the investors who subscribe to the units of the InvIT. The unit-holders are the eventual beneficiaries of the InvIT assets.

across the globe (see Box 6.1). The objective of the REIT structure is to broad-base financing options for the real-estate developers, create more real-estate infrastructure, while also giving more exit options to real-estate investors. REITs are established as trusts under the Indian Trust Act, 1882 and regulated under the SEBI (Real Estate Investment Trusts) Regulations, 2014.

India has seen three REIT transactions, all in the private sector, since the regulations were introduced (Table 6.3). Given the availability of industrial parks and public-sector-warehousing assets of corporations such as Central Warehousing Corporation and silos and other such facilities of

Table 6.3 REITs in India

	REIT	Sector	Public/ Private	Listing month	Assets under management (Rs. crore)
1	Embassy REIT	Office parks	Public	Apr 2019	33,000
2	Mindspace REIT	Office parks	Public	Aug 2020	22,500
3	Brookfield India REIT	Office parks	Public	Feb 2021	11,000

Source: NITI Aayog, Government of India. 2021. *National Monetization Pipeline, Volume 1: Monetization* Guidebook (https://www.niti.gov.in/sites/default/files/2021-08/Vol_I_NATIONAL_MONETISATION_PIPELINE_23_Aug_2021.pdf).

the Food Corporation of India, REITs can be used for leveraging private investment in such public-sector assets also through monetization.

India's first REIT was listed in April 2019—Embassy Office Parks REIT—in which the investors are Embassy Group (15 per cent), global investment firm Blackstone (55 per cent), FPIs (16 per cent), retail investors (12 per cent), and others (2 per cent). It initially raised about Rs.5,000 crore, followed by another Rs.3,680 crore through institutional placement, which was to be used for acquisition of the IT park, Embassy Tech Village for US$1.3 billion. This will make Embassy REIT the largest in Asia Pacific in terms of area. Embassy REIT has 32.3 million square feet of completed and operational commercial properties in Mumbai, Bengaluru, and Pune. Top occupiers by gross rent are IBM (12 per cent), Cognizant (9 per cent), NTT (4 per cent), and ANSR (3 per cent).

India's second REIT is Mindspace Business Parks REIT, backed by K Raheja Corp (63 per cent) and Blackstone (9 per cent). It has a completed commercial portfolio of 23.9 million square feet across Hyderabad, Mumbai, Pune, and Chennai. It has raised Rs.4,500 crore. The tenants are largely MNC firms from diversified sectors which have helped bring in better realizations and lower volatility of cash flows. The average rent for the Mindspace Business Parks REIT was around Rs.60 per square feet per month.

The country's third REIT, Canadian major's Brookfield India REIT, has raised Rs.3,800 crore through a public issue and will be publicly traded. This is India's first REIT which is 100 per cent managed by an institution. Brookfield owns and operates a portfolio of infrastructure and real-estate assets, including 42 million square feet of office properties, of which about 10 million square feet is intended to be offered under the REIT.

Collectively, the three Indian REITs own around 98 million square feet of office space with a total operating area of 66.4 million square feet. This is 10 per cent of India's 650 million square feet of Grade A office stock in the top metro cities.

What makes the country attractive to institutional investment is not just the range of novel models (TOT) and instruments (InvITs and REITs) available now, but also the improved transparency in the governance of projects, auction systems for the allocation of licenses for public resources, the existence of a top tier of well-managed private companies and other market mechanisms such as the creation of funding platforms for infrastructure (NIIF).[10]

The Need to Mainstream BAM

BAM is a relatively novel concept in India (and the world, except for REITs), where it has been used mainly in the road and power transmission sectors. There is a need to replicate this success in other infrastructure sectors as well, which will require a clear policy, regulatory and institutional framework, transparent processes, and political commitment. It has been estimated that the existing stock of brownfield assets in India is about US$16 trillion,[11]monetization of even a small proportion of which (say, 15 per cent) should be able to provide enough resources for filling the infrastructure financing gap for many years.

Given the need for creating a viable monetization structure, not all brownfield assets in India can be monetized. Also given that the main concern is bridging mainly the public-sector infrastructure financing gap, an indicative potential asset monetization pipeline may be seen in Table 6.4.

In order to support channelization of more investment and institutional savings into infrastructure investments, both for equity and debt, the following steps would be important:

Incentives: One of the reasons for the success of Australia's Asset Recycling Initiative was a 15 per cent bonus payment by the central government for any asset monetization at the state level (this has been replicated in the Indian National Monetization Pipeline where there is a central government incentive for state-level asset monetization). To incentivize monetization, proceeds of any asset monetization needs to flow back to the monetizing entity (given that these could be their best core assets) rather than flowing into the Consolidated Fund of India.

---

[10] Wharton School, University of Pennsylvania. 2020. *What Will It Take for India to Reach Its Infrastructure Goals?* (https://knowledge.wharton.upenn.edu/article/will-take-india-reach-infrastructure-goals/).
[11] World Economic Forum. 2017. *Recycling our Infrastructure for Future Generations* (http://www3.weforum.org/docs/WEF_Recycling_our_Infrastructure_for_Future_Generations_report_2017.pdf).

Table 6.4 Potential asset monetization pipeline

Ministry/PSE	Assets identified
M/o Civil Aviation/ Airport Authority of India (AAI)	AAI has a total of 137 airports. The following may be considered for monetization: • AAI-owned metro airports—Chennai, Kolkata • Non-metro airports—airports in Tier-2 and Tier-3 cities with traffic of 2 million passengers and above per annum: Trichy, Amritsar, Varanasi, Bhubaneswar, Raipur, Indore • Residual government stake in PPP airports at Delhi, Mumbai, Hyderabad, and Bengaluru • AAI cargo services, storage assets
M/o Power/Power Grid Corporation of India Limited (PGCIL)	• Transmission line assets of PGCIL: • First phase: Tariff-based competitive bidding (TBCB) assets (gross block Rs.1,700 crore immediately and Rs.4,000 crore post-July 2020/21) • Second phase: Regulated tariff mechanism (RTM) assets that comprise 95% of PGCIL's asset base • State transmission grids • Electricity distribution companies • Renewable power generating assets with central/state government companies
M/o Shipping	• 11 assets including 10 berths currently operated by Port Trusts • International crude terminal at Goa Port • Corporatization and sale of terminals in major ports • Captive terminals/jetties owned by PSUs • LNG terminals and stakes in terminals owned by PSUs
MoRTH/NHAI	• 12 lots of National Highway bundles on ToT, in the period 2020–2024 (more than 6,000 km out of a total of 1,39,000 km of NH).Estimated value ~ Rs.1,00,000 crore • Bundle—5, 6 (2020/21); Bundle—7, 8 (2021/22); Bundle—9, 10 (2022/23); Bundle—11, 12 (2023/24) • Operational expressways; high-density state highways
M/o Railways (MoR)	• 150 passenger trains by private operators • 50 railway station re-development projects (out of 7,325 stations) • 4 mountain railways • 3 sports stadia • Dedicated freight corridor rail lines • Overhead electrification lines • Port connectivity projects • Coal transport focussed projects
M/o Petroleum & Natural Gas/Gas Authority of India Limited (GAIL), oil marketing companies (OMCs)	• Monetization of natural gas pipeline network of GAIL — about 10,000 km (~225 mmscmd) valued at ~Rs. 27,000 crore in 2–3 asset bundles • Oil and gas pipelines owned by other oil marketing companies (OMCs) like IOCL, HPCL, and BPCL • City gas distribution concessions

Table 6.4 Continued

Ministry/PSE	Assets identified
M/o Housing and Urban Affairs/ Delhi Metro Rail Corporation (DMRC)	Monetization of metro assets of DMRC: • Tentative valuation of Rs.28,000 crore–68,000 crore under different assumptions (depending on rights for 20/50/99 years on metro assets, rolling stock, and commercial development rights)
Department of Telecommunication (DoT)	• Monetization of 69,047 BSNL and MTNL telecom towers • Other assets including land of BSNL, MTNL • BharatNet Optical Fibre Cable (OFC) (3.5 lakh km out of 5.25 lakh km) and associated infrastructure of BBNL • BSNL and MTNL data centres
PSUs	• Inter-PSU stakes held particularly in oil sector • Subsidiaries of PSUs in oil and power sector • Captive power generation facilities
Agriculture and allied sectors	• Land monetization of Food Corporation of India • Warehouses of FCI, Central Warehouse Corporation (total 81.8 million tonnes warehousing capacity)
Social infrastructure	• Stadiums • Hospitals bundled with capacity augmentation

Note: 'Potential asset base' refers to the infrastructure assets under the purview of the central line ministries and CPSEs covered as part of the National Monetization Pipeline (NMP) exercise. Rather than focussing on the whole universe of assets under a ministry/CPSE, the potential asset base focusses on the assets that are sizeable and amenable to monetization. These include brownfield assets that are currently operational as well as assets that are expected to be operational over the NMP period.

Source: NITI Aayog, Government of India. 2021. *National Monetization Pipeline, Volume 2: Asset Pipeline* (https://www.niti.gov.in/sites/default/files/2021-08/Vol_2_NATIONAL_MONETI SATION_PIPELINE_23_Aug_2021.pdf); Ministry of Finance (Government of India). 2020. *Strategic Asset Recycling Initiative-* Draft Report by Sub-Group of Inter-Ministerial Steering Committee on Asset Recycling and Infrastructure Equity, p. 16

Removing tax barriers: Capital gains taxes: The land/building/assets of PSUs have low acquisition cost and high market value. A sale event of such assets attracts large tax outgo discouraging monetization. Government may consider a tax-exemption window contingent on the PSU reinvesting these proceeds in greenfield assets in the succeeding two financial years. Similarly, stamp duty may be waived for transfer of assets to InvITs and REITs.

Streamlining the investment guidelines of insurance and pension funds: The existing investment guidelines for insurance and pension funds limit the exposure of such funds to InvIT/REIT assets. The investment limits are as follows: (i) insurance funds—maximum exposure at the lower of

3 per cent of fund size of the insurer/5 per cent of the units issued by a single InvIT/REIT; (ii) pension funds under Employees' Provident Fund Organization (EPFO) are regulated to invest up to a maximum of 5 per cent of the funds in InvIT/REIT; (iii) mutual funds can invest up to 10 per cent of their AUM in a single InvIT/REIT. Thus, there are inconsistencies across categories at the level of exposure. Also, there are other constraints like IRDA regulations not permitting investment of insurance funds in unlisted InvITs, and at least an 'A' rating of the underlying project for investment by pension and insurance funds when the typical credit rating of project-financed infrastructure projects is 'BBB'. Hence, there is a need to streamline the investment guidelines to ensure consistency, as well as permitting insurance and pension funds to invest in unlisted InvITs and lower-rated infrastructure projects as long as there is reasonable security of their investment in some other metrics (like Expected Loss Credit Rating scale; discussed in Chapter 12).

Permit land-use change at a reasonable fee: Government/PSU land banks are typically subject to restricted end-use and are available only for specific purposes. Government may advise state governments to consider a window for change in land use for a fee payable upon the sale event. This would enable states to mobilize additional revenue and sellers to realize optimal value for the assets.

Sound project preparation and following a clear timeline for asset monetization: Starting and stopping the bid process leads to lost credibility for the monetizing agency and the loss of time and money for bidders. Therefore, the project should be bid out only after sound project preparation (including applicable approvals) by the concessioning authority. There should be a two-stage bidding process aimed at evaluating technical and financial eligibility in the first stage and financial bidding at the second stage (with a single bidding parameter) and be spread over about three to six months. Following a clear timeline will generate credibility for the asset monetization programme in India, generating more investor interest.

Importance of sound project-level data: It is important to provide good quality data to prospective investors. This will lead to efficient price discovery at the second stage (financial bidding) of the bidding process.

Writing robust concession contracts: Since asset monetization in regulated infrastructure may need to be done through a concession, writing bankable and legally robust concession contracts would be important for attracting the private sector. These concession contracts should provide a clear risk-return framework, KPIs and performance standards, incentives and penalties for performance, termination payments in case of premature termination, *force majeure* provisions and dispute-resolution provisions which augment the comfort level of the private sector, while also be protecting the public (value for money) and user interests. Model Concession Agreements already exist for road and port sectors (but mainly for greenfield investments) and there is a need to prepare similar documents for brownfield investments in these sectors and in other sectors. BAM may be especially challenging given the need for incorporating the legacy and employee issues of brownfield assets in concession contracts. It must also be ensured that once signed, the sanctity of contracts is maintained by both public and private parties, failing which there should be adequate safeguards for other stakeholders.

Need for a National Monetization Pipeline: Long-term investors, whether financial or strategic, domestic or international, use medium-term plans to deploy their capital year-on-year to manage their finances and to build up their capabilities in a country or sector. India is already seen as a major investment magnet due to its growth potential, demographics, and reforms. Building on these strengths, the announcement of an asset recycling plan, and an asset monetization pipeline would generate excitement not only among domestic investors but also internationally. The pipeline should have project wise data on KPIs, latent risks, and so on. A line ministry/department/PSU/state-specific plan could be prepared in consultation with Niti Aayog and Ministry of Finance. A typical plan for a line ministry/department/PSU/state government could be to identify assets worth 2X of their monetization target for the year. The business plan should aim to include: year-on-year target for monetization of existing assets to generate funds for creation of new assets; rolling five-year plan for each sector/ministry/department, updated every year. This has been addressed and a National Monetization Pipeline was launched by the Government of India in 2021 (Box 6.3).

Box 6.3 Government launches the National Monetization Pipeline

The Government of India launched the National Monetization Pipeline (NMP) in August 2021. The NMP is a four-year pipeline of the central government's brownfield infrastructure assets available for private investment and is co-terminus with the National Infrastructure Pipeline (NIP). Besides providing visibility to investors, NMP will also serve as a medium-term roadmap and target for the asset monetization initiative of the government. The salient features of the NMP are:

- Union Budget 2021/22 identified monetization of operating public infrastructure assets as a key means for sustainable infrastructure financing. Towards this end, the Budget provided for preparation of a 'National Monetization Pipeline (NMP)' of potential brownfield infrastructure assets. The launch of the NMP is in pursuance of this budget announcement.[a,b]
- NMP is expected to raise about Rs.6 trillion ($81 billion, either in the form of upfront accruals or by way of private-sector investment) over four years ending 2024/25 (of which Rs.0.88 trillion are budgeted for FY 2021/22, see Figure 6.4). However, the aggregate as well as year-on-year value under NMP is only indicative, with the actual realization for public assets depending on the timing, transaction structuring, investor interest, and so on.
- The indicative monetization value may be in the form of upfront consideration paid to the Government/PSU or by way of private-sector investment in brownfield assets (like airports). Under PPP-based mechanisms, additional revenue streams that may accrue to the government towards revenue share and/or concession fee over and above the private investment has not been included.
- Asset monetization needs to be viewed not just as a funding mechanism, but more importantly, as a means to boost efficiency in public-service delivery.
- The assets and transactions identified under the NMP are expected to be rolled out through a range of instruments. These include direct contractual instruments such as PPP concessions,

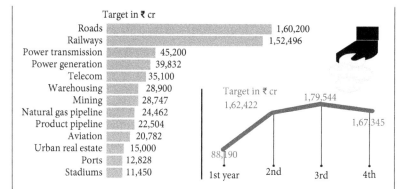

Figure 6.4 Sector-wise and annual roadmap of National Monetization Pipeline

Source: Times of India. 24 August 2021. Finance Minister Unveils Rs 6 lakh crore National Asset Monetisation Plan.

capital market instruments such as InvITs and REITs, and models like TOT in the road sector, and OMDA[b] in airports, among others. The choice of instrument will be determined by the sector, the nature of the asset, the timing of the transaction (including market considerations), target investor profile, the level of operational/investment control envisaged to be retained by the asset owner, and so on.

- Ownership of these assets would remain with the government (in the InvIT model) and there would be a mandatory hand-back of assets after a certain time period (in TOT model).
- NMP covers twenty asset classes spread over twelve ministries and thirteen sectors (see Figure 6.4). The top three sectors by value are roads (Rs.1.60 trillion; roads of 26,700 km), railways (Rs.1.52 trillion), and power (Rs.0.85 trillion; power transmission lines of 28,609 ckt km, hydro and solar power generation assets of 6 GW), together accounting for 66 per cent of the targeted NMP accruals.
- NMP lays the roadmap for monetizing de-risked core assets of the central government (and CPSEs) through BAM. Monetization through disinvestment and monetization of non-core assets (including land and buildings) have not been included in the NMP.
- The resources raised through monetization would be used for more and new infrastructure investment.

- Contractual partnerships (rather than outright privatization) for the implementation of the NMP will be with KPIs and performance standards to protect public and user interests.
- Incentive for state governments: A bonus of 33 per cent of the state's proceeds would be provided by the central government for monetizing an asset through the 'Scheme of Financial Assistance to States for Capital Expenditure'. This incentivizes state governments to recycle state-government-owned assets for fast-tracking greenfield infrastructure. This is akin to the Australian Asset Recycling Initiative, which also incentivizes states for undertaking BAM (see Box 6.1).
- As part of a multi-layered institutional mechanism for overall implementation and monitoring of the asset monetization programme, an empowered Core Group of Secretaries on Asset Monetization under the chairmanship of the cabinet secretary has been constituted.
- Seasoned infrastructure investors are likely to benefit from the NMP while domestic EPC players, power transmission companies, cement manufacturers, and so on, will benefit from more infrastructure spending by the government. The gains for these companies will depend on the NMP's successful implementation.
- The mainstreaming of BAM is crucial to the financing of the NIP (see Chapter 1) with estimated investments of Rs.111 trillion across over 6,800 projects to be implemented over FYs 2020–2025. Under the NIP, ministries are nudged to focus on generating more avenues of funding, including asset-monetization opportunities and funding mechanisms such as InvITs and securitization, and reduce reliance on gross budgetary support. The NIP has budgeted 2–3 per cent of the Rs.111 lakh crore target to come from asset monetization at the central-government level, while 1–2 per cent from asset monetization at the state level for a total of about Rs.3–5 trillion. The NMP, with a target of raising Rs.6 trillion by FY2024/25, supports the financing plan of the NIP.

An Assessment of the NMP

India has a large infrastructure deficit, existing along with a large pool of operational infrastructure assets, which can provide resources to bridge the infrastructure deficit through extensive use of BAM. Besides, the usage efficiency of infrastructure assets is also likely to improve through BAM. This is the spirit behind the NMP announcement. However, the implementation of NMP may falter. It has been stated that: 'When the government comes up with these mega pipelines—infrastructure pipeline earlier, monetisation pipeline now—the numbers are staggering, very big. There is absolutely no capacity, no clarity of structure. The sheer inability and the record of the government in carrying out such transactions'[c] makes for a large optimism bias. This poor record is evident from resource mobilization through TOT and InvIT models in the last five years (about Rs.1.7 lakh crore (or an average of Rs.34,000 crore per year), see Tables 6.1 and 6.2 and Figure 6.4 of this chapter, when the ask is about Rs.1.5 lakh crore per annum).

[a]Para 47 of the Finance Minister's Budget Speech 2021/22 states: 'Monetizing operating public infrastructure assets is a very important financing option for new infrastructure construction. A "National Monetization Pipeline" of potential brownfield infrastructure assets will be launched. An Asset Monetization dashboard will also be created for tracking the progress and to provide visibility to investors. Some important measures in the direction of monetization are:

   a. National Highways Authority of India and PGCIL each have sponsored one InvIT that will attract international and domestic institutional investors. Five operational roads with an estimated enterprise value of Rs.5,000 crores are being transferred to the NHAI InvIT. Similarly, transmission assets of a value of Rs.7,000 crores will be transferred to the PGCIL InvIT.

   b. Railways will monetize Dedicated Freight Corridor assets for operations and maintenance, after commissioning.

   c. The next lot of Airports will be monetized for operations and management concession.

   d. Other core infrastructure assets that will be rolled out under the Asset Monetization Programme are: (i) NHAI Operational Toll Roads (ii) Transmission Assets of PGCIL (iii) Oil and Gas Pipelines of GAIL, IOCL and HPCL (iv) AAI Airports in Tier II and III cities, (v) Other Railway Infrastructure Assets (vi) Warehousing Assets of CPSEs such as Central Warehousing Corporation and NAFED among others and (vii) Sports Stadiums.'

[b]Under the Operate-Maintain-Develop (OMD) structure, an asset, which is operational but due for augmentation, is handed over to the private party for augmentation and O&M over the concession period.

[c]Subhash Chandra Garg. 2021. MonetisationPlan Too Ambitious, No Likelihood of Getting Done: Subhash Garg, Former Finance Secretary. *The Economic Times* (https://economictimes.indiatimes.com/news/economy/finance/monetisation-plan-too-ambitious-no-likelihood-of-getting-done-subhash-garg-former-finance-secretary/articleshow/85648859.cms?from=mdr).

Value Capture Finance (VCF)

VCF relates to internalizing the externalities associated with large public infrastructure investments for making such investments more financially sustainable. It is well accepted that the creation of infrastructure like roads or metro rails increases property values in and around the area of development. VCF aims to capture this positive externality generated through public funding to improve the financials of the project by seeking to appropriate some of these unearned increases in property values through higher property taxes. The various value capture methods are shown in Table 6.5.

Two of the popular VCF methods are described below.[12] The first could be adapted for use in India for increasing the financial viability of metro-rail projects. The second is already being used in some states of India.

- Tax increment financing (TIF)—is one of the most popular value capture tools in many developed countries, especially the United States. In TIF, the incremental revenues from future increases in property tax or a surcharge on the existing property tax rate is ring-fenced for a defined period to finance some new investment in the designated area. TIF tools are especially useful to finance new investments in existing habitations.
- Premium on relaxation of rules or additional Floor Space Index/ Floor Area Ratio (FSI/FAR)—This is widely used in states such as Maharashtra, Karnataka, Gujarat, Tamil Nadu, and so on, to allow for additional development rights beyond the permissible limits in the state town planning laws and regulations. Sale of additional FAR is also an important value capture tool in Brazil and France. The French Land-use Policy restricts the landowner's building rights to a low baseline FAR and any additional FAR has to be purchased.

[12] Government of India, Ministry of Housing and Urban Affairs, (n.d.), *Value Capture Finance Policy Framework*. Available at http://mohua.gov.in/upload/whatsnew/59c0bb2d8f11bVCF_Po licy_Book_FINAL.pdf.

Table 6.5 VCF methods

	Value capture method	Frequency of incidence	Scale of intervention
1	Land value tax	Annual rates based on gain in land value	Area-based
2	Fees for changing land use (agricultural to non-agricultural)	One-time at the time of giving permission for change of land use	Area/Project-based
3	Betterment levy	One-time while applying for project development rights	Area/Project-based
4	Development charges (impact fees)	Annual but for a fixed period	Area-based
5	Transfer of development rights	Transaction-based	Area/Project-based
6	Premium on relaxation of rules or additional FSI/FAR	One-time	Area (roads, railways)/Project (Metro Rail)
7	Vacant land tax	Recurring	Area-based
8	Tax increment financing (TIF)	Recurring and for a fixed period	Area-based
9	Land acquisition and development	One-time up-front before project initiation	Area/Project-based
10	Land pooling system	One-time up-front before project initiation	Area/Project-based

Source: Government of India, Ministry of Housing and Urban Affairs (n.d.), *Value Capture Finance Policy Framework*. Available at http://mohua.gov.in/upload/whatsnew/59c0bb2d8f1 1bVCF_Policy_Book_FINAL.pdf.

In cases when projects are being established by central government ministries and their agencies, an agreement/MoU will have to be signed with the state government/urban local body, which will, inter alia, include details about the agency to levy and collect the value capture fund, sharing of funds, joint operation of accounts, and so on.

The importance of VCF for making metro-rail investments more sustainable is illustrated in Box 6.4.

Box 6.4 Sustainable metro-rail investments through VCF

The Government of India has declared its intention to have metro rail in fifty cities by 2025 (Halder, 2018).[a] Metro rails reduce pollution and congestion by substituting hundreds of thousands of personal vehicles for commuting in cities. But, for metro-rail operations to be financially sustainable, there is a requirement for huge footfalls, substantial non-fare revenue, and capturing value associated with appreciating property prices because of the metro-rail investment. The huge upfront capital costs of metro rail (estimated at about Rs.3 billion per km) combined with low passenger footfalls in some cities and the desire to keep fares even lower than the O&M costs of metro-rail means that they are perpetually loss-making entities. The losses of metro-rail companies will eat away the equity of the joint venture companies (JVCs) (most metro rails are 50:50 JVCs between central and state governments) and make them bankrupt in the near future. This will call for repeated bailouts of these JVCs like the power distribution companies in India.

With sustained operational losses and overall losses in metro rails across cities in India (Table 6.6), including Delhi,[b] where footfalls are about three million per day (3 million passengers and 6 million trips per day), it is clear from this cross-sectional analysis that the metro-rail sector in India faces substantial financial distress.

Table 6.6 Financial performance of major metro rails in India (Rs. billion)

Name of metro	Equity share capital	Operating profit[a] in 2018/19[b]	Profit after tax in 2018/19[b]
Delhi Metro	194.76	(–)7.22[c]	(–)4.64
Lucknow Metro	20.00	(–)1.48	(–)0.72
Kochi Metro	15.07	(–)1.21	(–)2.81
Jaipur Metro	16.94	(–)0.25[d]	(–)0.52[d]
Mumbai Metro	23.15	(–)0.14	0.04
Bangalore Metro	58.24	(–)5.02	(–)4.97
Chennai Metro	53.87	(–)3.84	(–)7.14

Table 6.6 Continued

Name of metro	Equity share capital	Operating profit[a] in 2018/19[b]	Profit after tax in 2018/19[b]
Nagpur Metro	15.39	(–)0.23	(–)0.18
Noida Metro	9.88	(–)0.71	(–)0.49

[a]Operating profit = operating revenue – operating expenses – employee benefits expense – depreciation and amortization.

[b]Operating profit and profit after tax columns show FY 2018/19 values or latest available year.

[c]While calculating the operating ratio, which indicates operational efficiency, DMRC excluded the depreciation and amortization expenses as part of the operating expenses, thereby reducing the operating expenses. Thus, DMRC was suffering an operational loss instead of earning operating profit. Even without considering the depreciation expenses, there has been a consistent increase in the operating cost ratio, from 48.99 per cent in 2011/12 to 80.55 per cent in 2019/20, which indicates inefficient operational performance of DMRC (Comptroller and Auditor General (CAG) of India. 2021. *Report of the Comptroller and Auditor General of India on Implementation of Phase-III Delhi Mass Rapid Transit System by DMRC.*)

[d]For Jaipur Metro operating profit and profit after tax refer to FY2017/18.

Source: Compiled by the authors from the annual reports of respective metro rails.

As metro rails spread across more cities in India, the financial distress of the JVCs running these metros will become more acute (Table 6.7).The estimated financial internal rate of return (FIRR) is projected as positive and reasonable for these projects in their detailed project reports. However, the record of negative profit after tax (PAT) in operational metros of India (Table 6.6) implies that there is '*optimism bias*' in the estimates, and actually, the FIRR would turn out to be much lower.[c]

Table 6.7 Planned metro rails in Indian cities

Name of metro	Total cost (Rs.billion)	Capital cost per km (Rs. billion)	Estimated financial internal rate of return (%)
Patna Metro	92.02	4.26	9.9
Kochi Metro Phase II	19.57	1.75	5.7
Ahmedabad Metro Phase II	53.84	1.91	5.9
Kanpur Metro	110.76	3.42	8.9
Indore Metro	75.01	2.38	8.2
Bhopal Metro	69.41	2.49	8.2
Agra Metro	83.80	2.85	10.1

Source: Compiled by the authors from detailed project reports of respective metro rails.

Financial analysis of some major metro rails

Delhi Metro Rail Corporation (DMRC) is the oldest, longest, and most developed metro rail in the country (392 km with 286 metro stations). Another major metro rail (relatively newer) is the Bangalore Metro Rail Corporation (BMRC). The financial performance trends of both these metro rails are examined in this time-series analysis to understand the financial sustainability of metro rails in India. Figure 6.5 shows the trends of PAT in these two metro rails.

The PAT trends in DMRC and BMRC confirm our findings that metro rails are loss-making ventures in India. The negative slope of the trendline in both metros points towards increasing financial unsustainability in the future.

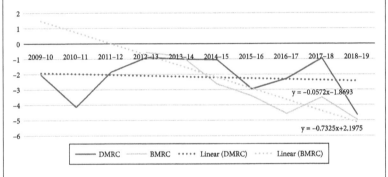

Figure 6.5 Profit-after-tax trends in DMRC and BMRC (Rs. billion)
Source: Annual Reports of DMRC and BMRC.

Impact of the Covid-19 pandemic on metro rail

FY2020/21 was disastrous for the financials of metro-rail JVCs as metros were locked down for more than six months because of the Covid-19 pandemic. Even as the metro services resumed in October 2020, the ridership has been adversely affected by social distancing requirements. Estimates suggest that instead of 1,800–2,000 passengers, a typical metro train in Delhi is carrying 350 to 400 passengers to ensure social distancing, implying a carrying capacity of metros of about a fifth of the business-as-usual levels. McKinsey[d] (2020) reports that Transport for London, the government body responsible for the public transportation system in Greater London, estimates that with 2 metres of physical distancing, the London Underground, or Tube, will be able to carry 13 per cent to 15 per cent of the passengers that it usually does, even at full service. Ways to augment ridership given the constraint of social distancing would be to stagger office and school hours so that the ridership is more even throughout the day, compulsory use of thermal scanners at stations with normal temperature as a requirement to avail of the services of the metro rail, and compulsory use of face masks, which can possibly increase the ridership to the range of about 40 per cent of the peak capacity. This supply destruction because of the pandemic is adversely affecting the already stretched financials of the metro rails. It has been estimated that the loss of daily revenue due to Covid-19 compared to business-as-usual is Rs.100 million per day for DMRC, Rs.16 million per day for Hyderabad Metro Rail, and Rs.9 million per day for Mumbai Metro One.[e]

Financial distress of the power sector and need for repeated bailouts

It is likely that the financial distress faced by the power distribution companies in India will be replicated in the metro-rail sector. The power sector faces inter-related problems of stressed assets, low capacity utilization (low plant load factor), bankrupt power distribution segment, and so on. The total financial losses of DISCOMs in the five years from 2013/14 to 2017/18 was Rs.2,456.40 billion, with Rs.333.65 billion losses in 2017/18.[f] These losses had increased to Rs.496.23 billion in 2018/19.[g] The government has been regularly bailing out the sector, the last one being Ujjwal Discom Assurance Yojana (UDAY).

UDAY was launched in 2015 for operational and financial turnaround of distribution utilities through targeted interventions to lower the interest costs, reduce the cost of power, increase revenues, and improve operational efficiencies. A total of twenty-seven states and five Union Territories joined the scheme. The total liability of Rs.2,690 billion was to be restructured under UDAY through issuance of bonds. Till 2019, bonds worth Rs.2,320 billion have been issued, consisting of state bonds of Rs.2,090 billion and DISCOM bonds of Rs.230 billion.[h]

The power sector woes are likely to increase in the future. In the recently concluded solar auctions, solar tariffs have reached a low of Rs.2 per unit of power (compared to Rs.6 per unit average cost of electricity supply for distribution utilities in India). The low cost of solar power means that it has reached grid-parity and more, which is the primary driver for its rapid growth. India currently has an installed capacity of 35 GW of solar capacity, which is about a tenth of the country's total installed power generation capacity. And there are ambitious plans to increase renewable (and solar) capacity as per India's nationally determined contributions as part of the Paris Accord. India has pledged a reduction in the emission intensity of its GDP by 33–35 per cent by 2030 from 2005 levels, and 40 per cent cumulative electric power installed capacity from non-fossil fuel-based energy resources by 2030. This would obviously mean more renewables in the energy mix, pursuant to which the government has targeted a renewable capacity of 175 GW by 2022 (and 450 GW by 2030), of which 100 GW would be solar power.

The falling solar prices benefits the cause of open access in the power distribution sector (with consumers having a choice of electricity supplier just as in the telecom sector). Using open access, DMRC, for example, is sourcing 32 per cent of its power requirements from the Rewa solar project in Madhya Pradesh. Open access in the power distribution sector is one of the neglected provisions of the Electricity Act, 2003, and operationalizing it would make the power sector competitive, which, in turn, would improve the cost competitiveness of the Indian economy.

However, the coming of age of solar power and open access in India would increase the power distribution sector's challenges, dominated by the public-sector DISCOMs. These DISCOMs have existing long-term power purchase agreements with mainly coal-based thermal power generating projects. Any decrease in thermal power demand due to cheaper solar power, and operationalization of open access would mean more financial stress for the DISCOMs as they would be required to pay the fixed costs of power, irrespective of actual power purchase. This may necessitate another DISCOM bailout soon, for which the government is ill equipped in the current Covid-19 pandemic times, with stressed fiscal deficit and growth rate.[i]

The AtmaNirbhar Bharat package includes about Rs.90,000 crore loan from the Power Finance Corporation (PFC) and Rural Electrification Corporation (REC) to DISCOMs for payment to the power generation companies. But, without tackling the issue of low-cost recovery (there is a revenue gap of 72 paise per unit of electricity sold in the country (PFC, 2020)), there is little likelihood of the power sector becoming financially sustainable. Therefore, there would be need for repeated bailouts in times to come. The path that the metro-rail sector is following is alarmingly similar to the power sector.

The case of the Hong Kong metro

However, there is nothing in theory that precludes financially sustainable operations of metro rails. We find that the Hong Kong metro is generating huge profits year after year. Hong Kong's Mass Transit Rail (MTR) system operates across 263 km, carrying 5.2 million passengers a day. MTR Corporation (MTRC), which built and operates the system, reported a whopping HK$12.09 billion (US$1.56 billion) net profit in 2019. In fact, in the last ten years (2010–2019), the net profits of the Hong Kong metro has been over US$18 billion, or an average of US$1.8 billion per year (Mass Transit Rail Corporation, n.d.).[j]

MTRC follows the rail plus property (R+P) model. This model is based on the concept of VCF, which internalizes the externalities generated from large public investments. It is well accepted that the creation of infrastructure like roads or metro-rail networks increases property values in and around the area of development. VCF aims to capture this positive externality generated through public funding to improve the financials of the project.

In Hong Kong, the government owns the land whose value is very high due to limited space. To develop the MTR system, the government entered into an agreement with MTRC, which has 70 per cent government shareholding. The government then transferred the land and development rights to MTRC at a pre-rail price. MTRC, in turn, transferred the developmental rights to private developers at an after-rail price.

After metro-rail development, the land value adjacent to the metro rail skyrocketed, and the difference between pre-rail and after-rail prices was substantial. The profit margin from this VCF mechanism was sufficient to meet the further development requirements of MTR. Also, the developer returned the land with premium value as a lease charge to the government, as well as shared a part of the profit with MTRC, making MTRC highly profitable. Changes were made in the local land-use law to drive property development around stations. In some districts, a floor-area ratio (FAR) of 10 was allowed to encourage dense development with a mix of residential and office facilities.

MTRC is one of the largest property managers in Hong Kong. As of 31 December 2019, MTR managed more than 1,04,000 residential units and more than 7,72,000 square metres of office and commercial space in Hong Kong.[k]

Profits from property development and related businesses of MTRC, including Hong Kong station commercial business and Hong Kong property rental and management business, accounted for more than 50 per cent of MTRC's total profit between 2000 and 2015. The R+P programme enabled MTRC to capture real-estate income to finance part of the capital and running costs of new railway lines and increase transit patronage by facilitating high-quality, dense and walkable catchment areas around stations.[l]

A more sustainable way for promoting urban transport in India

Cities are engines of growth for countries because of agglomeration economies. It has been estimated that while about a third of the Indian population lives in urban areas, it contributes two-thirds to GDP.[m] However, due to unplanned urbanization, there are pollution and congestion problems in Indian cities (six of the world's ten most polluted cities are in India, as per the World Economic Forum, 2020).[n] Urban transport is a major contributor to this pollution and congestion. Therefore, there is a need for more efficient urban transportation. However, the proliferation of metro rails across cities in India with little non-fare and property revenue, as is being done now, is financially unsustainable. The ameliorative measures that can be taken to improve the outcomes are suggested below.

First, it must be realized that metro rails are the most expensive form of public transport. Cheaper options like bus rapid transit system, light metro rail, and so on, may be used to achieve the objective of efficient urban transportation while managing the adverse financial fallout of a full-fledged metro-rail system.[o]

Second, if it is decided that metro rail is the preferred option, then user charges should cover at least the O&M costs of the metros. Low user charges and consequent inadequate cost recovery is widespread across infrastructure sectors like metro rail, power, water, transport, and social sectors like health and education (see Chapter 3 for a fuller discussion on user charges in infrastructure). In public utility services, full cost recovery, including both capital and O&M charges, may not always be desirable. However, reasonable user charges covering at least the O&M costs of assets would improve overall efficiency, help demand management, prevent waste, and would promote ownership and accountability (and thus, governance of infrastructure services). This is a measure that has been repeatedly emphasized by Finance Commissions, the Expenditure Management Commission, and so on.

Third, it is important that the operator generates non-fare revenue, including income generated through commercial, retail, advertising, consultancy, and other sector activity.[p] Depending solely on user charges for the financial sustainability of metro projects is problematic because of the high capital costs of such projects.

Fourth, as apparent from the financial success of Hong Kong's MTRC, there is a need for liberal use of VCF. The Hong Kong model has catalysed *transit-oriented development* (TOD, see Box 6.5) given the scarcity of land and the inherent need for high-density development above and near stations and depots, where accessibility is highest. Achieving this density has been part of a deliberate long-term strategy for maximizing scarce land use and driving viability for the metro. The rail and property[q] funding and delivery model for public transport projects is powerful—both for achieving financial sustainability and achieving development aims associated with transport. A key to making this work involves siting stations at the right location, providing foundations for future development. Developments are also carefully managed to ensure the mix of services that customers want. The result is developments that feed the metro in exchange for a metro that maximizes the value of developments (World Bank and RTSC 2017).[r] While Hong Kong is land-constrained and can generate substantial resources from VCF, the land constraint is quite pronounced in Indian cities too, making it possible to make efficient use of VCF tools (see Table 6.5).

Box 6.5   Features of transit-oriented development

- Aims to induce people to walk, cycle, and use public transport over personal modes.
- Influence zone to consist of a variety of high-density, mixed-use, mixed-income buildings within a short distance of mass transit systems.
- TOD to be developed as multimodal hubs ensuring seamless integration among various transport modes.

VCF, as known widely in the world, is based on the principle that private land and buildings benefit from public investments in infrastructure and policy decisions of governments (e.g. change of land use or floor space index). These benefits are externalities generated from public investment and hence should not be included in user charges. Therefore, there is a need to deploy appropriate VCF tools to capture a part of the unearned increment in land and buildings value. These can be used to fund projects being set up for the public by the central/state governments and urban local bodies. This generates a virtuous cycle in which value is created, realized, and captured, and used again for project investment. The Ministry of Housing and Urban Affairs has already developed a VCF policy that needs to be operationalized for metro-rail development to be financially sustainable.[5]

Finally, if we need to expand metro rail, monetizing existing networks can provide capital expenditure (capex) funding for future expansions—an idea whose time has come for Delhi metro. Delhi Metro Rail Corporation is the fourth largest metro system in the world with a network length of 392 km and daily usage by about 3 million passengers. Currently, Delhi Metro Phase IV, which is 62 km long, is being built at a total completion cost of Rs.249.48 billion, with an external loan component of Rs.129.31 billion. It would make more financial sense for DMRC to fund Phase IV's construction by monetizing (through the TOT model or the InvIT model) one of the three completed phases of the Delhi metro network. This will be another application of the BAM initiative for more greenfield investments, which is being pursued very vigorously in India's road and power transmission sectors (as we have seen).

[a]An earlier version of this section appeared as Kumar V. Pratap. 2021. Are We Creating Outcomes Similar to Power Sector by Proliferating Metro Rail across Cities in India? *Vikalpa*,46(1): 7–12 (https://journals.sagepub.com/doi/full/10.1177/02560909211015455).

[b]Delhi Metro is India's largest metro system, which is 392 km long with 286 metro stations, 3 million daily users and 6 million daily passenger trips.

[c]There was no minimum FIRR criteria for approval of a metro corridor before 2013. This resulted in sanctioning of two corridors (Badarpur-Faridabad and the Shiv Vihar extension) with negative FIRR. After Ministry of Housing and Urban Affairs instructions (August 2013), for minimum 8 per cent FIRR, detailed project reports for (i) Dilshad Garden to Ghaziabad, New Bus Adda, (ii) Noida City Centre to Noida Sector-62, (iii) Kalindi Kunj to Botanical Garden, (iv) YMCA Chowk to Ballabhgarh corridors were revised to make them viable and higher FIRRs of 12.23 per cent, 8.63 per cent, 9.85 per cent, and 11.01 per cent were computed as against the earlier 4.02 per cent, 2.03 per cent, 1.11 per cent, and 4.50 per cent, respectively. Increased Fare Box Revenue ranging from 111 per cent to 175 per cent has been considered to attain the FIRR of 8 per cent or more for sanctioning the projects. The comptroller and auditor general of India has recommended that DMRC should ensure at the project planning stage itself that detailed project reports are prepared with realistic assumptions for computation of FIRR to ensure the economic viability of the corridor(CAG. 2021. *Report of the Comptroller and Auditor General of India on Implementation of Phase-III Delhi Mass Rapid Transit System by DMRC*).

[d]McKinsey & Company (5 June 2020). *Restoring Public Transit amid COVID-19: What European Cities Can Learn from One Another* (https://www.mckinsey.com/industries/travel-transport-and-logistics/our-insights/restoring-public-transit-amid-covid-19-what-europ ean-cities-can-learn-from-one-another?cid=other-eml-alt-mip-mck&hlkid=bcb6a521d0c54 555a7405ffef83c0651&hctky=9579620&hdpid=d3f2a42e-78f6-452b-a794-bb46dbc15100).

[e]S. Roy.16 May 2020. Covid-19 Pulls the Chain: Delhi Metro Loses Rs 10 crore/day *Times of India* (https://timesofindia.indiatimes.com/city/delhi/covid-pulls-the-chain-metro-loses-rs-10cr/day/articleshow/75906591.cms).

[f]Government of India (2020), Rajya Sabha Unstarred Question No. 1421 answered on 3 March 2020 on Transmission and Distribution Losses of DISCOMs. Ministry of Power. Available at https://pqars.nic.in/annex/251/AU1421.pdf.

[g]Power Finance Corporation (2020). *Report on Performance of State Power Utilities, 2018–19* (https://www.pfcindia.com/DocumentRepository/ckfinder/files/Operations/ Performance_Reports_of_State_Power_Utilities/Report%20on%20Performance%20 of%20State%20Power%20Utilities%202018-19.pdf).

[h]Government of India. 2019. *Annual Report 2018–19*, p. 46. Ministry of Power. Available at https://powermin.nic.in/sites/default/files/uploads/MOP_Annual_Report_Eng_2018-19.pdf.

[i]Kumar V. Pratap.27 October 2020. Power Play: How Renewables' March Could End State Discom Era. *Financial Express* (https://www.financialexpress.com/opinion/power-play-how-renewables-march-could-end-state-discom-era/2114342/).

[j]Mass Transit Rail Corporation (n.d.) Financial Highlights of MTR (http://www.mtr. com.hk/archive/corporate/en/investor/10yr_stat_en.pdf).

[k]Mass Transit Rail Corporation (2019). Annual Report 2019, p. 20 (http://www.mtr.com. hk/archive/corporate/en/investor/annual2019/E09.pdf).

[l]Public-Private Infrastructure Advisory Facility (PPIAF), 2015. Case Study: Hong Kong MTR Corporation (https://ppiaf.org/sites/ppiaf.org/files/documents/toolkits/railways_tool kit/PDFs/RR%20Toolkit%20EN%20New%202017%2012%2027%20CASE5%20HK%20 MTR.pdf).

[m]S. Sankhe, I. Vittal, R. Dobbs, A. Mohan, A. Gulati, J. Ablett, ...and G. Setyy. 2010. *India's Urban Awakening: Building Inclusive Cities, Sustaining Economic Growth*. McKinsey Global Institute

[n]World Economic Forum. 2020. *Six of the World's Ten Most Polluted Cities Are in India* (https://www.weforum.org/agenda/2020/03/6-of-the-world-s-10-most-polluted-cities-are-in-india/#:~:text=6%20of%20the%20world's%2010,include%20Dehli%2C%20Hotan%20

and%20Raiwind.) More recent evidence suggests that things are going from bad to worse. Delhi has emerged as the most polluted capital and the fourth most polluted city in the world, according to 2021 World Air Quality Report by Swiss organization, IQAir. The report also said: thirty-five of the world's fifty most polluted cities are in India; sixty-three Indian cities are in the world's 100 most polluted cities; Bhiwadi (Rajasthan) is the most polluted city in the world, followed by Ghaziabad (UP), both falling in the NCR; vehicular emission is one of the major sources of urban pollution.

[o]In this context, the comptroller and auditor general has recommended that a guideline/criteria for selection of mode of transport for different scenarios, like the Light Metro, Bus Rapid Transit system, based on viability and an alternative analysis may be formulated (Comptroller and Auditor General of India. 2021. *Report of the Comptroller and Auditor General of India on Implementation of Phase-III Delhi Mass Rapid Transit System by DMRC*).

[p]As per the Detailed Project Report, Dwarka-Najafgarh metro corridor was not financially viable with assessed negative cash flow of ₹5,178 crore during the horizon period of 33 years. A requirement of 4.03 hectare of land at Najafgarh station for Property Development was, therefore, included in the Detailed Project Report to make the corridor viable. The metro corridor was completed in October 2019, but DMRC had not ensured availability of land for Property Development till December 2020 although Property Development from the land was the only way to make this corridor viable.

Since the metro corridor of Mundka-Bahadurgarh was not financially viable, 4 hectare land with 'residential' land use for Property Development at Ghevra (Delhi) and 1.56 hectare in Haryana was envisaged in Detailed Project Report to make it viable. Metro corridor has been completed in June 2018, but as on December 2020, 4 hectare land in Delhi portion has not been acquired by DMRC for Property Development. Further, out of 1.56 hectare land for Property Development in Haryana portion, only 0.8 hectare space is available, which also remained unutilised as of March 2020 (Comptroller and Auditor General of India. 2021. *Report of the Comptroller and Auditor General of India on Implementation of Phase-III Delhi Mass Rapid Transit System by DMRC*).

[q]For DMRC, the CAG of India has pointed out that as against consolidated targeted earning of ₹2,505 crore (from Phase-II and Phase-III) from property development as per sanction letters issued by Government of India, DMRC could generate only ₹657.13 crore (26.23 per cent) from property development up to 31 March 2020. For Phase-III and extensions, revenue from property business during 2016/17 to 2019/20 was estimated at ₹1,917.25 crore. DMRC generated only ₹76.06 crore during 2016/17 to 2019/20 from property business (CAG. 2021. *Report of the Comptroller and Auditor General of India on Implementation of Phase-III Delhi Mass Rapid Transit System by DMRC*).

[r]World Bank and RTSC (Railway and Transport Strategy Centre) at Imperial College London. (2017). *The Operator's Story: Emerging Findings*. Presented at the International Transport Forum, Organisation for Economic Co-operation and Development.

[s]Government of India, Ministry of Housing and Urban Affairs, (n.d.), *Value Capture Finance Policy Framework*. Available at http://mohua.gov.in/upload/whatsnew/59c0bb2d8f11bVCF_Policy_Book_FINAL.pdf; Ministry of Finance, Government of India. 2020. *Report of the Sub-group on Capital Markets for Financing of National Infrastructure Pipeline*; OECD. 2020. *Draft Progress Note on Asset Recycling*.

7

Moving from Bank Finance to Bond Finance—Credit Enhancement and Infrastructure Debt Funds

The main source of debt financing of infrastructure projects is bank credit, which suffers from asset–liability mismatch (ALM) as bank liabilities (deposits) are short term, while infrastructure assets are long term (the typical life of a conventional power or road project is thirty years or more). This chapter discusses how, despite banks not being the most efficient institution for debt financing of infrastructure projects, they continue to be major source of finance for such projects. This discussion leads to a discussion on the twin balance-sheet problem of infrastructure companies and banks, whereby the high leverage of infrastructure corporates are linked to the non-performing assets (NPA) of banks. Therefore, there is utility in moving from bank financing of infrastructure to bond financing, especially after cash flows have stabilized in the operational phase of projects. Since project financing (non-recourse financing) is generally used to finance private infrastructure projects, the general credit rating for such projects is only about BBB, while investment thresholds of institutional investors are AA or above. So, there is a requirement for credit enhancement (CE) of the bonds floated by these companies to make them amenable to institutional investment. In this context, the vehicle of infrastructure debt funds is also discussed.

Historically, India's infrastructure finance has largely been bank-led, with focussed non-banking financial companies (NBFCs) like the Power Finance Corporation (PFC), the Rural Electrification Corporation (REC), the India Renewable Energy Development Agency (IREDA), and the Indian Railway Finance Corporation, and so on, supplementing

Infrastructure Financing in India. Kumar V Pratap and Manshi Gupta, Oxford University Press.
© Kumar V Pratap and Manshi Gupta 2024. DOI: 10.1093/oso/9780198884934.003.0008

finance in targeted sectors and programmes. The National Infrastructure Pipeline (NIP) is a quantum leap over past periods in terms of vision, scale, and breadth of infrastructure creation and it needs broad-based financing modes to achieve its investment targets.

A variety of financing modes and instruments need to be developed to enable efficient financing of the NIP. Infrastructure assets over their life cycle have varying risk-return profiles (see Figure 7.1), and thus require a fit-for-purpose financing, with asset financing changing hands among various classes of financiers. For instance, during the early stage of planning and greenfield construction, equity investments and bank loans constitute the major part of financing. After project implementation and stabilization of cash flows (operational phase, brownfield infrastructure), long-term capital becomes important, which may be tapped via bond issuances to enable participation from a diverse range of retail and institutional investors. This will also reduce the cost of capital and improve the financial viability of projects.

Following the example set by the largest and deepest financial market in the world (the United States), where nearly 75 per cent of debt financing for businesses comes from capital markets, a wide spectrum of products and investors under a robust regulatory framework could eventually allow for a infrastructure financing number larger than the Rs.7 lakh crore envisaged to be raised from capital markets in the form of bonds by the NIP (see Chapter 1, Table 1.2).

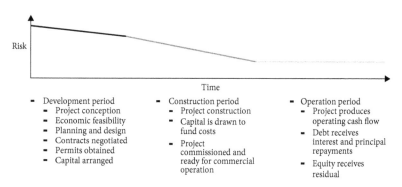

Figure 7.1 Changing risk profile of infrastructure projects over their life cycle

Source: Presentation made by Sherena Hussain, Schulich School of Business, York University, Canada.

Contribution of Capital Markets to Infrastructure in Global Markets

Bonds are increasingly becoming popular as a source of infrastructure finance (see Figure 7.2). Although bonds represented only about 20 per cent of private infrastructure financing in primary transactions in developing countries as of 2020, this has nearly doubled since 2015.[1]

Infrastructure bonds are closely associated with the development of bond markets, and therefore are primarily issued in developed economies with mature financial markets. Against this backdrop, development of local-currency bond markets also serves as an alternative avenue for infrastructure financing in emerging economies. Development of local-currency bond markets is also necessary for decreasing the need for foreign debt for financing infrastructure, a move in the right direction given that most infrastructure revenues are

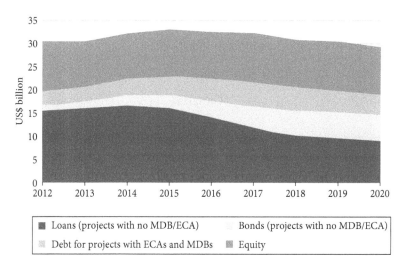

Figure 7.2 Private financing of primary infrastructure transactions in developing countries (three-year moving average)

Source: Based on Global Infrastructure Hub analysis of IJ Global data.

---

[1] Marie Lam-Frendo and Morgan Landy. 23 September 2021. If You Issue It, They Will Come: Lessons from Recent Infrastructure Bonds (https://blogs.worldbank.org/ppps/if-you-issue-it-they-will-come-lessons-recent-infrastructure-bonds?CID=WBW_AL_BlogNotification_EN_EXT).

Figure 7.3 Corporate debt market penetration, June 2018 (as % of GDP)
Source: Reserve Bank of India. 10 January 2019. India's Corporate Bond Market: Issues in Market Microstructure. *RBI Bulletin*, 73(1): 21. Available at https://rbidocs.rbi.org.in/rdocs/Bulletin/PDFs/BULLETINJANUARY2019_FBB1F301E2A264F8E8999CED9F9117658.PDF.

in local currency. Figure 7.3 shows corporate debt market penetration, by countries.

Canada and the United States have used capital markets efficiently for infrastructure creation as may be seen later in the chapter. The common factor across both these markets has been a developed local bond market, coupled with strong domestic investor appetite.

Canada

Canada is a leader in tapping capital markets to finance public infrastructure. It has a robust system of national/sub-national cooperation for implementing PPPs, project procurement processes prioritize the stability of long-term financing over shorter-term cost savings, a large defined benefit pension system that needs long-term inflation-linked investment assets to match their liabilities, generating steady demand for project bonds, and little competition from banks for longer-term financing due to their conservative lending approach and preference for shorter maturities.

Canadian pension funds have among the world's highest asset allocation to infrastructure, at approximately 5 per cent of assets, most of that in equity. Canadian pension funds like Canada Pension Plan Investment Board (CPPIB), Caisse de dépôt et placement du Québec (CDPQ), and the Public Sector Pension Investment Board (PSP Investments) are also very active in the Indian infrastructure market.

United States

Infrastructure financing is carried out by means of municipal bonds, which are used in financing more than 75 per cent of US public-sector infrastructure. In addition to this, there is an active non-municipal infrastructure debt market that connects institutional investor capital to infrastructure financing needs. This market is large, established, and attractive enough that many non-US infrastructure issuers choose to raise capital in the US bond market, often in conjunction with international bond offerings—although it is not generally used to finance social infrastructure.

Municipal 'revenue bonds' are project bonds whose payments are directly linked to an infrastructure project, and are a market-based instrument to finance infrastructure. Revenue bonds, though technically linked to an issuer, would not contribute to public deficits as the project returns would service these bonds. The special tax treatment of municipal debt in the United States, the high credit-worthiness of municipal borrowers (e.g. Fitch ratings in March 2021 has rated New York City Municipal Water Finance Authority's water and sewer revenue bonds AA+), and disclosures have contributed to the growth of this market while keeping borrowing costs low for municipalities and projects. The US municipal market is by far the most developed of its kind in the world with the total municipal debt outstanding currently being about US$4 trillion or Rs.300 trillion (lakh crore). About 98 per cent of this debt was long term or with a maturity of thirteen months or longer, while the remaining 2 per cent was short term. Of the total municipal debt, roughly 40 per cent was issued by states and 60 per cent by local governments.[2] The municipal bond market has facilitated easy access to decentralized capital planning, financing, and implementation in a federal system of government.

However, the Indian municipal bond market is quite underdeveloped, with the urban local bodies (ULBs) overly dependent on grants from higher tiers of the government to subject themselves to the discipline

---

[2] Tax Policy Centre, Urban Institute and Brookings Institution. 2020. *What Are Municipal Bonds and How Are They Used* (https://www.taxpolicycenter.org/briefing-book/what-are-municipal-bonds-and-how-are-they-used).

of capital markets, combined with the low credit worthiness of the ULBs. The share of municipal bonds in India in the total debt market is insignificant—only 1 per cent of urban body financial demands are met through municipal bonds. The Ahmedabad Municipal Corporation was the first to make a bond offering in 1998. Since 1998, local bodies in other cities like Nashik, Nagpur, Ludhiana, and Madurai have issued municipal bonds, without state guarantees. Tamil Nadu created the Water and Sanitation Pool Fund which was the first entity in the country to mobilize resources on the pooled finance framework. Following this, the Pooled Finance Development Fund was approved by central government in 2006. In the last three years, eight AMRUT cities have raised Rs.3,390 crore by issuance of municipal bonds on the back of an interest subvention scheme introduced by the Ministry of Housing and Urban Affairs. However, the low credit-worthiness of ULBs as a result of the weak state of their finances continues to impede the growth of this market in India.

The key drivers for the success of the municipal bond market are:

- Municipal bonds generally provide a tax benefit which provides investors with higher returns on an after-tax basis. However, tax-free bonds are not allowed in India currently.
- Municipal borrowers have a high creditworthiness and have maintained high credit ratings, even without any government guarantees (albeit some defaults have been seen on account of Covid-19).
- Financial information and other disclosures about these borrowers are also easily available, which ensures transparency with investors.

Capital Market Contribution in Indian Infrastructure Markets

As discussed earlier, the Indian municipal debt market is underdeveloped. Indian corporate debt markets are constrained by detailed primary issuance guidelines, high costs (costs for a public issue can average about 4 per cent of the amount raised), lengthy processes in the enforcement of default laws, and an absence of long-term investors. Long-term providers of capital, such as insurance and pension funds, are constrained partly by regulations (details in Chapter 8). Retail investors prefer to invest in postal savings and provident funds, where returns are artificially pegged at higher rates.[3]

Nevertheless, Indian domestic capital market issuance volumes have been on an upward trend in the last few years—with a compound annual growth rate of about 14 per cent between financial year (FY) 2009 and FY 2019 with volumes reaching a peak of over Rs.7 trillion in FY 2017. In 2020/21, corporate bond issuance increased to Rs.7.8 trillion (only to come down to Rs.5.9 trillion in FY 2021/22 as equities performed well and bank interest rates were low).

An analysis of issuances by non-financial corporations shows that debt market access is limited to large established corporations. Sector-wise primary issuance data shows that issuance volumes have been dominated by domestic financial institutions and some high-quality private-sector corporate issuers. The majority of bonds issued are in the two- to five-year tenor category (~56 per cent) and 85–90 per cent of issuance volumes have been in AA category and above, with AAA rated papers accounting for more than half of the total amount outstanding in the primary segment.

Given the contours of the debt capital markets in India, infrastructure financing via capital markets in the past few years has been relatively shallow and restricted to a few sectors and has largely financed low-tenor and brownfield investments that provide an avenue for capital re-allocation. Most of the infrastructure debt paper issuances that have been successfully placed in the market have been from issuers/projects with sound off-taker backing and a strong visibility of cash flows over the life of the project, such as the National Highways Authority of India (NHAI) annuity projects, transmission projects backed by the Power Grid Corporation of India Ltd pooled collection system, issuances supported by the Solar Energy Corporation of India Ltd, and so on. At this stage of the market, greenfield infrastructure finance risk may not be palatable to domestic institutional and retail investors.

---

[3] Anupam Rastogi and Vivek Rao. 2011. *Product Innovations for Financing Infrastructure: A Study of India's Debt Markets.* Asian Development Bank South Asia Working Paper Series No. 6.

From an international bond markets perspective, ratings pose a challenge for corporate issuers, as a result of which only limited number of Indian issuers have been able to tap the international bond markets within the applicable regulatory all-in-cost cap. Since 2015, the international debt capital markets have seen volumes of about Rs.5.6 lakh crore (US$75 billion) from India across 253 tranches, of which volumes in the infrastructure segment constitute about 20 per cent. The transactions have been dominated by high-quality issuers, with either an asset base of strategic importance or those with diversified and credit-worthy off-taker profiles. There is also a strong interest in restricted group bonds from offshore investors specifically through US$ bonds, wherein the off-take risk is diversified.[4]

Recent trends suggest that corporate fund-raising, by at least the better-rated companies, may have permanently moved to the bond market, shaking off their dependence on bank loans. Lower-rated companies, however, are still heavily dependent on banks for their funding needs. The corporate bond market is still dominated by financial companies, but non-financial companies have marked their presence in recent years. In FY 2019/20, non-finance companies raised Rs.6.11 trillion from the Indian market, of which issuance from nodal agencies for infrastructure stood at about Rs.80,000 crore (US$10.9 billion) whereas other infrastructure issuance volumes stood at about Rs.18,000 crore (US$2.45 billion). An additional amount of about Rs.37,500 crore (US$5 billion) was raised for the infrastructure sector from offshore bond issuances by Indian issuers in FY 2019/20. The reasons for the increasing popularity of bonds are a lower effective rate of interest, and the characteristic of bonds of being easily re-financeable.

The government has also unveiled a slew of measures to unleash the bond route to raising finances, for example, market regulator, Securities and Exchange Board of India (SEBI) in June 2021 allowed real estate investment trusts, infrastructure investment trusts (InvITs) and other specifically created entities in the real-estate and infrastructure space with less than a three-year track record to tap the bond market. However, such issues should be through the SEBI's bond-trading platform and only

---

[4] Ministry of Finance, Government of India. 2020. *Report of the Sub-group on Capital Markets for Financing of National Infrastructure Pipeline.*

institutional investors will be allowed to participate in it. In addition, unlisted entities cannot tap this fund-raising route.

To further popularize the bond route to financing infrastructure, the following new initiatives can be considered:

- Tax-paid bonds: Government owned banks, NBFC-IFCs and their subsidiaries may be allowed to issue tax-paid bonds to tap funding from retail investors. The proposed tax-paid bond features would be a combination of both the taxable bond and tax-free bond. Proposed tax-paid bonds will have no tax implications for the investors as the tax impact will be shared between the issuer and the government. Further, to make the instrument attractive to channelize resources, a special tax rate of 10 per cent may be notified. The tenor of the bonds would be long term only, that is, ten–twenty years. The main advantage of the proposed tax-paid bond is that the government will not lose the entire tax revenue on interest as with a tax-free bond as tax paid by the issuer will partially offset the tax loss to the government and the issuer will be able to raise funds at a cheaper rate.

- Zero coupon bonds (ZCBs) are bonds in respect of which no payment and benefit is received or receivable before maturity. ZCBs carry lower tax as they do not have annual coupons. ZCBs would help in better management of the asset portfolio of banks and FIs and are ideal for greenfield asset financing. ZCBs are also preferred for financing operational projects, making such projects flexible and resilient in overcoming volatility in operational cash flows for example, operational BOT road projects.

Investors in ZCBs pay capital gains tax on a redemption premium (instead of income tax on a coupon as in the case of plain vanilla bonds), which gives them a higher return. This will enable the tapping of funds from retail investors, high-net-worth individuals, charitable and religious trusts, family offices, debt mutual funds, and corporate treasuries for infrastructure.

However, Central Board of Direct Taxes (CBDT) approval under IT Rule 8B is required for issuing ZCBs. The application is to be submitted at least three months prior to the launch of the issue which may be a long period considering the immediate liquidity requirement and volatile bond markets. Hence, it is recommended that an automatic approval route in line with external commercial borrowing may be given to government-owned banks and NBFC-IFCs for which no prior approval may be required from any authority up to a certain limit of fund-raising.

CE for Facilitating Bond Financing of Infrastructure

In India, like elsewhere, banks have been the major source of debt financing of infrastructure. However, bank lending to infrastructure suffers from the problem of ALM. This is because banks' liabilities (deposits) are of much shorter tenure compared to the tenure of infrastructure assets, which is long (typically thirty years or more). Accordingly, banks are beginning to step back from infrastructure financing due to exposure constraints, capital constraints, rising NPAs, stressed asset levels, and so on.

Excessive bank lending also gave rise to the so-called twin balance-sheet problem whereby the infrastructure companies had high leverage (high debt-equity ratio) and they were unable to service their bank loans. This was a major contributory factor to the NPA problem of banks. In the decade since 2007/08, the debt of the top ten stressed corporate groups (Essar, Adani Power, GMR, Lanco, etc.) had multiplied five times, to more than Rs.7.5 trillion (lakh crore). Even with such a large infusion of funds, corporates had problems servicing their debts, so much so that by September 2016, no less than 12 per cent of the gross advances of public-sector banks had turned non-performing. With balance sheets under severe strain, the private corporate sector has been forced to curb its investments, while banks have been reducing lines of credit in real terms. To sustain economic growth, these trends will need to be rectified and reversed.[5]

Therefore, there is a need to develop alternate sources of financing through market-based instruments to supplement resources for infrastructure financing. CE will improve the credit-worthiness of a bond issuer by providing first loss support and guarantees to the lenders. In

---

[5] Arvind Subramanian. 2018. *Of Counsel—The Challenges of the Modi-Jaitley Economy.*

this way, CE would reduce the credit risk associated with the debt and improve the credit rating of the bonds issued. This will not only deepen the market of infrastructure bonds, but also develop alternate sources of financing based on market principles.

One of the attractive avenues is to source funds for infrastructure from holders of long-term patient capital, that is, pension funds, insurance funds, and sovereign wealth funds. However, these sources have an appetite only for higher-rated debt (AA or above), while the credit rating of infrastructure projects/companies is typically BBB grade, because of the non-recourse nature of financing associated with infrastructure project financing. CE of these bonds to AA category would bring a large set of projects into the 'acceptable' category for investments by pension and insurance companies. Hence, CE mechanisms providing first loss support/ guarantee are needed to boost investor confidence and help deepen the corporate bond markets. A first loss support of around 20 per cent of the project cost by government or multilateral/developmental institutions (e.g. World Bank/Asian Development Bank (ADB)—this could be in the form of guarantees from such institutions for securing timely payment under PPP) may be considered for completed infrastructure projects having an external rating of minimum BBB+, and for greenfield national importance projects with rating up to BBB.

Such CE would enable bonds floated by infrastructure companies to improve their credit rating, allowing them to raise resources from the bond market, thus enabling an alternative source of financing for such projects. A CE company would also help de-risk the banking sector and move some infrastructure funding to the capital markets. In addition, it will enable financing of infrastructure from pension, insurance, and sovereign wealth funds without ALM as the liabilities of such institutional investors are also long term, which would match the infrastructure asset tenure.

The CE of infrastructure bonds would assist in the development of non-banking markets in infrastructure finance by linking institutional and capital markets with infrastructure projects. Through this, it will contribute to the deepening of financial markets for infrastructure in India and help in the development of more appropriate risk-sharing mechanisms for sustainably supporting the sector. It would facilitate financing of the infrastructure sector with broader non-bank markets, including debt capital markets and institutional investors. This would release the exposure limits of banks for supporting new pipeline generation and scaling up infrastructure investments. This will not only diversify the resource mobilization avenues for infrastructure projects through the bond market, but also de-risk the banking sector and strengthen its fundamentals. Improved fundamentals would in turn lower the capital requirements of the banking sector. Moreover, it would assist the infrastructure projects raise cost-effective fixed-rate long-term funds and also better structure their liabilities with the receivables leading to a significant reduction in their financing cost.

Considering that infrastructure projects are capital intensive and highly leveraged, financing costs are a major expense. CE support would lead to improved viability of projects, lower user charges for the end-users and also de-risk banks' balance sheets. Hence, this is an innovative initiative for the infrastructure sector that will improve infrastructure financing thereby having multiplier effects for the entire economy.[6]

Globally, project bonds are being increasingly used for financing infrastructure (Figure 7.2). Specialized institutional initiatives have also been taken to enhance the credit rating of infrastructure projects enabling them to raise cost-effective funds. For example:

- The European Investment Bank (EIB) has established the Project Bond Initiative (PBI) to provide CE to infrastructure projects. So far, seven projects with a total project cost of 5.3 billion euros (Rs. 40,426 crore) have been supported under PBI.
- Similarly, Danajamin Nasional Berhad (DNB) is Malaysia's first financial guarantee insurer to ensure Malaysian companies' access to long-term financing from the corporate bond market by providing financial guarantees for bonds. Established in May 2009, it provides financial guarantee insurance for bond issuances to viable Malaysian companies to enable access to the corporate bond market. DNB is wholly owned by Bank Pembangunan Malaysia Berhad. It is rated AAA by both RAM Rating Services Bhd and Malaysia Rating Corporation. DNB has total assets of RM 2.7 billion (~Rs. 4,574

[6] Kumar V. Pratap and Mira Sethi. 2019. Infrastructure Financing in India—Trends, Challenges, and Way Forward.

crore) and total shareholders' equity of RM 1.8 billion (~Rs.3,049 crore) as of 31 December 2018 with a guarantee portfolio of nearly RM 5 billion (~ Rs.8,407 crore).

- ADB supported Credit Guarantee and Investment Facility (CGIF) in the ASEAN + 3 region (ASEAN members plus China, Japan, Republic of Korea), which provides guarantees for local currency-denominated bonds issued by investment grade corporations in the region. CGIF had received initial capital contribution of US$700 million from ASEAN, the People's Republic of China, Japan, Republic of Korea and ADB. As of June 2019, CGIF's capitalization stands at US$ 1,003.8 million. S&P and Fitch Indonesia have rated CGIF as AA and AAA respectively. CGIF's guarantee portfolio reached a total outstanding amount of US$1,157 million by the end of 2018. The guarantee portfolio now comprises of twenty-three bond issuances by fifteen companies from six countries.

In India, RBI has allowed banks, NBFCs, and HFCs to provide CE to a project as a non-funded subordinated facility in the form of an irrevocable contingent line of credit which will be drawn in case of a shortfall in cash flows for servicing the bonds, thereby improving the credit rating of the bonds. With a view to meeting the credit needs of the infrastructure sector in India and given that most infrastructure bonds are unable to get the rating required to meet the regulatory requirements of investors, RBI introduced guidelines on partial CE (PCE) to bonds dated 24 September 2015, allowing banks to extend PCE to enhance the credit rating of the bonds issued to enable corporates to access funds from the bond market on better terms. However, the guidelines are subject to a cap in terms of the extent to which the CE can be provided (50 per cent of issue size) and the amount of CE that an individual bank can provide (20 per cent of issue size) and mandate stringent timelines for top-up, which has made it challenging for issuers to avail of the scheme.

Generally, the CE required for a one notch upgrade in the rating of corporate papers is in the range of 8–10 per cent. With a cap of 50 per cent, most of the projects (rated BBB) can get a post enhancement rating in the A category, which is low compared to the AA+/AA rating preferred by the insurance and provident fund segment. Hence, there is a need to re-look at the 50 per cent cap. Given the stringent requirement to undertake assessments and a cap of 20 per cent CE for individual banks, we would need at least three banks to provide 50 per cent CE. It has been difficult to arrange three banks willing to provide CE on a single project and hence the 20 per cent cap per bank may be removed. The requirement to top up the utilization of CE within thirty days is also seen to be too onerous. A mechanism to get the top-up from the cash flows of the project will help in addressing this concern. The investors would be more comfortable with the CE being structured as a partial guarantee rather than a line of credit. A guarantee structured as an unconditional and irrevocable instrument has been the norm in the market. Therefore RBI may make the above changes to its existing CE scheme to enable more effective use of CE by existing institutions (e.g., India Infrastructure Finance Company Limited (IIFCL)) or CE can be offered by a specialized financing institution with a clear focus on infrastructure sector.

India recently mooted a specialized CE company for the infrastructure sector. India's central bank, the Reserve Bank of India, specified the regulatory framework for the CE company. It enumerated a differential set of prudential norms for the CE company in addition to the applicable guidelines for Type-II NBFCs. The salient features of the proposed CE company are:

- Given the scale of infrastructure financing needed in the country (which needs to be scaled up from about $110 billion per annum to about $250 billion per annum in line with the NIP), it is necessary that the proposed CE company is suitably capitalized and therefore it was proposed that the initial paid-up and authorized share capital of the company would be Rs.2,000 crore and Rs.20,000 crore respectively.
- In order to offer cost-effective CE services, it is essential that the CE company gets and maintains the highest level of rating (viz. AAA). One way of achieving this would be through equity contribution from the Government of India. It was therefore proposed that the Government of India's (GoI) equity contribution to the CE company will be 49 per cent of equity share capital. It is necessary that the proposed CE company develops into a professional company deriving its strength from a prudent business model including a suitable risk-mitigation strategy, and sound corporate governance principles.

Therefore, GoI equity has been deliberately capped at 49 per cent, giving it a minority stake in the proposed company.

- The proposed CE company would have a broad-based shareholding. The envisaged equity contribution from other financial institutions such as IIFCL, Life Insurance Corporation of India, PFC, REC, IREDA, State Bank of India, Bank of Baroda, National Housing Bank, and other public and private institutions, was to be 51 per cent of the equity share capital. Care had to be taken to ensure that no institution has a controlling interest in the shareholding to avoid conflict of interest.

- The GoI's contribution to the CE company was to be determined based upon the total contribution from the other financial institutions. Any shortfall in the CE company's initial paid-up capital (i.e. Rs.2,000 crore) that could not be funded through common equity (from the government and the financial institutions) was to be met through cumulative and convertible preference shares to be subscribed by the GoI.

- The proposed CE company would provide longer-term CE in the form of non-fund-based products initially, and fund-based products in the later years of operation. Some of the products (fund- and non-fund-based) that the CE company may use are as follows:

  o Partial credit guarantees—to cover risks such as delay in payment by power distribution companies, delay in the annuity payment by the concessioning authority, like NHAI, and so on. While the partial credit guarantee has not taken off for single assets due to a jump to default risk, it is expected to work well for pooled structures like securitization, InvITs, and so on. If there are multiple assets, the CE provided will take care of underperformance of one or two infrastructure assets and investors will also not run the jump to default risk associated with credit enhancing a single asset. Hence, once issuers start using pooling structures, they will see the benefits of the PCE schemes. However, the partial guarantee would need to work like a subordinated tranche that gets paid post senior financing (repayment from surplus cashflow can be explored) and may not have the right to initiate default proceedings. On invocation of guarantee, the interest rate on drawn amounts would need to be kept in line with subordinated debt in order to ensure that the sponsors manage businesses well.

Further, for the PCG facility, the CE company may, in the initial years, focus only on brownfield projects that have been completed and therefore represent relatively less risky assets (see Figure 7.1). In later years, based on the risk appetite and absorption capacity of the CE company, and demand in the market, the PCG may gradually and carefully be extended to cover greenfield projects.

o Subordinated debt—to undertake fund-based exposure in projects, which is subordinated to the guaranteed bonds/senior loans in terms of escrow waterfall and/or security interest for the devolved portion of the guarantees.

o Project completion risk guarantee—to guarantee additional interest burden beyond the envisaged quantum in the original project cost during financial closure, until project completion.

An array of CE products on the above lines would facilitate improved credit rating of debt and hence enhanced credit rating of bonds. The proposed CE company is expected to support projects worth about Rs.7 trillion (lakh crore) in the first ten years of its operations. However, the government is re-thinking about the proposed dedicated CE company.

Infrastructure Debt Funds

Infrastructure debt funds (IDFs) are an innovative solution to multiple challenges in infrastructure financing in India, including the ALM of banks, channelizing insurance/pension funds to infrastructure, enhancing the viability of projects by providing long-term fixed-rate solutions and deepening the bond market in India. In the current market, IDF-NBFCs are the only significant refinancers of long-term infrastructure assets that enable movement of assets out of the books of banks, enabling them to lend afresh to infrastructure. IDF-NBFCs are also the only long-term (fifteen-year) fixed-rate infrastructure project financiers in India. Refinancing the debt of completed projects by IDF-NBFCs enables banks and NBFC-IFCs to recycle resources that can be used for greenfield asset financing.

Currently, there are four IDF-NBFCs in India (L&T IDF, ICICI—Bank of Baroda joint venture called India Infradebt, NIIF IFL, and Kotak

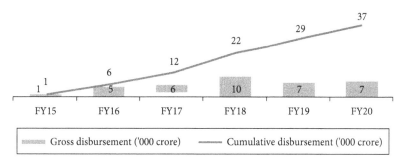

Figure 7.4 Infrastructure Debt Fund (IDF-NBFC) financing of
infrastructure

Source: Ministry of Finance, Government of India. 2020. *Report of Project Finance/Refinance Sub-Group Constituted under IMSC for Enabling Financing of Infrastructure Projects under National Infrastructure Pipeline,* p. 17.

IDF), which have provided gross financing (i.e. gross disbursement) of Rs.36,600 crore over the past five years[7] (see Figure 7.4).

The performance of IDFs has been exemplary. IDF-NBFCs have been consistently rated AAA and have delivered a return on equity of more than 12 per cent per annum to their investors. There have also been no impaired assets (i.e. 0 per cent NPA) on the books of IDF-NBFCs.

Some suggestions for increasing the contribution of IDFs to infrastructure financing are stated below. The 'Pattern of Investment' for Employee Provident Fund Organization (EPFO) notified by the Ministry of Labour and Employment applicable from 2019, permits investment of a minimum 20 per cent in 'debt and related instruments' with sub-points on 'listed debt securities issued by corporate engaged in development ... operation of infrastructure' and 'listed securities by IDFs operating as NBFCs'. To direct more EPFO resources into IDFs, a mandatory sub-limit of 1 per cent for IDF-NBFCs may be prescribed, albeit with more stringent criteria which could include past five-year track record of continuous profitability, corporate governance and reputation, past impeccable regulatory compliance, asset quality (NPA < 5 per cent) and an AAA rating from at least two rating agencies approved by RBI/SEBI.

---

[7] Ministry of Finance, Government of India. 2020. *Report of Project Finance/Refinance Sub-Group Constituted under IMSC for Enabling Financing of Infrastructure Projects under National Infrastructure Pipeline.*

Currently IDF-NBFCs are permitted to re-finance road sector BOT (Toll and Annuity) projects. Specific approval is required with respect to TOT (toll–operate–transfer) projects in the road sector. Since TOT projects satisfy RBI's requirement of having satisfactory operations post-commercial operation date (COD) of at least one year, it is recommended that IDF-NBFCs be allowed to finance TOT projects. In fact, IDF-NBFCs may be permitted to re-finance all PPP projects (including airport projects) with a project authority.

8

Priority of Governments the World Over—Institutional Investment into Infrastructure

Governments desire institutional investment (from pension, insurance, and sovereign wealth funds (SWF)) into infrastructure rather than bank financing, which is currently the predominant means of financing infrastructure debt. Institutional investment into infrastructure does not suffer from asset–liability mismatch issues, which is typical of bank financing of infrastructure. Infrastructure investments should also be attractive to institutional investors given that they provide long-term steady returns, which are not generally correlated to business cycles. For example, pension funds and insurance companies hold more than 90 per cent of the stock of infrastructure bonds in Chile. However, in the case of India, institutional investors have not been investing much in infrastructure. The chapter explores the reasons for this, as well as suggesting policy measures, including the need for a specialized credit enhancement (CE) company for infrastructure bonds, for domestic institutional investors to invest in infrastructure (as foreign, mainly Canadian pension funds, are already major investors in Indian infrastructure). This chapter also discusses the importance of infrastructure projects aligning with the environmental, social, and governance (ESG) criteria, increasingly being used by these investors for their investments. In this context, the chapter discusses the role of India's own SWF, the National Investment and Infrastructure Fund (NIIF), to facilitate such institutional investment in infrastructure.

Infrastructure Financing in India. Kumar V Pratap and Manshi Gupta, Oxford University Press.
© Kumar V Pratap and Manshi Gupta 2024. DOI: 10.1093/oso/9780198884934.003.0009

Covid-19 and the Infrastructure Financing Gap

We saw one estimate (McKinsey Global Institute)[1] of the infrastructure financing gap in Chapter 2: there is a US$5.5 trillion spending gap globally between now and 2035 between need and expected actuals, with regional variations. India spent 5.6 per cent of GDP on economic infrastructure in the period 2010–2015, and the gap is 0.7 per cent of GDP for the period 2017–2035.

Another estimate is presented here. According to G20 Infrastructure Monitor (2020),[2] global infrastructure needs are US$94 trillion up to 2040—US$15 trillion more than projected spending based on prevailing trends. To close the infrastructure financing gap, it estimated that annual infrastructure investment would need to increase from 3 per cent of global GDP to 3.5 per cent. Part of the difference in the two estimates may be related to different definitions of infrastructure and the different time periods covered. But what is clear is that the world needs to spend more on infrastructure to be able to meet its needs.

The World Bank (2021)[3] has projected negative global growth at (–)4.3 per cent in 2020 and a mere 4.2 per cent in 2021 with a wide negative output gap and a high rate of unemployment. Sustainable growth requires prioritizing investment in infrastructure in general and green infrastructure in particular for growing out of the Covid-19 induced recession as well as providing a foundation for inclusive development.

There exists very little room for fiscal stimulus to further public investment in infrastructure. In July 2020, the International Monetary Fund (IMF) estimated that global fiscal commitments in response to Covid-19 amounted to US$11 trillion, and this number can be expected to grow in the near to medium term. This along with exacerbated debt levels is creating macroeconomic distress the world over. Global debt was 230 per cent of GDP in 2019 (government debt being 83 per cent of GDP).

[1] McKinsey Global Institute. 2017. *Bridging Infrastructure Gaps: Has the World Made Progress?* (https://www.mckinsey.com/business-functions/operations/our-insights/bridging-infrastructure-gaps-has-the-world-made-progress).

[2] G20 (Global Infrastructure Hub). 2020. *Infrastructure Monitor 2020*, p. 13 (https://cdn.gihub.org/umbraco/media/3241/gih_monitorreport_final.pdf).

[3] World Bank. 2021. *Global Economic Prospects*, p. 26 (https://openknowledge.worldbank.org/handle/10986/34710).

Emerging markets and developing economies witnessed elevated debt levels at 176 per cent of GDP led by private debt of 123 per cent of GDP. Central government fiscal deficit in India was an unprecedented 9.2 per cent in 2020/21. In this scenario, countries, including India, have prioritized infrastructure investment for sustainable recovery.

This implies that fiscal resources would be under stress (though there is room for improving the efficiency of infrastructure investments— a recent IMF study provides evidence that, on average, 30 per cent of spending on infrastructure creation and maintenance is 'lost' due to poor governance) and much of the increased requirement for infrastructure investment would have to come from the private sector. Although traditional channels for financing infrastructure development remain relevant, there is a requirement for innovative mechanisms to crowd-in private capital. This can be achieved through better project preparation, risk mitigation, and developing infrastructure as an asset class for investment. In this context of overall scarcity of investible capital into infrastructure, the role of institutional investment (from pension, insurance, and SWFs) into infrastructure becomes even more important.

Institutional Investment into Infrastructure

Traditionally, the heterogeneous group of institutional investors has been seen as a source of long-term capital with investment portfolios built around two main asset classes (bonds and equities) and an investment horizon tied to the often long-term nature of their liabilities. They are constantly searching for opportunities that can provide stable returns to match their long-term liabilities. Operational (as opposed to under-construction) infrastructure assets are particularly attractive to them due to their time horizons, relatively inelastic demand, inflation-hedging characteristic, relatively high expected yields, and stable returns that have a low correlation with business cycles, thereby providing opportunities for portfolio diversification and downside risk protection. A long-term investment horizon can also bring direct benefits to institutional investors, as they can take advantage of long-term risk premia, including an illiquidity premium rewarding them for exposure to less liquid, long-term assets (such as infrastructure).

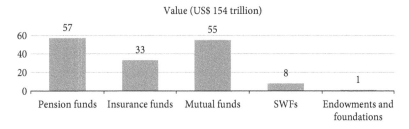

Figure 8.1 Assets under management of institutional investors
Source: Thinking Ahead Institute. 2021. *Global Pension Assets Study*, p. 9
(https://www.thinkingaheadinstitute.org/content/uploads/2021/02/GPAS__2021.pdf).

Globally, assets under management with pension funds, SWFs, mutual funds, insurance funds, and endowments and foundations are very high at US$154 trillion[4] at the end of 2020 (Figure 8.1). The largest share is that of pension funds (37 per cent). Ninety-two per cent of these pension funds are concentrated in P7 countries: Canada, the United States, Switzerland, the United Kingdom, the Netherlands, Australia, and Japan. Comparing the amount of pension assets to the size of the economy, measured by GDP, gives a better picture of the relative importance of retirement saving plans domestically. Within the OECD area, eight out of thirty-seven countries had assets at the end of 2019 above 100 per cent of their GDP, for example Australia has 138 per cent and the United States has 150 per cent. The corresponding number in other countries, including some rapidly developing countries, was below 20 per cent (e.g. China, India).[5]

The pension fund asset allocation of P7 countries reveals a preference for equities over bonds and others (alternate assets), partly explained through risk and returns, by asset class, as shown in Figure 8.2. High dividend yields, lower trading prices, and lower volatility are the key factors driving the attractiveness of infrastructure equities. Asset allocation for pension funds in these countries, at the end of 2020, is 43 per cent in equities, 29 per cent in bonds, 26 per cent in others, and 2 per cent

[4] Willis Towers Watson. 2021.*Global Pension Assets Study*, p. 7, 9 (https://www.thinkingahe adinstitute.org/content/uploads/2021/02/GPAS__2021.pdf).
[5] OECD. 2020. *Pension Markets in Focus* (https://www.oecd.org/daf/fin/private-pensions/ Pension-Markets-in-Focus-2020.pdf).

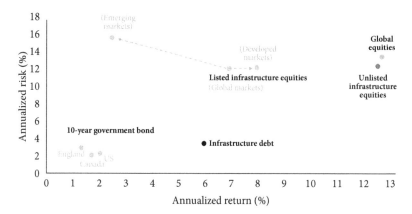

Figure 8.2 Ten-year risk-return, by asset class
Source: Global Infrastructure Hub. 2021. *Infrastructure Monitor.*

cash.[6] However, the share of equity has declined over time and that of others has increased. This points towards institutional investors' growing appetite for 'engineered financial products' if they suit their risk-return preference. In India, the figures stand at 13.1 per cent in equities and 68.6 per cent in bills and bonds.[7] Reasons for the high proportion of investments in government bonds in some countries, including India, include a lack of other investment opportunities domestically and the need for a fixed, low-risk, and guaranteed income. Typically, in non-OECD countries, portfolios were tilted towards safer assets.

India shares the characteristic of a preponderance of pension fund allocations to government bonds with select African countries (except South Africa, Figure 8.3), co-existing with the need for huge investments in infrastructure (US$130 billion–US$170 billion per year in Africa as reckoned by African Development Bank). Local pension funds in Africa manage about US$350 billion of assets in sub-Saharan Africa but struggle to find avenues to invest. In Nigeria, for example, pension funds put just 0.5 per cent of their assets into infrastructure.[8]

[6] Willis Towers Watson. 2021, *Global Pension Assets Study*, p. 7, 9 (https://www.thinkingahe adinstitute.org/content/uploads/2021/02/GPAS__2021.pdf).

[7] OECD. 2020. *Pension Markets in Focus* (https://www.oecd.org/daf/fin/private-pensions/Pension-Markets-in-Focus-2020.pdf).

[8] *The Economist*. 8 October 2021. Pension Funds—Building Bridges (https://www.economist.com/middle-east-and-africa/2021/10/02/african-pension-funds-have-grown-impressively).

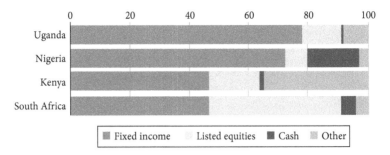

Source: Uganda Retirement Benefits Regulatory
Authority; National Pension Commission of Nigeria;
Kenya Retirement Benefits Authority

Figure 8.3 Pension fund asset allocation, 2021 (or latest available) (%)

Source: The Economist. 8 October 2021. Pension Funds—Building Bridges (https://www.
economist.com/middle-east-and-africa/2021/10/02/african-pension-funds-have-grown-impre
ssively).

It has been estimated that the global retirement savings gap, currently
estimated at US$70 trillion, will grow to US$400 trillion by 2050. In addition to challenges stemming from ageing populations, low interest rates
and bond yields have also contributed to the problem. The result is that
pension fund assets have not grown as fast as their liabilities, so their
deficits—the gap between the money they have and the money it will take
to pay their pensioners—have widened (see Figure 8.4 for an example). In
an attempt to offset these growing unfunded liabilities, national and state
pension funds have been increasing their investment levels in infrastructure over recent years. Fund managers are looking beyond the traditional

Figure 8.4 Why are institutional investors keen on infrastructure?
Source: Ontario Teachers' Pension Plan.

asset classes of equities, bonds, cash, and real estate. These investors need low-risk, long-term and inflation-hedged investments, which explains the increased level of interest in mature operating infrastructure assets.[9]

The Ontario Teachers' Pension Plan (OTPP) administers pension payments of over US$6 billion annually. In 1990, there were four teachers for every pensioner with an average pension life of twenty-five years. However, by 2018, the ratio was down to 1.3 active teachers for every pensioner, and a pension life of thirty-two years. As a result of these demographic trends, OTPP is looking for low-risk, long-term and inflation-hedged investments, which explains their increased interest in infrastructure assets.

An empirical evaluation of the performance of infrastructure investment over the 2002–2021 period and its comparison with five other asset classes—private equity, real estate, stocks, bonds, and cash—has shown that it meets the criteria of inflation hedging, portfolio diversification, stable income yield, and downside risk protection.[10] Infrastructure has strong portfolio diversification benefits and these benefits can be further improved by investing in different subsectors. Comparing returns of all asset classes during the Global Financial Crisis (2008–2009) and the 2020 Covid-19 downturn, Ravenhorst and Brounen have concluded that infrastructure exhibits least downside risk after bonds whereas private equity and real estate have witnessed maximum drawdown. Hence, in case of a market downturn, investors may seek to increase their exposure to infrastructure assets. Due to the underlying characteristics of infrastructure such as a long gestation period, regulated returns, long-term contracts and stable cash flows, it provides a dividend yield that is more stable than other illiquid assets and strong compared to stocks. The inflation-hedging property rests on various determinants like business model, regulation, contract provisions, and so on. With appropriate determinants, individual infrastructure assets and subsectors may function as an inflation hedge. Hence, capital allocation to infrastructure by institutional investors can be increased by developing it as a distinct asset class.

---

[9] World Economic Forum. 2017. *Recycling our Infrastructure for Future Generations* (http://www3.weforum.org/docs/WEF_Recycling_our_Infrastructure_for_Future_Generations_report_2017.pdf).

[10] Ivo Ravenhorst and Dirk Brounen. 2022. *Why Infrastructure?*

The proportion of institutional investment into infrastructure is low

The actual proportion of institutional investment into infrastructure is still low.[11] As of February 2020, institutional investment by OECD-based institutions into infrastructure was US$3.3 trillion, of which 70 per cent was through listed structures (Figure 8.5). Investment through securitized structures like YieldCos,[12] infrastructure investment trusts (InvITs), real estate investment trusts (REITs) and master limited part-nerships (MLPs) accounted for 43 per cent of the total investment. Asset managers are the major investors in infrastructure mainly through listed instruments as they invest on behalf of other clients and thus have lower risk appetite. Stocks and securitized instruments have benefits of liquidity and stable returns. These stock investments do not channel capital to the investee company and therefore cannot direct capital to new invest-ments. In contrast, pension funds mainly allocate investment through unlisted funds representing an affinity towards illiquidity premium and long-term capital appreciation. The exposure of insurance funds is very modest in infrastructure contributing 4 per cent of total investment. SWFs too play a small role as they move towards co-investment models mobilizing capital for specific policy purposes. SWFs of this nature may be capitalized by national governments, as in the case of the NIIF in India (see Box 8.1).

Infrastructure as an asset class provides attractive investment op-tions for investors to diversify and optimize their portfolio. Research by EDHECInfra (EDHECinfra 2021), suggests that the optimal portfolio al-location to infrastructure should be about 10 per cent, with allocation

---

[11] OECD. 2020. *Green Infrastructure in the Decade for Delivery: Assessing Institutional Investment*, ch. 2 (https://www.oecd-ilibrary.org/sites/f51f9256-en/index.html?itemId=/cont ent/publication/f51f9256-en)

[12] Globally private institutional funds have complemented debt funds in financing infrastruc-ture investment. There has been a global consensus on the potential for tapping large institu-tional investors (including pension funds, sovereign wealth funds, etc.) as well as retail investors towards infrastructure asset class, especially brownfield assets that have lower risk levels. Two specific instruments seen in the United States which have been fairly successful in tapping in-stitutional investors into infrastructure assets are: Yieldcos and Master Limited Partnerships (MLPs), which are similar to InvITs (Mauricio Franco Mitidieri. 13 April 2020. *The Evolution of the YieldCos Structure in the United States*).

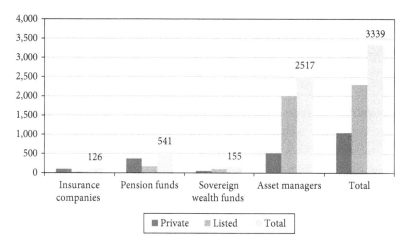

Figure 8.5 Investment in infrastructure by institutional investors ($ billion)
Source: OECD, NIIF Research (https://www.oecd-ilibrary.org/sites/aaa8a6c2-en/index.html?ite
mId=/content/component/aaa8a6c2-en#section-d1e2504).

between equity and debt varying based on the investor profile. Currently,
for most investors, the portfolio allocation to infrastructure as an asset
class is less than 5 per cent.[13]

However, institutional investment's contribution to global investment in developing-country infrastructure is minuscule—only 0.67
per cent—according to the World Bank's Private Participation in
Infrastructure (PPI) database. This may partly be because developed
markets provided higher risk-adjusted returns than emerging markets for all types of equities across all regions of the world.[14] There may
be some causality between stage of development and macroeconomic
environment conducive to institutional investment into infrastructure. Developed countries have better infrastructure, higher competitiveness, more developed capital markets, and the existence of sizeable
assets under management as a consequence of a good pension system.
These factors create a virtuous circle for institutional infrastructure
investment.

[13] Global Infrastructure Hub. 2021. *Infrastructure Monitor.*
[14] Global Infrastructure Hub. 2021. *Infrastructure Monitor.*

Box 8.1 India's quasi SWF—The National Investment and Infrastructure Fund (NIIF)

SWFs are state-owned investment funds established mostly from the country's reserves—balance-of-payments surplus, fiscal surplus, or excess foreign-exchange reserves. These funds are invested in capital assets and alternate funds like hedge funds and private equity to garner sustainable resources for the government through portfolio diversification, while helping the development of national economies. As per one estimate, the number of SWFs stands at 153 with assets under management of US$10.3 trillion.[a] The largest SWF is that of Norway (US$1.15 trillion) followed by the China Investment Corporation.

Globally, SWFs are moving away from the Limited Partner (LP) model, where they are passive investors, and increasingly rely on a General Partner (GP) who manages the funds, and towards various combinations of a LP/GP model involving collaborative investments.[b] India's NIIF is a hybrid SWF where anchor LPs are also majority owners of NIIF.[c] NIIF was established in India in 2015 in the context of the country's infrastructure deficit, limited fiscal space, and the advice of the country's central bank, the Reserve Bank of India (RBI), against using the country's forex reserves for infrastructure.

NIIF is a Category II Alternate Investment Fund (with a corpus of Rs.40,000 crore) under the Securities and Exchange Board of India (SEBI) regulations to provide long-term equity and debt capital to commercially viable greenfield, brownfield, and stalled infrastructure projects. While the Government of India is the anchor investor in the NIIF (49 per cent stake), the balance 51 per cent is held by international and domestic institutional investors, including the Abu Dhabi Investment Authority (ADIA), Australian Super, Singapore's Temasek, Canada's Ontario Teachers' Pension Plan, and Canada Pension Plan Investment Board (CPPIB), as founding LPs. This could be achieved through 'generous' co-investment terms whereby each of NIIF's international LPs—in contrast to the government and local partners—have a 3:1 investment right, that is, if they invest US$250 million, they have a US$750 million priority co-investment right.[d] NIIF manages over US$ 4.5 billion of equity capital commitments across its three funds

(Master Fund, Fund of Funds (FoF), and Strategic Opportunities Fund (SOF)), each with its distinct investment strategy.[e]

a. NIIF Master Fund (target size: US$ 2.3 billion)[f] primarily invests in operating assets in core infrastructure sectors such as roads, power, airports, and so on. These often operate in regulated environments or under concession or long-term agreements thus providing predictable inflation-hedged and stable cash flows. NIIF follows the strategy of establishing sector-specific companies in partnership with prominent companies.

Financing activities: The current projects under this fund include a ports and logistics platform, Hindustan Infralog Private Limited (HIPL), in partnership with DP World (HIPL acquired a 90 per cent stake in Continental Warehousing Corporation (Nhava Seva) Ltd., an integrated multimodal logistics player in India in March 2018); Ayana, the renewable energy platform, to invest in solar and wind power plants; and a smart meters platform called IntelliSmart Infrastructure Private Limited, which is a joint venture created by NIIF and Energy Efficiency Services Limited to implement, finance, and operate the smart meter roll-out programme of power distribution companies. NIIF has also set up Athaang Infrastructure Private Limited, to operate and manage a portfolio of mature operational road assets with a diverse mix of BOT–Toll, BOT–Annuity and Hybrid Annuity Model (HAM) assets, large size expressways and roads with greenfield and brownfield expansion requirements. The NIIF road portfolio includes Devanahalli Tollway (a strategic arterial 22 km six-lane toll road in the state of Karnataka, connecting Bengaluru city and its airport); Dichpally Tollway (a 60 km four-lane toll road in the state of Telangana, an important link between two key industrial hubs, Hyderabad and Nagpur, and serves long distance commercial traffic); and Navayuga Quazigund Expressway Private Limited (an operational tunnel road in the union territory of Jammu and Kashmir; four-laned 16.3 km expressway between Quazigund and Banihal Section of NH-1A; one of the largest annuity projects awarded by the NHAI on a BOT basis; project receives fixed, semi-annual payments from NHAI, providing stable and predictable cash flows). NIIF has also invested in the Mumbai Airport.

b. NIIF FoF (target size: US$1 billion)[g] invests in funds managed by fund managers focussed on some of the most dynamic sectors in India such as climate infrastructure, middle-income and affordable housing, digital consumer platforms and other allied sectors. The fund managers are selected on the basis of investment strategy and focus on risk management and compliance (including ESG risks). With the help of funds from FoF (NIIF), these fund managers are able to garner more funds from other institutional investors. As of February 2021, the FoF has made commitments to four funds aggregating over Rs.27.50 billion, which are focussed on (i) green energy and climate; (ii) middle-income and affordable housing; (iii) entrepreneur-driven mid-market growth companies; and (iv) affordable healthcare. The managers of the four funds have successfully raised over US$1.1 billion equivalent alongside NIIF's commitments.

Financing activities: Green Growth Equity Fund (GGEF) established in collaboration with the UK government, each contributing GBP120 million, has EverSource Capital as the fund manager; the core focus of GGEF is investing in scalable opportunities related to no-carbon and low-carbon solutions that cut greenhouse-gas emissions and reduce environmental impacts; HDFC Capital Affordable Real Estate Fund 2 (H-CARE 2), an investment platform managed by HDFC Capital Advisors, where NIIF has invested Rs.6.60 billion with other investors including the ADIA and HDFC Ltd to provide structured debt solutions to developers of mid-income and affordable urban housing projects; Multiples Private Equity Fund III, a Category II AIF, managed by Multiples Alternate Asset Management Pvt Limited where NIIF has committed Rs.8.78 billion to catalyse the capital-starved mid-market segment; and Somerset Indus Healthcare India Fund ('Fund II'), managed by Somerset Healthcare Investment Advisors Private Limited where NIIF has committed Rs.1.25 billion, to enable the provision of equity capital into small to medium-sized companies run by capable local entrepreneurs.

c. NIIF SOF (target size: US$2.1 billion) is a private equity fund that invests in large, scalable businesses that are fundamental, strategic, and key enablers to the India growth story.

Financing activities: SOF has invested equity at scale across the two companies: NIIF Infrastructure Finance Limited,[h] a non-banking financing company (NBFC) registered with the RBI as an infrastructure debt fund (NBFC-IDF), to help operating infrastructure assets with satisfactory commercial operations for more than one year by re-financing loans originally taken for project development; and Aseem Infrastructure Finance Limited (AIFL), an NBFC registered with the RBI as an infrastructure finance company (NBFC-IFC), to lend across infra-structure assets at different phases of implementation. The NIIF IFL and the AIFL together form the NIIF infrastructure debt financing platform.

Governance structure: The activities of NIIF are overseen by the Governing Council headed by the Indian finance minister and represen-tatives from the Government of India, economists, and professionals. NIIF Limited is the investment manager, comprising professional ex-perts. NIIF has an arms-length relationship with the Government of India in terms of decision-making. This has helped catalyse govern-ment seed capital with market rate returns. NIIF also takes into account potential ESG risks from an investment. These risks are integrated into investment decisions, making NIIF ESG compliant and making it more attractive to global impact investors. The association of foreign pension funds and SWFs indicates that NIIF is doing things right.

[a]Global SWF Data Platform. Sovereign Wealth Funds and Public Pension Funds (https://globalswf.com/, accessed on 15 October 2021).

[b]Boston Consulting Group and Sovereign Investment Lab. 2019. *The Rise of Collaborative Investing—Sovereign Wealth Funds' New Strategies in Private Markets* (https://bafficarefin.unibocconi.eu/sites/default/files/media/attach/Sovereign-Wealth-Funds-Approach_LOW RES_V11.pdf).

[c]Sarah Rundell. 2020. *The Rise of the Sovereign Wealth Fund* (https://www.top1000funds.com/2020/03/the-rise-of-the-sovereign-wealth-fund/).

[d]Sarah Rundell. 2020. *India's NIIF Gathers Steam* (https://www.top1000funds.com/2020/02/indias-niif-gathers-steam/).

[e]National Investment and Infrastructure Fund. 11 February 2021. National Investment and Infrastructure Fund Limited (NIIFL) Announces USD 100 Million Investment from New Development Bank (NDB) into the NIIF Fund of Funds (FoF). Available at https://www.niifindia.in/uploads/media_releases/Press%20Release%20-%20NIIFL%20announces%20USD%20100%20million%20investment%20from%20New%20Development%20Bank%20(NDB)%20into%20the%20NIIF%20Fund%20of%20Funds%20(FoF)%20(2)-converted.pdf.

[f]In December 2020, NIIFL announced that it had officially closed the Master Fund, with US$2.34 billion in commitments, from two SWFs (ADIA, US$1 billion; Temasek, US$0.4 billion), four PPFs (AustralianSuper, US$0.25 billion; CPPIB, US$0.6 billion; OTPP, US$0.25 billion; and PSP), US DFC, and a number of domestic investors such as ICICI Bank, HDFC Group, Axis Bank, and Kotak Mahindra Life Insurance.

[g]NDB has announced US$100 million into the NIIF Fund of Funds (FoF). Including this, so far FoF has secured US$800 million in commitments. NDB joins the Government of India, Asian Infrastructure Investment Bank (AIIB), and Asian Development Bank (ADB) as an investor in the FoF.

[h]NIIF IFL has announced an investment of Rs.21 billion in Manipal Hospitals. This is one of the largest PE investments in the country by a domestic fund.

Sectoral Composition of Institutional Investment into Infrastructure

Energy (41 per cent) followed by telecommunications (30 per cent) attracted the major share (71 per cent) of institutional investment into infrastructure (Figure 8.6). The renewable energy subsector attracted investment mainly through YieldCos and fossil fuel through MLPs. Pension funds made large investments in renewable energy, especially from those of Iceland, Denmark, the Netherlands, and Canada. The Icelandic Pension Fund of Commerce and LSR invested respectively 80 per cent and 70 per cent of their portfolio into renewable energy. The Danish PFA invested US$912 million (60 per cent of its portfolio) in renewable energy, mainly in offshore wind and other renewable energy. In telecommunications, the investment went towards mainly wireless communication infrastructure (including telecom towers, fibre-optic cables, data centres, etc.), which has shown high resilience during Covid-19 pandemic.

The transport sector has well-established project finance structures and offers steady revenue streams, often through concessions or availability payments. The use of securitized products for transport infrastructure is relatively modest compared to the energy and telecommunications sectors. However, InvITs are a noteworthy recent addition

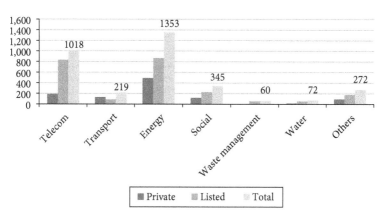

Figure 8.6 Sectoral composition of investment by institutional investors ($ billion)

Source: OECD, NIIF Research (https://www.oecd-ilibrary.org/sites/aaa8a6c2-en/index.html?ite mId=/content/component/aaa8a6c2-en#section-d1e2504).

to the transport investment landscape. This is driven by a rising interest in monetizing operational assets, both by the public and private sectors, to free construction-stage equity in certain markets (e.g. India). Pension funds have invested in these assets given the alignment between their long-dated liabilities and the long-term predictable revenues from transport assets.

Social infrastructure has attracted 10 per cent of total investment mainly in the form of funding of REITs, comprising mainly buildings. Water supply and waste management infrastructure experienced a modest level of funding owing to structural issues like low user charges (and associated political sensitivity), hardly covering even operational expenditures, let alone fair return on capital investment. The UK water sector is a notable exception, as water supply services in England and Wales were privatized in 1989. The sector has an independent economic regulator, OFWAT, which oversees tariff setting and capital investment planning of water operators. According to the investment data, 56 per cent of the water assets held by domestic and international institutional investors are located in the United Kingdom.

Instruments like pooled and blended finance may be used to harness long-term capital for critical social infrastructure. Blended finance structures that combine public and philanthropic capital with private investments using CE instruments can be useful, for example, the Philippines' Water Revolving Fund blends aid and public funds with commercial finance to offer a lower cost of capital to water service-providers. Water Equity's WCIF3 Fund uses a blended approach through low-interest loans and first-loss guarantee. Pooled funds—such as the Kenya Pooled Water Fund, which pools domestic pension and institutional money— also fits into this category.[15]

Pension funds' ESG strategy varies. Pension funds based in Australia, the Netherlands, Sweden, and Norway tend to report more detailed ESG or socially responsible investment strategies. Some funds do not have a separate, ESG-oriented investment strategy, but consider ESG factors along with other risk and opportunity factors during the investment

---

[15] Namita Vikas, Sourajit Aiyer, and Cymoran Vikas. 2021. *4 Ways to Scale up Finance for India's Water Sector* (https://www.weforum.org/agenda/2021/05/4-ways-to-scale-up-finance-for-indias-water-sector/).

decision-making process. Several funds consider ESG in the context of the long-term investment horizon. Common among funds is to have a climate-change strategy in place, including a carbon footprint measure to make the investments more resilient to climate change over the long term.[16]

Current holdings of institutional investment in *green* infrastructure amounts to US$314 billion. This equals 30 per cent of all institutional investment in infrastructure (excluding listed structures). Pension funds from the United Kingdom and Denmark lead capital allocation to green infrastructure. Among insurance companies, German insurers hold the largest amount in green infrastructure assets, followed by companies from Denmark.[17]

The challenges to institutional investment into infrastructure include: the (actual and perceived) political, regulatory, and micro risks; regulations, fiduciary duty, and investor mandates; investor capacity and costs; specific constraints for less-liquid investments like transport or water/sewerage projects. These challenges explain the investment choices of institutional investors, like brownfield assets compared to greenfield assets, developed country infrastructure compared to developing country infrastructure, green and renewable energy investments compared to fossil-fuel investments, and so on.

Institutional Investment in Indian Infrastructure

The Indian economy is estimated to have contracted by 6.6 per cent in financial year 2020/21. The Covid-19 pandemic has triggered a massive increase in global debt levels, including in emerging market and developing economies (EMDEs) like India. Among EMDEs, government debt is expected to increase by 9 percentage points of GDP in 2020—its largest increase since the late 1980s when EMDEs saw a series of debt crises. The

[16] OECD. 2021. *The Application of ESG Considerations in Infrastructure Investment in the Asia-Pacific.*

[17] OECD. 2020. *Green Infrastructure in the Decade for Delivery: Assessing Institutional Investment,* ch. 2 (https://www.oecd-ilibrary.org/sites/f51f9256en/1/3/2/index.html?itemId=/content/publication/f51f9256-en&_csp_=7d5d22ec82800d8235fe1f2706f7224f&itemIGO=oecd&itemContentType=book).

jump in government debt has been broad-based, with a large increase in all regions and all major EMDEs. South Asia has seen the steepest increases, with India's government debt expected to rise by 17 percentage points of GDP[18] amid a severe output contraction. Since the fiscal space with the government is constrained, there is an added imperative to attract institutional investment for infrastructure investment in general, and implementation of the National Infrastructure Pipeline (NIP) in particular.

Pool of domestic savings to finance infrastructure

As can be seen from Table 8.1, India has a huge pool of domestic savings which if efficiently channelized can be effectively utilized for infrastructure financing. Also, the risk-reward profile of operational infrastructure assets, as discussed earlier, are in consonance with the liability demands of institutional investors who look for long-term stable returns. Institutional investment into operational infrastructure will also help reduce stress on bank balance sheets, which are the primary vehicles for debt financing of infrastructure.

The investment criteria and behaviour of the domestic institutional investors so far as investment into infrastructure is concerned, are discussed below.

Insurance funds

Among the insurance funds, the largest participant is Life Insurance Corporation of India and a few other private insurance companies. They are active investors and typically invest in long-term securities via primary and secondary markets. Their investments remain concentrated primarily in the AAA category and a handful of AA rated papers. While insurance funds remain the second-largest holders of corporate bonds, the share of insurance companies has dropped over time due to reducing allocation to corporate bonds and a shift to central and state government securities.

---

[18] World Bank. 2021. *Global Economic Prospects*, p. 34 (https://openknowledge.worldbank.org/handle/10986/34710).

Table 8.1   Corpus with domestic institutional investors

Description	Estimated Corpus (Rs. trillion)
1. Employee Provident Fund Organization	12[a]
2. National Pension System	5.90[b]
3. Public Provident Fund	5
4. Life Insurance Funds	39[c]
5. General and Health Insurance Funds	3.60[d]
Total corpus	65.5 (~US$870 billion)

[a]Employee Provident Fund Organization estimated corpus as of 31 March 2019.

[b]National Pension System estimated corpus as of 31 March 2021 (NPS Trust Annual Report) National Pension System Trust, Government of India. 2021. *Annual Report 2020–21*, p. 31. Available at:
http://npstrust.org.in/sites/default/files/Annual%20Report%20of%20NPS%20Trust-%20FY%202020-21%20%281%29.pdf.

[c]Life Insurance Funds estimated corpus as of 31 March 2020 (IRDAI Report).

[d]General and Health Insurance Funds estimated corpus as of 31 March 2020 (IRDAI Report).

As of 31 March 2020, investments made by the Indian insurance industry stood at Rs.42.6 trillion (lakh crore). The share of life insurers stood at 91.5 per cent. As against a requirement of investment in infrastructure and social sectors of not less than 15 per cent of their corpus, the housing and infrastructure sector investments made by life insurers stood at Rs.2.75 lakh crore or about 7 per cent of their total investments. Infrastructure investments by general insurers and reinsurers stood at Rs.0.55 lakh crore or 15 per cent of their total investments. So, for the insurance sector as a whole, investment in the housing and infrastructure sectors stood at Rs.3.3 lakh crore or about 8 per cent of their total investments.[19]

Pension funds

State-run Employees' Provident Fund Organization (EPFO) is the largest PF in the country. There are also a number of widely scattered provident funds of corporates. EPFO and exempted trusts have grown steadily on the back of a steady growth of subscribers and salary/wage increases, which have driven corpus and thus investment in corporate bonds. They

---

[19] Insurance Regulatory and Development Authority of India. 2020. *Annual Report 2019–20*.

prefer long-tenor bonds (ten to fifteen years) to match their liability pro-files. However, from an investment perspective, they invest in a handful of AAA-rated papers.

Schemes such as the Employees' Provident Fund (EPF), are regulated by the EPFO, and schemes such as the National Pension System (NPS) are regulated by the Pension Fund Regulatory and Development Authority. The Public Provident Fund (PPF) is a defined contribution scheme man-aged by the government and offers a fixed rate of return. Schemes under EPFO are for individuals working for establishments employing more than twenty employees; NPS schemes are for state and central govern-ment employees, self-employed individuals, and other entities; while the PPF is a voluntary scheme. With the advent of the NPS scheme, individ-uals have been allowed to have an exposure to financial assets other than government securities in their pension corpus.[20]

Scheduled commercial banks

Allocation to corporate bonds by banks surged between fiscals 2014 and 2017. Among other factors, lowered SLR and limited growth in the lending book due to a weak credit outlook drove investments into cor-porate bonds. While credit is expected to grow over the next few years, factors such as large corporate exposure guidelines and the traditional preference of banks to lend through loans would limit their percentage allocation to corporate bonds.[21]

As would be apparent, treasuries (G-secs) dominate in the asset port-folio of domestic institutional investors. Share of infrastructure invest-ment is as low as 7 per cent by life insurers and 15 per cent by general insurers.[22] While insurance and pension funds have longer-tenor liabil-ities, they lack the sophistication to invest into infrastructure debt in-struments, given that these instruments are more structured and require in-depth analysis. Further, there are regulatory restrictions for pension/insurance/provident funds for participation in private limited companies'

---

[20] Anupam Rastogi and Vivek Rao. 2011. *Product Innovations for Financing Infrastructure: A Study of India's Debt Markets.*

[21] Ministry of Finance, Government of India. 2020. *Report of the Sub-group on Capital Markets for Financing of National Infrastructure Pipeline.*

[22] IRDAI, *Annual Report 2019–20*, p. 212 (https://irdai.gov.in/document-detail?documentId=696019).

issuance, investment restrictions linked to net worth of issuer, caps, and so on, which makes it challenging for them to invest into infrastructure bonds. Regulatory restrictions on investment pattern mandates majority investment into AAA-rated papers, which makes it difficult for pension funds to invest into infrastructure projects which are typically lower rated, though in theory their investment threshold has been reduced to A-rated paper recently.

While greenfield projects and construction risk do not fit well with pension and insurance investments, there is usually a strong business case for such investments in the case of operating yield-generating infrastructure assets. Brownfield (operating) infrastructure is typically perceived as lower risk, with the potential capability to match the risk-reward and term profile sought by long-duration investors such as pension, insurance, and SWFs. This is the idea behind the brownfield asset monetization initiative being sought to be mainstreamed in India (see Chapter 6).

Foreign savings in Indian infrastructure
Foreign institutional investment
Investment by foreign portfolio investors (FPIs) grew sharply in India post fiscal 2014 (Figure 8.7). Investment by FPIs is largely driven by regulatory limits, besides macroeconomic stability, currency exchange rates, and global interest rates. Most FPI entities presently consist of overseas branches of banks or corporates investing for strategic purposes through the FPI route. From a tenor perspective, given the lack of hedges for longer tenors, investments are largely concentrated within one- to three-year tenor buckets.

Figure 8.8 shows that the share of listed Indian infrastructure companies in FII holdings has remained at about 4 per cent.

Other offshore investors
Offshore investors primarily invest in international bonds issued by Indian issuers via the external commercial borrowing (ECB) route. Given that the ECB route permits investors from Financial Action Task Force- or International Organization of Securities Commissions–compliant jurisdictions, this allows a wide set of investors to invest through this route. Investor classes range from asset/fund managers, insurance funds,

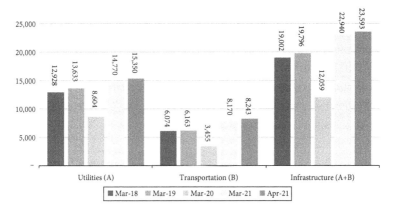

Figure 8.7 Foreign institutional investment(FII) in listed Indian infrastructure companies at the end of month, FY 2018–22 (US$ million)

Source: OECD, NIIF Research (https://www.oecd-ilibrary.org/sites/aaa8a6c2-en/index.html?ite mId=/content/component/aaa8a6c2-en#section-d1e2504).

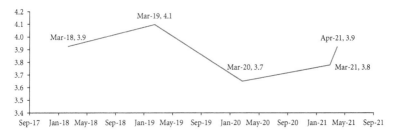

Figure 8.8 Share of listed Indian infrastructure companies in FII holdings (%)

Source: OECD, NIIF Research (https://www.oecd-ilibrary.org/sites/aaa8a6c2-en/index.html?ite mId=/content/component/aaa8a6c2-en#section-d1e2504).

pension funds, SWFs, and private banks. In accordance with ECB guidelines, tenor preference is generally three or five years. For longer tenor investments, issuers are generally restricted by the all-in-pricing cap which only allows high-quality issuers to access the markets for long tenors. Long-tenor issuances are generally anchored by insurance funds and pension funds, given their liability profiles.

From the above analysis, it is clear that there are constraints in using foreign savings for Indian infrastructure. In the case of FPIs, there is a challenge that investors face when it comes to hedging for longer tenors, which is why investments from FPIs are typically restricted to one- to three-year tenor buckets. Offshore investors are constrained by the all-in pricing cap (currently Libor+450 bps), under the extant ECB guidelines, and issuers are not able to access longer-tenor financing within the applicable price cap. Further, given that infrastructure projects generally generate revenues in domestic currency, issuers face challenges in booking hedges for longer tenors.

General low level of institutional investment into infrastructure

The World Bank finds that the current level of institutional investor activity in new infrastructure deals is abysmally low and constitutes a mere 0.7 per cent of total infrastructure investment in EMDEs in the period 2011–2017.[23] There are several risks and barriers to institutional investment in infrastructure. Although, on the demand side there is a need for more resources to finance infrastructure and on the supply side institutional investors are looking for steady, long-term returns, matching the two has been a challenge, resulting in an extremely low share of institutional investment in EMDE infrastructure.

The reasons for the mismatch include the lack of a significant pipeline of well-prepared and well-structured infrastructure projects in EMDEs, differing mandates and lower risk appetite of institutional investors, lower yields compared to risks associated with infrastructure projects, foreign-exchange risk, and limited resources to set up the specialized infrastructure teams that are essential to assess and track investments in EMDEs. The high-risk perception for infrastructure projects stems from the experience of implementation delays, cost overruns, poor cost recovery, and issues faced in the stabilization of these projects. Institutional investors are credit-risk averse and restricted by regulations and/or internal investment policies from investing in securities rated below the AA category. They are also taken aback by political sensitivity and corruption often associated with infrastructure projects. User charges in many infrastructure sectors are way below

---

[23] World Bank. 2017. *Contribution of Institutional Investors to Private Investment in Infrastructure.*

cost-recovery levels (e.g. water, power, metro trains, railways). For the long-run sustainability of these assets and for institutional investors to show investment interest, there would be a need to raise user charges to cost-recovery levels, which would subject any such move to political sensitivity, and possible failure. Similarly, since infrastructure projects involve large investments (e.g., a 4 GW thermal power project may cost about US$4 billion; the cost estimate of the Mumbai-Ahmedabad High Speed Rail Project is about US$16 billion), they suffer from charges of corruption in their procurement, which is an interest dampener for institutional investors.

However, despite these challenges, the CPPIB is a major investor having investments in India totalling C$19.6 billion across all asset classes (as of 31 December 2021), including real estate, infrastructure, public and private equities, funds, and credit. This formed 3.6 per cent of CPPIB's total worldwide assets.

Among CPPIB's key holdings in the infrastructure space in India are:

- Investment of a combined US$668 million for an approximately 20 per cent stake in ReNew Power Ventures Pvt. Ltd., one of India's leading clean energy companies with about 10.3 GW of capacity diversified across wind, utility-scale solar and rooftop solar-power-producing assets.
- In May 2018, L&T Infrastructure Development Projects Limited (IDPL) launched the first private infrastructure investment trust in India: IndInfravit Trust, with an initial portfolio of five operating toll roads which has grown over time. CPPIB now has a stake of 43.8 per cent in L&T IDPL.
- CPPIB has acquired 25 per cent of the units in National Highways Infra Trust, an infrastructure investment trust sponsored by the National Highways Authority of India (NHAI), for Rs.1,503 crore (C$257 million). The trust acquires brownfield toll roads from NHAI, the government agency responsible for developing, maintaining, and managing national highways.[24]

---

[24] Canada-India Business Council. 2022. Why India? Unlocking Canada's opportunity in the Indo-Pacific (https://canada-indiabusiness.com/why-india).

While Canadian pension funds (Caisse de dépôt et placement du Québec (CDPQ) has also invested C\$8 billion in India across infrastructure, real estate, fixed income, and private equity) have invested in Indian infrastructure, the same has not been the case with those of the United States, which has a much larger pool of pension-fund resources to be deployed in projects which provide steady returns over the long term. The challenge is to attract other such institutional investors (like CPPIB) to Indian infrastructure.[25] A wide-ranging effort would have to be made to attract more institutional investment into infrastructure.

How Can Institutional Investment in Infrastructure Be Improved?

As already stated, the cross-border institutional investment in infrastructure that does take place is primarily targeted at assets located in developed markets. Institutional investors have moved into emerging markets since the 1990s, mostly by buying securities of large, listed companies (such as financial, utilities, or telecom companies) or government bonds. More investors are now gaining exposure to EMDEs via private equity/ debt or infrastructure funds as these generally offer higher returns and further portfolio diversification opportunities. Some large investors are undertaking direct investments, for example, in renewable energy. This highlights the critical role of domestic policy frameworks and an investment-grade enabling environment to attract and scale up institutional investment in EMDEs like India.

General interventions

- *Investment environment*: Good governance in a reasonably stable legal and political environment is paramount. The less developed a country, the more public institutions international—must work

---

[25] Kumar V. Pratap, and Mira Sethi. 2019. *Infrastructure Financing in India—Trends, Challenges, and Way Forward.*

to provide confidence to institutional investors to invest in that country.

- *Pipeline of investable assets*: Governments need to work out a pipeline of assets that are suitable for private-sector investors. Clarity on the projects and their parameters will facilitate financing and investing. In this context, India's first NIP (details in Chapter 1) and the National Monetization Pipeline (launched in India in August 2021, details in Chapter 6), with particulars on shovel-ready infrastructure projects are useful.

- *Co-investing with multilateral development banks (MDBs)*: MDBs have useful convening power and many international investors find co-investing alongside MDBs a good way of entry into 'more difficult' countries and riskier, less liquid assets. This provides comfort in terms of risk mitigation, local knowledge, political clout, and experience of investing in these countries.

- *Co-investment vehicles*: Equity co-investment vehicles for riskier countries and sectors are still underdeveloped. Both commercial and blended finance[26] vehicles (e.g. with certain limited CE or insurance) targeting investors of different risk appetites could help. Blended finance has grown in the past decade. In 2021 it represented an aggregate financing of over US$160 billion, with annual capital flows averaging approximately US$9 billion since 2015. Blended finance has achieved notable success in Sub-Saharan Africa, attracting 61 per cent of global concessional financing in 2020, most of which went into supporting climate-smart agribusiness and off-grid renewable energy investments.[27] Between 2010 and 2020, IFC deployed US$1.6 billion of concessional donor funds to support 266 projects in over fifty countries, leveraging US$5.8 billion in IFC financing and more than US$6.8 billion from private sources.

---

[26] 'Blended finance'—the use of public or philanthropic finance alongside commercial finance to reduce the cost of capital and thereby increase private-sector investment in impactful investments and development.

[27] Emelly Mutambatsere and Maud de Vautibault. 2022. Blended Finance Can Catalyze Renewable Energy Investments in Low-income Countries (https://blogs.worldbank.org/ppps/blended-finance-can-catalyze-renewable-energy-investments-low-income-countries?CID=WBW_AL_BlogNotification_EN_EXT).

- *Domestic investors*: As their asset base grows, domestic investors in EMDEs can play an increasing role not only in domestic and regional investments, and also help in crowding-in international investors. This source of capital avoids foreign-exchange exposure and risks. It can help develop domestic capital markets and the financial sector and thus contribute to economic growth and development. Indian domestic institutional investors are not active in financing infrastructure and this needs to change.
- *Sustainability and impact investing*: Responsible investor boards are keen to raise their ESG and SDG profiles, opening a new door. Such demand could be increasingly satisfied in EMDEs as green and social bonds gain momentum. Tentative steps are also being taken towards investing in low-income countries via impact funds, for example in water, housing, and other community projects.

However, expectations need to be realistic about the potential of institutional investors, particularly in less-developed countries. Policymakers, DFIs, and investors should not just focus on a few headline policy vehicles. They need to better utilize the full spectrum of investment routes: impact, blended, and especially commercial finance. Even small re-allocations of capital can have a big impact on the ground.[28] The following specific interventions would also help.

Specific interventions

- *Financial engineering, risk allocation and mitigation*: Infrastructure development is characterized by many risks which can materialize at different stages of a project's life cycle. These risks include construction, completion, currency, revenue stability, environmental, and those arising out of demand fluctuations. Other risks arise as a result of a project's jurisdiction, including risks stemming from

---

[28] Georg Inderst. 12 May 2021. Institutional Investors: Time to Get Involved in Development and Blended Finance (https://blogs.worldbank.org/ppps/institutional-investors-time-get-invol ved-development-and-blended-finance?CID=WBW_AL_BlogNotification_EN_EXT).

the macroeconomic, political, and regulatory environment. The viability of infrastructure as an asset class requires that these risks are addressed, mitigated, and allocated to relevant stakeholders. Addressing foreign-exchange risks of infrastructure projects is of particular importance as infrastructure revenues are generally denominated in local currency, creating mismatches when foreign equity and debt are used in project financing. Adequate diversification of financial instruments and use of CEs are examples of tools that can better allocate the risks of a project and thereby have a catalysing effect on investment. Mechanisms such as blended finance can also provide a base to effectively crowd-in private funding, lower the cost of capital, and enhance risk mitigation. One of the most compelling aspects of blended finance is that it uses relatively small amounts of donor funding to rebalance a project's risk profile. With this small infusion of concessional funding, pioneering investments become attractive to private investors.

Institutional investors prefer liquid assets. This highlights the potential of securitized structures such as InvITs and REITs to scale up real-economy infrastructure investments. Asset managers have the largest holdings of green infrastructure assets owing to their investments in REITs and YieldCos. Another category that might receive increased investor attention is social infrastructure. REITs can be especially useful to scale up capital allocation towards health-care and education assets. There are ways to improve the financing ecosystem for water in India, which has 18 per cent of the global population but which ranks a dismal *120th on the Water Quality Index.* India is on track for a 50 per cent shortfall in its water supply by 2030, lending urgency to improving the financing of the sector. Reasonable cost recovery through water tariffs, and the use of blended and pooled finance may help. Additionally, infrastructure spending will form an essential pillar in government efforts around the world to fuel economic activity post Covid-19. This will add to the momentum in the private sector and create an opportunity to build green infrastructure that can avoid long-term emission lock-in and ensure public health and well-being.

- *Regulatory frameworks and capital markets*: Appropriate and effective legal, regulatory, tax, governance, and accounting frameworks play a role in attracting investment in infrastructure. It is important that these frameworks ensure well-functioning markets for infrastructure financing, protect investors, and ensure efficiency, transparency, stability, promote integrity and anti-corruption, while minimizing unnecessary regulatory burden.

Insurance Regulatory and Development Authority (IRDA) regulations mandate life insurance companies to invest a minimum of 15 per cent of controlled funds in the infrastructure and social sectors. For non-life and/or general insurance companies this figure is 10 per cent. Life insurance companies which are dominated by public life insurance companies, such as Life Insurance Corporation of India (LIC), have not been able to reach this limit, and most of their investments in the infrastructure sector have been in infrastructure created by the public sector. This is because of a high degree of risk aversion[29] and related regulatory guidelines.

- *Reducing project related risks by pooling structures*: A viable and cost-efficient way to address project-related risk is to diversify the risk across multiple projects by creating pooling structures which help in bridging cash deficit from one project with surplus from other projects in the pool. A few options that have worked well in India are InvITs (debt and equity units; e.g. around sixty HAM projects are near completion,[30] and thus will have a low-risk operational cash flow structure. This makes them suitable for securitization or monetization through InvITs) and the creation of restricted groups (RGs) in fund-raising done through offshore bonds, particularly in the case of renewable projects. Under this structure, there is a co-obligor structure, wherein typically a group of SPVs jointly and severally guarantee the payment of principal and interest on the instrument. To facilitate this, the Indian Companies Act (2013) should (a) recognize co-obligor issuance structure and (b) simplify inter-company

---

[29] Anupam Rastogi and Vivek Rao. 2011. *Product Innovations for Financing Infrastructure: A Study of India's Debt Markets*.

[30] CRISIL. 2021. *Yearbook on the Indian Debt Market* (https://www.crisil.com/en/home/our-analysis/reports/2021/02/crisil-yearbook-on-the-indian-debt-market-2021.html).

lending rules (Section 185 and 186) for infrastructure SPV assets which aids in moving cashflows across RG entities. Taxation should be moved to the pool level instead of SPV level to avoid any claims on the entity with surplus cash flows transferring funds for meeting deficit entities' obligations.

Securitization by the special purpose vehicle (SPV) route allows the sale of a pool of loans to a 'bankruptcy remote' SPV in return for an immediate cash payment and enables repackaging and selling the security to third-party investors by issuance of tradable debt securities. The RBI guidelines require originating banks to securitize loans only after these have been held by them for a minimum period in their books, to ensure that the project implementation risk is not passed on to the investors, and a minimum recovery performance is demonstrated. Changes should be made to the Indian Stamp Act to implement lower and uniform rates of stamp duty across states for assignment of debt instruments, as has been done for debentures, to make it cost effective.

- *CE*: The typical credit rating of a PPP non-recourse project funded on a project finance basis is BBB, which needs to be enhanced to AA level or so, which is the minimum threshold for funding by some of the institutional investors like pension and insurance funds. A well-capitalized CE agency through full or partial guarantees can enhance credit quality of project debt, improving the bankability of projects, enabling them to raise funds from institutional investors (see Chapter 7 and Box 8.2).
- *Refinancing/take-out guarantee*: For addressing issues on the availability of long-term financing beyond ten years, government guarantee on stub portions which will need to be refinanced at the end of the bond tenor can be explored. This will give confidence to investors to run refinancing risk beyond say ten/twelve years.
- *Modifications to domestic rating criteria*: To better capture the unique risk characteristics of the infrastructure sector and provide a rating output that would make infrastructure assets attractive to a wider set of investors, Indian domestic rating agencies have been advocating a scale incorporating the benefits of asset recovery analysis (Loss Given Default analysis) into the conventional rating scale based

---

Box 8.2 How guarantees can accelerate the mobilization of sustainable finance

---

Guarantco (a private infrastructure development group company) was established in 2005 to enable long-term financing of infrastructure in local currency in low-income countries across Asia and Africa. This is achieved primarily through appropriately structured guarantees like partial risk and partial credit guarantees, first-loss guarantees, and tenor extension guarantees among others, thus transferring risks.

In 2018, Sindicatum Renewables Energy Co. Pte. Ltd, a Singapore based developer issued US$40 million Indian rupee synthetic green bonds (issued and settled in US$). The proceeds were to be used to finance renewable energy projects in India. Guarantco provided for 100 per cent of principal and interest through unconditional and irrevocable guarantee. This provided a strong rating to the bond issued—A1 by Moody's and AA—by Fitch, which in turn attracted institutional investors successfully (GuarantCo—Guarantees for Development. 2021. *Who We Are and What Do We Do* (https://guarantco.com/).

---

on Probability of Default (based on factors that affect the ability of the issuer to meet debt obligations in a timely manner, which are liquidity and cash flow, and do not factor in post-default recovery prospects). This would make the Expected Loss scale more suitable for rating infrastructure projects, which is arrived at by multiplying the Probability of Default (the conventional scale) by Loss Given Default. Internationally this is done by providing notch-ups to issue rating for high recovery prospects (or low Loss Given Default) to arrive at an issue rating that is higher than the issuer rating (dealt with at length in Chapter 12).

- *Demand-side measures*: SEBI has notified the SEBI (Infrastructure Investment Trusts) Regulations, 2014 on 26 September 2014, providing for registration and regulation of InvITs in India. However, given the ambitious NIP capex targets and ever-evolving financial structures and regulations, there is also a strong need to bring in some regulatory interventions so as to enable increased investment in InvITs (see Chapter 6 for more details on InvITs).

o *Insurance funds, global and domestic, including ESIC and LIC*: Insurance funds should be permitted to participate in debt issuances of InvITs, securitization papers, and so on, and necessary amendments should be made to Insurance Regulatory and Development Authority (Investment) Regulations, 2000.

o *Pension funds, global and domestic, including EPFO and NPS*: Permitting participation in InvITs/securitization papers would help boost interest from this investor segment and changes should accordingly be made to the Pension Fund Regulatory and Development Authority Act. EPFO is mandated to invest in AAA rated papers which needs to be relaxed (EPFO has recently been permitted to invest in government-sponsored InvITs). There are other limits for investing by pension and insurance funds, partly because of their fiduciary duty to their clients. However, some relaxation in allowing them to invest in up to EL2-rated instruments (on the Expected Loss scale) as long as these instruments have investment grade rating on the Probability of Default scale may help infrastructure financing without compromising on their fiduciary duties.

o *SWFs*: The Indian markets have seen participation from SWFs primarily through the external commercial borrowings (ECB) route. To increase participation from this segment, it would be important to further liberalize the ECB and Foreign Portfolio Investment (FPI) guidelines for investment into the infrastructure sector like permitting InvITs as Eligible Borrower under ECB guidelines and allowing FPIs to participate in debt units of InvITs (announced in the Budget 2021/22), flexibility from all-in-cost perspective (currently capped at LIBOR + 450 bps) along with a specific swap window from RBI (for tenor in excess of ten years), allowing long tenor financing access with fixed rupee cost, permitting different asset-specific financing entities to target specific liquidity pools, given that investor pools are targeted specifically towards ESG, the renewable sector, the rural development sector, and so on. This will help in accessing new pools of liquidity from the ESG investor and impact investor base. Issuance in the form of green bonds (already prevalent in substantive amounts in India) and social bonds can be explored (depending on the sector being financed) for accessing a wider and deeper global investor base. ESG finance may come cheaper as global funds would be interested in investing in environmentally and socially responsible projects backed by a sound corporate governance framework.

- *Repo window with RBI*: Currently, investors who invest in long-term paper do not have ample secondary market liquidity to exit in case of liquidity concerns/redemption pressures. A long-term repo window for 50–70 per cent of the exposure issue size can, therefore, be explored for investors in pooled financing structures.
- *Encouraging municipal bond markets*: The finances of ULBs in India are very weak. Cross-country comparison shows that total own revenues of ULBs is a mere 1 per cent of GDP in India as compared to 5 per cent in Brazil and 4.5 per cent in Poland. Property taxes and user charges are the main sources of revenue for ULBs, but are narrow, inflexible, and lack buoyancy (property tax to GDP ratio is 0.15 per cent in India compared to 4.1 per cent in the United Kingdom, 4 per cent in Canada, 3 per cent in the United States, 1.1 per cent in Germany, and 0.3 per cent in Mexico). In addition, there are low/no charges for some municipal services. This leads to own revenue sources not keeping pace with the rising cost of the provision of services making them financially unsustainable, suffering from low credit worthiness, and highly dependent on grants from state and central government. A third of all municipal corporations were facing severe financial stress in 2017/18 as measured by fiscal balance, fiscal autonomy, and committed expenditures. This, in turn, is attributed to slow governance reforms, inadequate accounting standards and low institutional capabilities. Revenues of ULBs need to be improved and a partial CE mechanism needs to be put in place to help develop the Indian municipal bond market, in which institutional investors can also participate. What is encouraging is that 469 out of 485 AMRUT (Atal Mission for Rejuvenation and Urban Transformation) ULBs have received a credit rating, with 163 having investment grade rating. Eight AMRUT cities have already raised Rs.3,390 crore by issuance of municipal bonds in the last three years (backed by

interest subvention by the Ministry of Housing and Urban Affairs).
Pooled bond issuances may also help.

- *Posing most infrastructure projects as ESG-compliant projects*: Renewable energy including solar and wind projects, mass transit like metro-rail projects, four- and six-lane road projects, dedicated freight corridor projects, water and sewerage projects can all be posed as environmentally benign projects, and as long as they comply with social and governance requirements, they can be attractive to institutional investors.
- *Develop hedging instruments which are long tenor, low cost, and flexible*: Since infrastructure companies borrow long term and want capital from institutional investors, lack of adequate hedging instruments and shallow financial markets result not only in a high cost of borrowing due to currency risks, but also a lack of demand for long tenor securities. This results in FPI investments restricted to one–three-year tenor, thus limiting their utility for infrastructure projects. Box 8.3 provides a snapshot of a currency hedging initiative that can be help India too.

Some measures announced in the Budget 2021/22 to ease the flow of institutional capital to infrastructure (in addition to those already mentioned) are as follows:

- Ministry of Finance has revised the investment pattern allowing the non-government provident funds, superannuation, and gratuity funds to invest in Category I and II Alternate Investment Funds (AIFs) registered with SEBI. Further, IRDAI vide circular dated 5 April 2021 has allowed investment by domestic insurance companies into the FoF (of NIIF), which complies with section 27E of the Insurance Act.
- National Bank for Financing Infrastructure and Development (NaBFID):[31] Following an announcement in the Budget, the NaBFID has been set up. NaBFID would be developed as the

---

[31] PRS Legislative Research. 2021. *The National Bank for Financing Infrastructure and Development (NaBFID) Bill*, 2021 (https://prsindia.org/billtrack/the-national-bank-for-financing-infrastructure-and-development-bill-2021).

Box 8.3 The Currency Exchange Fund (TCX)

The Currency Exchange Fund (TCX) was established in 2007 by a group of donors, microfinance investment vehicles, and DFIs to provide long-tenor cross-country currency hedging products. Currently there are twenty-two investors including International Finance Corporation, German KfW, French Development Agency (AFD), EBRD, and others participating in this initiative. TCX provides two types of products—Forward Contracts and Cross-Country Swaps. By reducing exchange-rate risks, it helps local borrowers access long-term financing in local currency thus reducing the cost of borrowing for them. It manages its own risk via portfolio diversification. Currently it provides hedging in seventy currencies with tenor ranging from a minimum of seven years to thirty years. Thus, TCX helps de-risk development finance, supports the mobilization of private capital and deepens financial markets in local currencies in developing countries by repackaging currency risks into different baskets making it attractive to various investors. Up until 2020, TCX had de-risked US$985 million of external lending in emerging and frontier countries.

Source: TCX. 2021. *About the fund.* (https://www.tcxfund.com/)

---

principal development finance institution (DFI) for infrastructure financing in India. NaBFID has both financial as well as developmental objectives. Financial objectives are to directly or indirectly lend, invest, or attract investments for infrastructure projects located entirely or partly in India. Developmental objectives include facilitating the development of the market for bonds, loans, and derivatives for infrastructure financing. Functions of NaBFID include: (i) extending loans and advances for infrastructure projects, (ii) taking over or refinancing such existing loans, (iii) attracting investment from private-sector investors and institutional investors for infrastructure projects, (iv) organizing and facilitating foreign participation in infrastructure projects, (v) facilitating negotiations with various government authorities for dispute resolution in the field of infrastructure financing, and (vi) providing consultancy services in infrastructure financing (see Chapter 12 for a fuller discussion on DFI for India).

Conclusion

A number of reforms need to be carried out to mobilize institutional investment into infrastructure. The above recommendations, many of which have been actioned, are aimed at encouraging institutional investors to act in line with their investment horizon and risk-return objectives and facilitate the flow of capital into infrastructure. They help address regulatory and institutional impediments to long-term investment by institutional investors into infrastructure. These recommendations are also in accordance with the G20/OECD roadmap to 'developing infrastructure as an asset class'.[32]

[32] OECD. 2018. *Roadmap to Infrastructure as an Asset Class* (https://www.oecd.org/g20/roadmap_to_infrastructure_as_an_asset_class_argentina_presidency_1_0.pdf).This Roadmap addresses common barriers to the emergence of infrastructure as an asset class, including the heterogeneous nature of infrastructure assets, the lack of a critical mass of bankable projects and insufficient data to track asset performance. The Roadmap is organized into three overarching pillars with the principal objectives of: i) improving project development; ii) improving the investment environment for infrastructure; and iii) promoting greater standardization.

9

Environmentally and Socially Responsible Infrastructure Finance

For sustainable infrastructure, projects have to be financially, economically, environmentally, and socially sustainable. While countries like India have traditionally been looking at financial and economic viability through metrics like the financial internal rate of return (FIRR), net present value (NPV), economic internal rate of return (EIRR), and so on, not much attention has been given to environmental and social sustainability. However, being responsible entities, and as multilateral financial institutions and institutional investors look at environmental and social sustainability also before committing investments, these concerns have to be on-boarded. This chapter looks at these issues, while also being cognizant of the fact that much of infrastructure is under-priced and any additional concerns that are incorporated would have financial viability implications.

The alignment of environmental principles with infrastructure investments and projects is necessary for sustainable development, as also their financing. Many financial institutions have voluntarily adhered to Equator Principles (EPs), Carbon Principles, and Climate Principles, thereby preventing them from financing projects that are not aligned with these principles. Green bonds are also being increasingly used for financing infrastructure projects. For India, green bonds would be the key to meeting the ambitious target of building 175GW of renewable energy (RE) capacity by 2022 and 450GW of RE capacity by 2030. The chapter explores the Equator, Carbon, and Climate Principles, as also the green bond, climate bond, and social bond avenues for financing infrastructure projects. By posing infrastructure finance in a broader setting, this chapter also connects to India's obligations for mitigating climate change (Paris Accord), which is expected to make India's infrastructure

Infrastructure Financing in India. Kumar V Pratap and Manshi Gupta, Oxford University Press.
© Kumar V Pratap and Manshi Gupta 2024. DOI: 10.1093/oso/9780198884934.003.0010

more sustainable, environmentally, socially, and financially. In addition, it discusses the future of coal-based power generation projects, given that India is abundant in this resource. In this context, the chapter discusses some Indian projects to illustrate the trade-off between growth and environment. In addition, the chapter discusses whether exploitation of RE (through the case study of Solar Energy Corporation of India Ltd.) is the silver bullet that side-steps the traditional trade-off between growth and environment to enable sustainable development.

> Human influence on the climate is now 'unequivocal': it is why the world is 1.1°C (2°F) hotter than it was in the late 19th century; it has moved jet streams, shrunk glaciers, stripped away Arctic sea ice, contributed to two decades of increased melting of the Greenland ice sheet, warmed the oceans and driven the past 50 years of sea-level rise.[1]
>
> *The Economist*, 9 August 2021, commenting on the latest Intergovernmental Panel on Climate Change (IPCC) Report

Climate change has emerged as the most important threat to mankind and there is an urgent need for action (honouring Paris Accord commitments, Net Zero emissions, etc.). The G20 has adopted the Principles for Quality Infrastructure Investment in 2019. One of the Principles exhorts the G20 members to integrate environmental considerations in infrastructure investments thus: both positive and negative impacts of infrastructure projects on ecosystems, biodiversity, climate, and weather and the use of resources should be internalized by incorporating these environmental considerations over the entire process of infrastructure investment, including by improving disclosure of environment-related information, and thereby enabling the use of green finance instruments. Infrastructure projects should align with national strategies and nationally determined contributions for those countries determined to implement them, and with transitioning to long-term low emissions strategies, while being mindful of country circumstances.[2]

---

[1] Global mean sea level rose at an average of 4.5mm per year over the period 2013–2021 as per the World Meteorological Organization's 'State of Climate' Report (2021). This is more than double the rate between 1993 and 2002 due to the accelerated loss of ice mass from the ice sheets. This has major implications for coastal dwellers and increases vulnerability to tropical cyclones.

[2] G20 Principles for Quality Infrastructure Investment.

Development of infrastructure usually has environmental implications like destruction of natural habitats of flora and fauna. A recent report[3] has estimated that infrastructure is responsible for 79 per cent of all greenhouse gas emissions and 88 per cent of all adaptation costs. This is apparent, for example, when coal blocks beneath virgin forests would have to be exploited for feeding a pit-head coal-based power plant, or when hydroelectric power is sought to be exploited by building a dam in densely forested areas. Issues like these are posed as a trade-off between environment and development in many developing countries, including India. One of the earliest contests between environment and development in India occurred in the case of Silent Valley Project in Kerala (Box 9.1).

However, the environmental impacts of projects can be mitigated by adequate pre-planning, as captured in the requirement for 'environmental impact assessment' (EIA), and taking corrective action accordingly (like compensatory afforestation for forest land 'diverted' for development projects, which is not, however, a perfect solution as virgin forests are replaced with plantations). In India, the concern for the environment, partly based on the Chipko and the Silent Valley movements, started in 1976–1977 when the Planning Commission asked the Department of Science and Technology to examine the river-valley projects from an environmental angle. The federal Department of Environment came into being in 1980, which was turned into the Ministry of Environment and Forests in 1985 (and Ministry of Environment, Forest, and Climate Change in 2014). The Seventh Five-Year Plan (1985–1990) made the requirement widespread, stating that 'the Department of Environment would oversee approval of projects from the environmental angle.' The outlay for environment and ecology was substantially increased from Rs.40 crore in the Sixth Five Year Plan to Rs. 428 crore in the Seventh Five Year Plan. In January 1994, the federal Ministry of Environment and Forests (MoEF), Government of India, under the Environmental (Protection) Act 1986, promulgated an EIA notification making environmental clearance (EC) mandatory for expansion or modernization of any activity or for setting up new projects listed in Schedule 1 of the notification. The theme of the

---

[3] UN Office for Project Services (UNOPS), UN Environment Programme (UNEP) and University of Oxford. 2021. *Infrastructure for Climate Action* (https://www.unep.org/news-and-stories/press-release/new-report-reveals-how-infrastructure-defines-our-climate).

Box 9.1 Silent Valley project in Kerala

From colonial times, India has witnessed several environmental calamities in the form of forest depletion, unbridled resource exploitation, and hydroelectric dam controversies. Environmental movements in India have been a response to these challenges. After independence, in its quest for rapid economic growth, India witnessed an accelerated trade-off between growth and the natural environment.

Environmentalism as a movement started in India in the 1970s and blossomed with the *Chipko* movement (grassroots movement in the present-day Uttarakhand state of India where forests became the focal point of both environment and livelihood issues). Most of these movements followed the Gandhian model of decentralized democracy and village self-rule, or *Swaraj*, and relied on the Gandhian values of careful management of resources and ecological prudence. At the same time, some movements like the Silent Valley movement in Kerala synthesize both Marxian and Gandhian ideologies. The emergence of environmental movements across the country paved the way for a new development paradigm called 'sustainable development'.[a]

Silent Valley Project

The Silent Valley movement involved protest against the state to protect a pristine evergreen rainforest in Kerala, in south India. Silent Valley was the continuation of a debate about development, which had already started in India with the Chipko movement. It led to the transformation of the Marxist notion of nature as a 'resource base' to nature as a 'treasure' to be protected.

Silent Valley is in Palakkad district of Kerala. It has one of India's last substantial stretches of tropical evergreen forests. The Silent Valley project envisaged the construction of a dam across Kunthipuzha, a tributary of Bharathappuzha, flowing through the Silent Valley to produce 60MW of electric power and to facilitate irrigation of 10,000 hectare of land in Palghat district. It would have submerged 830 hectares of rich, tropical, Silent Valley rainforest.

In 1951, the Kerala state government undertook the first survey for the hydroelectric project, and in 1973 the Indian Planning

Commission approved the dam project. In 1976, the National Committee on Planning and Coordination (NCEPC) recommended a stay order to study its environmental impact. Kerala Natural History Society and Bombay Natural History Society demanded the cessation of the project in 1978. Focusing attention on the threat to the endangered lion-tailed macaque, the International Union for Conservation of Nature (IUCN)[b] passed a resolution to preserve the Silent Valley at its fourteenth General Assembly held at Ashkabad in the USSR in September 1978. The central and state governments had appointed several committees on the subject but those led by M. S. Swaminathan and M. G. K. Menon strongly opposed the project because of its environmental impact. The supporters of the dam argued that those who opposed the power project were against development and the national interest. The debate went on for years and at last in 1983, the then prime minister, Indira Gandhi, advised the state to abandon the project and declared Silent Valley a National Park.

Analysts have found that the project was neither unavoidable nor the best immediate solution.[c] The stated economic benefits of the project were also disputed. Kerala State Electricity Board (KSEB) argued that the Malabar area was short of electricity. The average per capita consumption in the four districts of Malabar was just 33 units. But this could not just be attributed to energy shortage as Kerala exported 40 per cent of its energy production to neighbouring states. Moreover, the maximum potential per capita hydro-energy availability was only about 300 units, not sufficient to meet the energy demand–supply gap expected in the future. This made tapping of other sources of energy inevitable. Regarding irrigation, lift irrigation was argued to be more reliable, regulatable, and with a lower capital investment per hectare.

The Silent Valley movement in Kerala, a people's movement, saved a pristine moist evergreen forest in Kerala's Palakkad district from being destroyed for a hydroelectric project. Although the campaign did not have any centralized planning, it was highly effective. This movement brought the notion of ecological Marxism[d] to the forefront as Marxists consider capitalism to be the major factor in the degradation of the environment.

[a]The United Nations Commission on Environment and Development defines sustainable development as follows: 'Sustainable development is the development that meets the

needs of the present without compromising the ability of future generations to meet their own needs' (World Commission on Economic Development (WCED) 1987: 43).

[b]Warrieron S.Gopikrishna. 2018. Silent Valley: A Controversy That Focused Global Attention on a Rainforest 40 Years Ago. (https://vikalpsangam.org/article/silent-valley/)

[c]M. P. Parameswaran.1979. Significance of Silent Valley. *Economic and Political Weekly*, 14(27):1117–19 (https://www.jstor.org/stable/4367757?read-now=1&refreqid=excelsior% 3Ab71944efafa8baee999d8c1a54c5da96&seq=1)

[d]A. S. Sasikala.2014. *Gandhi and Ecological Marxists: The Silent Valley Movement.* (http://www.satyagrahafoundation.org/gandhi-and-ecological-marxists-the-silent-valley-movement/)

Twelfth Five Year Plan (2012–2017) was 'faster, more inclusive, and sustainable growth'.

The 1994 EIA notification was replaced with a modified draft in 2006. The EIA 2006 divided the projects into three categories: category A projects are appraised at national level by the Impact Assessment Agency and the Expert Appraisal Committee, while category B projects are appraised at the state level. Category A projects require mandatory EC, while category B projects are further subdivided into B1 and B2 categories after screening. Category B1 projects require mandatory EIA while those in category B2 do not.

The government of India has now come up with draft EIA, 2020 Notification. The new notification is being brought in to make the process more transparent and expedient by implementation of an online system, further delegation, rationalization and standardization of the processes. The draft EIA, 2020, removes several activities from the purview of public consultation. A number of projects have been included under the B2 category, expressly exempted from the requirement of an EIA, including offshore and onshore oil, gas, and shale exploration; hydroelectric projects up to 25MW; inland waterway projects; expansion or widening of highways between 25 km and 100 km with defined parameters; aerial ropeways in ecologically sensitive areas; and so on.

Earlier, the projects were first screened by an Expert Appraisal Committee and then categorized as B2. However now, it is proposed that the activities listed in the schedule are automatically exempted. The draft notification also gives central government the power to categorize projects as 'strategic'. The draft notification states that no information related to such projects shall be placed in the public domain. In the new proposed scheme, coal and non-coal mineral prospecting and solar photovoltaic (PV) projects do not need prior EC. The draft also cuts the notice period for a public hearing from thirty days to twenty days. A new provision for postfacto EC of projects executed without prior clearance is also provided in the draft. The projects in violation of environmental regulations can be given postfacto approval with conditions, including remediation of ecological damage. The draft also liberalizes the norms for project modernization and expansion—only those above 25 per cent expansion will require an EIA, and only those above 50 per cent will require public consultation or public hearings. If the new draft kicks in, the project proponents will need to submit only one annual report on compliance with conditions, compared to the existing two.

While the above developments show that in the trade-off between environment and development, the country has opted to accord primacy to development, there have been other developments that show that the country is steadfast in its pursuit of sustainable development. One of the major pillars of sustainable development is the development of RE in India, which, by providing sustainable energy for development side-steps the traditional trade-off between environment and development.

Renewable Energy Development in India

As per the Harmonized Master List of Infrastructure of the Government of India (Box 1.3, Chapter 1), RE is included under the 'electricity generation' sub-sector in 'infrastructure'. As per India's Nationally Determined Contributions (NDCs), as part of the Paris Accord voluntary obligations, India has pledged reduction in the emission intensity of its GDP by 33 to 35 per cent by 2030 from 2005 levels, and 40 per cent cumulative electric power installed capacity from non-fossil-fuel-based energy resources by 2030. These commitments have been upscaled in the 2021 Glasgow Summit declarations—reduction in emission intensity of GDP by 45 per cent (as against 33 to 35 per cent earlier) by 2030 from 2005 levels, and 50 per cent of cumulative electric power installed capacity (from 40 per cent earlier) from non-fossil fuel sources by 2030. This would obviously mean more renewables in the energy mix, pursuant to which the government has targeted a RE capacity of 175 GW by 2022, which includes 100 GW from solar, 60 GW from wind, 10 GW from biomass, and 5 GW from small hydro. The target for non-fossil-fuel-based energy has been scaled up to 450GW (which has further been increased to 500 GW) RE installed capacity by 2030. India is well on its path to achieving the NDCs by 2030.

The government has taken several measures to increase production from RE sources in the country: permitting foreign direct investment (FDI) up to 100 per cent under the automatic route in the RE sector; waiver of Inter-State Transmission System (ISTS) charges for inter-state sale of solar and wind power for projects to be commissioned by 30 June 2023; fiscal incentives such as accelerated depreciation, goods and services tax (GST) at lower rates, concessional custom duty, and so on; setting up of ultra-mega RE parks providing land and transmission on a plug-and-play basis; schemes such as Pradhan Mantri Kisan Urja Suraksha evam Utthaan Mahabhiyan (PM-KUSUM), Solar Rooftop Phase II, 12,000MW CPSU Scheme Phase II, and so on; laying of new transmission lines and creating new sub-station capacity under the Green Energy Corridor Scheme (central and state transmission utilities are mandated to build a 'green corridor' to evacuate RE-based electricity, including from solar energy generators); notification of standards for deployment of solar PV system/devices; setting up of a project development cell for attracting and facilitating investments; system operators mandated to dispatch the electricity generated by solar plants as 'must-run' plants, irrespective of the tariff quoted as the social marginal cost of such generation is zero; and the issue of standard bidding guidelines for tariff-based competitive bidding process for procurement of power from grid-connected solar PV and wind projects. The government has also mandated that power shall be dispatched against a letter of credit or advance payment to ensure timely payment by distribution licensees to RE generators.[4]

Globally, India stands fourth in terms of renewable power, with a cumulative RE capacity of 100 GW (excluding large hydro) up to August 2021, which includes 45.20 GW from solar (fifth largest in the world), 39.60 GW from wind (fourth), 10.31 GW from biomass, and 4.75 GW from small hydro power. If we include large hydro which is also RE, the total installed RE capacity as of August 2021 becomes 146 GW.

---

[4] Lok Sabha Unstarred Question No. 1786 answered on 11 February 2021.

In this framework, the thrust towards solar energy is also a way in which the energy demands for development are satisfied in an environmentally benign way. Solar energy has tremendous benefits over conventional energy as it is clean and renewable energy, reduces greenhouse gas emissions (than business-as-usual scenarios), reduces oil imports, saves foreign exchange, avoids fossil-fuel dependence, is now cheaper than conventional energy, and helps in achieving energy security for the country. The distribution companies (DISCOMs) procured RE earlier because of RPOs and now, increasingly because of its cost effectiveness. We look at the case study of Solar Energy Corporation of India Ltd. (SECI) (see Box 9.2), a central public-sector undertaking, which is providing a boost to the development of solar energy in the country.

There are ways in which environmental concerns are incorporated in ventures. One is through regulations and we have seen how EIA is mandatory for many activities. While EIA incorporates environmental concerns through the regulatory structure, the thrust nowadays is to augment financing of environmentally and socially responsible infrastructure projects. Thus, many of the environmental, social, and governance (ESG)[5] features adopted by companies make them responsible corporate citizens, while also augmenting and diversifying their sources of financing.

Infrastructure Financing and ESG Concerns

The term ESG dates back to 2004. The idea is that investors should evaluate firms based not just on their commercial performance but also on their environmental and social record and their governance, typically using numerical scores.[6] As environmental concerns become

---

[5] ESG investing is an approach that seeks to incorporate environmental, social, and governance factors into asset allocation and risk decisions, in order to generate sustainable, long-term financial returns. For example, the FT Lexicon explains: 'ESG (environmental, social and governance) is a generic term used in capital markets and used by investors to evaluate corporate behaviour and to determine the future financial performance of companies. ESG factors are a subset of non-financial performance indicators which include sustainable, ethical and corporate governance issues such as managing the company's carbon footprint and ensuring there are systems in place to ensure accountability' (OECD. 2021. *The Application of ESG Considerations in Infrastructure Investment in the Asia-Pacific*)

[6] *The Economist*. 29 July 2022. Three Letters That Won't Save the Planet.

Box 9.2 Solar Energy Corporation of India Ltd.

SECI, a central public-sector undertaking (CPSU) under the administrative control of the Ministry of New and Renewable Energy (MNRE), was set up on 20 September 2011 to facilitate the implementation of Jawaharlal Nehru National Solar Mission (JNNSM) and the achievement of targets set therein. It is the only CPSU dedicated to the solar energy sector. Its vision is to build 'Green India' through harnessing abundant solar radiation and to achieve energy security for the country. Its mission is to become the leader in the development of large-scale solar installations, solar plants, and solar parks and to promote and commercialize the use of solar energy to reach the remotest corners of India and to become the leader in exploring new technologies and their deployment to harness solar energy. The mandate of the company has been broadened recently to cover the entire RE sector.

SECI, being the implementing agency of MNRE, has been assisting MNRE in: (i) conducting several rounds of tenders for development of projects in Power Purchase Agreement (PPA) mode across India; (ii) procuring RE power at the central level, thereby reducing the off-taker risk of developers; (iii) implementation of government schemes and disbursal of central financial assistance (CFA) (viability gap funding, subsidies, etc.); (iv) setting up of own innovative and pilot projects for commercialization of RE; and (v) providing consultancy services to other government organizations and public-sector undertakings.[a]

Among its important functions, SECI acts as intermediate procurer, selecting developers through transparent bids for setting up RE generation projects, procuring power from them and selling it to DISCOMs as the government has prescribed RPO that mandates the electricity DISCOMs to purchase a minimum share of renewable power, including solar power. In this role, SECI floats tenders for selecting developers to set up solar projects (and solar–wind hybrid projects) on a pan-India/ state-specific basis. After developers have been selected on the basis of tariff-based competitive bidding, SECI signs twenty-five-year PPA for procurement of power from these projects, and the power procured is in turn sold to DISCOMs through twenty-five-year power supply agreements (PSAs). Implementation of tenders for wind power projects runs on similar lines. SECI's initiatives have brought rationalization of solar and wind power tariffs through a system of competitive procurement thus enabling inter-state transfer of RE power. It has cumulatively signed PPAs of 23.5 GW and was trading RE with twenty-five states and union territories in 2019/20.[b]

SECI, by functioning as intermediate procurer, has reduced off-taker risks as PPAs are signed by RE power producers with SECI and not financially weak, state DISCOMs. This brings certainty and stability in expected revenue streams of renewable power project developers. This financial assurance, in turn, reduces risks attached with any debt instrument floated by them to finance green projects thus attracting institutional investors. This creates a deeper and more liquid market for the climate/green bonds issued by project developers to finance their green projects and hence facilitates their cheaper and easier access to capital.

Implementation of projects by SECI

A solar park is a concentrated zone of solar power generation projects. The parks are characterized by well-developed infrastructure where the project development risk and the gestation period of projects is minimized. Infrastructure like transmission systems, water and road connectivity, and communication network, and so on are well developed in these parks. The concept of solar parks[c] has emerged as a powerful tool for the rapid development of solar power projects. Assured availability of land and transmission infrastructure are the major benefits of a solar park. The recent downward trend in solar tariffs may be attributed to factors like economies of scale, and assured availability of land and power evacuation systems in solar parks. The scheme for the development of solar parks and ultra-mega solar projects was introduced in December 2014 by MNRE, Government of India. The plan is to set up at least fifty solar parks, targeting around 40,000 MW of solar power installed capacity by 2021–22 through these parks. As against these targets, as of the end of 2020, forty-two solar parks with a cumulative capacity of 26,801 MW have been sanctioned in fifteen states. These solar parks are at different stages of development. The mode of selection of solar power park developers (SPPDs) is stated in Table 9.1.

Table 9.1 Solar Power Park Developers (SPPDs) scheme: mode of selection of power developers

SPPD modes	Selection criteria
Mode-1	The state-designated nodal agency or a state government PSU or a special purpose vehicle of the state government
Mode-2	A JV company of state-designated nodal agency and SECI
Mode-3	The state designates SECI as the nodal agency
Mode-4	Private entrepreneurs with equity participation from the state government or its agencies based on open and transparent bidding process
Mode-5	By central public-sector undertakings (CPSUs) like SECI, NTPC etc., in own or leased land
Mode-6	Private entrepreneurs without any CFA from MNRE
Mode-7	SECI acts as the SPPD for development of RE parks (solar or wind or hybrid or other RE parks)
Mode-8	Ultra-mega renewable energy power parks (UMREPP)

Source: Radheyshyam et al. (2019).

The SPPD is tasked with acquiring the land for the park, levelling it, and allocating the plots for individual projects. Apart from this, the SPPD is also entrusted with providing the necessary facilities like approved land for installation of solar projects and required permissions including change of land use and so on, road connectivity, telecommunication facilities, power evacuation facility, housing facility for basic manpower wherever possible, parking, warehouses, and so on. The entire cost of development including the cost involved in acquiring land forms the total cost of the project for which the SPPD may raise funds by selling/leasing out the plots to prospective project developers, imposing a one-time registration fee (per project or per MW), and/or put in some of its own equity and it can raise loans, depending on the availability of funds and requirements.

SECI is also engaged in setting up projects for generating renewable power through joint ventures (JVs) (Mode 2, Table 9.1). So far, the following JVs have been formed by SECI (Table 9.2). These JVs have been set up primarily for large scale solar parks and related infrastructure and as of the end of 2020, solar parks with a combined capacity of 7.6 GW have been developed through them.

Table 9.2 Joint ventures of SECI

Serial number	Name	Shareholding pattern
1	Andhra Pradesh Solar Power Corporation Private Limited	SECI (50%) and APGENCO (41%) and NREDCAP (9%)
2	Karnataka Solar Power Development Corporation Private Limited	SECI (50%) and KREDL (50%)
3	Lucknow Solar Power Development Corporation Limited	SECI (50%) and UPNEDA (50%)
4	Renewable Power Corporation of Kerala Limited	SECI (50%) and KSEB(50%)
5	Rewa Ultra Mega Solar Limited	SECI (50%) and MPUVNL(50%)
6	Himachal Renewables Limited	SECI (50%) and HPSEBL (50%)

Source: Solar Energy Corporation of India Ltd. 2020. *Annual Report 2019–20.*

Major challenges in solar power development include land acquisition and transmission infrastructure. To address these challenges, a new mode (Mode-8, Table 9.1), namely, ultra-mega renewable energy power parks (UMREPP) has been introduced in the solar park scheme to take up large projects. Mode-8 stipulates a SPPD to be any central or state public-sector undertaking (PSU), state government organization or any of their subsidiaries, or a JV. The state government or any state-designated government organization will provide necessary assistance to the SPPDs in identifying and acquiring land for setting up UMREPPs and also facilitate all required statutory clearances. For the various activities undertaken by state government or its designated organization they would be paid a facilitation charge of Rs.0.05 per unit of power generated from the projects in the UMREPPs for the entire PPA period of the project. Land will be made available on the condition that project development will be completed within two years, to be extended for another year only in rare cases. The SPPD will be entitled to compensation under CFA for the development and management of the UMREPP. Projects can be developed in a developer mode through tariff-based competitive bidding or through the engineering–procurement–construction (EPC) mode or any combination of both.

SECI also plays the role of disbursing CFA to project-implementing agencies on the basis of pre-defined scheme milestones. The state government will first nominate the implementing agency for the solar park and also identify the land for the proposed solar park. It will then send a proposal to MNRE for approval along with the name of the implementing agency. The implementing agency may be sanctioned a grant of up to Rs.25 lakh for preparing a detailed project report (DPR) for the solar park, conducting surveys, and so on. The DPR must be prepared in sixty days. Thereafter, application may be made by the implementing agency to SECI for the grant of up to Rs.20 lakh per MW or 30 per cent of the project cost including grid-connection cost, whichever is lower. The approved grant will be released by SECI as per project milestones.

The various solar schemes are as follows:

i. Solar Parks Scheme: As has already been discussed, the scheme for 'Development of Solar Parks and Ultra-Mega Solar Power Projects' was sanctioned in December 2014. The implementing agency is termed a solar power park developer (SPPD) and may be selected in any of the eight modes as per the Solar Park Scheme (Table 9.1).

ii. Canal Top/ Canal Bank Scheme: This encourages utilization of areas available on canal tops and canal banks for development of solar projects.

iii. Scheme for Defence Establishments: This encourages defence establishments to set up solar power projects.

iv. CPSU scheme, Phase-II (Government Producer Scheme): This encourages CPSUs to set up solar power projects.

v. Scheme for Distributed Grid-connected Solar PV Power Projects in Andaman and Nicobar Islands and Lakshadweep Islands with capital subsidy from MNRE.

Progress and status

SECI has played a major role in the development of the RE sector by assuming strategic risks: financial risks; contractual risks and exposures; commercial risks; legal, regulatory, and compliance risks; external risks; and risks associated with power trading, project management consultancy, project development, and scheme implementation.

Around 50,000 MW of RE projects are under implementation of which SECI's share is 54 per cent. The production of solar energy has increased in the country during the last three years and the weighted average tariffs discovered in the country through competitive bidding have reduced, reaching a low of Rs.2.68 per unit (kWh) in 2019/20[d] and further to a new record-low tariff of Rs.2 per unit ($0.027/kWh) in the SECI auction on 23 November 2020. The tariff-based bidding was conducted for the selection of solar power developers to set up 1,070 MW of grid-connected solar PV projects on a 'build-own-operate' (BOO) basis in Rajasthan (Tranche-III). Saudi Arabia-based Aljomaih Energy and Water Co. and Sembcorp Energy's India arm Green Infra Wind Energy Ltd. were the lowest (L1) bidders with a tariff of Rs.2 per unit for 200 MW and 400 MW capacities respectively. The downward trend in solar tariffs may be attributed to factors such as economies of scale, assured availability of land, and power evacuation systems under the solar park scheme.[e]

The share of solar energy in meeting the total energy demand in the country has increased from 0.63 per cent in 2015/16 to 3.61 per cent in 2019/20, and SECI has played a major role in this process. The Indian finance minister in her budget speech of 2021/22 announced additional capital infusion of Rs.1,000 crore in SECI. This will enable SECI to float 15,000 MW of tenders, attracting investment of more than Rs.60,000 crore, generating employment of 45,000 job years and reducing emissions by 28.5 million tons of CO_2.

SECI has been a national aggregator of RE. This has provided assurance of steady revenue and streamlined payment process. While this certainty has created a positive environment for investors from all over the world, it is critical to ensure that the model is scalable to the tune of investments needed up to 2030. Delays in payments by DISCOMs in some states, delays in adoption of tariffs arrived at through competitive bidding by concerned State Electricity Regulatory Commissions, reopening of PPAs by the State Government of Andhra Pradesh threatening contractual sanctity, and so on, are challenges that have to be addressed. It is also important that PPAs with SECI are equally backed by PSA between SECI and DISCOMs to be able to maintain financial viability of the organization.

[a]Solar Energy Corporation of India Ltd. 2020. *Annual Report 2019–20.*

[b]Solar Energy Corporation of India Ltd. 2020. *Annual Report 2019–20.*

[c]MNRE, Government of India. 2014. Implementation of a Scheme for Development of Solar Parks and Ultra-Mega Solar Power Projects in the Country Commencing from 2014 to 2019, p. 5 (https://mnre.gov.in/img/documents/uploads/d9f99dc08abd4b6988ba7ee3be288 ee1.pdf).

[d]Lok Sabha Unstarred Question No. 1702 answered on 11 February 2021.

[e]PIB. 2021. Budget 2021–22 Augments Capital of SECI and IREDA to Promote Development of RE Sector (https://pib.gov.in/PressReleaseIframePage.aspx?PRID= 1696498).

centre stage, with extreme weather and climate change becoming top global risks, we may be at an inflection point. Consider the following statistics:

- In 2006, when the UN Principles for Responsible Investing (UNPRI) was initiated, there were sixty-three signatories with assets under management (AUM) of US$6 trillion. As of May 2021, there were four thousand signatories of UNPRI with AUM of US$110 trillion.
- Volumes in sustainable banking and investing have been growing at a double-digit rate for a number of years (Figure 9.1).
- The Glasgow Financial Alliance for Net Zero (GFANZ), whose members hold about US$130 trillion of assets, will try to cut emissions from their lending and investing to net zero by 2050.
- The Network for Greening the Financial System, launched in 2017, now includes eighty-three central banks and supervisors (including RBI, see Box 9.3); a major focus is on recommendations for disclosure of climate risk by banks.
- The EU recently announced that banks in member countries will be required to 'systematically identify, disclose and manage' ESG risks, including climate-related risks.
- More than thirty insurance companies have announced restrictions on underwriting coal projects, essential for obtaining finance.

Sustainable banking seems to have grown fast, as indicated by the Global Alliance for Banking on Values

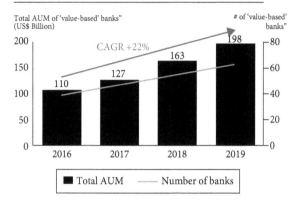

Sustainability-dedicated funds control ~$850 billion in assets and rising fast (+10% CAGR)

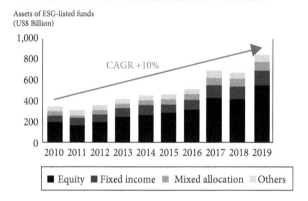

Figure 9.1 Volumes in sustainable banking and investing (by years)

Note: Value-based banks based on membership of Global Alliance for Banking on Values.

Source: Global Alliance for Banking on Values membership (https://www.gabv.org/members/); IMF Global Financial Stability Report, October 2019—Sustainable Finance (as shown in B20 Italy. 2021. *Finance and Infrastructure Policy Paper*).

- Multiple pension funds and endowments with almost US$40 trillion under management have promised to divest from fossil fuels.[7]

---

[7] Alan S. Miller. 2021. A Brief Introduction to the Critical, Complex World of Climate Finance (https://alanmiller-64880.medium.com/a-brief-introduction-to-the-critical-complex-world-of-climate-finance-120001f4ca61).

In consonance with rest of the world, in India too, ESG issues in infrastructure are becoming important as apparent from these numbers:

- $28 billion of international socially responsible investment (SRI) funds allocated to India.
- $1.6 billion AUM of the ten ESG funds in India as at the end of March 2022. The AUM of funds linked to the ESG theme have seen a five-fold jump in the last four years.
- Acuite Ratings & Research, a domestic rating agency, will incorporate ESG norms into its credit ratings and analysis. It is the first rating outfit from India to sign the UNPRI.[8]

With the country abundant in coal, it was but natural that it was emphasized as the main feedstock for power plants. This is expected to change with ESG concerns increasingly occupying centre stage these days. Given the increasing frequency and devastation from floods, storms, forest fires, and similar climate-related events, the Covid-19 pandemic provides an opportunity to 'build back better', where ESG concerns are mainstreamed. ESG factors have become increasingly important for private investors—not only as a means to manage and mitigate risk, but also as a mechanism to enhance financial performance and returns.[9] Similarly, in India, while social issues like job creation and balanced regional development have been emphasized, the representation of women in infrastructure is still quite poor and it is time that gender parity is brought into focus (which ESG also underlines).

Post-Covid-19: The Opportunity for a Green Recovery

With governments prioritizing Covid-19-related budget expenditures, they are exploring ways to draw more private financing into infrastructure development. Covid-19 has also forced corporations to scrutinize their responsibilities and role in society (purpose) as their most important

---

[8] *Business Standard*. 30 September 2021. Acuite Ratings 1st Rater in India to Sign Up for ESG.
[9] Global Infrastructure Hub. 2021. *Infrastructure Monitor*.

stakeholders—investors, customers, employees—want it.[10] One strategy to match the demand with the supply would be to frame infrastructure as an ESG investment to capitalize on the desire of institutional investors to move trillions into assets that produce benign ESG outcomes (sustainable investing). The rising focus on environmentally and socially sustainable outcomes from infrastructure investment not only has the potential to improve lives but also to ease the ability to attract the capital needed to fill the infrastructure investment gap.[11]

Both the 2008 economic crisis and the Covid-19 pandemic painfully reflect our vulnerability to global shocks. Managing all stakeholders has been the biggest challenge for businesses in this ongoing uncertainty, which is proof that economic health cannot be built in isolation. Society and environment are equally important for businesses to flourish and going forward all ESG risks will have to be managed to build resilience into the system.[12] Industry and academic studies also suggest that ESG investing can, under certain conditions, help improve risk management and potentially lead to attractive risk-adjusted returns; going forward, this would lead to strong growth in investors' interest in ESG-attentive companies.

Adherence to ESG principles is increasingly becoming necessary to attract investments. The McKinsey Global Survey on valuing ESG programmes, finds that 83 per cent of C-suite leaders and investment professionals say they expect that ESG programmes will contribute more shareholder value in five years than today (in fact the green boom is already under way and firms with ESG characteristics are already producing more shareholder value—since the start of 2020, *The Economist* portfolio of companies that benefit from energy transition, has risen by 59 per cent, twice the increase in S&P's 500, the United States' main equity index;[13] in the last ten years, wind and solar equities have generated a compound annual return of 16 per cent, higher than the compound annual return of listed (6 per cent) and unlisted (12 per cent) infrastructure

---

[10] McKinsey & Company. 2022. *The Role of ESG and Purpose.*
[11] World Economic Forum. 2021. *4 Big Infrastructure Trends to Build a Sustainable World* (https://www.weforum.org/agenda/2021/01/four-big-infrastructure-trends-for-2021/).
[12] Ernst &Young. 2020. *Risk, Returns and Resilience: Integrating ESG in the Financial Sector.*
[13] *The Economist.* 22–28 May 2021. Climate Finance—The Green Meme.

equities).[14] They also indicate that they would be willing to pay about a 10 per cent median premium to acquire a company with a positive record for ESG issues over one with a negative record. Maintaining a good corporate reputation and attracting and retaining talent continue to be cited most often as ways that ESG programmes improve financial performance.[15] So, ESG does not come at the expense of profitability but, in many cases, drives outperformance.

However, there are data limitations to make a deterministic claim about ESG adherence and financial returns. In 2019, EDHECinfra investigated the link between ESG performance and financial performance in unlisted infrastructure firms using the EDHECinfra and GRESB ESG rating databases on infrastructure companies. Due to data limitations, this research covered only three years of ESG performance data, even though the relationship between ESG performance and financial performance is generally expected to be a long-term one. The study did not find a positive relationship between ESG performance and financial performance, nor a negative one.[16]

Echoing these concerns, *The Economist*[17] points out that ESG suffers from three fundamental problems. First, it lumps together a dizzying array of objectives and makes no coherent guide for investors and firms to make the trade-offs that are inevitable in any society, for example closing down a coal-mining firm is good for the climate but awful for its suppliers and workers. Second, it is not being straight about incentives—the link between virtue and financial outperformance is suspect. Third, ESG has a measurement problem—the various scoring systems have gaping inconsistencies and are easily gamed—for example, one could assess labour practices based on employee turnover, while another could count labour-related court cases against the firm; or, the mere act of disclosing well-crafted climate strategies determines the 'E' score in many cases,

---

[14] Global Infrastructure Hub. 2021. *Infrastructure Monitor.*

[15] McKinsey & Company. 2020. *The ESG Premium: New Perspectives on Value and Performance* (https://www.mckinsey.com/business-functions/sustainability/our-insights/the-esg-premium-new-perspectives-on-value-and-performance?cid=other-eml-ttn-mip-mck&hdpid=b62e2 c93-e9a5-425d-8a55-12e52d307fa6&hctky=9579620&hlkid=43078758859542b2923b61248 e74a845).

[16] OECD. 2021. *The Application of ESG Considerations in Infrastructure Investment in the Asia-Pacific.*

[17] *The Economist.* 29 July 2022. Three Letters That Won't Save the Planet.

rather than the quality of interim targets or the steps actually taken to reach them. In other words, ESG may be too imprecise to be a shadow tax on a company's negative externalities.

Sign of the Times

Despite the data limitations, the ESG wave is gaining ground. Norway's US$1.15 trillion sovereign wealth fund blacklisted fifteen companies in 2020 for ethical (corruption, human rights violations) or sustainability (environment damage) reasons. These firms included Canadian Natural Resources, Imperial Oil, and Suncor Energy.[18]

An increase in extreme weather events such as floods, droughts, and cyclones risk are souring debt of more than Rs.6.2 trillion ($84 billion) at India's biggest financial institutions [State Bank of India (Rs.3.83 trillion), HDFC Bank (Rs.1.79 trillion), IndusInd Bank (Rs.0.46 trillion), and Axis Bank (Rs.0.08 trillion)] as per CDP, an international non-profit organization based in the United Kingdom that helps companies and cities disclose their environmental impact. The banks have exposure to environmentally sensitive businesses including cement, coal, oil, and power.

As investors look at funding companies based on ESG disclosures,[19] companies are increasingly reporting climate risks to their portfolio.

---

[18] However, the rise of ESG investing and the stigma faced by publicly listed energy firms is having an unintended side-effect. Public firms, including European oil majors such as Shell, and large listed mining outfits, are selling their most polluting assets to please ESG investors and meet their carbon reduction targets. But these oil wells and coal mines are not being shut down. Instead they are being bought by private companies and funds that have alternative sources of capital and stay out of the limelight. Private equity firms have snapped up US$60 billion worth of fossil-fuel-linked assets in the last two years alone, from shale fields to pipelines. This retreat to private ownership is part of a broader global trend. More opaque institutions are taking over dirty assets. This is problematic for two main reasons: the claims being made by listed firms (and ESG funds) that they are helping to decarbonize the planet are questionable; selling a polluting asset does not, in itself, reduce emissions at all, if it keeps pumping oil or digging up coal. Second, as dirty assets pass into private hands, it becomes harder to tell if their owners plan to reduce their output over time, or expand it. What can be done? First, impose more carbon taxes or carbon prices. Such tools are the best way to align the profit motive with the imperative to cut emissions, and so unleash the power of markets to reallocate capital quickly and efficiently. Second, investors should question the idea that the best way to make polluters pollute less is to dump their shares. Instead, green investors should hold onto dirty shares and work with managers to reduce emissions (*The Economist*. 18 February 2022. Green Investing—A Dirty Secret)

[19] Pension Fund Alecta (Sweden) reported that it invested nearly 43 per cent of its portfolio in green equity and 4 per cent in green bonds. It considers ESG factors in all of its investment decisions, including new investment strategies, product mandates, and investment proposals.

CDP, which gathered data on behalf of 515 investors with US$106 trillion in assets, said it received responses from 220 small and large Indian companies. SBI said it may face reputational risks if it is involved in lending to environmentally sensitive projects, which may have significant public opposition. More than fifty Indian companies are preparing for future policy and regulatory changes by voluntarily committing to cutting their carbon footprint. For example, HDFC Bank has unveiled plans to be more environment friendly and become carbon neutral by 2031–32. It will focus on offering loans for green products like electric vehicles at lower rates and incorporate ESG scores into its credit decisions. The aim is to fund ESG segments by floating green bonds which attract socially and environmentally conscious investors who want their money deployed in only green projects.[20] Increased investor pressure and stronger disclosure norms are compelling companies to address climate concerns (see Figure 9.2).[21]

Formal rules are also being framed out of concern that climate change poses a threat to financial stability. Climate change can affect the financial system in three ways. The first is through what regulators describe as 'transition risks'. These are most likely to arise if governments pursue tougher climate policies, which is inevitable. As a result, the economy restructures: capital moves away from dirty sectors (e.g. coal) and towards cleaner ones (e.g.RE). Companies in polluting industries may default on loans or bonds; their share prices may collapse. The second channel is financial firms' exposure to the hazards of rising temperatures. The US Financial Stability Board has estimated that global economic losses resulting from weather-related catastrophes increased from US$214 billion in the 1980s (in 2019 prices) to US$1.62 trillion in the 2010s, roughly trebling as a share of GDP. These losses are often borne by insurers, but ultimately by customers through higher premia. The third channel is the impact of the financial system to wider economic damage caused by

---

Another pension fund, PME (Netherlands) reported 36 per cent of its total portfolio to be held in green equities (OECD. 2021. *The Application of ESG Considerations in Infrastructure Investment in the Asia-Pacific*).

[20] *Times of India*. 4 June 2021. HDFC Bank, TCS Aim for Carbon Neutral Tag.
[21] Archana Chaudhary. 4 March 2021. Extreme Weather Puts Rs.6.2 Trillion Bank Debt at Risk. *Business Standard*.

climate change, say if it triggered swings in asset prices. Academic estimates of the effect of 3°C of warming (relative to pre-industrial temperatures) veer from financial losses of 2 per cent to 25 per cent of world GDP. The value of financial assets exposed to transition risk is potentially very large. According to Carbon Tracker, a climate think tank, around US$18 trillion of global equities, US$8 trillion of bonds and perhaps US$30 trillion of unlisted debt are linked to high-emitting sectors of the economy. This compares with the US$1 trillion market for collateralized debt obligations (CDOs) in 2007, which were at the heart of the Global Financial Crisis.[22]

These concerns have forced financial regulators to take pre-emptive action. The thinking is that climate change is too big a risk to the financial system to deal with under the old rules. The US Securities and Exchange Commission (SEC) has created a taskforce to examine ESG issues, and said it will 'enhance its focus' on climate-related disclosures for listed firms. It looks poised to introduce, among other things, rules forcing firms to reveal how climate change or efforts to fight it may affect their business. Since September 2020, regulators in Britain, New Zealand, and Switzerland have said they plan to make such climate-related disclosures mandatory. So, too, have stock exchanges in Hong Kong, London, and South Korea. The EU has already implemented the Non-Financial Reporting Directive [requiring companies to report how they manage social and environmental challenges]. Many watchdogs are pinning their hopes on the Task Force on Climate-related Financial Disclosures (TCFD), set up in 2015 by the Financial Stability Board (FSB), a global group of regulators. The TCFD has recommended a reporting standard made up of eleven broad categories, from carbon footprints to climate-risk management. Regulators like it because it focuses on material risks rather than environmental impacts, and because it asks for information about firms' future plans.

These qualities also appeal to financiers. Financial firms make up almost half of the 1,800 or so companies that back the TCFD's recommendations. Together they hold assets worth over US$150 trillion and include the world's ten biggest asset managers and eight of its ten biggest

---

[22] *The Economist.* 10 September 2021. Hot Take—Could Climate Change Trigger a Financial Crisis?

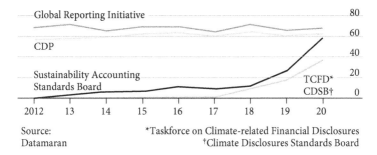

Figure 9.2 Greener postures—S&P 500 companies, reporting standards mentioned in sustainability reports (%)

Notes: TCFD: Taskforce on Climate-related Financial Disclosures; CDSB: Climate Disclosures Standards Board.

Source: The Economist. 13 March 2021. Regulators Want Firms to Own Up to Climate Risks.

banks. Their clients and regulators are egging them on to adopt the standard, so the financial firms in turn are prodding companies to do so too, causing an uptick in its use.[23] Clear and consistent definitions are required to support transparency, comparability, and monitoring of such major global initiatives.

Similar developments are in happening in India too. As per a Reserve Bank of India research paper,[24] transition to a net-zero carbon emission target will entail adjustment in the production processes of industries that are directly or indirectly exposed to excessive use of fossil fuel. Concomitantly, due to the exposure of Indian banks to these industries, there can be spillover effects on them. Three sectors with direct exposure to fossil fuels—electricity, chemicals, and automobiles—account for about 24 per cent of credit to the overall industrial sector, but only 10 per cent of total outstanding non-retail bank credit, which implies a limited spillover effect to the banking system. Several other industries, however, indirectly use fossil fuels and therefore any transition to green energy

---

[23] *The Economist.* 13 March 2021. Regulators Want Firms to Own Up to Climate Risks(https://www.economist.com/business/2021/03/13/regulators-want-firms-to-own-up-to-climate-risks?utm_campaign=the-climate-issue&utm_medium=newsletter&utm_source=salesforce-marketing-cloud&utm_term=2021-03-22&utm_content=ed-picks-article-link-4&etear=nl_climate_4).

[24] SaurabhGhosh, SiddharthaNath, Abhinav Narayanan, and Satadru Das. 2022. Green Transition Risks to Indian Banks. *Reserve Bank of India Bulletin* (https://rbidocs.rbi.org.in/rdocs/Bulletin/PDFs/03AR_17032022266D3EFB505B744DB9B32A37C162E0680.PDF).

can have implications for their income and consequently their interest coverage ratio (ICR). Therefore, the gross non-performing assets (GNPA) ratio of such industries may be sensitive to green energy transition, and their impact on the overall banking system needs to be monitored closely.

In May 2021, the RBI set up a new unit, Sustainable Finance Group, to effectively counter climate-related financial risks, and for leading the regulatory initiatives in the areas of sustainable finance and climate risk ('which are far-reaching, non-linear, and have mostly irreversible consequences').

The Indian capital market regulator, SEBI, has floated a Consultation Paper on the Format for Business Responsibility and Sustainability Reporting as another indication of the mainstreaming of the ESG concerns. SEBI, in 2012, mandated the top 100 listed entities by market capitalization to file Business Responsibility Reports (BRR) as per the disclosure requirements emanating from the 'National Voluntary Guidelines on Social, Environmental and Economic Responsibilities of Business' (NVGs). The requirement for filing BRRs was extended to the top 500 companies by market capitalization from the financial year (FY) 2015. In December 2019, SEBI extended the BRR requirement to the top 1,000 listed entities by market capitalization, from the FY2019/20.

India Ratings & Research (Ind-Ra), the Indian arm of the global major Fitch, has announced that it will look into fourteen different factors under its ESG framework for rating companies, including a company's greenhouse-gas emissions, energy and water management processes, community and labour relations, ownership and board structure. The factors are drawn from Sustainability Accounting Standards Board's Global Sustainability Framework with fourteen factors.[25]

The philosophy of responsible business is based on the principle of business being accountable to all its stakeholders, which are increasingly seeking businesses to be responsible and sustainable towards the environment and society. In light of ever-increasing global challenges relating to climate change, environmental risks, growing inequality, and so on, business leaders have been compelled, and have also found

---

[25] *Times of India*. 11 December 2021. Ind-Ra: Ratings to Have ESG Factor.

it to be in their interest, to re-imagine the role of businesses in society and not view them merely as economic units for generating wealth. The performance of a company must be measured not only on the return to shareholders, but also on how it achieves its environmental, social, and good governance objectives. Therefore, globally there is a growing recognition and emphasis on stakeholder models of governance, including, among others, institutional investors. As such, SEBI has recommended that the Business Responsibility Report (BRR) be called the Business Responsibility and Sustainability Report (BRSR). These disclosures, which are from an ESG perspective that have been recommended in the BRSR, are intended to enable businesses to engage more meaningfully with their stakeholders, and encourage them to go beyond regulatory financial compliance and report on their social and environmental impacts.[26]

ESG metrics are also being built and increasingly used. EDHECinfra is developing tools to measure the current and evolving risks and impacts that ESG considerations bring to infrastructure investment. The main objective of the project is to develop a set of indicators to measure the magnitude of infrastructure assets' contribution to climate change, as well as climate-related risks faced by the assets. Another initiative is the Global ESG Benchmark for Real Assets (GRESB) that collects and analyses data on the ESG characteristics of infrastructure investments through its annual Infrastructure Assessments, which are aligned with international reporting frameworks. Many pension funds that reported infrastructure investment have indicated that they use GRESB data and analytical tools in their investment management and engagement process, including almost all Australian pension funds. The SuRe standard (Global Infrastructure Basel Foundation), CEEQUAL (BRE Global Limited), the IS rating scheme (Infrastructure Sustainability Council) and the Envision rating tool (Institute for Sustainable Infrastructure) are also being used. Fitch Ratings ESG scores (ESG.RS) provides insight into the credit relevance and materiality of ESG factors for the infrastructure

---

[26] Securities and Exchange Board of India (SEBI). 2020.*Consultation Paper on the Format for Business Responsibility and Sustainability Reporting* (https://www.sebi.gov.in/reports-and-statist ics/reports/aug-2020/consultation-paper-on-the-format-for-business-responsibility-and-sus tainability-reporting_47345.html).

sector. The scores show how ESG factors affect global infrastructure and project finance issuer or transaction ratings.[27]

Various initiatives are also being developed to address the need for a label for sustainable infrastructure. The Finance to Accelerate the Sustainable Transition-Infrastructure (FASTInfra)[28] initiative attempts to establish a consistent, globally applicable labelling system for sustainable infrastructure assets. Through this labelling system, the market can easily signal the sustainability of the asset, and investors can trust that their money is going to projects that meet environmental, social, resiliency, and governance needs and contribute to the Sustainable Development Goals (SDGs). A sustainable infrastructure label will ensure that governments and project developers embed high environmental, social, governance, and resiliency standards into new infrastructure at the design and pre-construction phases, on the grounds that only assets incorporating such standards will obtain the label. Additionally, it is developing financial mechanisms to mobilize private investment at scale for the financing of labelled projects. The initiative was founded in 2020 by the Climate Policy Initiative (CPI), HSBC, the International Finance Corporation (IFC), OECD and the Global Infrastructure Facility. Over fifty global entities, representing governments at all levels, the financial sector, investors, DFIs, insurers, rating agencies, and NGOs are participating in the FASTInfra initiative.[29]

Central bank regulations have been increasingly incorporating, within the transaction-based frameworks, granulated climate-related risks from the standpoint of financial intermediation and, concomitantly, financial stability. The country's central bank, the Reserve Bank of India (RBI), has also joined the Network for Greening the Financial System (NGFS) (see Box 9.3).

At its most basic, these ESG regulations, standards, and metrics make intermediaries recognize the possibility of climate-risk drivers that alter

---

[27] OECD. 2021. *The Application of ESG Considerations in Infrastructure Investment in the Asia-Pacific.*

[28] FAST-Infra is a public-private initiative to raise private investment in developing world sustainable infrastructure, conceived in early 2020.

[29] SamieModak.29 June 2021. India Inc Does Well on ESG. *Business Standard* (https://www.business-standard.com/article/economy-policy/india-inc-fares-well-on-environmental-social-and-governance-disclosures-121062800371_1.html)

Box 9.3   RBI joins Network for Greening the Financial System

---

The RBI joined the central banks and supervisors Network for Greening the Financial System (NGFS) as a Member on 23 April 2021. Launched at the Paris One Planet Summit on 12 December 2017, the NGFS is a group of central banks and supervisors willing to share best practices and contribute to the development of environment and climate risk management in the financial sector, while mobilising mainstream finance to support the transition towards a sustainable economy.

The Reserve Bank expects to benefit from the membership of NGFS by learning from and contributing to global efforts on Green Finance which has assumed significance in the context of climate change.

Source: RBI Press Release 2021–2022/131.
(https://www.rbi.org.in/Scripts/BS_PressReleaseDisplay.aspx?prid=51496).

(reduce) borrowers' ability to repay and service debt. This includes the likelihood that, in some extreme circumstances, the recovery of a loan could be impaired—an event of default. By and large, the recognition translates into apposite (usually higher) pricing of risk for the borrower and setting aside of additional bank capital by the intermediary.[30]

Indian companies have done relatively well when it comes to ESG disclosures. Refinitiv, a financial-data provider, has analysed the level of transparency in public disclosure of ESG strategies and performance data across 163 Indian companies, and compared that to markets, such as South Africa, Brazil, China, and Hong Kong. India Inc fared better on a number of parameters. The study showed 98 per cent of domestic companies respected and promoted human rights as compared to 46 per cent of the overall universe; the figure for Brazil is 52 per cent, China is 31 per cent, and Hong Kong 72 per cent. Also, 64 per cent of Indian businesses

---

[30] Urjit R.Patel.9 September 2021. Central Banks Must Stop Pussyfooting on Climate. *Business Standard*

respected and promoted the well-being of employees, including those in their value chains under trade union representation. Parameters where India scored high included policy on equal voting rights (100 per cent), policy on community involvement (99 per cent), and CSR sustainability reporting (98 per cent). Factors where India Inc scored low included carbon offsets (1 per cent), products recovered to recycle (1 per cent), and written consent requirements (1 per cent). A separate study released by CRISIL said IT and financial firms have relatively high ESG scores, given their inherently lower natural resource intensity, resulting in lower emissions, waste generation, and water usage. In contrast, oil and gas, chemicals, metals and mining, and cement firms have lower ESG scores, reflecting high natural resource intensity, and thereby higher emission levels, extractive use of natural resources, and potentially adverse environmental and community impact.

Reflecting these trends, many Indian companies are riding the ESG wave headlong. Reliance has declared its commitment to make itself a net carbon zero company by 2035. Tata Power was the first power company to declare a net zero target by 2050. It will make no new investment in the thermal power sector, and focus solely on expansion of RE. India's largest thermal power company, NTPC, has an installed capacity of 66 GW, with thermal (coal + gas) capacity of 61 GW, hydro of 3.7 GW, solar of 1 GW, and the balance being wind. It has incorporated a wholly owned subsidiary, NTPC RE, in 2020 and plans to add 60 GW of RE by 2032. NTPC plans to retire existing coal-fired plants before that timeline, or hive them off. The world's biggest miner of coal, Coal India Limited, will invest in a solar park in Bikaner (Rajasthan), and is targeting 3 GW of solar capacity by FY 2024 from the current level of about 300 MW.[31]

Some of the more recent tie-ups aimed at riding the ESG wave are shown in Table 9.3.

Phasing down of coal is reflected also in India giving the green nod (environmental clearance, EC) to only one non-captive coal-fired plant (2,400 MW NLC Talabira Thermal Power Project 3*800 MW in Odisha) in 2021 [as compared to five with capacity of 8,900 MW in 2015, five (6,360 MW) in 2016, nine (15,300 MW) in 2017, two (1,520 MW) in

---

[31] *Times of India*. 15 October 2022. CIL's US$970 mn Deal to Add Solar Cap.

Table 9.3 Riding the green wave

Company	Tie-Up with	Purpose
Reliance Jio-bp	Mahindra, Zomato	Charging solutions for Mahindra vehicles, RIL's captive fleet, and Zomato
Reliance New Energy Solar	Sterling & Wilson	EPC business in green power generation
Reliance BP Mobility Ltd	BluSmart	Green energy solutions for Jio-bp branded outlets and fuel retailing business
L&T	ReNew Power	Green hydrogen
Bharti Airtel	Avaada Energy	Solar power sourcing
MG Motor India	Attero	EV battery recycling

Source: Mukul (2021).

2018, three (3,860 MW) in 2019, three (3,060 MW) in 2020]—the least since it joined over 195 other nations in approving the Paris Agreement on climate change in 2015. This could be attributed to lack of financing and competition from RE. Banks and insurance companies are now moving away from coal-powered power plants due to concerns over climate change, high risk due to social opposition and large number of stranded assets where existing power plants are not able to find takers for the power generated. EC is a useful indicator of power generation trends as it is a pre-requisite to set up a power project in India.

And there are adverse impacts on companies that are perceived not to be ESG-friendly. India's largest state-owned commercial bank, State Bank of India (SBI) has been considering loaning A$1 billion to the Adani's controversial Carmichael coal mine project in Queensland, Australia. In December 2020, climate-conscious investors like Amundi have sold US$20 million worth of SBI bonds held in its green fund, Amundi Planet Emerging Green One, launched in 2018 in partnership with IFC. Ranked among the top ten globally, Amundi is Europe's largest asset manager with a portfolio of 1.76 trillion euros.[32]Large foreign investors such as

---

[32] V.Keshavdev.2021. SBI Loan to Adani's Coal Project Stuck.*Fortune India*

AXA IM and NNIP also divested their holdings of SBI green bonds in response to SBI's proposed loan to Adani Group's Carmichael coal project.

Green Finance

As a corollary to these developments, green finance is increasingly being used to fund environmentally sound projects. Green finance is defined as comprising 'all forms of investment or lending that consider environmental effect and enhance environmental sustainability'.[33] The growing importance of green finance is evident in that 'a cool $178 billion flowed into green-tinged investment funds in the first quarter of 2021'.[34] It is important to align the financial system—banking, capital markets, and insurance—with sustainable development. Aligning the financial system with sustainable development will require actions across the entire financial system and the involvement of all actors, including international financial institutions, banks, institutional investors, market-makers such as rating agencies and stock exchanges, as well as central banks and financial regulatory authorities. As we have seen, this alignment is happening across multiple stakeholders in India, and also abroad. Box 9.4 presents green finance developments in India and the world.

Gender Gap in Infrastructure

Though the 'social' in ESG could refer to a number of aspects including balanced regional development, effects on vulnerable populations, preservation of cultural heritage, protection of human rights, improvement in quality of life, inclusion, diversity and equality, making infrastructure services accessible, employment practices, maternity and paternity leaves, labour relations, investment in human capital and communities, and so on, we restrict our discussion to the specific issue of gender gap in infrastructure.

---

[33] U. Volz, J.Böhnke, L.Knierim, K.Richert, G.-M. Röber, and V. Eidt.(2015).*Financing the Green Transformation: How to Make Green Finance Work in Indonesia*.Basingstoke: Palgrave Macmillan.
[34] *The Economist*. 12 June 2021. How Green Bottlenecks Threaten the Clean Energy Business.

Box 9.4 Green finance in India and the world

India stands seventh in the Global Climate Risk Index 2021.[a] This implies that the country is quite vulnerable to climate-related risks, which would increasingly have an influence on the economy and raises the prospect of future downgrades. A transition to low-carbon, climate-resilient growth is needed to avert worsening consequences of climate change and natural resource scarcity. Public policy plays a crucial role in this by avoiding price distortions (e.g., subsidies on fossil fuels) and applying policies that manage natural resources to reduce emissions, mitigate climate risk. India also needs massive investment in green infrastructure.[b] It will need to invest US$1.4 trillion in clean energy technology during the current decade to achieve 450 gigawatts (GW) of RE capacity by 2030. This financing requirement cannot be covered by public sources alone and private financing would have to be tapped to support climate action. This private financing is increasingly subject to environmental sustainability norms.

Financial firms can play a large role in reducing greenhouse-gas emissions. Such firms' direct emissions are usually small—some pollution will be released while generating electricity to light offices and power computers, for instance. But that is not the case for their 'financed emissions', those associated with their lending, investing, or insuring activities. A new study from CDP, a non-profit group, finds that on average financed emissions are usually 700 times greater than operational ones. Some financial firms are trying to measure their financed emissions. Some are also setting targets to reduce them. They plan to do that by divesting dirty assets or pressing polluters to shape up.

Financial firms tend to say they set green goals out of a sense of purpose. But self-interest also plays a part. Asset managers can charge their clients more for climate-friendly funds than for conventional ones. A green tinge helps impress customers too. ABN AMRO, a Dutch bank, tells some clients the size of their portfolio's carbon footprint. Moreover, a reputation as a polluter can be bad for business.[c]

In October 2002, ABN AMRO and the IFC—the organization in charge of private projects for the World Bank Group—invited major international financial institutions engaged in project finance activities, to assemble in London with the intention to come up with environmental and social risk-management guidelines for private financial institutions. As a result of this meeting, Citigroup, ABN AMRO, Barclays, and West LB in collaboration with IFC, created a framework of managing environmental and social risks. The *Equator Principles* (EPs) were thus formulated in June 2003. EPs are a set of voluntary guidelines adopted by financial institutions to ensure that large-scale development or construction projects appropriately consider the associated potential impacts on the natural environment and the affected communities. EPs were first revised in July 2006, to align them with the IFC Performance Standards. Most recently, EP4 was launched in November 2019. EP4 applies to a broader range of transactions and requires further environmental and social assessments such as climate change and human rights. As of March 2021, 116 financial institutions in thirty-seven countries have adopted these Principles. The EPs apply globally, to all industry sectors and to five financial products: project finance advisory services, project finance, project-related corporate loans, bridge loans and project-related refinance, and project-related acquisition finance.

In February 2008, three leading banks, Citibank, JPMorgan Chase, and Morgan Stanley, announced common coal-power financing policies, known as the *Carbon Principles*. When the Carbon Principles were created, they were one of the first industry-wide statements from the banking sector specifically addressing climate change and carbon-intensive investments. The *Climate Principles* are a similar framework for climate-change best practices for the financial sector launched by The Climate Group. The adopting institutions include Crédit Agricole, BNP Paribas, F&C Investments, Standard Chartered, Swiss Re, and HSBC.

In 2019, the Principles for Responsible Banking were developed by a core group of thirty founding banks, representing more than US$17 trillion in assets around the world, through an innovative global partnership between banks and the UNEP Finance Initiative (UNEP FI). It provides the framework for the sustainable banking system of the future. It is expected to align the banking industry with society's goals as expressed in the SDGs and the Paris Climate Agreement. Yes Bank is the only Indian bank amongst the thirty founding banks of the Principles for Responsible Banking. Through it, the banking sector (220 banks had joined by March 2021) will usher in a new-age, twenty-first-century economy geared towards sustainable and equitable growth.

Green bonds: A green bond is a debt security that is issued to raise capital specifically to support climate-related or environmental projects. In addition to evaluating the standard financial characteristics (such as maturity, coupon, price, and credit quality of the issuer), investors also assess the specific environmental purpose of the projects that the bonds intend to support.[d] Green bonds are the most important innovation in the field of sustainable finance. Financing through green bonds has been rising in recent years, particularly in high-income countries (Figure 9.3).

The benefits for issuers include investor diversification, and help to build a market that has attracted investors with its focus on socially responsible investing (SRI) and those that incorporate ESG criteria as part of their investment analysis.

At an international level, green bonds were first issued in 2007. In response to the growing green bond market in early 2014, a group of banks initiated the development of the *Green Bond Principles* (GBP)—a set of voluntary guidelines about the issuance of green bonds. The GBP encourage transparency, disclosure, and integrity in

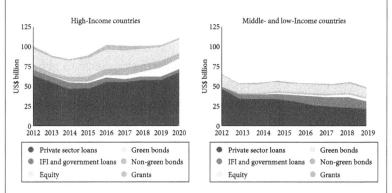

Figure 9.3 Private investment in infrastructure projects by instrument type and income group (three-year moving average, US$ billion)
Source: Global Infrastructure Hub. 2021. *Infrastructure Monitor.*

the development of the green bond market. The International Capital Markets Association (ICMA) acts as the GBP's secretariat and facilitates the work of its members, including issuers, investors, banks underwriting green bonds, and other market participants.

The sustainable debt market consists of green, social,[e]pandemic, and sustainability bonds. This market is traditionally dominated by green bonds (accounting for 58 per cent of the volume in 2011–2020, at US$195 billion). However, the share of other themes has been growing, both in terms of amount issued and number of issuers. Looking at the recent developments, the following inferences follow:

- 2020 has seen the overall sustainable debt market growing, with a total half-year figure of over US$250 billion versus US$341 billion for the full year of 2019. However, its composition is noticeably different, with a more even split among themes than previous years. The pandemic theme, which emerged in China in February 2020, was the second largest in 2020 and already almost as large as the entire social theme.[f] As an example, on 15 July 2021, the New Development Bank (NDB) issued its three-year US$2.25 billion Pandemic Support and Sustainable Bond. The net proceeds from the bond was to be used for financing Covid-19 emergency support loans and sustainable development activities of the member countries of the Bank.[g]
- Bloomberg New Energy Finance (BNEF) expected as much as US$900 billion of sustainable finance to be mobilized in 2021. A record sum of US$732 billion was raised in 2020, with green bonds and social bonds accounting for the largest chunk of issues[h] (see Figure 9.4). It is estimated that private actors provided 49 per cent of total climate finance, an average of US$310 billion per year in 2017 to 2019.
- In 2020, thirty-two emerging-market countries issued sustainable debt products—twice as many as five years prior—even as the overall emerging-market issues fell 17 per cent YoY.
- Governments are joining the bandwagon. More than twenty countries have already issued green debt, notably Germany.

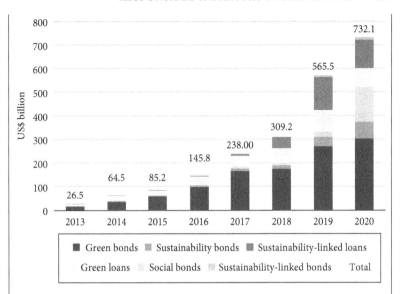

Figure 9.4 Annual global sustainable debt issuance, 2013–2020
Source: Adapted from Bloomberg data.

Governments have together raised more than US$100 billion through the green bond route by October 2021.[i]

- The cumulative issuance of global green bonds crossed the US$1 trillion mark in 2020. India is the second largest green bond market among the emerging markets, after China.[j]

- Green bonds have been used for financing RE projects. New solar installations are expected to have surpassed 200GW in 2021 for the first time. Wind installations, including offshore wind, are projected to be 88GW.

- As per Bloomberg, cumulative sustainable investing assets had grown to US$35.3 trillion in 2020. The sustainable investment industry had grown by 15 per cent over a two-year period to 2020, and accounted for 36 per cent of all professionally managed assets across the United States, Canada, Japan, Australasia, and Europe.[k]

Green financing in India

In 2015, the RBI included lending to social infrastructure and small RE projects within the priority sector targets.[l] As of the end of March 2020, the aggregate outstanding bank credit to the non-conventional

(RE) energy sector was about Rs.36,543 crore, constituting 7.9 per cent of the outstanding bank credit to power generation.[m]

Green bonds in India: Yes Bank issued the first Indian green bond in 2015, soon followed by Export-Import Bank of India and IDBI later that year. SEBI issued a circular on 30 May 2017 setting out disclosure norms which would govern the issuance and listing of 'green bonds' (Green Bond Guidelines). The guidelines on issuance of green bonds in India are in line with international standards: the ICMA Green Bond Principles and the Climate Bonds Initiatives Taxonomy. The launch of green indices such as S&P BSE CARBONEX (in 2012), MSCI ESG India (in 2013), and S&P BSE 100 ESG Index (in 2017) allows passive and retail investors to invest in 'green' companies. As of 24 December 2020, eight ESG mutual funds had been launched in India.[n]

As of 12 February 2020, the outstanding amount of green bonds in India was US$16.3 billion. Indian issuances of green bonds since January 1, 2018 constituted about 0.7 per cent of all bonds issued in the Indian financial market. Most of the green bonds issued since 2015 had maturities of five years or above, but less than ten years. Around 76 per cent of the green bonds issued in India since 2015 were denominated in US dollars.[o] India, however, attracted less than a tenth of China's total in 2019 (see Figure 9.5), but nevertheless remains the second-largest emerging market for such finance.

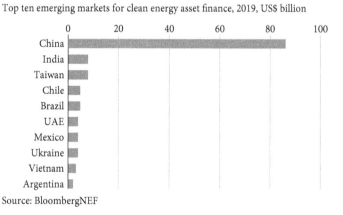

Top ten emerging markets for clean energy asset finance, 2019, US$ billion

Source: BloombergNEF

Figure 9.5 Clean energy asset finance, by country
Source: Bloomberg NEF.

In 2021, Indian companies attracted US$9.7 billion[p] in green bonds, beating the previous record of US$3.43 billion in cumulative green bond issuance in 2017 (US$3.23 billion in 2019 and US$875 million in 2020) and nearly as much as in the previous five years combined, demonstrating that green bonds have become a key financial instrument for mobilizing cost-effective foreign debt capital into the Indian renewables market. The importance and popularity of Indian green bonds is likely to increase: they offer an opportunity for clean energy companies to leverage global finance for projects that will help India meet its RE targets (450GW by 2030) and offer relatively higher and less volatile yields for global investors. The yields are relatively stable because most of the RE projects in India have long-term PPAs with government entities. This ensures a less volatile cashflow and thus timely debt service payments by the bond issuer. For example, Azure Power Global Limited (Azure) raised US$414 million in August 2021 via a green bond issued through Azure Power Solar Energy Private Limited, a wholly owned subsidiary of Azure. The bond had been issued at a coupon rate of 3.575 per cent which is the lowest-ever coupon for any borrower in India. Azure will use the proceeds of the bond to refinance its 5.50 per cent US$500 million green bond issued in 2017 which is due in 2022. It is estimated that the refinancing would reduce Azure's debt cost by 200 basis points (bps) in hedged rupee terms.[q]

To give a further impetus to green bonds in India, the government, in the FY 2023 budget, announced that as a part of the government's overall market borrowings in 2022/23, sovereign green bonds will be issued for mobilizing resources for green infrastructure, which help in reducing the carbon intensity of the economy. The proceeds will be deployed in public-sector projects.[r]

Challenges in the Indian green finance market

i. High borrowing costs: The average coupon rate for green bonds issued since 2015 with maturities between five and ten years has generally remained higher than the corporate and government bonds with similar tenure. This could be on account of asymmetric information, higher risk perception, and other governance issues as green projects often have high upfront cost with some cost-saving features only applicable over the long term.[s] However, this is unusual as there is empirical evidence that green bonds around the world trade at a higher price (lower yields) compared to the corresponding non-green bonds both in primary as well as in secondary markets.

ii. Maturity-mismatches: Indian green loans are mostly loans to utility-scale RE projects. These projects are generally based on PPAs of up to twenty-five years, and thus are ideally financed by long-term debt. However, green investors provide relatively shorter-term debt. This increases the cost of borrowing.

iii. Absence of a universal definition of green finance: There is no detailed taxonomy of green finance, so issuers have scope to define *green* for themselves. For instance, the category *renewable and sustainable energy*, covers not just RE but also 'other sources of energy which use clean energy' opening the door for green bonds to continue funding fossil-fuel power generation with energy-efficiency technology and limited carbon capture, which are excluded from the Climate Bonds Taxonomy.[t]

To gain creditability in the eyes of investors, issuers should consider using green labelling schemes like national standards or Climate Bonds Initiative's internationally recognized specific standards. These are available for an increasingly broad range of assets (energy, buildings, water infrastructure, transport, forestry), but there are some sectors where green tagging is harder to devise (e.g. sustainable agriculture) or metrics may not be available (e.g. low carbon buildings and energy-efficiency metrics). This information asymmetry often results in 'greenwashing', wherein investors end up receiving false signals about green bonds.

iv. While India does monitor greenhouse gas emissions through various reporting mechanisms including PAT (perform-achieve-trade) and RPO (renewable purchase obligation), like many other countries, it does not have a national measurement, reporting, and verification platform for tracking climate finance.[u]

What can be done?

- Define green finance, enhance transparency of information by promoting disclosure standards for carbon and environmental risks, and green certification. Clearly defining green finance will help in accurate tracking of capital flowing in green sectors, enable better reporting and disclosure thus removing information asymmetry between investors and recipients and also reducing transaction costs. To address the problem of asymmetric information, it is important to enhance disclosure standards for carbon and environmental risks and related information flows. Making climate-related financial information publicly available will help investors better understand the performance of their assets, consider the risks of their investments, and ultimately make more informed investment choices. Thus, there is a need for green data definition, standardization, collection, verification, and disclosure.

  The lack of commonly agreed definitions of what constitutes sustainable lending and investment practices contributes to fragmentation of sustainable finance markets, delays the development of even more vibrant green financial markets, and risks green-washing.[v] *The Economist* points out an additional factor contributing to green-washing: the inter-play of value-driven marketing by the finance industry with a hunger for the higher fees that an ESG designation fetches. In support, it quotes a study that found that companies in ESG investment portfolios of American mutual funds between 2010 and 2018 violated labour laws, paid more fines, and had higher carbon emissions than those in non-ESG portfolios sold by the same institution.[w]

  Building on existing market-driven and public initiatives, principles and guidelines for green finance should be developed for all asset classes, including bank credit, bonds, and secured assets. For instance, there is a need to harmonize standards in the green bond market and develop common green bond ratings criteria.[x] The Green Bonds Principles established by the International Capital Market Association are a good example in this field. International regulatory standards such as Basel III for banks and Solvency II for insurers should consider environmental risks by including exceptions for capital and liquidity requirements for green investments. For India, it is recommended that both RBI and SEBI should use well-accepted green standards while formulating their own guidelines for green bonds, which would be useful to attract international investors in this market segment.

- Deepening of corporate bond market and more innovative green finance products like green equity, green bank, and green fund. Infrastructure Debt Funds (IDFs) were designed as mutual funds or NBFCs to refinance long-term infrastructure assets. NBFCs and IDFs can raise resources from long-term investors such as pension funds and insurance companies, using green bonds. Asset aggregators including the Infrastructure Investment Trust can issue green bonds to improve and balance distributable cash flows.

- Establish a Green Project Pipeline on the lines of National Infrastructure Pipeline: This is required for better insight into the market potential, with in-depth analysis of green segments, growth, issuers, use of proceeds, and so on. This will help in better assessment of investment potential in green projects and assist in financial innovation to meet those investment needs.

- Credit enhancements: Deals from ReNew Power and Porbandar Solar Power (who issued unlabelled bonds financing climate-aligned assets) benefitted from a guarantee from the state-owned India Infrastructure Finance Company Limited. These deals show that credit enhancement support can make bond investments from corporates attractive to risk-averse institutional investors. Such credit enhancement could mobilize India's substantial domestic savings for infrastructure projects, facilitating market access for the private sector, and lengthening bond tenors (see Chapter 7 for details).

- Aggregation, warehousing credit line: The distributed nature of renewables and energy-efficiency projects lends itself to warehousing of loans and raising of asset-backed securities. In the rural sector, aggregation can be used to accumulate the fund and invest it in green bonds issued by various public- and private-sector bodies. NABARD, public-sector banks, and NBFCs can facilitate securitization, and the funds raised can be utilized in various infrastructure projects in rural India. Securitization refers to the process of transforming a pool of illiquid financial assets (e.g. mortgages or lease receivables for a rooftop solar PV system) into tradable financial instruments: the so-called asset-backed securities (ABS). Green ABS are securities where the collateral assets or the assets that would be funded with the proceeds (the investment assets) conform to established guidelines such as the Climate Bonds Taxonomy.

- Amend prudential norms: RBI may reduce the risk weightage of green bonds by lowering the related capital adequacy requirements. RBI may also consider green bonds as 'Treasury investments' to increase liquidity and set a target for investment in green securities.
- Tax concessions: Similarly, tax-credit green bonds can be introduced so that investors receive tax credits when they invest in such bonds.

The above analysis shows that the role green finance is playing in the overall transition to more sustainable and responsible fixed-income markets depends not only on absolute trading volumes in green bonds, but also on the level of financial innovation and increased transparency around connecting the source of funding with the intended objectives. To reach meaningful scale and contribute to abating climate change, active public policy and continued private engagement will help green finance reach its full potential.

[a]David Eckstein, Vera Künzel, and Laura Schäfer. 2021. Global Climate Risk Index 2021. Germanwatch. p. 8 (https://germanwatch.org/sites/default/files/Global%20Climate%20 Risk%20Index%202021_1.pdf).

[b]International Energy Agency. 2021. *India Energy Outlook 2021*,p. 169 https://www.iea. org/reports/india-energy-outlook-2021.

[c]*The Economist*. 3 May 2021. The Climate Issue.

[d]The World Bank. 2015. *What Are Green Bonds?* p. 23 (http://documents1.worldbank. org/curated/en/400251468187810398/pdf/99662-REVISED-WB-Green-Bond-Box3932 08B-PUBLIC.pdf).

[e]'Social' investments refer broadly to investments made into companies, organizations, funds, and financial instruments with the intention to generate social impact alongside financial returns. Social impact bonds and development impact bonds are examples. Impact investing is a rather new phenomenon and there is yet to a emerge a widely agreed upon definition. However, one major impact investment transaction has happened recently in India: Mahindra and Mahindra (M&M) has raised US$250 million from UK impact investor British International Investment (BII) for its new electric vehicle unit at a valuation of US$9.1 billion (Source: *Times of India*, 9 July 2022).

[f]Miguel Almeida, Lionel Mok, and Krista Tukiainen. 2020. *Sustainable Debt Global State of the Market H1 2020: Climate Bonds Initiative*, p. 4 (https://www.climatebonds.net/sys

tem/tdf/reports/cbi-sustainable-debt-global-sotm-h12020.pdf?file=1&type=node&id=
54589&force=0).

[g]New Development Bank Press Release.

[h]Vandana Gombar. 05 May 2021. Offshore Wind, Jobs, Hydrogen. *Business Standard*.

[i]*The Economist*. 15 October 2021. Climate Investing—The Virtues of Green Government
Bonds May Be More Political Than Economic.

[j]Ministry of Finance, Government of India. 2021. *Economic Survey 2020–21*.

[k]Bloomberg. 2021. European ESG Assets Shrank by $2 Trillion after Greenwash Rules
(https://www.bloomberg.com/news/articles/2021-07-18/european-esg-assets-shrank-by-
2-trillion-after-greenwash-rules?sref=hyzKRfwE).

[l]Ministry of Finance, Government of India. 2021. *Economic Survey 2020–21*.

[m]*RBI Bulletin*. 2021. Green Finance in India: Progress and Challenges (https://www.rbi.
org.in/Scripts/BS_ViewBulletin.aspx?Id=20022).

[n]Ministry of Finance, Government of India. 2021. *Economic Survey 2020–21*.

[o]*RBI Bulletin*. 2021. Green Finance in India: Progress and Challenges (https://www.rbi.
org.in/Scripts/BS_ViewBulletin.aspx?Id=20022).

[p]*The Economist*. 12 November 2021. Pollution—Baby, It's Toxic Outside.

[q]Institute for Energy Economics and Financial Analysis. 2021. Green Bonds Are Driving
Cost-effective Finance to Clean Energy in India (https://ieefa.org/ieefa-green-bonds-are-
driving-cost-effective-finance-to-clean-energy-in-india/).

[r]Government of India, Ministry of Finance. 2022. Budget Speech of the Finance Minister
(https://www.indiabudget.gov.in/doc/Budget_Speech.pdf).

[s] *RBI Bulletin*. 2021. Green Finance in India: Progress and Challenges(https://www.rbi.
org.in/Scripts/BS_ViewBulletin.aspx?Id=20022).

[t]Prashant Vaze, Sandeep Bhattacharya, Neha Kumar, Monica Filkova, and Diletta
Giuliani. 2019. *Securitisation as an Enabler of Green Asset Finance in India: Climate Bonds
Initiative*, p. 17 (https://www.climatebonds.net/files/reports/securitisation-as-an-enabler-
of-green-asset-finance-in-india-report-15052020.pdf).

[u] Labanya Prakash Jena and Dhruba Purkayastha. 2020. *Accelerating Green Finance in
India: Definitions and Beyond. Climate Policy Initiative*.

[v]The term green-washing was coined by environmentalist Jay Westerveld in 1986. Green-
washing is considered an unsubstantiated claim to deceive consumers into believing that a
company's products are environment friendly.

[w]*The Economist*. 29 July 2022. Asset Managers—The Saviour Complex.

[x]Each rating system involves its own sourcing, research, and scoring methodology, resulting in a single company being rated differently by different ESG rating agencies. This can
pose a challenge to investors.

There is a large gender gap in provisioning of infrastructure, which is
an example of social concern in infrastructure. For example, poor women
in particular must commit large shares of their income and time to
obtaining water and fuelwood, as well as to carrying crops to market. This
time could otherwise be devoted to high priority domestic duties, such as
childcare, or to income-earning activity.[35]

---

[35] World Bank. 1994. *World Development Report—Infrastructure for Development*.

The infrastructure industry continues to attract and employ far fewer women than men, and women users of infrastructure still face safety and other issues from infrastructure that has not been designed to work for everyone. Women's roles in infrastructure development need to be encouraged for greater gender inclusiveness throughout the industry—in alignment with the G20's agenda of social inclusion as an integral component of quality infrastructure. There are benefits that follow when diverse groups of infrastructure users are consulted to create infrastructure that works, and when there is diversity among the people responsible for delivering infrastructure.[36]

Infrastructure is not gender neutral, and the examples of how infrastructure impact gender outcomes are powerfully clear. They can be found in the way infrastructure investments are planned, designed, constructed, and operated, not to mention infrastructure's reach, and the quality and prices of the services it provides. Urban transit systems that are mapped against job locations for women, designed to provide security, and operated to remove uncertainty of arrival times, are essential to balancing labour opportunities for female workers. The design and pricing of water and power systems that recognize and value the disproportionate productivity losses of women and children having to collect water, firewood, or other alternative sources of basic services for their families will look different than those that do not weigh those costs. The expansion of network infrastructure—from highways to pipelines to hydropower projects—may result in disruption to communities. To ensure this disruption does not worsen the existing power imbalances between women and men, and put women at risk of sexual harassment and gender-based violence, proper consultation and contracting mechanisms are essential. This begins with the earliest stages of project design and continues throughout the supervision and oversight of the project's implementation.[37]

India's status and concerns on gender gap in infrastructure is a reflection of the country's position in the Gender Gap Report (GGR) 2022

---

[36] Global Infrastructure Hub blog. Meet Four Women Leaders Who Are Transforming Infrastructure Development in Latin America (https://www.gihub.org/blog/women-in-infrastructure-in-latin-america/).

[37] World Bank. 2019. *Gender Equality, Infrastructure, and PPPs—A Primer* (https://library.pppknowledgelab.org/documents/5720/download).

Table 9.4 Representation of women in India

	Measure	Percentage of women
1	Members of Parliament (2019)	14.4
2	Ministers (2021)	14.1
3	Supreme Court	12.1
4	High Courts	11.9
5	Managerial positions (all workers)	18.7
6	Managerial positions (listed companies)	19
7	Share of elected women in Panchayati Raj Institutions (all India)	45.6

Source: Government of India, Ministry of Statistics and Programme Implementation. 2021. Women and Men in India.

published by the World Economic Forum. India ranks 135 out of 146 countries in terms of gender parity in the GGR. India's ranking in the Gender Gap Index (GGI) has fallen steeply, making it the third-worst performer in South Asia, ahead only of Pakistan and Afghanistan. This is reflected in representation of women in India across occupations (Table 9.4). The table also shows what affirmative action can do, for example, the share of elected women in Panchayati Raj Institutions is much higher at 46 per cent, compared to other indicators.

Women have been the biggest casualties not just of the impact of the Covid-19-induced lockdowns but of the 2016 demonetization, which saw unemployment soar to a forty-five-year high. Well before the pandemic, women's participation rate in the workforce was at a low 24.8 per cent (down from 33.1 per cent in 2011–12). Widespread joblessness following the lockdown in 2020 reduced that to 22.3 per cent, and research shows that though men gradually returned to work in the post-Covid-19 recovery, far fewer women did. Women's representation on boards in India had increased to 17.3 per cent in 2021; however, it remained significantly below the global average of 24 per cent (France leads with 45 per cent board representation).[38] Based on current trends, India will take eighteen years to achieve the world average of 24 per cent gender diversity on boards.

[38] Credit Suisse Research. 2021. CS Gender 3000.

Oxfam estimates a 43 per cent rise in GDP if Indian women had the same workforce participation rate as men. Much of India's decline is on account of key empowerment indicators—in the number of women parliamentarians (the proportion of women in the 779-strong Parliament is still a low of 14 per cent or 110—eighty-one in Lok Sabha and twenty-nine in Rajya Sabha), ministers, and in management and boardroom positions. These are symptomatic of systemic, societal discrimination against women, which remains a huge drag on Indian society, though the government prioritizes women's equal participation in the economy and protection from violence. The estimated average earned income of women is one-fifth that of men, putting India among the bottom ten globally on this indicator. Similarly, India wallows at the bottom on account of poor access to health and education. The history of the developed world shows that prosperity cannot be achieved if almost half a nation's population is excluded.[39] The Economist adds to this prognosis by saying that nations that fail women fail.[40]

Given the evidence, sustainable mechanisms for women's inclusion in infrastructure and PPPs can be created by:

- Institutionalizing strong incentives for women's inclusion in PPP frameworks by either creating gender sub-units or institutionalizing the role of gender specialists in national PPP units. Other measures include ensuring representation of women's civil society organizations (CSOs) in PPP steering committees (typically established before procurement) if they exist and recruiting women with a background in activism or community service as gender specialists.
- Enhancing transparency by institutionalizing external communications regarding project activities so that women's CSOs are kept abreast of latest developments and by conducting procurement online in fora accessible to the public.
- Facilitating coordination of women as users, planners, and builders of infrastructure in the project cycle. This would entail building

---

[39] *Business Standard.* 2 April 2021. The Slip Is Showing—India's Gender Gap Is Wider Than Ever.
[40] *The Economist.* 11 September 2021. Why Nations That Fail Women Fail.

networks among women in target communities, project teams, PPP units, and private developers.

These mechanisms leverage the idea that there is power in numbers and go beyond the conventional recommendation to just hire more women in PPP units and project operations.[41] Though there may be short-term costs in bringing about gender parity in infrastructure, they may pay for themselves by bringing in more efficiency and effectiveness in infrastructure service delivery that would be reflected in better outputs and outcomes.

There are isolated examples that show that things may be changing for the better, as the need for gender parity finds increasing traction. Ola has announced that its electric scooter factory will be run entirely by women. Its Future Factory plans to employ at least ten thousand women, which will make it the largest all-women factory in the world. Companies like Kirloskar and HUL have already created all-women plants. This is heartening as women currently constitute barely 12 per cent of the Indian industrial workforce.[42]

[41] Maria Waqar and Jade Shu Yu Wong. 2021. Making Gender Matter in Infrastructure PPPs (https://blogs.worldbank.org/ppps/making-gender-matter-infrastructure-ppps?CID=WBW_AL_BlogNotification_EN_EXT).

[42] *Times of India*. 18 September 2021. Women at Work—Industrial Jobs Can Tackle a Key Gender Imbalance.

10

Generic Issues for Sustainable Infrastructure Financing—Sanctity of Contracts and Autonomous Regulation of Infrastructure

Infrastructure projects require huge investments, which are in the nature of sunk costs, with returns that are spread over decades. As such, the sanctity of contracts needs to be upheld as the private sector has used these contracts to model their returns and submit bids accordingly. This chapter looks at one case study (the Hyderabad Metro Rail Project) to illustrate the point about upholding the sanctity of contracts for sustainable financing of infrastructure projects.

Because of the characteristics of infrastructure, autonomous tariff regulation is very important for sustainable financing of infrastructure projects. If there is regulatory capture, either by the public or the private sector, the returns of infrastructure projects are affected, including the regulatory risk and its impact on the cost of capital. In this context, the chapter examines infrastructure regulation in India to evaluate whether some of the decisions taken by infrastructure regulators are increasing regulatory risk. This discussion leads to a case for other regulatory options like 'regulation by contract' and multi-sectoral regulators, rather than creating an independent sectoral regulator for each sector opened up for private participation.

Infrastructure Financing in India. Kumar V Pratap and Manshi Gupta, Oxford University Press.

Promoting Private Participation in Infrastructure through Upholding the Sanctity of Contracts—Case Study of the Hyderabad Metro Rail Project

Abstract

Investment in infrastructure is necessary for economic growth and development.[1] However, because of the fiscal resource crunch and general low efficiency of public-sector-operated infrastructure, many countries are increasingly turning to the private sector to build and operate the required infrastructure. But the outcomes of private participation in infrastructure may not always be satisfactory for stakeholders, especially if big private-sector companies behave opportunistically and the public sector does not do adequate project preparation. This segment uses the Hyderabad Metro Rail Project as a case study to illustrate this assertion, using the issues associated with the financial incentive scheme (viability gap funding) of the Government of India, to demonstrate how the users of this metro rail project and the government may be getting adversely affected by the opportunistic behaviour of an influential private partner.

The case study offers the following key learnings: (i) sanctity of contracts needs to be upheld as the contracts define the risk-return framework among stakeholders, which is the basis for competitive bidding of projects. The sanctity of contracts also needs to be upheld for fairness of outcomes to stakeholders, the government, the private sector, and the users. (ii) Renegotiation of contracts is a bilateral process (between the concessionaire and the public authority) where equilibrium occurs through negotiations and could, therefore, be non-transparent and risks frittering away the gains of competitive bidding. Therefore, contracts should not be renegotiated, and there should be safeguards for preventing opportunistic renegotiations. (iii) Allowing post-contract changes in the obligations of the private sector through renegotiation of contracts will promote more aggressive bidding and threaten the private participation

---

[1] The contribution of Shubham Goyal, assistant director in the Infrastructure Policy and Finance Division of Department of Economic Affairs, Ministry of Finance, in the preparation of this case study is gratefully acknowledged. Views expressed in the case study are those of the authors and not of the Government.

in infrastructure regime of countries. (iv) Adequate project preparation by the public sector, including land acquisition, is expected to improve project outcomes and value for money to the public sector, while also decreasing the chances of renegotiations.

Highlights

- Many countries, both developed and developing, are using public–private partnerships (PPP) to bridge their infrastructure deficit. However, the public sector has to be vigilant in contract administration so that the expected benefits materialize. Otherwise, there are chances of poor returns to the public sector from entering into PPPs.
- Sanctity of contracts needs to be upheld for fairness of outcomes to stakeholders, the government, the private sector, and the users.
- Renegotiations and post-award changes in contracts risks frittering away the gains of competitive bidding of infrastructure projects. Therefore, contracts should not be renegotiated, and there should be safeguards for preventing opportunistic renegotiations.
- Allowing post-contract changes in the obligations of the private sector through renegotiation of contracts will promote more aggressive bidding and threaten the private participation in infrastructure regime of countries.
- Adequate project preparation by the public sector, including land acquisition and environment and forest clearance, is expected to improve project outcomes and value for money to the public sector, while also decreasing the chances of renegotiations.

Introduction

The availability of quality infrastructure is a pre-requisite for achieving broad-based and inclusive growth on a sustained basis. Economic infrastructure including telecommunications, electricity, roads, railways, metro rail, airports, and ports, and social infrastructure including education, health, solid waste management, water treatment and supply are important for economic growth and development. Infrastructure works on growth both from the supply and the demand side through enhancing productivity and efficiency leading to enhanced cost-competitiveness and industrialization, thus kindling the virtuous cycle of more infrastructure investment leading to higher growth. Therefore, countries across the world, both developed and developing, are trying to increase infrastructure investment.

Infrastructure investment is generally characterized by large and lumpy upfront expenditures, sunk costs, long gestation periods, natural monopolies, large externalities, and public-good characteristics like non-excludability and non-rivalness in consumption, which make for long payback periods and market failure.[2] Owing to these characteristics of infrastructure, it has traditionally been provided by the public sector. However, governments the world over, are facing a resource crunch, while the demand for infrastructure is increasing, forcing them to invite the private sector into infrastructure provisioning. Private participation in infrastructure is also seen to lead to more efficient delivery of services (either qualitatively superior services or at lower cost, or both) than pure public-sector delivery. Therefore, countries have increasingly turned towards the private sector to provide essential infrastructure to the masses. The rough worldwide split between public and private investment in infrastructure is two-thirds to one-third.[3]

India has prioritized infrastructure investment, and with some success. It is estimated that India spent US$1.1 trillion on infrastructure in the ten-year period from 2008 to 2017, of which more than a third came from the private sector.[4] While this is a substantial amount, India needs to spend much more on infrastructure. Fast-growing countries of East Asia in their fast-growing phases have annually spent about 7–8 per cent of

[2] Kumar V. Pratap and Rajesh Chakrabarti (2017). Public–Private Partnerships in Infrastructure: Managing the Challenges, pp. 11–15.

[3] Boston Consulting Group (2013). Bridging the Gap—Meeting the Infrastructure Challenge with Public–Private Partnerships, p. 6 (https://web-assets.bcg.com/img-src/Bridging_the_Gap_Feb_2013_tcm9-99579.pdf).

[4] Niti Aayog, Government of India (2017). Appraisal Document of Twelfth Five Year Plan (2012–17), pp. 178–9 (http://164.100.94.191/niti/writereaddata/files/document_publication/Appraisal%20Document%20Five%20Year%20Plan%202012%20-%2017-Final%20%281%29.pdf); Ministry of Finance, Government of India (2020). Report of the Task Force on National Infrastructure Pipeline, Volume 1, p. 26 (https://dea.gov.in/sites/default/files/Report%20of%20the%20Task%20Force%20National%20Infrastructure%20Pipeline%20%28NIP%29%20-%20volume-i_1.pdf).

their GDP on infrastructure.[5] Using this proportion and with a GDP of US$2.8 trillion in 2018/19, India needs to spend about US$200 billion per annum on infrastructure. Under-investment on infrastructure (average annual spend of US$110 billion as against the need for about US$200 billion) is reflected in India's low-quality power supply especially in rural areas, over-crowding and frequent accidents and associated loss of lives in the road and railway sectors, the high turnaround time of ships in the port sector, and the generally poor quality of public health and education institutions. Given the fiscal resource crunch, the required step-up in annual infrastructure investment has to come mainly from the private sector.

Private investment in infrastructure primarily comes in the form of PPPs, where the private sector provides public services on the basis of a concession agreement signed between the public and the private sector. Well-managed PPPs help in addressing the infrastructure resource gap as well as improving efficiency in infrastructure service delivery. As per the Private Participation in Infrastructure (PPI) database of the World Bank, India is ranked second among developing countries both by the number of PPP projects as well as the associated investments.[6] Much of the Indian success in PPPs is attributed to the development of a robust institutional structure, financial support in the form of viability gap funding (VGF),[7] and use of standardized documents, both process documents like the Model Request for Qualification (RfQ) and the Model Request for Proposal (RfP), as well as substantive documents like the Model Concession Agreements (describing, inter alia, the risk allocation among stakeholders), across infrastructure sectors.

India is among the leaders in the developing world in PPPs, as per the PPI database of the World Bank (ppi.worldbank.org). However, issues do

---

[5] World Bank (2008). The Growth Report: Strategies for Sustained Growth and Inclusive Development, p. 35 (https://openknowledge.worldbank.org/bitstream/handle/10986/6507/449860PUB0Box3101OFFICIAL0USE0ONLY1.pdf?sequence=1&isAllowed=y).

[6] World Bank. Private Participation in Infrastructure Project database (ppi.worldbank.org).

[7] Recognizing that externalities engendered by infrastructure projects would not be reflected in project revenues, the Viability Gap Funding Scheme was introduced in 2006 to enhance the commercial viability of competitively bid infrastructure projects that are justified by economic returns, but do not meet standard thresholds of financial viability. Under the scheme, grant assistance up to 20 per cent of project capital cost can be provided by the Central government to PPP projects (in economic infrastructure; in social infrastructure the VGF is larger), thus leveraging scarce budgetary resources to access the larger pool of private capital. An additional grant up to 20 per cent of project costs can be provided by the project sponsoring entity.

arise in implementing PPPs in India and the case study highlights some of these issues, particularly the hold-up problem[8] in contracting. The objective of this segment is to present the case study of a major infrastructure project in India, which is trying to subvert the competitive bidding process by effectively renegotiating the contract. The segment shows that this opportunistic behaviour of the private sector is detrimental to the public interest and the interest of the most important stakeholder, the users.

The plan of the rest of the segment is as follows. The second section provides the literature review. The third section discusses investment in metro-rail projects in India and finds that most investments in the sector are being made by the public sector. The fourth section deliberates on the private concessionaire of Hyderabad Metro Rail Project (L&T Metro Rail (Hyderabad) Limited). The fifth section describes the regulatory system including the financial incentive scheme (VGF) of the government, and the bidding process, while the sixth section applies the regulatory system to the Hyderabad Metro Rail Project. The seventh section presents the analysis of the user charges of the project in terms of a comparison between 'what it should be' and 'what it is'. The chapter then describes the issues that would arise if the contention of the private concessionaire is accepted followed by a discussion of what can be done to prevent opportunistic renegotiations. The final section describes the key learnings from the case study.

Literature review

The case study is about upholding the sanctity of contracts and the issues that arise when projects are renegotiated, including compromising public interest by being unfair to many other stakeholders, including the users and the government. Concession contracts have evolved and include

---

[8] The Theory of Incomplete Contracts avers that actual contracts are incomplete. They are poorly worded, ambiguous, and leave out important eventualities including unanticipated contingencies. The right to decide about the missing eventualities is called right of residual control. This leads to the 'hold-up' problem. The source of the hold-up power is the ownership over right of residual control which generally lies with owner of the asset. (Oliver Hart. 2017. Incomplete Contracts and Control. *American Economic Review*. 107 (7): 1731-52).

many mechanisms aimed at reducing the chances of renegotiations like inflation-indexing of user charges, dispute resolution clauses providing for a three-step process consisting of mediation, arbitration, and adjudication, *force majeure* clauses dealing with unforeseen events, and so on. The importance of an effective dispute resolution mechanism in reducing contractual stresses has been emphasized by many, including Wells and Gleason (1995).[9] The contract between the state government and the private party for the Hyderabad Metro Rail Project included most of these mechanisms, but despite this, the contract got into trouble because of, what we feel was, the opportunistic behaviour of the private sector.

Renegotiations have become increasingly common in long-term infrastructure contracts (Guasch 2004).[10] Though Guasch (2004), after studying more than a thousand concessions granted in the Latin America and Caribbean region during 1985–2000, found the overall renegotiation rate to be 30 per cent, and the corresponding rates for transport and water sector contracts to be 55 per cent and 74 per cent respectively, the renegotiation rate in some countries like Portugal has been higher (average renegotiation rate 67 per cent), particularly in transportation and water projects, where 100 per cent of the contracts have been renegotiated (Cruz and Marques 2013).[11] This high incidence shows that renegotiations have become the rule rather than the exception.

Most governments go in for competitive bidding for infrastructure projects to ensure competition *for* the market, which very often are natural monopolies (and therefore, preclude competition *in* the market). Competitive bidding for infrastructure projects is expected to compete away the monopoly rents that may be available to some of these projects. However, competitive bidding may also be forcing some bidders to submit aggressive bids, who after winning the bid, look at ways to manage their obligations, and renegotiations offer a way out. While aggressive bidding improves the chance of winning the bid, renegotiations offer a

---

[9] L. T. Wells and E. S. Gleason. 1995. Is Foreign Infrastructure Investment Still Risky? *Harvard Business* Review 73, no. 5 (September–October 1995): 44–55

[10] J. L. Guasch. 2004. *Granting and Renegotiating Infrastructure Concessions: Doing It Right.*

[11] C. O. Cruz and R. C. Marquez. 2013. Exogenous Determinants for Renegotiating Public Infrastructure Concessions: Evidence from Portugal. *ASCE Journal of Construction Engineering and Management* Vol. 139, Issue 9

way out to the winning bidder not to suffer the consequences of aggressive bidding.

The Hyderabad Metro Rail case is a typical concessionaire-led renegotiation (Guasch (2004) found that in 61 per cent of cases, concessionaries requested renegotiation and in 26 per cent of the cases, governments' initiated renegotiation) to raise the tariff beyond what was prescribed in the concession agreement (this qualifies to be renegotiation[12] as per Guasch (2004)). This was a large project (total project cost, about US$2 billion) and therefore more adversely affected by problems of demand forecasting, delays in finalization of the route alignment, and land acquisition, which made it more likely to be renegotiated. This was also a case where the concessionaire changed the fares (from what was mentioned in the concession contract) from day one of the operation of the project (Guasch (2004) found that most renegotiated concessions underwent renegotiation very soon after their award, with an average of 2.2 years between concession award and renegotiations), despite the concession period being thirty-five years. There is no independent regulatory body for metro rails in India and the Hyderabad Metro Rail Project was regulated by its concession contract (Guasch (2004) found that renegotiation was much more likely when a regulatory agency was not in place (61 per cent) than when one was in place (17 per cent)). And the de facto[13] renegotiations ended up benefitting the concessionaire to the detriment of the users. The reasons for, and results of renegotiations in the case study are broadly in accordance with those found in the literature.

Investment in metro rail projects in India

As per the 2011 census, more than 377 million people (or about a third of the Indian population) lived in urban areas.[14] Indian urban areas are also

---

[12] Guasch (2004), p. 12: Renegotiation has occurred if a concession contract underwent a significant change or amendment not envisioned or driven by stated contingencies in any of the following areas: tariffs ... Standard scheduled tariff adjustments and periodic tariff reviews are not considered renegotiations.

[13] The concessionaire increased the fares from day one of the project operation, beyond what is stated in the concession contract. So, this amounts to de facto renegotiations.

[14] Census of India (2011) https://en.wikipedia.org/wiki/2011_Census_of_India, accessed 15 April 2020.

among the most polluted in the world,[15] the major reason for which is vehicular pollution. To address this and to attend to the problem of general over-crowding of cities, many cities have taken up mass rapid transit system (MRTS), of which the metro rail system is the most popular and also the most expensive.

Recent experience in India suggests that it costs an average of about US$40 million per km (averaged over underground and above-ground segments) for the construction of metro rail in cities.[16] As metro rail is a MRTS system, its tariffs have to be 'affordable'. The high capital costs and the need for tariffs to be affordable, implies that in some cases, actual tariffs are so low that they are not able to recover even the operation and maintenance costs of the MRTS (see Chapter 6 for a discussion about cost recovery in metro rail in India). This non-commercial nature of the metro-rail MRTS also implies that it would mostly be implemented by the public sector and the losses of the system would be funded by the state. This is supported by the record in India, where eleven cities have a functional metro-rail system, of which only three have some degree of private participation.

However, because of the fiscal resource crunch, governments and the public sector are unable to fund the entire needed infrastructure,

---

[15] World Economic Forum. 2020. Six of the World's 10 Most Polluted Cities Are in India (https://www.weforum.org/agenda/2020/03/6-of-the-world-s-10-most-polluted-cities-are-in-india/).

[16] The following table gives the capital cost per km of planned metro rails in Indian cities. The average cost, over both underground and above-ground sections, comes to Rs.272 crore per km, which is a shade below US$40 million per km at the current exchange rate.

Planned metro rails in Indian cities

Name of metro	Total cost (Rs. crore)	Capital cost per km (Rs. crore per km)
Patna Metro	9,202	426
Kochi Metro Phase II	1,957	175
Ahmedabad Metro Phase II	5,384	191
Kanpur Metro	11,076	342
Indore Metro	7,501	238
Bhopal Metro	6,941	249
Agra Metro	8,380	285

Source: Compiled by the authors from the detailed project reports of respective metros.

including metro rails, and therefore there is a need to attract the private sector to do so. Given the non-commercial nature of metro-rail operations, there is a need for VGF to make such economically viable metro-rail projects also commercially viable. This case study discusses the Hyderabad Metro Rail Project, which was tendered out to the private sector with VGF as the bidding parameter. The winning private-sector bidder was Larsen & Toubro (L&T) Limited (selected on the basis of least-quoted VGF), which created a special purpose vehicle (SPV), L&T Metro Rail (Hyderabad) Limited, to implement the project.

In this case study, we discuss the construction and operation of a metro-rail system solely by the private sector, while the majority of metro-rail systems in the country are built and operated by the public sector. Though other public–private arrangements are possible and have been tried in the road sector, including construction by the public sector and operation by the private sector, the metro-rail sector is a late entrant to the private space, and only a few transactions of private construction and operation have taken place. Therefore, other public–private arrangements in the metro-rail sector are not discussed further in this segment.

Larsen & Toubro Metro Rail (Hyderabad) Limited

Larsen & Toubro Limited, commonly known as L&T, is a large Indian multinational company headquartered in Mumbai in the Maharashtra state of India. The company has diverse business interests in basic and heavy engineering, construction, realty, manufacturing of capital goods, information technology, and financial services. As of 31 March 2019, the L&T Group comprises 110 subsidiaries, eight associates, twenty-seven joint venture companies and thirty-one joint operations. L&T Metro Rail (Hyderabad) Limited, the subject of this case study, is one of the major subsidiaries of L&T. The L&T group had revenues of Rs.1,41,007 crore[17] for financial year[18] (FY) 2019 registering a growth of 18 per cent over FY 2018. Profit after tax touched an all-time high of Rs.8,905 crore

---

[17] One crore is 10 million. The dollar–rupee exchange rate as of 13 April 2020 was US$1 = Rs.76.36 (https://dbie.rbi.org.in/DBIE/dbie.rbi?site=statistics).

[18] Indian financial year is from April 1 to March 31.

in FY 2019 showing a substantial growth of 21 per cent over FY 2018. As of 31 March 2019, the company had 44,332 permanent employees, out of which 2,822 were women and forty-one were employees with disabilities.[19]

The equity shares of the company are listed on the Bombay Stock Exchange (BSE) and the National Stock Exchange (NSE) of India. The company's shares constitute a part of the BSE 30 Index of the BSE Limited as well as the NIFTY Index of the NSE. Its global depository receipts are listed on the Luxembourg Stock Exchange and the London Stock Exchange. Its market capitalization is about Rs.2,14,000 crore as of 14 February 2021[20] and is ranked 18th among Indian companies on this metric. L&T is a large reputable company with sound governance practices and diverse public ownership constituted by mutual funds (15 per cent), insurance companies (18 per cent), foreign portfolio investors (21 per cent), employee trusts (14 per cent), and so on.

L&T incorporated an SPV—L&T Metro Rail (Hyderabad) Limited (L&T MRHL) to implement the Hyderabad Metro Rail Project on Design–Build–Finance–Operate–Transfer (DBFOT) basis. L&T's holding company, Larsen and Toubro Limited, holds 99.99 per cent of the company's shares.[21]

L&T Limited was awarded the Hyderabad Metro Rail Project by the then government of Andhra Pradesh in India. The company signed the concession agreement with the then government of Andhra Pradesh on 4 September 2010 and completed the financial closure of the project on 1 March 2011. The SPV was to construct, operate, and maintain the metro rail, which consisted of three elevated corridors from Miyapur to LB Nagar (Corridor I), Jubilee Bus Station to Falaknuma (Corridor II), and Nagole to Shilparamam (Corridor III) in Hyderabad, covering a total distance of 71.16 km, in accordance with the provisions of the concession agreement. The project cost is funded by the promoters' share capital, VGF of the Government of India, and term loans from a consortium

[19] Larsen & Toubro. *Annual Report 2018–19*. (http://investors.larsentoubro.com/upload/AnnualRep/FY2019AnnualRepFull%20Annual%20Report%202018-19.pdf).

[20] Bombay Stock Exchange (BSE) website, accessed 14 February 2021: (https://www.bseindia.com/stock-share-price/larsen--toubro-ltd/lt/500510/)

[21] L&T Metro Rail (Hyderabad) Limited. *Annual Report 2017–18* (https://corpwebstorage.blob.core.windows.net/media/38559/annual-report-2017-18-ltmrhl.pdf).

of ten banks with the State Bank of India (SBI) as the lead bank.[22] This is the largest debt funding tie-up in India for a non-power infrastructure PPP project.[23]

L&T MRHL started its commercial operations from 29 November 2017, on the stretch of about 30 km between Nagole—Ameerpet—Miyapur. The 16 km metro-rail stretch between Amarpreet and LB Nagar was opened to the public on 24 September 2018. The third section Ameerpet-Hitec City (10 km) came into operation on 20 March 2019. Another 1.5 km stretch from Hitec City to Raidurg was commissioned in November 2019. With the launch of another 11 km stretch on 7 February 2020 (total, 68.5 km), Hyderabad Metro Rail has become the second-largest metro-rail network in the country after Delhi.

Gross sales and other income for L&T MRHL for FY 2018 were Rs.69.53 crore (including fare and non-fare revenue). The loss after tax from continuing operations including extraordinary and exceptional items was Rs.58.36 crore for FY 2018.

Regulatory framework for metro rail in India and the bidding process

Since metro rail is a public utility, the user fees (tariffs) and service obligations need to be regulated. The metro-rail sector does not have an independent sectoral regulator in India and what is practiced in the sector is 'regulation by contract'. The contract, signed between the public authority (Government of Andhra Pradesh, now Telangana) and the private concessionaire (L&T MRHL) has provisions on user fees (basic fare with inflation indexation) that can be charged by the concessionaire from the passengers over the thirty-five-year concession period.

Infrastructure projects are often not commercially viable on account of high project cost, long gestation period, and returns spread over decades. However, they continue to be economically viable. Accordingly, the

---

[22] L & T Metro Rail (Hyderabad) Limited. *Annual Report 2017-18*, p. 65 (https://corpwebstorage.blob.core.windows.net/media/38559/annual-report-2017-18-ltmrhl.pdf).

[23] L & T Metro Rail (Hyderabad) Limited website (https://www.ltmetro.in/about-us/about-lt-metro-rail-limited/).

Scheme and Guidelines for Financial Support to Public Private Partnerships in Infrastructure (Viability Gap Funding (VGF) Scheme)[24] was formulated by the Ministry of Finance, Government of India, to provide financial support to infrastructure projects undertaken through PPPs with a view to make them commercially viable. VGF under the scheme is normally in the form of a capital grant at the stage of project construction. The quantum of VGF is restricted to the lowest bid for capital grant subject to a maximum of 20 per cent of the total project cost (TPC).

For grant of VGF under the scheme, the project has to be accorded 'in-principle' and 'final approval' by the Empowered Committee seated in the Ministry of Finance. At the stage of 'in-principle' approval, project agreements (such as the concession agreement, the state support agreement, the substitution agreement, the escrow agreement, the operation and maintenance agreement, and the shareholders' agreement, as applicable) along with RfQ and RfP are examined. After the 'in-principle' approval, bids are invited by the concerned ministry, state government, or statutory entity, and the concessionaire is selected through a transparent and open competitive bidding process. The bidding parameter is VGF and the bidder who asks for the least VGF is the selected bidder. After the selection of the bidder, their proposal is submitted for 'final approval' under the VGF scheme along with signed copies of all the project agreements. After 'final approval', the project becomes eligible for VGF support in accordance with the terms and conditions of the scheme. So far, sixty-three projects with a TPC of Rs.34,161 crore and VGF of Rs.5,620 crore have been granted 'final approval' by the Government of India.

Under the VGF scheme, VGF for amounts below Rs.200 crore may be sanctioned by the Empowered Committee, consisting of the following members: the secretary, Department of Economic Affairs (chair); secretary, Department of Expenditure; CEO, NITI Aayog; and secretary of the line ministry dealing with the subject. VGF above Rs.200 crore may be sanctioned by the Empowered Committee with the approval of the finance minister.

---

[24] *Scheme and Guidelines for Financial Support to Public–Private Partnerships in Infrastructure (VGF Scheme)*, Ministry of Finance (2013) (https://www.pppinindia.gov.in/documents/20181/21751/VGF_GuideLines_2013.pdf/999e4386-9623-47bb-b372-38246ede1a0f).

Prior to disbursement of VGF, the government (Department of Economic Affairs, Ministry of Finance), lead financial institution (LFI) and the private-sector company (concessionaire) enter into a tripartite agreement.[25] The project sponsoring authority signs the tripartite agreement as the confirming party. VGF is disbursed only after the private-sector company has subscribed to and spent the equity contribution on for the project and is released in proportion to debt raised from LFI.

Regulatory framework as applied to Hyderabad Metro Rail Project

After a failed initial bidding, the re-bidding of the project was done in July 2010. In the re-bidding, L&T emerged as the winning bidder with the VGF requirement of Rs.1,458 crore. The next two bidders were Transstroy India consortium, which had sought VGF of Rs.2,200 crore and Reliance Infrastructure consortium, which had sought VGF of Rs.2,991 crore. The cost of the project was estimated to be Rs.12,132 crore (TPC) at this point in time.

The 'in-principle' approval for VGF support for Hyderabad Metro Rail Project on DBFOT basis was accorded at the 12th meeting of the Empowered Committee[26] held on 29 July 2010. The offer of L&T was accepted by Government of Andhra Pradesh, which awarded the project to the L&T SPV called 'L&T Metro Rail (Hyderabad) Limited' (L&T MRHL) and entered into a concession agreement with it on 4 September 2010. The Empowered Committee in its 17th meeting held on 6 May 2013[27] recommended the granting of 'final approval' for VGF of Rs.1,458 crore under the scheme, which was approved by the finance minister. The project was to be funded with debt of about Rs.11,480 crore by a consortium

[25] Format of Tripartite Agreement is available in the Scheme and Guidelines for Financial Support to Public–Private Partnerships in Infrastructure (VGF Scheme), Ministry of Finance (2013), p. 21 (https://www.pppinindia.gov.in/documents/20181/21751/VGF_GuideLines_2013.pdf/999e4386-9623-47bb-b372-38246ede1a0f).

[26] Record of Discussion of the 12th Meeting of Empowered Committee (https://www.pppinindia.gov.in/documents/20181/22340/12+EC+minutes+29.07.2010-+HMR.pdf/a3ee67fc-a0a0-4c07-aaad-a47b9eb7bd57?version=1.0).

[27] Record of Discussion of the 17th Meeting of Empowered Committee (https://www.pppinindia.gov.in/documents/20181/22340/17th+EC+Minutes++06.05.2013.pdf/7672db31-d525-483d-8d0f-239a7d4a0ade?version=1.0).

of banks led by the State Bank of India (LFI) and the equity component of the project was expected to be around Rs.3,440 crore (including the VGF) at this point in time.

The tripartite agreement, as prescribed under the VGF scheme, was signed by the government (Department of Economic Affairs, Ministry of Finance), the LFI (SBI), and the concessionaire (L&T MRHL) on 1 October 2015. The sponsoring authority (Hyderabad Metro Rail Ltd, a Government of Andhra Pradesh, now Telangana, entity) was the confirming party to the tripartite agreement. Out of the total approved VGF of Rs.1,458 crore, Rs.1,204 crore (about 83 per cent of the approved amount) was disbursed by the Department of Economic Affairs to the concessionaire up to December 2017, after which further disbursal of VGF was suspended.

It must be noted that VGF is the single bidding parameter, while other parameters (including the user charges) are frozen in the concession agreement. The concession agreement between the Government of Andhra Pradesh (now Telangana) and the winning bidder has a schedule on user charges (Schedule-R), which describes both the base user charges as well as its escalation on account of inflation over the concession period. This schedule is crucial for protecting user interests and that of the concessionaire and is summarized below.

Provisions regarding user charges as per Schedule-R of the concession agreement

The basic fares, as mentioned in Table 10.1, were to be increased annually, without compounding, by 5 per cent for a period of fifteen successive years commencing from 1 April 2014. The first increase of 5 per cent was to take effect on 1 April 2015, and the last and fifteenth such increase was to be effected on 1 April 2029. Such increased rates were to be deemed to be the base rates for the purpose of these rules. This implies that for a rail system commissioned on 1 April 2015, the basic fare for a journey of less than 2 km shall be Rs.8.40 per trip (Rs.8 + 5 per cent of Rs.8 or Rs.0.40).

The applicable basic fare was also to be revised annually with effect from 1 April each year to reflect the variation in the Wholesale Price Index (WPI) between the week ending 31 January 2009 and the week ending on or immediately after 31 January of the year in which such revision is undertaken, but

Table 10.1 Basic fare for Hyderabad Metro Rail as per Schedule R of the Concession Agreement

Serial no.	Distance to be travelled (in km)	Basic fare (in Rs.)
1	Up to 2	8
2	More than 2 and up to 6	10
3	More than 6 and up to 10	12
4	More than 10 and up to 14	14
5	More than 14 and up to 18	16
6	More than 18	19
7	Unlimited use for the day	40

Source: Concession Agreement between the then Government of Andhra Pradesh and L&T MRHL.

such revision was to be restricted to 60 per cent of the increase in Wholesale Price Index. This provides inflation-indexation to the user charges.

The formula for determining the fare due and payable under these rules was:

$$\text{Fare} = b + \left[b * \left(\text{WPI}_B / \text{WPI}_A \right) - b \right] * 0.6 \qquad (10.1)$$

where:

'b' is the basic fare determined for the rail system;

'WPI_B' is the Wholesale Price Index (WPI) of the week ending on or immediately after 31 January of the year in which such revision is undertaken; and

'WPI_A' is the WPI of the week ending on 31 January 2009.

Rounding off fares: fares to be collected under these rules were to be rounded off to the nearest rupee.

Analysis

On the basis of Table 10.1 and the rules stated in Schedule-R of the concession agreement and summarized earlier, the basic fare of the metro-rail system is calculated in Table 10.2.

Table 10.2 Basic fare for Hyderabad Metro Rail system (yearly progression) as per Schedule R of the Concession Agreement (in Rs.)

Serial no.	Distance to be travelled (in km)	Basic Fare	1 Apr 15	1 Apr 16	1 Apr 17	1 Apr 18	1 Apr 19	1 Apr 20
1	Up to 2	8	8.4	8.8	9.2	9.6	10	10.4
2	More than 2 and up to 6	10	10.5	11	11.5	12	12.5	13
3	More than 6 and up to 10	12	12.6	13.2	13.8	14.4	15	15.6
4	More than 10 and up to 14	14	14.7	15.4	16.1	16.8	17.5	18.2
5	More than 14 and up to 18	16	16.8	17.6	18.4	19.2	20	20.8
6	More than 18	19	19.95	20.9	21.85	22.8	23.75	24.7
7	Unlimited use for the day	40	42	44	46	48	50	52

Source: Authors' calculations.

The final fare after escalating the above basic fares for inflation as per the rules mentioned in Schedule-R of the concession agreement are calculated in Table 10.3.

The concessionaire vide its fare notification dated 25 November, 2017[28] has fixed the final fare (Table 10.4) which is at variance and much higher than the one shown in Table 10.3, which is derived from the concession agreement. The quantum of fare variation between 'what it should be' (as per the concession agreement) and 'what it is' (as per the fare notification of L&T MRHL) is shown in Table 10.5.

The higher fare fixation by the concessionaire (as shown in Table 10.5) amounts to a violation of the VGF scheme, the tripartite agreement and Schedule-R of the concession agreement. This violation is explained below.

To be eligible under the VGF scheme, the project must provide the service against the payment of a pre-determined tariff (Schedule-R of the

---

[28] Fare Notification issued by L&T MRHL in November 2017 (http://corpwebstorage.blob. core.windows.net/media/35991/press-release-25th-november-2017-fare-chart-hyderabad-metro-rail.pdf).

Table 10.3 Final fare as on 1 April 2020 for Hyderabad Metro Rail system after escalation, as per Schedule R of the Concession Agreement

Serial no.	Distance to be travelled (in km)	Final fare calculation as per Equation 10.1 above	Final fare as per equation 10.1 (in Rs.)	Rounding off of fare (in Rs.)
1	Up to 2	10.4 + (10.4*(191.72/124.4) – 10.4) *0.6	13.78	14
2	More than 2 and up to 6	13 + (13*(191.72/124.4) – 13) *0.6	17.22	17
3	More than 6 and up to 10	15.6 + (15.6*(191.72/124.4) – 15.6) *0.6	20.67	21
4	More than 10 and up to 14	18.2 + (18.2*(191.72/124.4) – 18.2) *0.6	24.11	24
5	More than 14 and up to 18	20.8 + (20.8*(191.72/124.4) – 20.8) *0.6	27.55	28
6	More than 18	24.7 + (24.7*(191.72/124.4) – 24.7) *0.6	32.72	33
7	Unlimited use for the day	52 + (52*(191.72/124.4) – 52) *0.6	68.89	69

Note: Wholesale Price Index (WPI) of January 2009 = 124.40; WPI of January 2020 = 191.72 (Source of WPI: http://eaindustry.nic.in).

Source: Authors' calculations.

Table 10.4 Final fare as per Notification dated 25 November 2017 issued by the Concessionaire (L&T MRHL)

Serial no.	Distance to be travelled (in km)	Fare
1	Up to 2	10
2	More than 2 and up to 4	15
3	More than 4 and up to 6	25
4	More than 6 and up to 8	30
5	More than 8 and up to 10	35
6	More than 10 and up to 14	40
7	More than 14 and up to 18	45
8	More than 18 and up to 22	50
9	More than 22 and up to 26	55
10	More than 60	60

Source: Fare Notification of November 2017 by L&T MRHL (http://corpweb storage.blob.core.windows.net/media/35991/press-release-25th-novem ber-2017-fare-chart-hyderabad-metro-rail.pdf).

Table 10.5 Hyderabad Metro Rail fares—'what it should be' and 'what it is'

Distance travelled (in km)	Projected fares, as per Concession Agreement, as of 1 April 2020:'what it should be'	Adjusted fares as per L&T MRHL Notification issued in November 2017: 'what it is'	Variation (%)
Up to 2	14.00	10.00	−29%
More than 2 and up to 6	17.00	20.00	18%
More than 6 and up to 10	21.00	32.50	55%
More than 10 and up to 14	24.00	40.00	67%
More than 14 and up to 18	28.00	45.00	61%
More than 18 and up to 22	33.00	50.00	52%
More than 22 and up to 26	33.00	55.00	67%
More than 26	33.00	60.00	82%
Simple average (mean)	25.38	39.06	46%

Source: Authors' calculations.

concession agreement), and which was taken into account by the bidders when submitting their financial bid. However, by fixing the fares much higher than that mentioned in Schedule-R of the concession agreement (as shown in Table 10.5), the eligibility condition of the VGF scheme regarding pre-determined tariff is violated.

As stated earlier, prior to disbursement of VGF, the government (Department of Economic Affairs, Ministry of Finance), LFI (SBI) and the private-sector company (concessionaire, L&T MRHL) enter into a tripartite agreement. The project-sponsoring authority signs the tripartite agreement as the confirming party. In accordance with the tripartite agreement,[29] further disbursement of VGF was suspended (as already

---

[29] Relevant provisions of the Tripartite Agreement signed under the VGF Scheme are:

Clause 3.1 (c) - the confirming party i.e. Project Authority, represents, warrants and confirms that project shall provide the service against payment of pre-determined tariff/user charge as set forth in the Concession Agreement;

Clause 6.1 (d) - if any of the representations or warranties of the owner are found at any time to be false or incorrect, and owner fails to cure within a cure period of five business days, it would be considered as VGF default.

In this case, since the concessionaire has fixed higher fare vis-à-vis that mentioned in the Concession Agreement, the warranty of the Project Authority (Hyderabad Metro Rail Ltd, the

mentioned, Rs.1,204 crore of the approved Rs.1,458 crore VGF had already been disbursed to the concessionaire) by the Department of Economic Affairs, Government of India, after the L&T MRHL fare notification. The legal justification given by the concessionaire for fixing higher fares[30] is 'Change in Law', that is, the project has been brought under the ambit of Metro Railway (Operation & Maintenance) Act, 2002 (Central Metro Act)[31] by notification in January 2012, while the original concession agreement was signed under the Andhra Pradesh Municipal Tramways (Construction, Operation and Maintenance) Act, 2008. As per the concessionaire, this change in the governing law for metro rail allows it to fix a substantially higher fare[32] than the fare prescribed in the

Government of Andhra Pradesh (now Telangana) public sector outfit) is violated. Therefore, this needs to be considered as VGF default in terms of Clause 6.1(d) of the Tripartite Agreement. The remedy for VGF default is given in Clause 2.4(iii) of the Tripartite Agreement, which is stated below:

Clause 2.4(iii) - Notwithstanding anything to the contrary, in the event of occurrence of VGF Default, the disbursement of VGF would be suspended or terminated.

In accordance with the Tripartite Agreement clause 2.4(iii), further disbursement of VGF was suspended by the Department of Economic Affairs, Government of India, after issue of the L&T MRHL Fare Notification.

[30] Record of Discussions of the 32nd Meeting of Empowered Committee (https://www.ppp inindia.gov.in/documents/20181/22340/RoD+of+32nd+EC+Meeting/7b4160ee-1405-4c2a-b637-3993ad6e6ce9?version=1.0).
[31] Metro Railway (Operation & Maintenance) Act, 2002 (http://mohua.gov.in/upload/uplo adfiles/files/MetroRail_Act_2002.pdf).
[32] Section 33 of the Metro Railway (Operation & Maintenance) Act, 2002 states that:

The metro railway administration shall, from time to time, on the recommendations made to it by the Fare Fixation Committee constituted under sub-section (1) of section 34, fix, for the carriage of passengers, fare for travelling from one station to another of the metro railway; Provided that the metro railway administration may fix the fare under this section without recommendations of the Fare Fixation Committee on the initial opening of the metro railway.

As per Section 2(j) of Metro Railway (Operation & Maintenance) Act, 2002, 'metro railway administration' in relation to:

i. a Government metro railway means the General Manager of that railway; or
ii. a non-Government metro railway means the person who is the owner or lessee of that metro railway or the person working that metro railway under an arrangement with the owner or lessee of that metro railway.

Section 2(j)(ii) makes the lessee of the Hyderabad Metro Railway (L&T MRHL), the *metro railway administration* (MRA), who, therefore, has the right to fix the fare at the time of initial opening of the metro railway without the recommendation of the Fare Fixation Committee (FFC). Since there is no provision in the Metro Railway (Operation & Maintenance) Act, 2002 which defines the period of initial opening, the concessionaire can continue with the higher fares till the time the Fare Fixation Committee is constituted in accordance with section 33 of the Metro Railway (Operation & Maintenance) Act, 2002.

concession agreement[33]. The Department of Legal Affairs, Government of India, was also consulted in this regard, which upheld the stance of the concessionaire.[34]

Issues in accepting the concessionaire's contention

i. The concession agreement dated 4 September 2010 was signed between the Government of Andhra Pradesh and L&T Metro Rail Hyderabad Ltd (concessionaire) under the provisions of Andhra Pradesh Municipal Tramways (Construction, Operation and Maintenance) Act, 2008 and subsequently, in January 2012, the project was brought under the ambit of the Central Metro Act. Therefore, it becomes relevant to examine the 'Change in Law'[35] provisions of the concession agreement. This examination reveals that the Central Metro Act became applicable to the project in January 2012 while the bidding for the project was completed in July 2010. Therefore, the event of bringing this project under the ambit of the Central Metro Act should be treated as 'Change in Law' as per Clause (c) of these provisions.

---

[33] As per section 103 of the Metro Railway (Operation & Maintenance) Act, 2002: 'The provisions of this Act shall have effect notwithstanding anything inconsistent therewith contained in any enactment other than this Act or in any instrument having effect by virtue of any enactment other than this Act.'

[34] The Department of Legal Affairs, Government of India opined that:

   i. In view of the notification dated 24.01.2012, the Concessionaire is the Metro Railway Administration (MRA) under the Central Metro Act and can fix the fare as per section 33 of the Act.

   ii. In view of i above, revision of fare as elaborated in Schedule-R of the Concession Agreement stands altered and fare determination should be under the Central Act only.

   iii. In setting the initial fare, a FFC recommendation is not necessary and therefore an FFC need not to be constituted for this. For subsequent revision, FFC is a must.

[35] As per the Concession Agreement, 'Change in Law' is defined as the occurrence of any of the following after the date of Bid:

   a) the enactment of any new Indian law as applicable to State;

   b) the repeal, modification or re-enactment of any existing Indian law;

   c) the commencement of any Indian law which has not entered into effect until the date of Bid;

   d) change in the interpretation or application of any Indian law by a judgment of a court of record which has become final, conclusive and binding, as compared to such interpretation or application by a court of record prior to the date of Bid; or

   e) any change in the rates of any of the Taxes that have a direct effect on the Project.

The remedy for 'Change in Law' is provided in clause 41.1 of the concession agreement.[36] Accordingly, since the concessionaire has benefitted from the higher fares to the extent of much more than Rs.1 crore (Table 10.6), it has to be brought to the same financial position in net present value (NPV) terms as would have prevailed before the 'Change in Law'. Since the estimated gains to the concessionaire because of the higher fares is about Rs.5,000 crore in NPV terms (Table 10.6), and the amount of approved VGF is Rs.1,458 crore, the already disbursed VGF (Rs.1,204 crore) should be recovered from the concessionaire and the balance VGF (Rs.254 crore) should be terminated.

ii. The Central Metro Act did not prescribe any fare for the metros. Therefore, even if the concessionaire was the *metro railway administration* (see footnote 32), it could have fixed the fare that was prescribed in Schedule-R of the concession agreement and to which it was a signatory. However, the concessionaire willingly opted for the higher fare than that prescribed in the concession agreement, to its advantage and to the detriment of the most important stakeholder, the users of the metro rail.

iii. In a similar case of Mumbai Metro Line-I (Mumbai Metropolitan Region Development Authority versus Fare Fixation Committee), Writ Petition No. 2605 of 2015, the Bombay High Court[37] had observed that:

> Applying the principles of statutory interpretation, it is not possible to accept the extreme position that the concession agreement totally stands obliterated on account of non-obstante clause contained in section 103 of the Metro Act (see footnote 33). The section itself states that the provisions of

---

[36] Clause 41.1 of the Concession Agreement states that:

If as a result of Change in Law, the Concessionaire benefits from a reduction in costs or increase in net after-tax return or other financial gains, the aggregate financial effect of which exceeds the higher of Rs.1 crore (Rupees one crore) and 0.5% of the Realizable Fare in any Accounting Year, the Government may so notify the Concessionaire and propose amendments to this Agreement *so as to place the Concessionaire in the same financial position as it would have enjoyed had there been no such Change in Law.*

[37] Bombay High Court Order (https://indiankanoon.org/doc/140387429/).

Table 10.6 Estimated gains to the Concessionaire because of higher fares

Financial year	Fare as per Concession Agreement (Rs.) (2)	Actual fare of L&T MRHL (Rs.) (3)	Ridership per day (4)	Estimated gains (in Rs. crore) = (3-2)*4*365/ 10^7 (5)
2017/18	20.75	39.06	70,000	15.90[a]
2018/19	22.13	39.06	2,50,000	154.55
2019/20	23.75	39.06	3,50,000	195.62
2020/21	25.38	39.06	3,67,500	183.60
2021/22	27.02	41.66	3,85,875	206.19
2022/23	28.78	44.44	4,05,169	231.56
2023/24	30.65	47.40	4,25,427	260.05
2024/25	32.64	50.56	4,46,699	292.03
2025/26	34.77	53.92	4,69,033	327.95
2026/27	37.03	57.51	4,92,485	368.28
2027/28	39.43	61.34	5,17,109	413.57
2028/29	42.00	65.43	5,42,965	464.42
2029/30	44.73	69.79	5,70,113	521.51
2030/31	47.63	74.43	5,98,619	585.62
2031/32	50.73	79.39	6,28,550	657.60
2032/33	54.03	84.68	6,59,977	738.43
2033/34	57.54	90.32	6,92,976	829.17
2034/35	61.28	96.33	7,27,625	931.06
2035/36	65.26	102.75	7,64,006	1,045.45
2036/37	69.50	109.59	8,02,206	1,173.89
2037/38	74.02	116.89	8,42,317	1,318.10
2038/39	78.83	124.68	8,84,433	1,480.00
2039/40	83.96	132.98	9,28,654	1,661.77
2040/41	89.41	141.84	9,75,087	1,865.85
2041/42	95.22	151.28	10,23,841	2,094.96
2042/43	101.41	161.36	10,75,033	2,352.19
2043/44	108.01	172.11	11,28,785	2,640.98
2044/45	115.03	183.57	11,85,224	2,965.18
2045/46	122.50	195.79	12,44,485	3,329.16
2046/47	130.47	208.83	13,06,710	3,737.77
	NPV of estimated gains as on 1 April 2020 till FY 2019/20 (Rs. crore) (actuals)			388.66

(continued)

Table 10.6 Continued

Financial year	Fare as per Concession Agreement (Rs.) (2)	Actual fare of L&T MRHL (Rs.) (3)	Ridership per day (4)	Estimated gains (in Rs. crore) = (3-2)*4*365/ 10^7 (5)
	NPV of estimated gains as on 1 April 2020 from FY 2020/21 (Rs. crore) (projected)			4,580.35
	NPV of total estimated gains as on 1 April 2020 (Rs. crore) (actuals + projected)			4,969.01

[a] Estimated gains based on 124 days of FY 2017/18 as the metro became operational on 28 November 2017.

Note: The following assumptions have been made in the above analysis: (a) discount rate for NPV calculation is 12 per cent; (b) annual increase in actual fare (from FY 2021/22) has been assumed as 6.66 per cent on the basis of Delhi Metro (a publicly implemented metro and the largest metro system in India) Fare Fixation Committee Report in which the annual increase for FY 2015/16 is calculated as 6.66 per cent; (c) annual increase in the fare (from FY 2021/22) as per concession agreement has been assumed as 6.50 per cent; (d) increase in ridership from FY 2020/21 has been assumed as 5 per cent.

Source: Authors' calculations.

the Metro Act shall prevail over 'anything inconsistent there-with' in any instrument having effect by virtue of any enact-ment other than the Metro Act. Therefore, it becomes relevant and necessary to determine whether there is anything incon-sistent between the Concession Agreement and the provi-sions of the Metro Act ... The extreme position that section 103 of the Metro Act completely obliterates the Concession Agreement, or even obliterates the portions of Concession Agreement not inconsistent with the provisions of Metro Act is not acceptable.

iv. The concessionaire has claimed the higher fares as well as the VGF on account of various reasons: time and cost overrun due to the delay in the conditions precedent to be fulfilled by the govern-ment, additional cost due to change of scope and *force majeure*, lower traffic than expected, and so on.[38] However, all these issues

[38] Record of Discussions of the 34th Meeting of Empowered Committee (https://www.ppp inindia.gov.in/documents/20181/22340/Record+of+Discussions+of+the+34th+EC+Meeting. pdf/68979c66-0498-4d39-9d33-834cf38b6c91?version=1.2).

are already dealt with in the concession agreement[39] (Article 4: Conditions Precedent, Article 16: Change of Scope, Article 29: Effect of Variations in Traffic Growth, and Article 34: *Force Majeure*).[40] On examination of the relevant clauses in the concession agreement, it is found that for the delay in fulfilment of conditions precedent, the public authority has to pay the damages at the specified rate. The payment for change of scope of the project has

---

[39] Concession Agreement of the L&T MRHL project (https://www.pppinindia.gov.in/docume nts/20181/34422/5.+Hyderabad+Metro+Rail+project.pdf/7fd98761-d514-4087-b56f-33db5 6472cb8?version=1.0).

[40] As per clause 4.2 of the Concession Agreement, if the Government does not procure any or all of the Conditions Precedent within the period specified and the delay has not occurred as a result of breach of this Agreement by the Concessionaire or due to Force Majeure, the Government shall pay to the Concessionaire, Damages in an amount calculated @0.1% of the performance security for each day's delay until the fulfilment of such Conditions Precedent, subject to maximum of 20% of performance security.

As per clause 16.3.2 of the Concession Agreement, all cost arising due to Change of Scope (in excess of 0.25% of Total Project Cost) would be paid by the Authority to the Concessionaire in accordance with clause 16.3.1. Within 7 days of the Change of Scope Order, the Government shall make an advance payment to the Concessionaire in a sum equal to 20% of the cost of Change of Scope. The Concessionaire shall after commencement of work, present to the Government bills for payment in respect of Work in Progress or completed works. Within 30 days of receipt of such bills, the Government shall disburse to the Concessionaire such amount as certified by the Independent Engineer.

As per clause 29.2.1 of Concession Agreement, in the event that Actual Average Traffic shall have fallen short of the Target Traffic, then for every 1% shortfall as compared to the Target Traffic, the Concession Period shall, subject to payment of Concession Fee in accordance with this Agreement, be increased by 1.5% thereof; provided that such increase in Concession Period shall not in any case exceed a maximum period of 7 years. In clause 29.1.1, the Target Date for determination of traffic variation is mentioned as October 1, 2024. Therefore, any shortfall in traffic needs to be assessed only in October 2024.

Further, as per clause 34.7 of the Concession Agreement,

A. upon occurrence of any Force Majeure Event prior to the Appointed Date, the Parties shall bear their respective costs and no Party shall be required to pay to the other Party any costs thereof;

B. Upon occurrence of a Force Majeure Event after the Appointed Date, the costs incurred and attributable to such event and directly relating to the Project (the "Force Majeure Costs") shall be allocated and paid as follows:

a) upon occurrence of a Non-Political Event, the Parties shall bear their respective Force Majeure Costs and neither Party shall be required to pay to the other Party any costs thereof;

b) upon occurrence of an Indirect Political Event, all Force Majeure Costs attributable to such Indirect Political Event, and not exceeding the Insurance Cover for such Indirect Political Event, shall be borne by the Concessionaire, and to the extent Force Majeure Costs exceed such Insurance Cover, one half of such excess amount shall be reimbursed by the Government to the Concessionaire; and

c) upon occurrence of a Political Event, all Force Majeure Costs attributable to such Political Event shall be reimbursed by the Government to the Concessionaire.

to be made by the public authority. For traffic shortfall, the remedy is provided in terms of the modification of the concession period. *Force majeure* costs are allocated between the concessionaire and the public authority depending on the nature of the *force majeure* event. The concessionaire should pursue the remedies as per the concession agreement and not give them as reasons for higher fares from those mentioned in the concession agreement. In fact, L&T MRHL is actually also 'working on favourable resolution of … compensation for delays and scope change, concession period extension and other issues pending with the State Government,'[41] and therefore, the unilateral change in user charges by the concessionaire amounts to double counting of claims.

While all the above remedies are provided in the concession agreement, it needs to be emphasized that better-prepared projects by the public sector would decrease the chances of renegotiations. In this specific case, a better-prepared project with adequate land acquisition would have led to conditions precedent being fulfilled in a timely manner, while also decreasing the need for changing the scope of the project.

v. As we have seen, there were finally three financial bidders for this project. The winning bid was that of L&T MRHL with a VGF demand of Rs.1,458 crore. The difference between the VGF bid of the winning bidder and the losing bidder (Transstroy India Consortium with a VGF demand of Rs.2,200 crore) was Rs.742 crore. The NPV of the extra gains from higher fares, as per Table 10.6, is about Rs.5,000 crore, which is much more than the difference in their bids. Therefore, the losing bidder may challenge this post-contract benefit to the winning bidder, saying that if this benefit was forthcoming, it would have bid even lower than the winning bidder.

As Guasch (2004) observes, 'when used opportunistically or strategically by an operator or government, to secure additional benefits, and not

---

[41] Larsen & Toubro. *Annual Report 2018–19*, p. 265 (http://investors.larsentoubro.com/upl oad/AnnualRep/FY2019AnnualRepFull%20Annual%20Report%202018-19.pdf).

driven by the incompleteness of a contract, renegotiation can undermine the integrity of a concession, reduce welfare … Renegotiation, particularly opportunistic renegotiation, can reduce or eliminate the expected benefits of competitive bidding.' This case study is an illustration of this observation.

What can be done to prevent opportunistic renegotiations?

Renegotiations do away with the sanctity of contracts. With easy renegotiations, everything would be negotiable even after the contract has been awarded, with the result that the benefits of a competitive auction would be lost. Since many infrastructure projects enjoy a monopoly in the delivery of services, competitive bidding ensures competition *for* the market (as distinct from competition *in* the market) and competes away the monopoly rents available to service providers, thus keeping user charges for infrastructure services reasonable. Once renegotiations are institutionalized and they become routine, competitive bidding would not lead to the selection of the most efficient service provider, but the one who is most adept at renegotiations, which is a perverse outcome. Thus, opportunistic infrastructure players would bid low to get the project awarded, and then get the contract terms changed through renegotiations (Guasch 2004). And these renegotiations are a bilateral process between the selected service provider and the government, which is not subject to the discipline of competition.

Experience in many countries suggests that changing or upsetting the balance of risk-sharing through renegotiations typically results in higher tender prices, delays in completion, additional time and cost claims, and, in the worst cases, major protracted disputes leading to arbitration, and sometimes to contract termination.

Given this, the sanctity of contracts must be upheld by both the public and the private sectors. It is important that there is adequate project preparation and that the detailed project reports are of high quality which bridge any information asymmetry between the government and the bidders. This would allow contractors to bid with greater confidence and thereby enable more efficient price discovery, and in turn make the contract less incomplete.

To limit demand for renegotiations, there is a need to write better contracts with unambiguous delineation of risks and rewards across stakeholders and include all foreseeable eventualities in the contract document. There may be a need to adopt global best practices by following International Federation of Consulting Engineers (FIDIC) contracts.

Also, once written, these contracts need to be strictly enforced because the sanctity of bids needs to be upheld through, say, higher performance bonds. As a further deterrent, the government needs to specify that it would not entertain any demand for renegotiations for say, the first five years of a contract. After this period, the private sector would need to deposit a fee, which should be related to the TPC, for the regulators to consider any request for renegotiation. This fee would be refunded in the event that the renegotiation request is approved by the regulator. In evaluating these requests, regulators should be able to distinguish between renegotiation demands based on incomplete contracts and those based on opportunistic behaviour, and only the former kind needs to be considered for any relief. In such cases, the relief should be strictly limited to bringing the concessionaire to the same financial position as would have prevailed if the event which made the contract incomplete had not occurred. Opportunistic renegotiation demands based on aggressive bidding are bad in principle and practice, produce perverse incentives and outcomes, and therefore should not be entertained.

Key learnings

Metro-rail systems are natural monopolies. Therefore, competition *in* the market is precluded by definition. To mimic the outcomes of a perfectly competitive market (the most socially optimal outcomes), it needs to be ensured that there is competition *for* the market. In accordance with this, a two-stage (RfQ and RfP) competitive bidding process has been prescribed in India for major infrastructure projects. The bidding is done on the basis of a draft concession agreement that is part of the bidding documents shared with the prospective bidders. The draft concession agreement defines the risks and rewards to the private sector (including the user charges that we have analysed extensively earlier) and is the basis for bidding by the private sector. In this context, maintaining the sanctity of

Table 10.7 Indicator-wise rank of India in Ease
of Doing Business rankings 2020

Serial no.	Indicator	Rank
1	Starting a business	136
2	Dealing with construction permits	27
3	Getting electricity	22
4	Registering property	154
5	Getting credit	25
6	Protecting minority investors	13
7	Paying taxes	115
8	Trading across borders	68
9	Enforcing contracts	163
10	Resolving insolvency	52
Overall		63

Source: World Bank's Ease of Doing Business rankings (https://www.
doingbusiness.org/content/dam/doingBusiness/country/i/india/
IND-LITE.pdf) (accessed 13 April 2020).

contracts is at the heart of achieving equitable outcomes for stakeholders through private participation in infrastructure.

India has one of the highest infrastructure deficits in the world. To bridge the infrastructure deficit and to attract foreign investment into infrastructure, India is trying to improve its position in the World Bank's Ease of Doing Business[42] (EoDB) assessment. India ranks sixty-three among 190 countries in the current rankings. The indicator-wise rank[43] of India in World Bank's EoDB 2020 is given in Table 10.7.

Enforcing contracts is one of the ten business-climate parameters considered for arriving at the country rankings. As per Table 10.7, India's rank in enforcing contracts is 163 out of 190 countries and is the worst among all parameters. In this segment, focus has been on the Hyderabad Metro Rail Project as an example of a major infrastructure project where

[42] World Bank. 2020. *Doing Business 2020: Comparing Business Regulation in 190 Economies* (https://openknowledge.worldbank.org/handle/10986/32436).
[43] World Bank's Ease of Doing Business rankings (https://www.doingbusiness.org/content/dam/doingBusiness/country/i/india/IND-LITE.pdf) (accessed 13 April 2020).

a contract needs to be enforced. The segment draws significantly from the concession agreement of the project. As we have seen, the concessionaire is seeking to violate the VGF guidelines, the tripartite agreement, as well as the concession agreement.

Any post-award changes in the contract, which is what allowing the concessionaire to charge a higher tariff than allowed in the concession agreement implies, amounts to a renegotiation of the contract and risks frittering away the gains of competitive bidding. Renegotiation of a contract is a bilateral process between the winning bidder and the public authority, where equilibrium occurs through negotiation and could, therefore, be non-transparent.

Allowing higher fares amounts to a windfall gain to the concessionaire to the detriment of the users and other stakeholders. This also promotes aggressive bidding by the private sector, as they would be assured that an aggressive bid would get them the contract and they would then work on the system to modify the concession contract after winning the contract. As per the PPI database of the World Bank (ppi.worldbank.org), India has the second highest number of PPP projects in the developing world and the associated investments. Condoning this type of behaviour sets a bad precedent and will promote more aggressive bidding by the private sector and later renegotiations, threatening the entire PPI regime in the country.

As we have seen, some of the reasons given by the concessionaire for charging higher fares than those mentioned in the concession agreement were related to non-fulfilment of conditions precedent by the public authority. Notwithstanding the remedy for non-fulfilment of conditions precedent provided in the concession agreement, this highlights the need for better project preparation by the public authority, which can be expected to improve project outcomes for all stakeholders.

Exploring Optimal Regulatory Options for Indian Infrastructure

Abstract

The Ministry of Railways and the Ministry of Coal, respectively, recently opened up their passenger-train and commercial coal-mining segments to private participation. With this, there is a growing clamour to set up independent regulators for these sectors.[44] This segment argues that given the envisaged role of the regulator in the passenger-train and coal mining segments, and the record of the independent sectoral regulators across infrastructure sectors in India, railways and coal may be better off 'regulating by contract' or the independent sectoral regulators in related sectors may be given the regulatory responsibility of railways and coal, respectively. The latter recommendation would also be in accordance with the worldwide trend towards multi-sectoral regulators.

The clamour for an independent regulator for railways has been gaining ground since the time private passenger trains were mooted. It is reasoned that with an incumbent public-sector monopolist in the sector, private investment would not be forthcoming in the absence of unbiased regulation, which purportedly translates into the requirement for an independent sectoral regulator. After the RfQ for private participation in passenger-train services was issued (1 July 2020) and interest shown by only two bidders at the RfP stage, of which one is the public sector IRCTC, the clamour has become shriller. The objective of private participation in this market segment is to introduce modern technology rolling stock with reduced maintenance requirements, reduced transit time, job creation, enhanced safety, a world-class travel experience to passengers, and reduced demand-supply deficit in the passenger transportation sector. As per the plan, 151 private trains are to be operated over 109 routes, which will bring in private investment of about Rs.30,000 crore. The concession period would be thirty-five years and the bidding parameter would be revenue share to railways. The concessionaires would have to pay fixed haulage charges for path, stations, access to railway infrastructure, and energy charges based on actuals. The first private passenger trains under this initiative were expected to start operations in 2023.

Similarly, the coal sector has recently been opened up to the private sector for commercial mining. Thirty-eight explored coal blocks were offered for which forty-three bids were received. For nineteen blocks, there were more than two bids, while for three, there was a single bid. To

---

[44] An earlier version of this segment appeared as Kumar V Pratap. 2023. Autonomous Regulation and Regulatory Risk - Why Railways and Coal Should Not Have Independent Sectoral Regulators, Economic and Political Weekly, Volume LVIII No 28 (July 15, 2023)

take this initiative to fruition, Ministry of Coal is open to the idea of a coal regulator.

However, to decide whether an independent railway or coal regulator is needed or not, we need to understand why we want to regulate the railway and coal sectors, the experience with independent regulators in infrastructure sectors so far, international best practices, and given all this, how do we address the issue of regulatory risk to prospective bidders in railway passenger trains and coal-mining segments.

The need for regulating infrastructure services

Given the need for attracting private investment into infrastructure, the Eleventh Five Year Plan aimed at, inter alia, developing an environment which is both attractive to investors and also seen to be fair to consumers, especially since many infrastructure projects have an element of monopoly. This called for an environment in which either the market itself is competitive giving consumers a choice among different suppliers, as in the case with telecommunications or freight container carriers; or concessions are given to the most competitive bidders in an environment where the regulatory system limits user charges to reasonable levels and sets appropriate standards of service as in the case of airports, ports, and roads. The rationale for regulating railway and coal services remains the same.

There is substantial regulatory risk in infrastructure sectors, because of characteristics of infrastructure, among which is high asset specificity, with little alternative use of these assets, and the consequent sunkcost nature of infrastructure investments. So, once capital is invested in building or refurbishing an airport, a port, a road, a passenger train or coal mine, the investor should not be subjected to arbitrary decisions regarding user charges or output price; otherwise, there would be no investment forthcoming. Tariff risk is the most important regulatory risk and refers to the risk that the regulator would not allow cost-recovering user charges. One of the ways of mitigating regulatory risk is by setting up independent sectoral regulators, who would, inter alia, regulate user charges/output price and service standards.

Independent and autonomous regulation guards against politically motivated government intervention or 'hold-up' by the private sector. It is also expected to provide a level playing field with incumbent public and private players. For example, autonomous regulation will guard against arbitrary action by the public-sector departmental undertaking, Indian Railways, or the public-sector company, Coal India Limited, which could lead to stranded private investments. Autonomous regulation would be a great source of comfort for the new private players planning to enter these erstwhile public monopoly sectors.

A perfectly competitive market is the gold standard for benign outcomes for society, including consumers, captured in the sentence, while 'he intends only his own gain … he is … led by an *invisible hand* to promote an end which was no part of his intention … By pursuing his own interest he frequently promotes that of the society more effectually than when he really intends to promote it' (Adam Smith 1776). In long-term equilibrium in a perfectly competitive market, price is equal to marginal and average cost so that the users do not have to pay any rent or extraordinary profits and the providers make just enough money to make it viable to provide the services. However, large segments of infrastructure markets are a monopoly, that is, we cannot, for example, have competing power transmission lines catering to the same consumers as it would be economically and financially unviable to do so. Similarly, private passenger trains would be having a monopoly for the time that railways would not be able to run competing trains from the same station.

Regulation is aimed at producing competitive outcomes in the absence of such markets. So, there is a need for regulating these services, so that passenger service standards (punctuality, reliability, upkeep of trains, etc.) are reasonable in order to lessen the chances of monopolistic exploitation of users (normally, both the user charges and service standards are regulated, but user charges are not being regulated for private passenger trains and the selected bidder would be free to set the user charges).

The experience with independent sectoral regulators in infrastructure so far

Given the need for regulating infrastructure services, there are four infrastructure regulators in the country, namely, Telecom Regulatory Authority of India (TRAI), Central Electricity Regulatory Commission

(CERC) and states have the State Electricity Regulatory Commission, Tariff Authority for Major Ports (TAMP), and the Airport Economic Regulatory Authority (AERA). India probably already has the highest number of independent sectoral regulators, which has complicated and delayed decision-making and has increased uncertainty regarding the business environment, raising the regulatory risk premium and, thus, the cost of capital.

The question we need to answer is whether the existing sectoral regulators have been able to mitigate the regulatory risk in their respective sectors. It has been alleged that in the case of TRAI, there has been regulatory capture by the private sector, which is apparent from alleged partisan decisions of the regulator, whether it is reducing the interconnection usage charge (IUC), and the one whereby both Vodafone and Airtel were being prevented from practicing valid market segmentation strategies. In the case of CERC, the regulatory flip-flops in the case of tariff fixation for the Tata Mundra project are well-known. For TAMP, we are well too aware of the case of Nhava Sheva International Container Terminal, where the revenue share to be paid to the public authority was made a part of the costs to be taken into account in tariff fixation for the project, thus rendering the whole idea of competitive bidding with revenue share as a bidding parameter, a farce. If the bidders are assured that the outgo (revenue share) on account of the bid would be compensated through higher tariffs, then there would be no effective limit to what bidders would bid, because any amount that is bid would be compensated by increasing the user charges. This would make competitive bidding of projects a meaningless exercise.

AERA has also been accused of approving development fees imposed on consumers for Mumbai and Delhi airports post-contract, to the detriment of passenger interests. The comptroller and auditor general (CAG) pointed out that Delhi International Airport Limited (DIAL) had financed about 27 per cent of the capital costs through development fees, levied on the passengers since 2009 (CAG 2012). Thus, development fees enriched DIAL by Rs.3,415 crore at the expense of passengers. It is also anticipated that while Adanis have bid aggressively for the recent bouquet of six airports in India, they would petition AERA to include the bid parameter (per passenger fee) as a cost element, while fixing airport charges for the airlines and the passengers, which would reduce the competitive bidding exercise for airports to a farce. Actually, the revenue share or passenger fee (bidding parameters in port and airport sectors, respectively) are a distribution of profits and should not be included as a cost element while determining tariffs or user charges.

The disquiet with the functioning of the existing sectoral regulators has been expressed at the highest levels of the government. For example, the prime minister, in his 2011 Independence Day speech said:

> In recent years, we have established independent regulatory authorities in many areas. These authorities discharge many responsibilities which were earlier in the domain of the government itself. We have no legislation which would enable monitoring of the work of these regulatory authorities and make them more accountable, without, however, compromising their independence. We are also considering enactment of such a law.

On the other hand, in the road sector, India has the highest number of PPP projects in the world (486 projects accounting for an investment of US$90 billion as per the PPI database of the World Bank) without having an independent sectoral regulator. What is practiced in the sector is 'regulation by contract', whereby the concession contract has clauses that govern the relationship between the public authority and the private sector, ranging from non-fulfilment of conditions precedent, *force majeure* events like the ongoing Covid-19 pandemic (which is classified as a non-political *force majeure* event, the relief for which is extension of the concession period by the *force majeure* period), premature termination, and so on. It is not that the road sector does not have issues in private participation including disputes with the private sector but it has devised strategies for tackling them to make the road sector, the most happening sector in Indian infrastructure.

It is well accepted in the regulatory firmament, that quality human resources are scarcer than money (Tremolet and Shah 2005). The appointment of regulators in India may have led to issues in regulatory capacity leading to compromised regulatory substance, in terms of quality of decisions, that damages credibility. As long as independent sectoral regulators are seen as a perch for retired bureaucrats (after all, all the four infrastructure regulators are headed by retired bureaucrats), they will not be autonomous and look to central and state governments before taking decisions. Thus, though the Electricity Act (2003) recognizes the principle that tariffs should be cost-reflective (Section 61), we find that the difference between the average cost of supply of power and average revenue realization has widened to Rs.0.72 per unit of power in the country, lately (Power Finance Corporation 2020). So, it can be surmised that the role of independent sectoral regulators in infrastructure sectors of India in addressing regulatory risk has been quite suspect thus far in India.

We should also be cognizant of the fact that even in sectors with independent sectoral regulators, the government is thinking in terms of parallel regulatory structures, for example, the new Electricity Act (Amendment) Bill proposes creation of the National Electricity Contract Enforcement Authority, thus eating into the domain of the existing electricity regulators. The mandatory and advisory functions of the Electricity Regulatory Commissions include, for example, the following: to adjudicate upon disputes involving generating companies or transmission licensee; to specify and enforce standards with respect to quality, continuity, and reliability of service by licensees; the promotion of investment in the electricity industry. Therefore, this move to create parallel regulatory structures may not be optimal in theory for the evolution of infrastructure regulation in the country.

So, there is nothing automatic about autonomous regulation once an independent sectoral regulator has been created. Much depends on whether the regulator has *decision-making independence* (make regulatory decisions without de facto prior approval of government), *institutional and management independence* (the regulator has control over internal administration and protection from removal from office for political reasons), and *financial independence* (the regulator has an earmarked, secure, and adequate source of funding). The Indian infrastructure sectoral regulators are wanting in many of these aspects.

The recommended regulatory option for railways and coal

As we have seen, in the passenger-train segment user charges are unregulated, while the service standards mentioned in the concession contract would have to be enforced by the proposed railway regulator. This is too limited a role for an independent sectoral regulator.

It should also be noted that the Ministry of Railways already has Cabinet approval for a Rail Development Authority (in May 2017, and Rail Tariff Authority in January 2014), but it has not been actioned for many years now. India has one of the lowest per km tariffs for passengers (National Transport Development Policy Committee (Volume III Part I) 2014: 51), while having one of the highest per ton-km tariff for freight to allow for cross-subsidization. The result is that though railways are a much more economically and environmentally efficient mode of transport and the idea behind the proposed Rail Tariff Authority, inter-alia, was to set this imbalance right, the proposal has not been actioned. If the Ministry of Railways could not implement the Cabinet approval for so many years despite the overwhelming rationale for setting the tariff imbalance right, the advent of private participation in passenger-train services may not be enough reason for actioning this Cabinet approval.

So, just like the road sector, the Ministry of Railways may practice 'regulation by contract' with balanced risk-sharing between the public and the private sectors. Concession agreements define the 'rules of the game' so that service providers can build financial models and bid. Concession agreements have provisions regarding tariff determination (which has been left to the bidders in the passenger-train segment) and performance standards, which provide greater predictability and clarify risks and rewards for the private sector.

Alternatively, AERA may also function as the regulator for the railways, thus creating a multi-sectoral regulator. Multi-sectoral regulators would be a check against proliferation of regulators, help build capacity and expertise, promote consistency of approach, prevent regulatory capture, and save on costs. The United States has a multi-sectoral regulator in the form of the Federal Communications Commission, the United Kingdom and Sri Lanka are mulling regulatory reforms including multi-sectoral regulators to streamline the regulatory framework and eliminate overlapping regulations, and most states in Australia have multi-sectoral regulators (Planning Commission 2008). The railway safety regulator (Commission of Railway Safety) is already functioning under the aegis of the Ministry of Civil Aviation, so this idea about AERA being made a multi-sectoral regulator for the civil aviation and railways sectors would only cement the relationship between these two modes of transportation for the common good.

The same rationale holds for the proposed coal regulator, whereby the Ministry of Coal should be practicing 'regulation by contract' or alternatively, CERC may also function as the regulator for coal, thus creating a multi-sectoral regulator.

11

Covid-19 Pandemic and Its Impact on Infrastructure and Its Financing

The Covid-19 pandemic is a black swan event and has had a major impact on infrastructure and its financing. The impact on infrastructure has been both from the demand and the supply side. In terms of its treatment, the Covid-19 pandemic is a non-political *force majeure* event in the Indian road sector's Model Concession Agreement and the relief provided is an extension of the concession period by the *force majeure* period. To address the issue of the concessionaire's liquidity during this period, the country's central bank (Reserve Bank of India, RBI) has put in place a moratorium period for loan repayment up to August 2020. However, bank financing was already grappling with non-performing assets of 8.5 per cent of their portfolio, which is expected to go up because of the Covid-19 pandemic (however, the actual numbers are much lower), with consequent impact on bank financing of infrastructure. Implementation of India's first National Infrastructure Pipeline (NIP, April 2020) has been impacted adversely at least in the first two years (financial years (FYs) 2020 and 2021) as public-sector resources were constrained because of the high-priority expenditures associated with the pandemic and private-sector investments suffered from increased risk. However, since the NIP is a six-year infrastructure development plan, the slack in the first two years may be covered in the later years given the infrastructure green shoots that have appeared even in the midst of the pandemic.

The Covid-19 pandemic is a black swan event and has had a major impact on all economic parameters. While the world growth rate in 2020 is estimated to be (−)3.3 per cent by the IMF, the severe contraction has had particularly adverse employment and earning impacts on certain groups, highlighting the human costs of the pandemic (sometimes recognized as

Infrastructure Financing in India. Kumar V Pratap and Manshi Gupta, Oxford University Press.
© Kumar V Pratap and Manshi Gupta 2024. DOI: 10.1093/oso/9780198884934.003.0012

the twin threats to lives and livelihoods). Youth, women,[1] workers with relatively lower educational attainment, and the informally employed have generally been hit the hardest. Income inequality is likely to increase significantly because of the pandemic. Close to 95 million more people worldwide are estimated to have fallen below the threshold of extreme poverty in 2020 compared with pre-pandemic projections.[2] The potential economic impact of the pandemic on Asia and the Pacific could range from US$1.7 trillion to US$2.5 trillion[3] (across different containment scenarios).

The human and health crisis engendered by the pandemic is more troublesome. Before the current pandemic, some twenty-five to thirty people migrated to Indian cities every minute. The pandemic has triggered a reverse migration back to rural areas with economic shutdowns, job losses, and a lack of livelihoods for migrants. Knowledge workers are also migrating away from cities, looking for open spaces. The future of cities has become uncertain and constrained by diminishing revenues due to the economic downturn and already limited infrastructure services.[4]

The widespread nature of the pandemic is also creating unprecedented problems to lenders and investors trying to insure against *force majeure* risks. To the extent that some of such risks are uninsurable, lenders may take a portfolio approach. Portfolios are constructed to include investments in diverse geographies, and across many sectors. For example, if the oil price suddenly collapses, fossil-fuel investments do poorly, but airline and shipping investments do better, and a portfolio may be constructed including these diverse assets. However, during the current pandemic, transportation and fossil-fuel sectors are collapsing together. Likewise, geographic diversification may be unhelpful because of the widespread nature of the pandemic.[5]

---

[1] Centre for Monitoring Indian Economy (CMIE) data showed that urban India had 22.1 per cent fewer women employed in 2021 than in 2019.

[2] International Monetary Fund. April 2021. *World Economic Outlook*.

[3] ADB. 2021. *An Updated Assessment of the Economic Impact of COVID-19*.

[4] Abha Joshi Ghani. 2020. How COVID-19 will impact our cities in the long term (https://www.weforum.org/agenda/2020/11/what-will-our-cities-look-like-after-covid-19/).

[5] Herb Ladley. 2020. COVID-19 and Infrastructure: Why Governments Must Act to Protect Projects (https://blogs.worldbank.org/ppps/covid-19-infrastructure-why-governments-must-act-protect-projects).

The Covid-19 pandemic has had a major adverse impact on infra-structure and its financing. The impact on under-construction projects in infrastructure was disproportionate. In contrast to the operational phase of projects, the construction phase is labour-intensive and vulner-able to supply-side impacts such as workplace restrictions for construc-tion workers, the unavailability of material and equipment, and longer lead times caused by this impact. For example, bottlenecks in wind-power supply chains have created shortages of the key components for wind turbines, which have led to delays. The People's Republic of China (PRC) is estimated to account for 40–50 per cent of the global wind-energy supply chain. Vestas, the world's largest supplier of turbines, and Siemens Gamesa, a Spanish manufacturer, both have assembly facilities in the PRC that were forced to shut down. Both recorded net losses in their mid-year results, which was attributed to supply-chain disruptions. Similar dynamics would also have been observed elsewhere across global supply-chain networks because of lockdowns and disruptions across dif-ferent countries.[6] While there have been supply-chain disruptions, the impact is more acute for international than domestic supply chains be-cause of a drop in international trade volumes, shipping disruptions (e.g. containers were stranded in ports because of movement restrictions), and delays caused by labour restrictions and inspections. Also, import-dependent human-resource expertise and raw materials were severely impacted leading to further disruptions downstream. On-site product-ivity had gone down because of the requirements of social distancing, staggered work hours, and workforce rotation.

There are some estimates of project disruptions in Phase 1 (2020) of the Covid-19 pandemic. The World Bank using an artificial intelligence (AI) model to collect data found that 256 projects have been reported as cancelled or delayed. Project disruptions in pipeline peaked in April, stabilizing since then. For projects already under construction, the number of projects facing disruptions peaked in May and have also been decreasing[7] since then (Figure 11.1).

[6] Asian Development Bank. 2021. Covid-19 and Public–Private Partnerships in Asia and the Pacific Guidance Note (https://www.adb.org/sites/default/files/publication/681536/covid-19-ppps-asia-pacific-guidance-note.pdf).

[7] Makhtar Diop. 2020. What Can AI Tell Us about COVID-19's Impact on Infrastructure? (https://blogs.worldbank.org/ppps/what-can-ai-tell-us-about-covid-19s-impact-infrastructure).

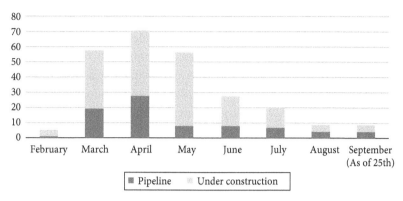

Figure 11.1 Number of Covid-19-affected infrastructure projects (Phase 1, 2020), by month

Source: Makhtar Diop. 2020. What Can AI Tell Us about COVID-19's Impact on Infrastructure?

In operational projects also, like metro rail, there was supply destruction due to the enforcing of social-distancing measures. McKinsey reports that Transport for London, the government body responsible for the public-transportation system in Greater London, estimates that with 2 meters of physical distancing, the London Underground, or Tube, will be able to carry 13–15 per cent of the passengers than it normally does, even at full service (2020: 15–20).[8] This will have a debilitating impact on project revenues. Transport also suffered more generally: it has been estimated that compared with 2019, global air traffic fell by 65 per cent in 2020 with regard to passenger volume, while rail traffic dropped by between 40 per cent and 60 per cent among European countries.[9] The substantial declines in public transport would promote higher levels of personal transport and car use with consequent adverse impact on the

[8] McKinsey & Company. 5 June 2020. Restoring Public Transit amid COVID-19: What European Cities Can Learn from One Another (https://www.mckinsey.com/industries/travel-transport-and-logistics/our-insights/restoring-public-transit-amid-covid-19-what-european-cities-can-learn-from-one-another?cid=other-eml-alt-mip-mck&hlkid=bcb6a521d0c54555a 7405fffef83c0651&hctky=9579620&hdpid=d3f2a42e-78f6-452b-a794-bb46dbc15100).

[9] McKinsey & Company. 2021. *Built to Last: Making Sustainability a Priority in Transport Infrastructure* (https://www.mckinsey.com/industries/travel-logistics-and-infrastructure/our-insights/built-to-last-making-sustainability-a-priority-in-transport-infrastructure?cid=other-eml-dre-mip-mck&hlkid=608129efd7bb439e998c6e67ff9bca12&hctky=9579620&hdpid= 1f11f87d-0534-4c99-99b7-d818a439acb6).

environment. *Force majeure*, compensation, and change-in-law clauses might apply depending on case circumstances. However, given that the pandemic's impacts are expected to be limited to the short or medium term, project credit risk and access to financing may not change substantially.

However, if the impact is long-lasting (with disruptions in China in December 2022, the impact of Covid-19 has been running for three years now, and counting), bankability may be redefined and the private sector may seek to transfer more risks to the government and there may be increased demand for government guarantees. But, given their Covid-19-induced fiscal stress (in terms of Covid-19-induced expenditure and resultant public debt), the ability of governments to take on additional risks and contingent liabilities such as guarantees may be limited. Although fiscal prudence is more important than ever in light of the emergency spending that the current global crisis entails, issuing guarantees may be one way for governments to encourage continued economic activity in infrastructure through private-sector mobilization. Done carefully, this can have a positive effect during the recovery phase of the pandemic and help ensure that the infrastructure financing gap continues to be bridged.[10]

The impact of Covid-19 on public–private partnerships (PPPs) broadly relate to the following: (i) decreasing PPP project value and volume, (ii) increasing PPP project risk allocation to the private sector, and (iii) public sector perception that value for money may not currently be realized fully from PPP projects.

Since the start of 2020, existing infrastructure projects have been delayed or cancelled due to supply-chain disruptions, travel and shipping restrictions, and other obstacles. Decreased demand or required renegotiations also prevented or delayed many projects already in the pipeline from achieving financial closure. For infrastructure investors, the sudden evaporation of demand combined with cost increases, or at least cost uncertainty, likely overwhelmed the legal system and led to a tidal wave of contractual disputes.

---

[10] Jenny Chao and Jason Zhengrong Lu. 2020. *Using Government Guarantees Carefully As the Private Sector Redefines Bankability* (https://blogs.worldbank.org/ppps/using-government-guarantees-carefully-private-sector-redefines-bankability).

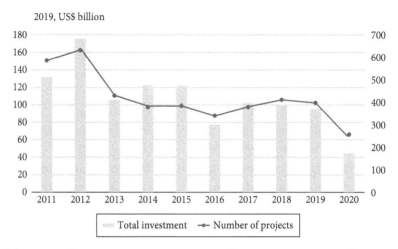

2019, US$ billion

Figure 11.2 Investment commitments in infrastructure projects with private participation in EMDEs, 2011–2020

Source: World Bank. 2021. *Private Participation in Infrastructure 2020 Annual Report.*

As per the Private Participation in Infrastructure database of the World Bank (ppi.worldbank.org), which tracks private infrastructure investment in low- and middle-income countries), private-sector investment in 2020 (US$45.7 billion in 252 projects)[11] dropped by an unprecedented 52 per cent compared to 2019[12] (Figure 11.2). Private investment commitments have not fallen to these levels since 2004, when investment totalled US$31.3 billion. Nevertheless, despite the ongoing pandemic, investments in the second half of the year (H2) increased by 15 per cent from the first half of the year (H1) (and to US$76.2 billion in 2021, marking a 49 per cent increase from 2020 and signalling a return to normalcy, though the number of PPI projects that reached financial

---

[11] This data is only for developing countries. As per the *Infrastructure Monitor, 2021* of the Global Infrastructure Hub, all countries, including high-income countries, saw US$156 billion invested in infrastructure projects by private investors in 2020 representing 0.2 per cent of global GDP and was little affected by the pandemic for HICs, while private investment in middle- and low-income countries declined significantly. The *Infrastructure Monitor* adds that HICs attract around three-quarters of all private investment in infrastructure projects. To put this in perspective, high-income countries represent around 60 per cent of global GDP and have about 50 per cent of total public and private investment in infrastructure.

[12] World Bank. 2021. *Private Participation in Infrastructure 2020 Annual Report.*

close dropped).[13] Transport sector investment commitments were the lowest in the past decade, both in terms of the number of projects and investment level as mass transit services and toll roads were affected due to lockdowns, and ports and railways were impacted with decreased volumes of passengers, containers, and cargo. Sudden and drastic declines in international travel have hurt airport PPPs. In 2020, air travel was at some 5–10 per cent of normal levels, and had been so for several months. Even after recovery, air transport is likely to suffer—2021 is likely to be 30 per cent lower than 2019. The entire air transport business model is evolving, with the potential permanent or semi-permanent reduction of lucrative business passengers—one of the key sources of revenues for airlines and airports alike.[14]

As already stated, private-sector infrastructure investment in low- and middle-income countries in 2020 dropped by an unprecedented 52 per cent compared to 2019. The drastic fall in the investment commitments reflects the pandemic shock as countries scrambled to contain the virus, and abrupt lockdowns and travel restrictions brought economies to a near standstill. By comparison, during the period of the Global Financial Crisis, investment levels dropped 14 per cent from the first half-year of 2009 to the first half-year of 2010, and then dropped again by 13 per cent in the first half-year of 2011, before rising by 19 per cent in the first half-year of 2012. The average (mean) project size in 2020 (US$183 million) was lower than the average project size in 2019 (US$243 million), as was the median project size—US$78 million in 2020, versus US$95 million in 2019. A decrease in larger projects was also seen in 2020, as indicated by the lower mean and median.

In 2020, South Asia received US$10.2 billion private investment across thirty projects, an 18 per cent decrease in investment from 2019 levels and approximately the same as the five-year average. However, the region's number of projects was the lowest in ten years. With US$5.3 billion commitments, across twenty-one projects, India was South Asia Region's

[13] Imad N. Fakhoury. 2022. New Data Shows Private Investment Lends a Hand as Public Debt Looms Large (https://blogs.worldbank.org/ppps/new-data-shows-private-investment-lends-hand-public-debt-looms-large?CID=WBW_AL_BlogNotification_EN_EXT).

[14] Jeff Delmon and Andy Ricover. 2020. Rebalancing Airport PPPs, Even As the COVID-19 Winds Still Blow (https://blogs.worldbank.org/ppps/rebalancing-airport-ppps-even-covid-19-winds-still-blow).

largest PPI investment destination (and third highest PPI among developing countries, but with a decreased share of PPI in terms of GDP, from 0.26 per cent to 0.18 per cent, Table 11.1). In the past, India's transport sector received the most PPI investments, but, in 2020, 65 per cent of investment commitments were made in energy. As the Covid-19 crisis continues to challenge the transport sector, the airport industry especially has turned to privatization, with the management and lease contracts of Lucknow, Ahmedabad, and Mangalore airports. The other projects in the transport sector were all brownfield road investments.

Bangladesh received the region's second highest private investment. Its 2020 private investment commitment of US$2.9 billion, across seven projects, was the highest in Bangladesh's history, placing it among the top five countries for the first time (see Table 11.1). While the risk perception of the private sector was high throughout the developing world, Bangladesh moved against the trend. However, most of its 2020 private investment commitments were channelled to a series of fossil-fuel-powered electricity plants—conventional power plants received US$2 billion in 2020, compared with US$133 million investment commitments for two renewable power plants. This trend is expected to continue for a while as Bangladesh, one of the world's fastest-growing economies, needs a robust power infrastructure that can sustain its long-term needs for electricity.

Even in the dismal 2020 infrastructure investment trends, there are silver linings: RE continues to be a significant part of new energy

Table 11.1 Top five countries with investment commitments in 2020

Country	2020 PPI (2019 US$ million)	2020 PPI as a share of GDP (%)	2019 PPI as a share of GDP (%)	Number of megaprojects in 2020
Brazil	7,733	0.42	1.01	1
China	6,285	0.04	0.18	1
India	5,251	0.18	0.26	1
Mexico	4,269	0.34	0.23	1
Bangladesh	2,948	0.97	0.34	1

Source: World Bank. 2021. *Private Participation in Infrastructure 2020 Annual Report.*

generation projects, accounting for 62 per cent of the sector's investment in the data World Bank tracked. Of the 129 electricity-generation projects, 117 were in renewables (in 2021, renewables constituted 95 per cent of the total electricity generation projects through private participation). This tells us that the private sector is already mostly on board with the decarbonization agenda. The most popular renewable technology in 2020 was solar, due to strong renewable programmes in India and Brazil. The next most popular was onshore wind technology, mainly due to high investments in Vietnam and Brazil.

Secondly, the role of institutional investors rose in 2020, due to the high levels of institutional debt involved in the New Burgos, Cactus, and Isthmus Corridor Pipelines in Mexico (US$4.0 billion). This project alone accounted for a quarter of total international debt, showing that institutional investors should be looked at as potential long-term partners, though they are constrained by risk exposure and scale of projects. This is notable because their role has been negligible up to now, with less than 1 per cent of total infrastructure investment in developing countries. There have been clear indications that institutional investors would like to be more active in this space and the potential is enormous. According to Swiss Re, long-term investors have huge resources under management that could be used for infrastructure projects in developing countries under the right conditions. What do they need to get there? Top on the wish lists are robust legal frameworks, regulatory certainty, asset class standardization, standard definitions for environmental, social, and governance (ESG) considerations and resilience indicators. Efforts are ongoing on all these fronts across the world (and India) pointing towards sustainable infrastructure investment in the future.[15]

While most sectors suffered, pandemic control and online activities contributed to the increase in investment in the social (health) and telecommunications (digital) sectors. But there is a need to invest still more in health infrastructure, Covid-19 treatment, and vaccination. However, with government finances already stretched (India's central government's fiscal deficit is estimated at 9.2 per cent of GDP in FY 2020/21 and 12.8

---

[15] Makhtar Diop. 26 February 2021. Private Sector's Retreat Jeopardizes Recovery (https://blogs.worldbank.org/ppps/private-sectors-retreat-jeopardizes-recovery?CID=WBW_AL_Blog Notification_EN_EXT).

per cent for centre and state combined), reliance would need to be put on private participation in infrastructure.

Aiming for an Infrastructure-Driven Recovery

Infrastructure development has been an oft-examined but difficult-to-implement tool for economic stimulus and growth. In a world shaken by the Covid-19 pandemic, an infrastructure-driven recovery is becoming an increasingly discussed solution. Many governments see the continuation of shovel-ready infrastructure and PPP projects as a feature of their recovery efforts. The US president's US$7 trillion 'Build Back Better' plan includes massive new infrastructure spending ($2 trillion) meant to revolutionize the United States' aging and neglected infrastructure systems. Infrastructure development will also play a key role in the implementation of the €1 trillion European Green Deal, while China is turning to infrastructure-led stimulus (US$0.5 trillion), much as it did after the 2008 Global Financial Crisis. The Global Infrastructure Hub has estimated that G20 countries, in total, have allocated US$3.2 trillion (4.6 per cent of G20 GDP) to infrastructure as a stimulus in the post-Covid-19 recovery.[16] Box 11.1 captures the evidence on effectiveness of infrastructure investment as a fiscal stimulus.

As countries emerge from lockdowns, buoyed by hopes of vaccinations and achieving herd immunity, the level of investment commitments is expected to rise in the coming years. As more infrastructure is built, it would have the following characteristics.

Embracing technology

In the future, infrastructure technology, or infratech, will be more widely embraced to improve safety, accelerate decarbonization, increase community engagement in the development process, and optimize operations

---

[16] Global Infrastructure Hub. 2022. *Transformative Outcomes through Infrastructure* (https://transformativeinfratracker.gihub.org/overview/?utm_source=PR&utm_medium=media&utm_campaign=FTpaid_May22).

Box 11.1 Evidence on the effectiveness of infrastructure investment as a fiscal stimulus

Multipliers associated with public expenditure and investments are on average about twice as high as those from tax cuts and fiscal transfers. Among public-spending categories, multipliers related to public investment display the highest values, typically at around 1.5, meaning that a rupee of public investment leads to 1.5 rupees of economic activity (Figure 11.3).

The size of multipliers is very sensitive to the economic context in which the stimulus takes place. In particular, public spending multipliers are significantly higher during downturns than during average periods or booms (where they are usually estimated to be negative and never significantly positive).

Fiscal stimulus may be particularly effective (and the multiplier correspondingly larger) when monetary policy is loose with near-zero interest rates. This is because higher government spending can be expected to increase inflation, which in turn drives the real interest into negative territory further boosting the economy by stimulating private consumption and investment spending.

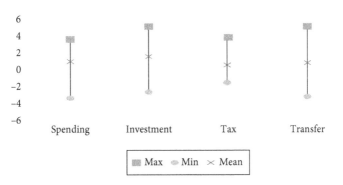

Figure 11.3 Range of fiscal multipliers depending on fiscal instrument used

Source: Foster, Vivien, Maria Vagliasindi, Nisan Gorgulu. 2022. *The effectiveness of infrastructure investment as a fiscal stimulus: What we've learned, pg 26* (https://blogs.worldbank.org/ppps/effectiveness-infrastructure-investment-fiscal-stimulus-what-weve-learned?CID=WBW_AL_BlogNotification_EN_EXT).

The most recent evidence suggests that public investment in developing countries may carry higher returns, as the size of the initial stock of public capital is much lower, and the baseline quality, quantity, and accessibility of economic infrastructure is often inadequate, meaning that improvements may be particularly beneficial.

The current Covid-19 crisis has many peculiarities that distinguish it from earlier ones and complicate inferences based on earlier crises. On the one hand, the context of the pandemic may depress public investment multipliers, due to stronger precautionary behaviour and hoarding of cash, amplified by fear of disease that prevents people from engaging in travel and social activities. At the same time, the severity of the economic downturn, accompanied as it is by loose monetary policy, present conditions that in the past have tended to enhance the efficacy of fiscal stimulus.

Source: Vivien Foster et al. (2022).[a]

[a]Vivien Foster, Maria Vagliasindi, and Nisan Gorgulu. 2022. The Effectiveness of Infrastructure Investment as a Fiscal Stimulus: What We've Learned (https://blogs.worldbank.org/ppps/effectiveness-infrastructure-investment-fiscal-stimulus-what-weve-learned?CID=WBW_AL_BlogNotification_EN_EXT).

and maintenance (big data for predictive maintenance) of infrastructure systems. There will be an increasing focus on digital infrastructure and smart mobility. Technology adoption, obsolescence, and resilience will become critical factors when investing scarce resources.[17]

New innovations like digital twin technology can revolutionize infrastructure planning and operation, building information modelling can vastly improve design, 3D printing is disrupting construction, and permeable pavements will reduce flood risk. These potentially powerful tools can help planners and developers tailor the delivery of infrastructure systems to meet the needs of communities and leverage technology as an enabler of better infrastructure that begets better outcomes.

New technologies for mitigating climate change will be a major play in the future. Digital applications including optimized movement sequencing, smart metering, and energy solutions can reduce *airports'*

[17] Richard Abadie. 2020. COVID-19 and Infrastructure: A Very Tricky Opportunity (https://blogs.worldbank.org/ppps/covid-19-and-infrastructure-very-tricky-opportunity).

carbon footprint, while the all-around digitization of the *shipping supply chain* (including cloud and IoT technology, advanced analytics tools to optimize freight scheduling and routing, and adoption of biofuels) could reduce the sector's emissions globally. For *roads*, the installation of charging infrastructure for electric vehicles (EVs) is among the most effective smart solutions to improve their sustainability footprint.[18]

There is an additional gender dimension of concern here. Even before the pandemic, women in low- and middle-income countries were 8 per cent less likely than men to own a mobile phone. And 300 million fewer women than men use mobile internet, representing a gender gap of 20 per cent. This digital gender divide is expected to worsen because of Covid-19 and pro-active measures will have to be taken to address this. The interventions could relate to access, affordability, knowledge and skills, safety and security, as well as make relevant content, products, and services more available to women.[19]

A focus on sustainability

The occurrence of extreme weather, extreme temperature, floods, and droughts have increased sharply over the past decades (see Figure 11.4). Climate change and its symptoms, like rising sea levels, more frequent and extreme weather events, and increasing global temperatures, can have lasting, damaging effects on existing and planned core infrastructure.[20] Natural disasters cost about US$18 billion a year in low- and middle-income countries through direct damage to infrastructure assets and impose US$391–US$647 billion of economic cost a year through service disruption. Climate-related damage of infrastructure will also have a significant impact on vulnerable populations and increase inequalities.

[18] McKinsey & Company. 2021. *Built to Last: Making Sustainability a Priority in Transport Infrastructure* (https://www.mckinsey.com/industries/travel-logistics-and-infrastructure/our-insights/built-to-last-making-sustainability-a-priority-in-transport-infrastructure?cid=other-eml-dre-mip-mck&hlkid=608129efd7bb439e998c6e67ff9bca12&hctky=9579620&hdpid=1f11f87d-0534-4c99-99b7-d818a439acb6).

[19] Mari Elka Pangestu and Mats Granryd. 2020. Equal Access to Digital Technologies: A Key to Resilient Recovery (https://blogs.worldbank.org/voices/equal-access-digital-technologies-key-resilient-recovery).

[20] Swiss Re Institute. 2021.*Closing the Infrastructure Gap.*

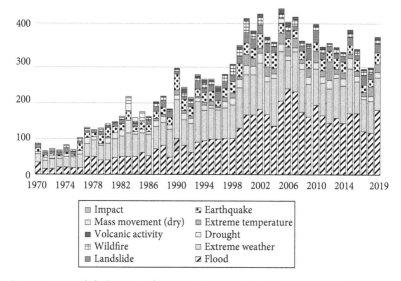

Figure 11.4 Global reported natural disasters by type, 1970–2019

Source: International Monetary Fund. 2021. *Strengthening Infrastructure Governance for Climate-responsive Public Investment.*

Infrastructure that is not climate-resilient will require additional routine and emergency maintenance over its lifespan and could lead governments to reallocate resources from productive capital to adaptation capital. Investing in retrofitting traditional technologies to adapt to climate change is usually more costly than the initial cost of ensuring climate-resilient infrastructure.[21]

This calls for investment in sustainable infrastructure, which is defined as infrastructure that is socially, economically, and environmentally sustainable throughout its entire life cycle, and is a key driver of economic growth and social progress and a critical enabler to achieving the SDGs and Paris Agreement commitments.[22] US President Biden's 'Build Back Better' plan places heavy emphasis on developing sustainable infrastructure at a cost of US$2 trillion, and both EU and Chinese plans focus on green infrastructure development to varying degrees.

---

[21] International Monetary Fund. 2021. *Strengthening Infrastructure Governance for Climate-responsive Public Investment.*

[22] B20 Italy. 2021. *Finance and Infrastructure Policy Paper.*

The imperatives of climate change means designing infrastructure plans that favour renewable energy (RE) production over fossil-fuel plants (e.g. the target of 450GW of RE capacity by 2030 for India), improved mass transit over car-centric transport infrastructure, and infrastructure that supports EVs[23] (see Box 11.2 for EVs). We will also likely see an increase in the use of nature-based solutions to improve infrastructure resilience in the face of climate change: wetlands and green roofs rather than high walls and expensive pipes to manage stormwater and improve flood control. Wider pavements, pedestrianized streets, dedicated bicycle lanes, electric-scooter pathways, or car-free zones, the health and safety benefits of such investments are even more important now. The business case is also strong: the Global Commission on Adaptation led a study suggesting that investing US$1.8 trillion in climate-resilient infrastructure by 2030 could amount to more than US$7 trillion in net benefits. In other words, in order to save money tomorrow, the government must spend wisely on sustainable infrastructure today.[24]

Seeking equity and justice through social outcomes

Infrastructure connects people and creates opportunities within communities. At its core, the development of infrastructure is a direct reflection of the values of a society. In the United States, an examination of legacy infrastructure reveals a history of systemic injustice that continues to the present day, resulting in disparities in public health and safety outcomes. The 2014 drinking water crisis in Flint, Michigan, echoed by a separate episode a few years later in Newark, New Jersey, resulted in lead contamination impacting thousands of working-class and minority families.

The pursuit of a truly resilient recovery must attempt to correct those inequalities in the existing built environment and deliberately aim to reach underserved populations. Taking a people-first and outcomes-focused approach will help to ensure all citizens have equal access to the

---

[23] However, given that there is a need for charging EVs, low greenhouse-gas benefits from their usage will accrue only if they are charged using non-fossil-fuel sources.

[24] Svitlana Orekhova and Guillermo Diaz-Fanas. 2020. Bouncing Back Is Not Enough. Let's Bounce Forward to Infrastructure Resilience (https://blogs.worldbank.org/ppps/bouncing-back-not-enough-lets-bounce-forward-infrastructure-resilience).

Box 11.2 EVs in India

The transport sector, the biggest contributor of GHG emissions (around 28 per cent), is bucking the general decarbonization trend. While other sectors such as industry and power are decreasing emissions annually by 1.5 per cent and 1 per cent respectively, the transportation sector is reporting a 0.8 per cent annual growth in $MtCO_2e$ (metric tonnes of carbon dioxide equivalent), with passenger cars accounting for the highest portion. It is incumbent on the transport sector to shoulder its part of the global responsibility toward shared environmental goals.[a] One way out is to increase use of EVs.

According to the International Council on Clean Transportation,[b] nearly 40 per cent of the global cumulative EV sales are concentrated in twenty-five global cities, called the EV capitals of the world. In 2020, fourteen of the world's EV capitals were in China and ten were in Europe or the United States. Since the Tesla Roadster became the first vehicle to use lithium-ion cells in 2008, the number of EVs on the road has grown.[c] In 2020, this number had grown to 10.2 million constituted by China (4.5 million), Europe (3.2 million), USA (1.8 million), and Rest of the World (0.7 million). As per the International Energy Agency's *Global EV Outlook*, electric passenger car sales climbed in 2020 (by 41 per cent) despite the total automobile industry contracting by 16 per cent. Bloomberg estimates total EV passenger car sales in 2021 more than doubled to 6.3 million vehicles, with China and Europe dominating.

Such is the dominance of EVs in future car outlook that while Toyota, Volkswagen, and Daimler have a combined market capitalization of US$506 billion, Tesla alone is worth more than twice that ($1,059 billion), while the market capitalization of the top three EV carmakers—Tesla, Rivian, and Lucid—is over US$1.3 trillion (November 2021). The automobile companies have recognized this trend towards EVs with plans to go all electric by 2030 and 2035 by Volvo and General Motors respectively. Ford reckons that 40 per cent of its global sales will be electric by 2030 (the deadline the US president would like to set for half of all new cars in America to be battery-powered).[d] At COP26, in November 2021, six major auto makers and thirty-one countries pledged to work towards phasing out sales of new petrol- and diesel-powered vehicles by 2040 worldwide, and by 2035 in 'leading markets'.

However, while the number of electric passenger cars in use globally increased from close to zero to 10.2 million in the last decade, electric cars and plug-in hybrids accounted for just 4.6 per cent of global passenger car sales in 2020. The projections for total EVs globally are 51.7 million in 2025 and 144.3 million in 2030 (IEA).

To achieve their all-electric goals, some cities have enacted a wide range of supporting policies to make EVs broadly attractive. These fall into several general categories: making EVs financially viable through incentives, promoting the development of convenient charging systems, and accelerating vehicle adoption in fleets. Germany has doubled incentives offered to buyers of battery-powered cars as part of a €130 billion (US$146 billion) economic recovery package that excludes internal-combustion cars from the stimulus programme.[e] In the massive infrastructure investment plan unveiled in the United States on 31 March 2021, US$174 billion will go on EVs—tax credits to help consumers afford them, to encourage states to build 5,00,000 public charging stations, and to boost domestic supply chains.[f]

EVs in India

The transport sector accounts for 18 per cent of total energy consumption in India translating to an estimated 94 million tonnes of oil equivalent energy, the demand for which is being met mostly through imported crude oil, thereby making this sector vulnerable to the volatile international crude oil prices. In response to growing urbanization and concomitant need for mobility, it is critical to introduce alternative means in the transport sector which can be coupled with India's rapid economic growth to safeguard the country's energy security. Electric mobility which is efficient, sustainable, and decarbonizing is the answer, with high fossil-fuel prices and the increasing focus on ESG by corporations helping to transform urban mobility towards EVs. However, though India is the fourth largest vehicle market in the world at present, EVs represent less than 1 per cent of the total vehicle sales in India. India's investment in EVs has been a cumulative US$0.68 billion so far, predominantly targeting electric buses and e-rickshaws. Over the past few years, India has announced a plethora of electric mobility policies and regulatory measures moving towards a coherent and effective EV policy.[g]

In 2013, India announced a National Electric Mobility Mission Plan (NEMMP) to promote hybrid and EVs over the conventional internal combustion engine (ICE) vehicles. The NEMMP 2020[h] provides the vision and the roadmap for the faster adoption of EVs and their manufacturing in the country. Under it, there is an ambitious target to achieve 6–7 million sales of hybrid and EVs year-on-year from 2020 onwards. As part of the NEMMP 2020, the Government of India has formulated a scheme for Faster Adoption and Manufacturing of (hybrid and) Electric Vehicles in India (FAME India) in the year 2015, with a total outlay of Rs.895 crore to promote manufacturing of electric and hybrid vehicles and to ensure sustainable growth. Phase I of the FAME India scheme was implemented through four focus areas namely: (i) demand creation, (ii) technology platform, (iii) pilot project, and (iv) charging infrastructure (according to the Society of Manufacturers of EV, there are 1,800 charging stations in India as of March 2021. It has been estimated that India will need 2.9 million charging points at an investment of Rs.21,000 crore by 2030).

The government approved Phase II of the FAME scheme, with an outlay of Rs.10,000 crore for a period of three years commencing from 1 April 2019 (2019/20 to 2021/22). The scheme includes incentives for customers for purchasing EVs, incentives for manufacturers for research and development, besides developing the charging infrastructure. Vehicles eligible under the FAME II scheme can cumulatively save 5.4 million tons of oil equivalent over their lifetime, worth Rs.17,200 crore. With this the government is aiming for an EV sales penetration of 30 per cent for private cars, 70 per cent for commercial cars, 40 per cent for buses, and 80 per cent for two- and three-wheelers by 2030. Emphasis is on electrification of public transportation, which includes shared transport. To encourage advanced technologies, the benefit of incentives will be extended to only those vehicles which are fitted with an advanced battery like the lithium-ion battery and other new-technology batteries. The scheme proposes the establishment of charging infrastructure whereby there will be availability of at least one charging station in a grid of 3 km x 3 km.

In a major thrust to the EV charging ecosystem, the government announced (in January 2022) that any entity can set up public charging stations (PCS) without any license. EV owners can also charge their vehicles at home or offices from existing connections at domestic tariffs. This also opened the door for government and private entities to use government land for setting up PCSs on a revenue-sharing basis. As per the announcement, the target is one PCS in every 3 square km grid in megacities and every 25 km on connecting highways in the next three years.[i]

Covid-19 and its consequential impact has realigned the focus on green investments. Covid-19-induced social distancing has spurred demand for personal vehicles. This coupled with higher petroleum product prices designed to collect fiscal resources and discourage dependence on fossil fuels along with higher prices of Bharat Stage-VI-compliant ICE vehicles will accelerate transition towards EVs. This can be gauged from the higher sales witnessed by the EV industry in recent years. The share of EVs in total vehicle sales rose in FY 2021 despite a dip in EV vehicle sales in absolute terms after the first lockdown. India had 69,012 EVs in 2017/18, which went up to 1,43,358 in 2018/19 and then to 1,67,041 in 2019/20.[j] The number of EVs at the end of 2021 in India was estimated at 8,70,141 (as compared to 295.8 million registered vehicles in India in 2018—a penetration rate of less than 0.3 per cent for EVs).The main manufacturers of EV sedans in India are Mahindra (eVerito) and Tata Motors (eNexon and eTigor). The outlook of EVs is also bright: for example, Ola Electric raised about US$200 million in October 2021 from a clutch of investors in a fresh funding round, valuing the EV maker at over US$5 billion.[k] Maruti Suzuki, the market leader in cars, has announced an investment of Rs.10,440 crore to develop an EV manufacturing and battery plant in India (March 2022). MG Motor will get an 'affordable and futuristic' EV in Rs.10–15 lakh range. Other companies like Mercedes and Volvo are also expected to launch EVs in India.

The Ministry of Road Transport and Highways (MoRTH), in its vehicle scrappage policy approved the scrapping of government vehicles older than fifteen years. The policy came into effect from 1 April 2022. This was in response to the slowdown in the auto industry in the aftermath of the Covid-19 pandemic. This will also spur the adoption of EVs.

Delhi EV Policy

Besides central government's FAME scheme, sixteen states and union territories have published their own draft EV policies or notified final policies detailing fiscal, non-fiscal, and other incentives to accelerate adoption of electric mobility.

The Government of National Capital Territory (NCT) of Delhi announced the Delhi Electric Vehicle Policy on 7 August 2020, with a vision to promote adoption of EVs in the city and to make Delhi, the EV capital of India. The policy objective is to improve Delhi's air quality and create an entire supply-chain ecosystem for this new segment of vehicles. The policy intends 25 per cent of all new vehicles to be battery-operated by 2024. It prioritizes two-wheelers, three-wheelers, public transport (buses), and taxi fleets. Delhi plans to add 50 per cent e-buses to public transport over the period 2019–2022.

The policy encourages long-term investment by dealers and charging facility providers to create enabling conditions for private and public charging infrastructure. It provides a unique electricity tariff for EV charging and encourages power distribution companies to work with owners of residential and non-residential buildings to ensure adequate power supply infrastructure for the installation of these charging points. Additionally, the policy also promises that the state will have public charging infrastructure at least every 3 km. The parking areas need to be made EV ready as per the policy, that is, at least around 20 per cent of the total area should have the equipment required for the charging of EVs. Road tax and registration fees will be waived for all battery EVs during the period of this policy. A purchase incentive of Rs.30,000 per vehicle would be given to owners of e-two wheelers or e-rickshaw or e-cart or e-autos and the government would pay 5 per cent of the interest on the loan for the purchase. The maximum purchase incentive for electric cars is Rs.1.5 lakh (Rs.10,000 per kWh of battery capacity). One hundred per cent subsidy has been allowed for the purchase of charging equipment (up to Rs.6,000 per charging point). This has been done to promote self-employment and wide ownership of EVs. The concept of feebate has been introduced, that is, inefficient polluting vehicles will incur a surcharge while efficient ones will receive a rebate. Every month, 50 per cent of the total amount collected under the Air Ambience Fund (collected from the surcharge levied on ICE vehicles) will be transferred to the EV fund as per the policy. A large number of new jobs can be created due to increasing EV adoption—for example, e-auto and e-cab drivers, charging-station operators and EV service mechanics. Vocational courses will be designed to train EV drivers, mechanics, and charging-station staff in partnership with auto OEMs and the energy operators.

The total number of EVs registered in Delhi up to June 2022 was 1,55,214 (1.1 per cent of total vehicles registered in Delhi), of which about 57,000 have been sold since the Delhi EV policy was announced. Furthermore, 25,890 EVs were registered in 2021 constituting 5.6 per cent of the total vehicles registered in that year.

Challenges and Way Forward

The EV market in India is marred by a number of problems such as inadequate charging infrastructure, reliance on battery imports, reliance on imported components and parts, the high cost of lithium-ion batteries, limited single-charge running range, inadequate electricity supply in parts of India, and a lack of quality maintenance and repair options. To address some of these problems and encourage 'Make in India' storage technologies, in March 2019, the government approved the National Mission of Transformative Mobility and Battery Storage, which includes phased manufacturing programmes, valid till 2024 for localization of the entire value chain for EVs, while being cognizant of the fact that this is a highly technology-intensive industry, providing avenues for innovation and start-ups, including battery swapping, and so on.

[a]McKinsey & Company. 2021. *Built to Last: Making Sustainability a Priority in Transport Infrastructure* (https://www.mckinsey.com/industries/travel-logistics-and-inf rastructure/our-insights/built-to-last-making-sustainability-a-priority-in-transport-infrastructure?cid=other-eml-dre-mip-mck&hlkid=608129efd7bb439e998c6e67ff9bc a12&hctky=9579620&hdpid=1f11f87d-0534-4c99-99b7-d818a439acb6).

[b]International Council on Clean Transportation. 2020. *Electric Vehicle Capitals: Cities Aim for All-electric Mobility*, p. 1 (https://theicct.org/sites/default/files/publications/ev-capit als-update-sept2020.pdf).

[c]*The Economist*. 31 March 2021. Lithium Battery Costs Have Fallen by 98% in Three Decades (https://www.economist.com/graphic-detail/2021/03/31/lithium-battery-costs-have-fallen-by-98-in-three-decades).

[d] *The Economist*. 28 September 2021. Ford and General Motors Fight It Out to Electrify.

[e]Christiaan Hetzner. 2020. Germany Doubles EV Incentives, Excludes Internal-combustion Cars from Stimulus Program (https://www.autonews.com/sales/germany-doub les-ev-incentives-excludes-internal-combustion-cars-stimulus-program).

^{f}*The Economist*. 1 April 2021. Joe Biden Unveils America's Most Ambitious Infrastructure Plan in Generations (https://www.economist.com/united-states/2021/04/01/joe-biden-unveils-americas-most-ambitious-infrastructure-plan-in-generations).

^{g}NITI Aayog and World Energy Council. 2018. *Zero Emission Vehicles (ZEVs): Towards a Policy Framework*, p. 4 (https://e-amrit.niti.gov.in/assets/admin/dist/img/new-fronend-img/report-pdf/EV_report.pdf).

^{h}Press Information Bureau, Ministry of Heavy Industries & Public Enterprises, Government of India. 08 July 2019. Implementation of National Electric Mobility Mission Plan (https://pib.gov.in/newsite/PrintRelease.aspx?relid=191337).

^{i}*Times of India*. 16 January 2022. In EV Push, Govt Eases Rules to Set Up Charging Stations.

^{j}Jyoti Mukul. 25 March 2021. EV Start-ups Feel the Spark of Recovery.

^{k}*Economic Times*. 8 October 2021. Ola Electric Raises $200 mn at over $5 bn Valuation: Sources (https://auto.economictimes.indiatimes.com/news/two-wheelers/ola-electric-rai ses-200-mn-at-over-5-bn-valuation-sources/86872969).

infrastructure services that underpin flourishing communities. In the future, there will be increasing attention paid to social outcomes and community engagement in infrastructure planning. Reference tools such as the ISI Envision Rating System and the GI Hub Inclusive Infrastructure and Social Equity tool can provide integrated frameworks to guide decision-makers.

Riding the ESG financing wave

With governments prioritizing Covid-19-related budget expenditures, they are exploring ways to draw more private financing into infrastructure development. One strategy is framing infrastructure as an ESG investment to capitalize on the desire of institutional investors to move trillions into assets that produce positive ESG outcomes (dealt with at length in Chapter 9). The rising focus on environmentally and socially sustainable outcomes for infrastructure investment not only has the potential to improve lives but also ease the availability of capital needed to fill the infrastructure investment gap.[25]

---

[25] World Economic Forum. 2021. *4 Big Infrastructure Trends to Build a Sustainable World* (https://www.weforum.org/agenda/2021/01/four-big-infrastructure-trends-for-2021/).

Impact of Covid-19 on Indian Infrastructure

The context

As per the Private Participation in Infrastructure (PPI) database of the World Bank (ppi.worldbank.org), India is second in the developing world both by the number of PPP projects as well as the associated investments (see Chapter 2). In India, the highest number of projects have come up in the transport sector (559 projects) (and within transport, in the road sub-sector, 488 projects). Most private investment has flowed into the energy sector (mainly electricity generation) at US$152 billion. The sector where there is tremendous infrastructure deficit and could gain immensely from private investment is the water and sewerage sector.

The year-wise breakup of Indian PPP projects is shown in Figure 11.5. As is apparent from Figure 11.5, there has been a pronounced slowdown in PPP procurement in India in the last two Covid-19-afflicted years. On average, India contracted thirty-five PPP projects accounting for an investment of US$8.77 billion per year (averaged over thirty-two years from 1990 to 2021). However, the number of PPP projects contracted in 2020 and 2021 are twenty-one and thirteen respectively, with the investments dwindling to US$5.25 billion and US$2.16 billion respectively. The numbers show that what India has achieved in the last two Covid-19-afflicted

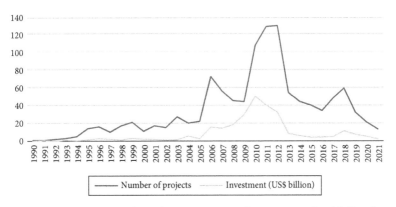

Figure 11.5 India—number of PPP projects and investment (US$ billion)

Source: Private Participation in Infrastructure database of the World Bank (ppi.worldbank.org) (viewed on 3 April 2022).

years in terms of number of PPP projects and the associated investments are still below the average achievements of a single year for the country. The reasons could be the private sector becoming more risk averse and their outlook changing to conserving cash from making investments in the extremely risky Covid-19 period. Contact-intensive sectors like aviation (airports and airlines), and hospitality (hotels, restaurants, and tourism) experienced disproportionate adverse impact.

The following section examines the impact of Covid-19 on Indian infrastructure in greater detail.

First wave

Following a strict national lockdown imposed from 24 March to early June 2020, the Covid-19 pandemic slowed down the infrastructure programme of the country, both from the demand and the supply side. Passenger traffic on roads, railways, and by air was locked down, and in the power sector, there was a major demand slowdown (about 28 per cent less than business-as-usual) with most industrial and commercial activity locked up. This had left airports and travel terminals largely underutilized, which denied those projects their usual source of air-side revenue (such as gate and landing fees) and land-side revenue (such as retail). Box 11.3 captures the impact of Covid-19 on one of the best airports in the world (the Delhi International Airport Limited).

Conversely, there was increased uptake and traffic for telecommunications infrastructure, as well as personal modes of transport. Health infrastructure is also experiencing increased demand. On the supply side, supply chains and the construction labour force were dislocated because of the pandemic. The net result was that India suffered a (–)24.4 per cent GDP growth rate in the period April–June (Q1) 2020, the largest decline among the G20 countries. But, the economy recovered progressively in later quarters (July–September (Q2) 2020 (–)7.5 per cent, October–December 2020 (Q3) (+)0.4 per cent, January–March (Q4) 2021 (+)1.6 per cent), with the overall real GDP growth being (–)6.6 per cent in FY 2020/21, the worst-ever performance in independent India to date (there have been only four years of negative GDP growth in independent India (excluding 2020/21): 1957–1958 (–0.5 per cent), 1965–1966

Box 11.3 Impact of Covid-19 on Delhi International Airport Limited

The Indian aviation sector, as a major component of the Indian growth story, was sailing smoothly before being buffeted by the Covid-19 wave in 2020. The number of airports in the country had risen from seventy-four in 2014 to 140 by 2021, and is further set to reach 220 by 2025. To match the growth in infrastructure, the aircraft fleet is also likely to grow from 710 today, by 110–120 every year, as well as expand the share of wide-bodied aircraft for greater long-haul connectivity.

Delhi International Airport Limited (DIAL) is one of 140 airports in the country. It is the special purpose vehicle for the Indira Gandhi International Airport at New Delhi and is the crown jewel of the Indian aviation story. The airport was bid out to the private sector for improving service delivery and for providing for expansion. The winning bidder (in 2006) was a consortium led by GMR Infrastructure Limited, and included Fraport of Frankfurt, Germany, and others. The winning bid provided for 45.99 per cent revenue share to the public entity. It is a brownfield project with the concession type being build–rehabilitate–operate–transfer. The original contract period is thirty years, with the option of extending the contract period by another thirty years provided certain conditions are met.

The modernized international airport in Delhi was opened for traffic in 2010 just in time for the 2010 Commonwealth Games. It became South Asia's largest hub, which handled about 36 million passengers in 2011/12 and 69.23 million in 2018/19. DIAL was rated the Best Airport in the over 40 million passengers per annum category in the Asia Pacific region by Airports Council International in the Airport Service Quality Programme 2019 rankings.

DIAL saw significant losses in 2010/11 and 2011/12 before turning into profit in 2012/13. Thereafter, it made profits for the next five years. In more recent years, its profitability has been very limited. In 2020/21, the losses increased (Rs.(–)188 crore) owing to less revenue generation due to Covid-19. The total number of passengers handled at DIAL came down sharply from 69.23 million in 2018/19, to 67.30 million in

2019/20 (3 per cent decrease from the previous year), and further to 22.58 million in 2020/21 (66 per cent decrease from the previous year).

DIAL demanded a relief package from the government on account of low traffic because of the Covid-19 pandemic ('cash support ... to sustain operations'). This was expected given the severe hit to airport financials as contact-intensive sectors like aviation (airports and airlines) and hospitality (hotels and restaurants) have borne the brunt of the Covid-19 pandemic.

(−2.7 per cent), 1972–1973 (−0.5 per cent), and 1979–1980 (−5.1 per cent)).[26] The negative growth rate in 2020/21 came at a time when the country's economy was already doing poorly with economic growth of barely 4 per cent in 2019/20, which implied that the economy's capacity to cope with a one-in-a-century pandemic was low.[27]

A Pew Research Center study estimates that India's middle class shrank by 32 million in 2020 as a consequence of the Covid-19-induced downturn, while the number of poor—with a daily income of US$2 (Rs.148) or less—is estimated to have increased by 75 million. India's numbers account for nearly 60 per cent of the global increase in poverty.[28]

Second wave

Just a year after the first wave struck India, the second wave impacted the country with high ferocity (the loss of life and caseload of infections were much higher than the first wave). High frequency indicators for April–May 2021 suggest that the biggest toll of the second wave was in terms of demand shock—loss of mobility due to local lockdowns, discretionary spending, and employment, besides inventory accumulation. The unemployment rate touched 14.7 per cent in the week ended 23 May 2021 (with youth unemployment in urban areas across India rising to 25.5 per cent in April–June 2021). There was also a disproportionate impact

---

[26] Government of India, Ministry of Finance. 2020. *Economic Survey 2019–20.*
[27] Shankar Acharya. 2021. *An Economist at Home and Abroad—A Personal Journey.*
[28] *India Today.* 23 August 2021. Distress Signals.

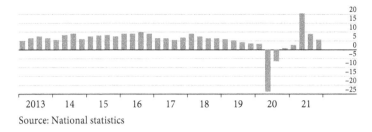

Source: National statistics

Figure 11.6 India—GDP growth rate, by quarter (%)
Source: The Economist. 2022. A New Formula.

of the pandemic on women, hurting gender parity (among women in the 15–29 years category, the unemployment rate was higher at 31 per cent in April–June 2021). Oxfam India estimates that women collectively lost US$800 billion in earnings in 2020, with 13 million fewer women working in 2021 than in 2019.

The state governments responded with local lockdowns which would impact the economy, but not to the same extent as the nationwide lockdown following the first wave. The second wave was also shorter (three months) compared to the first wave (six months). For both these reasons, the second wave had a much smaller impact on the economy compared to the first; accordingly, data showed that GDP grew by 20.1 per cent in April–June 2021 (Q1 FY 2022) (Figure 11.6), 8.5 per cent in July–September (Q2 FY 2022) 2021, 5.4 per cent in October–December 2021 (Q3 FY 2022), and 4.1 per cent in January–March 2022 (Q4 FY 2022), making it 8.7 per cent for full 2021/22 (against the estimated 11.5 per cent earlier). In April–June 2022, the growth was 13.5 per cent. With this, India is among the few countries that have recorded seven consecutive quarters of growth amid Covid-19 (Q3, Q4 of FY 2020/21; Q1, Q2, Q3, Q4 of FY 2021/22; and Q1 of FY 2022/23), reflecting the resilience of the Indian economy. The recovery was driven by a revival in services, full recovery in manufacturing, and sustained growth in the agriculture sectors.[29]

There are many indicators that point in the direction of a robust recovery: goods and services tax collections in April 2021 were Rs.1.40

[29] Ministry of Finance, Government of India. November 2021. *Monthly Review of the Indian Economy.*

trillion (lakh crore), followed by the highest-ever Rs.1.68 trillion in April 2022; and collections in September 2022 were Rs.1.47 lakh crore, the seventh month in a row when collections have been more than Rs.1.4 lakh crore. Gross non-performing assets (GNPA) of banks, earlier estimated to go up from 7.5 per cent of their portfolio (March 2021) to 12.5 per cent to 14.5 per cent because of the Covid-19 pandemic, with the consequent impact on bank financing of infrastructure, is now expected to go up to 9.8 per cent under the baseline scenario and to 11.2 per cent under a severe stress scenario.[30] However, the actuals have turned out to be far better—GNPA have declined from 8.2 per cent in March 2020 to 7.3 per cent in March 2021, and further to 6.9 per cent in September 2021. India has also set up a bad bank, the National Asset Reconstruction Company Limited to transfer some of the bad loans of the country's banks (initially Rs.900 billion of Rs.2 trillion) to this bank so as to clean up their balance sheets and unclog credit flow.

There is a need for rapid and universal vaccination of the population (2 billion vaccinations administered and 71 per cent of the Indian population fully vaccinated by 16 July 2022) to limit the human and economic costs of Covid-19, while also hoping for continued efficacy of vaccines in the face of numerous mutations of the virus (a new variant of Covid-19, named Omicron, was found to be quite virulent while also evading immunity from extant Covid-19 vaccines and was called a 'variant of concern' by WHO. This variant engendered the third wave of Covid-19 in India). The vaccination rate, incidentally, is now a macroeconomic indicator as it affects the fortunes of the economy. Effective control over the impending fourth wave is also extremely critical to strengthen an otherwise uneven and nascent economic recovery.

However, three shocks in the space of two years in India is estimated to have resulted in total Covid-19 infections of 43 million accounting for 4,93,000 deaths (as per official figures, as of 28 January 2022). This is likely to cause long-term damage to smaller enterprises and informal-sector employment.[31] The federal fiscal deficit is also very high at 9.2 per

---

[30] Reserve Bank of India. 2021. *RBI Releases the Financial Stability Report, July 2021* (https://rbi.org.in/Scripts/BS_PressReleaseDisplay.aspx?prid=51832).

[31] It has been estimated that over 1.6 billion workers worldwide (most of them in the informal sector) have been significantly impacted by the Covid-19 pandemic and their earnings have declined by over 60 per cent.

cent of GDP in 2020/21 (with the combined federal and state fiscal deficit being at an unprecedented over 12.8 per cent in that year) and 6.7 per cent of GDP in 2021/22 (and estimated at 6.4 per cent of GDP in FY 2022/23), leaving little room for a substantial fiscal stimulus.

More generally, risk aversion became a dominant depressant to economic recovery for enterprises, workers, and consumers. Contact-intensive sectors like airlines, railways, restaurants, hotels, tourism, and many other service sectors suffered disproportionately. User-fee-based infrastructure and PPP projects have suffered from demand slowdown, which has a direct impact on the revenues and therefore the financial viability of these projects (it is estimated that NHAI incurred a loss in toll revenue of Rs.3,513 crore in 2020/21 due to Covid-19-related restrictions). Projects based on availability-based payments (BOT annuity road projects, for example) would not have an immediate adverse financial impact but would stretch public-sector finances in an environment in which they are already stretched because of the high-priority demands of the pandemic.

There are implications of the pandemic on the NIP too. The government, in a major pro-active initiative, drew up the NIP with an ambitious plan to invest Rs.111 lakh crore (about US$1.5 trillion) on infrastructure in the period up to FY 2025, roughly planning to double the annual infrastructure investment compared to what has been achieved in recent years (see Chapter 1). As per estimates in the NIP Task Force Report, about 79 per cent of the required investment would come from the centre and state governments, and this would be constrained given the state of the Indian public finances and the higher-priority demands of the pandemic. Strong government expenditure was a key driver of economic growth in the years before Covid-19. Government consumption went up by an annual rate of 9 per cent between 2014 and 2019. This resulted in a significant expansion in borrowing and the pandemic further pushed up the fiscal deficit. Since the public debt has increased to about 89.4 per cent of GDP in FY 2021 from 74 per cent in FY 2020 (global debt has jumped to US$226 trillion in 2020, including debt of governments, households, and non-financial corporations, which is US$27 trillion above 2019 and the largest ever on record),[32] the government's ability to support growth with higher expenditure would remain limited.

---

[32] IMF. 2021. *Fiscal Monitor Report.*

This has adversely impacted the implementation of the NIP in FYs 2021 and 2022, with stretched public sector finances while private investment suffered from low sentiments and risk averseness. With only 8.5 per cent of the NIP projects implemented up to June 2022, accounting for only 3.8 per cent of the envisaged project costs (see Chapter 1), there is a high likelihood of the NIP targets not being attained even though NIP is a six-year infrastructure investment plan and infrastructure investment green shoots have appeared recently (see Box 11.4).

In terms of its treatment, the Covid-19 pandemic is a non-political *force majeure* event in the Indian road sector's Model Concession Agreement and the relief provided is an extension of the concession period by the *force majeure* period. The lockdowns may be covered under the 'Change in Law' provisions of the concession agreements where the prescribed relief is restoring PPP concessions to the same financial position in NPV terms that they would have been in if this change had not occurred, which would be of significant financial help. A moratorium of one year on the initiation of insolvency proceedings has also been allowed. To address the issue of concessionaire's liquidity during this period, the country's central bank (RBI) has put in place a moratorium period for loan repayment up to August 2020.

Box 11.4 Infrastructure green shoots

If we classify events as those occurring pre-Covid-19 (before March 2020) and after-Covid-19 (after March 2020), we find that even as infrastructure investment slowed down, there is anecdotal evidence that some notable deals happened. Noteworthy transactions pre-Covid-19 were:

- Successful awarding of NHAI toll–operate–transfer (TOT) bundle 3 to Singapore-based Cube Highways (November 2019);
- Award of Jewar Airport, a greenfield project, to the Swiss airport operator, Zurich AG (December 2019);
- Successful award of electricity distribution license in Odisha's five circles to Tata Power (December 2019).

After-Covid 19, noteworthy transactions have been:

- Adani Green Energy bagged the world's largest solar tender to construct 8GW photovoltaic power plant and 2GW solar cell and module manufacturing capacity at a total envisaged investment of US$6 billion (June 2020). It also signed the world's largest green PPA with SECI to supply 4,667MW of green power (December 2021).
- IRB Infrastructure achieved financial closure of Mumbai-Pune Expressway in a major brownfield asset monetization initiative at the state level for a total consideration of Rs.8,262 crore (June 2020);
- Spanish Solarpack Corporation won the bid at Rs.2.36 per unit for 300MW of solar power (June 2020, lowest solar bid in India until then) in a SECI tender. This was followed by successive lower bids by Saudi Arabia's Al Jomaih Energy and Water Co. and Singapore-based Sembcorp's Indian arm, Green Infra Wind Energy Ltd, who won bids at Rs.2 per unit for 200MW- and 400MW-capacity solar power projects, respectively (November 2020). Finally, Gujarat Urja Vikas Nigam Limited's (Phase XI) auction for 500MW of solar projects set a new record of Rs.1.99 per unit (or ~$0.027 per unit) in December 2020, which is the lowest solar bid in India to date.
- Acquisition by Reliance of Norway-based REC Solar Holdings (100 per cent stake for US$771 million), a well-established global player in solar cells, panel, and polysilicon manufacturing, and Sterling & Wilson Solar (40 per cent stake for US$379 million), a strong player for EPC and O&M services in the RE sector (October 2021). Reliance, subsequently, raised a US$736 million green loan to finance its largest overseas purchase, REC Solar Holdings, joining the growing list of Indian companies embracing sustainable finance to fund environment-friendly projects.[a] Reliance has been investing in new energy assets like Germany's NexWafe, Denmark's Stiesdal, United States' Ambri, and UK-based sodium-ion battery technology provider Faradion.
- The most noteworthy transaction was raising of Rs.1,52,057 crore by Reliance by selling just under a third of the stake of RIL in Jio Platforms (April–July 2020).

- The Adani Group has bagged the contract to build India's longest expressway project—the Rs.17,000 crore and 594 km long Meerut-Prayagraj eway—in Uttar Pradesh (December 2021). This would be a six-lane access-controlled expressway built on PPP (DBFOT) mode with a concession period of thirty years.
- CDPQ bought a 40 per cent stake in an Odisha toll road (the 67 km-long Shree Jagannath Expressway) for Rs.2,100 crore (December 2021).
- Ola Electric raised over US$200 million from Tekne Private Ventures, Alpine Opportunity Fund, Edelweiss, and others, valuing the EV maker at US$5 billion (January 2022).
- Blackrock Real Assets and Mubadala Investment Company put Rs.4,000 crore into Tata Power's RE business for an 11 per cent stake (April 2022).
- KKR, a leading global investment firm, and Ontario Teachers' Pension Plan Board (Ontario Teachers') signed an agreement under which Ontario Teachers' will invest up to US$175 million (C$220 million) in KKR's road platform in India, which includes Highway Concessions One (April 2022).
- Welspun sold six operational highway projects (five of these are contracted on the hybrid annuity model) to British PE investor Actis for an enterprise value of Rs.6,000 crore (US$775 million). This was funded by Actis Long Life Infrastructure Fund (June 2022).
- IndInfravit Trust, India's largest InvIT, led by Canada Pension Plan Investment Board, OMERS Infrastructure, and Allianz Capital Partners, entered into an agreement to buy the entire equity shareholding of five operational road projects from Brookfield in a deal valued at Rs.9,375 crore (US$1.2 billion) in one of the largest road transactions in the country (June 2022). The road portfolio comprises three toll roads and two annuity roads, with about 2,400 lane km in Andhra Pradesh, Bihar, Maharashtra, and Uttar Pradesh. IndInfravit currently holds a portfolio of thirteen operational road concessions with about 5,000 lane km spread across five states. This acquisition will expand the portfolio into three additional states, Andhra Pradesh, Bihar, and Uttar Pradesh.

- JSW Energy will acquire the renewable portfolio of Mytrah Energy (1.75GW) for Rs.10,531 crore. The deal leapfrogs JSW power-generation capacity by more than 35 per cent to 6.5GW and pushes it towards net-zero emissions.
- Mahindra Group sold a 30 per cent stake in its RE unit Mahindra Susten to Canadian pension fund, Ontario Teachers' Pension Plan for Rs.2,317 crore (nearly US$300 million) (September 2022).
- Global investment firm KKR and Hero Group invested US$450 million (around Rs.3,588 crore) in Hero Future Energies (HFE)—the RE arm of the Hero Group. HFE is an independent power producer with a diversified portfolio of 1.6GW of operating solar and wind projects (September 2022).
- NHAI raised Rs.6,267 crore from monetization of the Eastern Peripheral Expressway, half of the new ring road around the National Capital Region. Indian Highway Concession Trust, a JV of Maple Highways, a private company incorporated in Singapore, and CDPQ, a Canadian Pension Fund, bagged the project under the TOT model (November 2022).
- Singapore's Sembcorp Industries acquired Vector Green Energy, an Indian renewable-power producer for a base equity consideration of S$474 million or Rs.2,780 crore. Vector Green has an asset portfolio of 583MW including 495MW of solar and 24MW of wind energy in operation as well as 64MW solar projects under development (November 2022).

The total value of these transactions is about Rs.3 lakh crore, which has been achieved in the extremely difficult Covid-19 times. What is noteworthy about these transactions is the diversity of sectors—roads, airports, telecom, solar, and the most difficult, electricity distribution—which demonstrates the overall attraction of Indian infrastructure to investors; in addition to brownfield assets, investment has also been made in greenfield projects with high construction risk; transactions at both the federal and the state level; funding also from foreign investment, implying internalization of currency risk inherent in infrastructure investments, which in turn shows that foreign investors are betting on a stable Indian economy over the longer term;

and the large size of projects. All this augurs well for future infrastructure resource mobilization.[b]

[a]*Times of India.* 7 December 2021. RIL Makes Green Finance Debut with $736 mn Loan.

[b]Kumar V. Pratap. 2020. A New Normal in Infrastructure—Barring the Onset of Second Covid Wave, the Worst Is behind Us (https://www.financialexpress.com/opinion/a-new-nor mal-in-infrastructure-barring-the-onset-of-second-covid-wave-the-worst-is-behind-us/ 2033384/).

12

Some Questions

This chapter deals with four questions that repeatedly come up in discussions on augmenting infrastructure financing in India.

Is There a Case for Borrowings in Foreign Currency for Infrastructure Finance?

Indian infrastructure is largely a domestically financed story. However, infrastructure finance is scarce, more so now in Covid-19 times, and it has been repeatedly suggested that government liberalizes foreign-currency borrowings for filling up the infrastructure financing gap. However, there is an inherent foreign-currency risk in using foreign financing for infrastructure as infrastructure revenues are generally denominated in local currency (except in the airport and the port sectors), while servicing of foreign financing would require foreign exchange, which would increase the cost of such financing. As most infrastructure in India is also underpriced, this would be an additional constraint to infrastructure financing. Use of foreign financing also increases the risk of infrastructure project failure in macroeconomic crises as we have repeatedly seen in the cases of the Mexican Peso Crisis (1994), the East Asian Crisis (1997), the Argentinean Peso Crisis (2002) and the Global Financial Crisis (2008). However, many pension funds, especially the Canadian pension funds, are putting in foreign currency in Indian infrastructure. This section describes the various foreign sources of financing Indian infrastructure and recommends an appropriate approach for foreign financing of Indian infrastructure.

India has been spending about Rs.10 trillion ($135 billion) per annum on infrastructure in recent times with plans to double the investment as per

Infrastructure Financing in India. Kumar V Pratap and Manshi Gupta, Oxford University Press.
© Kumar V Pratap and Manshi Gupta 2024. DOI: 10.1093/oso/9780198884934.003.0013

the targets in the National Infrastructure Pipeline (NIP). Though there is private participation in infrastructure, availability of funds at cheaper rates remains an issue. Due to high fiscal deficit, the government also borrows from the domestic market, and in the process raises interest rates, thus dampening private investment. In this context, the increased use of foreign currency for infrastructure investment has repeatedly been mooted in India. What adds to the attraction of this proposition is that the world is flush with liquidity at low interest rates due to an accommodative stance of monetary policy in the wake of the Covid-19 pandemic.

There is an inherent foreign-currency risk in using foreign financing for infrastructure as infrastructure revenues are generally denominated in local currency (except in the airport and the port sectors), while servicing of foreign financing would require foreign exchange, which would increase the cost of such financing. As most infrastructure in India is also under-priced (e.g. power, metro rail, water, public health, and education, see Chapter 3), the use of foreign-currency financing would be an additional constraint to infrastructure financing. Use of foreign financing also increases the risk of infrastructure project failure in macroeconomic crises as we have repeatedly seen in the case of the Mexican Peso Crisis (1994), the East Asian Crisis (1997), the Argentinean Peso Crisis (2002) and the Global Financial Crisis (2008). These episodes of macroeconomic crises led to wholesale failure of infrastructure projects as foreign-capital servicing became very expensive with local currency depreciation and governments and public authorities in no position to raise user charges to match the depreciation.[1]

It has been suggested that a part of the huge foreign-exchange reserves of the country ($639 billion on 17 September 2021) be used for infrastructure financing. However, the country's central bank (Reserve Bank of India, RBI) has clarified that foreign-exchange reserves are accumulated from investment flows (and not from trade surplus) and have liabilities against them. Hence, the forex reserves work as a buffer against exchange-rate volatility and should not be deployed for funding projects, where the funds would be locked in for a considerable period of time.

---

[1] Clive Harris and Kumar V. Pratap. 2009. *What Drives Private Sector Exit from Infrastructure? Economic Crises and Other Factors in the Cancellation of Private Infrastructure Projects in Developing Countries.*

To avoid currency risk altogether, local-currency financing of infrastructure is preferable, and we have seen that banks are the main source of debt finance in the country, while there are pools of institutional finance available with pension and insurance funds, and NIIF, which are deployed to various degrees on infrastructure. However, this does not imply that foreign-currency financing be eliminated altogether. There are many other avenues for deploying foreign funds into infrastructure: external commercial borrowing (ECB), foreign direct investment (FDI), foreign portfolio investment (FPI), Masala bonds (where foreign-currency risk is borne by investors), and foreign institutional investment (pension, insurance, and sovereign wealth funds (SWFs), see Chapter 8)) into infrastructure. It has also been held that there is plenty of cheap money available in the country and abroad to finance viable infrastructure projects since central banks the world over, including India, have infused liquidity to battle Covid-19-induced recession and fuel demand.

ECB is already allowed for infrastructure projects, with the following limitations:

- All eligible borrowers can raise ECB up to US$750 million or equivalent per financial year (FY) under the automatic route;
- All-in cost ceiling per annum for ECBs is LIBOR + 450 basis points (bps) spread.

To tap longer-tenure funding from international markets for infrastructure financing, the following regulatory changes have been suggested:

- The US$750 million limit for raising ECB under the automatic route may be enhanced to US$1.5 billion for banks and NBFC-IFCs;
- The existing all-in cost ceiling of LIBOR + 450 bps under RBI ECB Guidelines may be rationalized and a suitable higher-upper-cap limit (LIBOR + 500 bps) may be prescribed for longer-tenor borrowings.

FDI is a preferable source of foreign money to be deployed in infrastructure as it is a relatively stable source of capital than FPI. Since 2000, there has been a remarkable increase in the total FDI flows into India (Figure 12.1). This is mainly due to factors like relative macroeconomic stability,

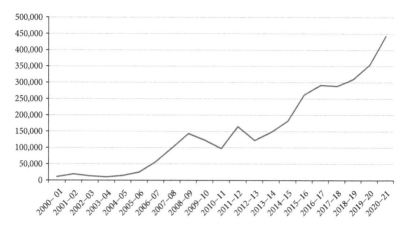

Figure 12.1 FDI equity inflows into India (2000–2021) (Rs. crore)

Source: Department for Promotion of Industry and Internal Trade (DPIIT), Government of India (https://dpiit.gov.in/sites/default/files/FDI_Factsheet_March%2C21.pdf).

raising foreign equity limits and allowing automatic FDI approvals in many sectors, capital market liberalization, and tax reforms.

However, despite impressive growth rates achieved as well as aggressive investment promotion policies, most of this investment is concentrated in a few non-infrastructure sectors. Total FDI equity inflows, from April 2000 to March 2021, have been of the order of Rs.31.75 trillion. The inflows into the construction development sector (townships, housing, built-up infrastructure, and construction development projects) and construction (infrastructure) activities stood at Rs.1.27 trillion and Rs.1.67 trillion, respectively adding up to 9.3 per cent of the total FDI inflows. One of the recent successes in terms of FDI, is awarding the Jewar Airport (Noida International Airport Limited), a greenfield project, to the Swiss airport operator, Zurich AG (December 2019).

Investment by FPIs in non-debt instruments are governed by the Foreign Exchange Management (Non-Debt Instrument) Rules 2019 (FEM (NDI) Rules 2019). Schedule-II of the rules provide that an FPI may purchase or sell capital instruments of a listed/to be listed Indian company on a recognized stock exchange in India. The total holding by each FPI or an investor group should be less than 10 per cent of the total paid-up equity capital of the Indian company on a fully diluted basis and the total holdings of all FPIs put together should not exceed the sectoral cap for FDI.

Debt investment by FPIs is governed by the Foreign Exchange Management (Debt Instrument) Regulations 2019. The investment in fixed-income securities such as government securities (G-Sec), state development loans (SDL), and corporate debt is subject to specified investments limits and conditions as notified from time to time by the RBI. FPIs have three routes to invest in corporate debt and G-Sec (including SDL): the Medium Term Framework (MTF; introduced in October 2015); the Voluntary Retention Route (VRR; introduced in March 2019); and the Fully Accessible Route (FAR; introduced in April 2020).

Investment under MTF is subject to macro-prudential controls such as limits on short-term and security-wise investments and concentration limits. In terms of total investment, the MTF route has the largest FPI investment; but there has been a secular decline in utilization of available limits from a high of 91 per cent in March 2018 to 31 per cent in June 2021. The VRR investments are broadly free of macro-prudential controls but are subject to a minimum retention period of three years. FPI investment through the VRR is almost entirely in corporate debt (98 per cent of the total investments as of 31 March 2021). FAR was introduced in pursuance of an announcement made in the Union Budget 2020/21 that certain specified categories of central G-Secs would be opened fully for non-resident investors without any restrictions. The scheme allows non-residents to invest, without any limit or macro-prudential control, in securities notified by RBI. Currently, thirteen securities are included under FAR. As of 25 June 2021, FAR has witnessed investment by FPIs of Rs.36,487 crore which indicates utilization of less than 10 per cent of the outstanding position of specified securities.

FPIs operate in the capital market in accordance with the provisions of Securities Exchange Board of India (Foreign Portfolio Investors) Regulations, 2019 notified in September 2019. FPIs are required to undergo mandatory registration under the FPI Regulations 2019, a process which entails Designated Depository Participants granting registration to FPIs on behalf of SEBI after necessary due diligence. As per eligibility conditions prescribed by SEBI's Regulation, NRIs/OCIs/resident Indians are allowed to be constituents of FPIs subject to the

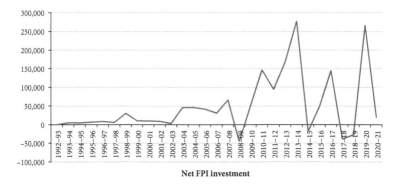

Figure 12.2 Trends in FPI in India (1992–2021) (Rs. crore)

Source: National Securities Depository Limited, Government of India (https://www.fpi.nsdl.
co.in/web/Reports/Yearwise.aspx?RptType=5) (accessed 9 September 2021).

condition that their contributions to the corpus of the FPI should be
below 25 per cent individually and below 50 per cent collectively.

FPI inflows started rising from 1992 onwards when the Government
of India allowed them to invest in financial markets (Figure 12.2). They
increased consistently until a decline in 1997–1998 in response to the
East Asian Crisis and the ensuing contagion effect. This reversal was
short lived and flows revived soon after. Due to proactive measures by
the government, like opening up more sectors and the derivatives market
and increased limits, FPI inflows rose again, followed by a sharp decline
in 2008–2009 due to a severe contraction of liquidity in global financial
markets as a result of the Global Financial Crisis. Quantitative easing in
global markets coupled with progressive reforms undertaken, like the enactment of the SEBI (Foreign Portfolio Investors) Regulations, 2014, and
FPIs being allowed to invest in exchange-traded currency derivatives,
caused FPI flows to increase again. However, the overall trend has been
erratic.

There were sharp outflows in net FPI investment (Figure 12.3) to the
tune of Rs.1,40,418 crore soon after the onset of the Covid-19 pandemic
in 2020, followed by a strong rebound in FPI flows from June 2020 largely
driven by equity investments. FPIs made a record equity investment of
Rs.2,74,032 crore during FY 2020/21 with the month of December wit-
nessing the highest-ever FPI equity inflow at Rs.62,016 crore. While the
initial months of FY 2021/22 saw an outflow of Rs.13,034 crore in equity

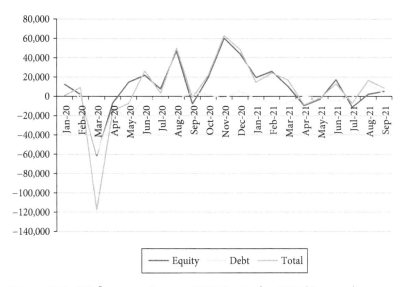

Figure 12.3 FPI flows over January 2020–September 2021(Rs. crore)

Source: National Securities Depository Limited, Government of India (https://www.fpi.nsdl.
co.in/web/Reports/Yearwise.aspx?RptType=6) (accessed 9 September 2021).

markets, a sharp recovery was seen in June 2021 with net investment touching Rs.17,215 crore. However, subsequent months witnessed outflows (July 2021) or lukewarm inflows (August 2021).

The FPI outflows from debt markets which began soon after the start of the pandemic have not reversed like equity flows. During FY 2020/21, FPI net investment in debt stood at Rs.(–)50,433 crore. The net outflow from debt markets continued into FY 2021/22, with net FPI investment of Rs.(–)22,170 crore as of 20 August 2021.

Analysis of sector-wise FPI investment (Figure 12.4) shows that FPI in infrastructure, such as oil and gas, telecom services, transportation, and utilities, is very small compared to sectors like financial services and software services.

Masala bonds are debt papers sold overseas by an Indian entity that are denominated in rupees, and so the exchange-rate risk is borne by the investors. An example of such bonds being issued for infrastructure finance is the Kerala Infrastructure Investment Fund Board (KIIFB) issue of masala bonds of Rs.2,150 crore on the London Stock Exchange in 2019. KIIFB is the first sub-sovereign entity in India to tap the offshore Rupee

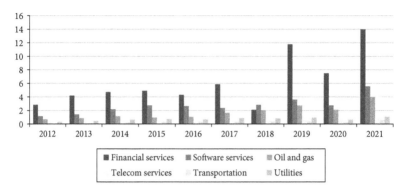

Figure 12.4 Assets under custody of foreign portfolio investors (as of 31 March) (Rs. trillion)

Source: National Securities Depository Limited, Government of India (https://www.fpi.nsdl. co.in/web/Reports/FPI_Fortnightly_Selection.aspx).

international bond market. The secured fixed-rate bond has 9.7 per cent coupon and a five-year tenor.

Following from the above, India could adopt the following approach for foreign-financing of Indian infrastructure:

- Foreign institutional sources of financing infrastructure like pension, insurance, and SWFs (exemplified by CPPIB, CDPQ, etc.) should be encouraged to participate in Indian infrastructure financing as they enable such financing without asset–liability mismatch (detailed steps in Chapter 8);
- FDI in Indian infrastructure (exemplified by Zurich AG investing in Jewar Airport) also needs to be encouraged as it augments both resources and the efficiency of infrastructure provisioning;
- As the country's central bank (RBI) has advised, foreign-exchange reserves should not be used for infrastructure financing. These foreign-exchange reserves are accumulated from investment flows (and not from trade surplus) and have liabilities against them. Hence, the forex reserves work as a buffer against exchange-rate volatility and should not be deployed for funding infrastructure projects, where the funds would be locked in for a considerable period of time.

- Foreign debt in infrastructure is coming through various routes—ECB, FPI, Masala bonds, and so on. While the regime may be liberalized to make it administratively simpler, there is no place for guarantees by the government (or exchange-rate risk devolving on to the government) for facilitating such inflows.

The Need for a new Development Finance Institution in India

Because of the ongoing difficulties in infrastructure financing in India (and for augmenting its quantum), it has been suggested that India needs a new development finance institution (DFI) on the lines of *Banco Nacional de Desenvolvimento Econômico e Social* (BNDES) of Brazil and the China Development Bank. Earlier, IDBI, ICICI, and IFCI were the DFIs that helped infrastructure financing in India. However, because of the closing of access to low-cost finance, competition from traditional banks, and the concentration risk of infrastructure financing, these DFIs converted themselves into universal banks (except IFCI, which, in any case, is performing poorly). India currently has many sectoral DFIs that have come up (e.g. PFC and REC in the power sector, IRFC in the railway sector, HUDCO in the housing sector, NABARD in the agriculture sector, etc.). In addition, there is IIFCL, which can function as a DFI. For all these reasons, this section highlights some issues so that the new DFI that has come up is able to fulfil its objectives while making a reasoned case for strengthening the existing DFIs in the country.

What is a DFI?

A World Bank survey defines a development bank as a bank or financial institution with at least 30 per cent state-owned equity that has been given an explicit legal mandate to reach socio-economic goals in a region, sector, or particular market segment.[2]

---

[2] As quoted in Gulzar Natarajan. 2020. *Designing a New Development Finance Institution for Infrastructure.* Available at https://papers.ssrn.com/sol3/papers.cfm?abstract_id=3517980.

Development banks or DFIs may be considered a form of government intervention in the financial system that aims to address market failures in the provision of finance and, more generally, to help achieve socio-economic objectives such as poverty reduction.[3] DFIs are meant to provide long-term finance to agriculture, industries, trade, transport, and basic infrastructure. DFIs provide financing for development activities at less than strictly commercial terms. They deliver this through technical assistance, grants, structured loans, different types of guarantees, and credit enhancement, and sometimes even equity. Commercial banks, as infrastructure financing entities, suffer from asset–liability mismatch (and the consequent problem of non-performing assets) and therefore, there may be a role for DFIs in infrastructure financing, especially at the construction stage of projects.

Global experience with DFIs

The multilaterals including the World Bank, Asian Development Bank, African Development Bank, and the Inter-American Development Bank for Latin America were all founded after the Second World War and are in the nature of DFIs. More recently, the New Development Bank and the Asian Infrastructure Investment Bank have come up.[4]

In Europe, late industrializers in the nineteenth century, such as France and Germany, benefitted from institutions that provided not only capital but also entrepreneurial skills and technological expertise. So, there was KfW in Germany, the European Investment Bank in Europe, and the Nordic Bank in Scandinavian countries. Today, there are fifteen European national DFIs, with eight of them having significant minority shareholding by domestic private entities. Government ownership guarantees their creditworthiness and thereby allows them to source private capital from global financial markets at cheaper rates. The United States too has a long history of DFIs, for example, the War

[3] Vladimir Popov. 2019. *Infrastructure Investment and Growth: Market Failures Can Be Corrected by the Government.* Available at https://carleton.ca/vpopov/wp-content/uploads/Infrastructure-investment-and-growthMarch-2019.pdf.

[4] Rakesh Mohan. 2021. New Development Finance Institution and Infrastructure Financing in India.

Finance Corporation (1918) and Reconstruction Finance Corporation (1932) funded infrastructure in addition to the war. More recently, the United States established its international Development Finance Corporation (DFC) in 2018.

The other main region where DFIs have been active is East Asia. Historically, in Japan tax-exempt and guaranteed-return post office savings by households, the largest savings pool in the world, was the principal source of low-cost funds for the Development Bank of Japan. Though China was a late adopter of DFIs, the largest development bank in the world currently is the China Development Bank.

The BNDES was created in 1952 to implement the Brazilian federal government's investment policy. The initial focus of BNDES was the development of infrastructure in the country, but it was later expanded to include technology and SME funding in line with the developmental and economic priorities of Brazil. It is now supporting programmes, projects, construction, and services related to the country's economic and social development. Since 2015, BNDES has focussed on catalysing third-party capital, driven in part by the removal of fiscal support. The Indonesian Development Bank, PT SMI, was established in 2009, to catalyse Indonesian infrastructure development. PT SMI focusses on debt products. There is a complimentary institution PTIIF, established in 2010 to act more in the private-sector space, but also provide equity, FDI, and support for capital market development.

Ownership structure, supervision and regulatory framework of some DFIs

BNDES (Brazil) is a federal public company, wholly owned by the government, whose board members are appointed by the president of Brazil and supervision and regulation is by the Central Bank of Brazil. PT SMI (Indonesia) is an NBFC, 100 per cent state-owned, whose board members are appointed by the Ministry of Finance (MoF) and supervision and regulation lies with the MoF. Almost three-quarters of DFIs surveyed by the World Bank are 100 per cent state-owned, 21 per cent have between 50 and 99 per cent state ownership, and only 5 per cent have minority ownership of government.[5] The rationale for predominant state owner-ship of DFIs is that they are expected to serve as the engine of infrastruc-ture growth of the country with significant public policy considerations and to finance projects with significant externalities which possibly cannot be addressed by private entities.

The Indian experience with DFIs

India too has a long history of DFIs with DFIs being set up right from the first decade of independence (see Table 12.1). Earlier, IFCI, ICICI, and IDBI were the DFIs that helped infrastructure financing in India. The three institutions focussed on term finance even as the commercial banks focused on working capital. Lending to infrastructure was almost

Table 12.1 History of DFIs in India

Early post-Independence period, 1947–1969	Pre-reform years 1970–1990	Post-reform years, 1991–
National development banks for supporting industrialization	National development banks for specific sectors	Infrastructure financing institutions for supporting PPPs
IFCI (1948) ICICI (1955) IDBI (1964) State industrial development banks in different states	Housing and Urban Development: HUDCO (1970) Agriculture and Rural Development: NABARD (1981) Trade: EXIM Bank (1981) Power: REC (1970); PFC (1986) Shipping: SCICI (1986) Railways: IRFC (1986) Renewable energy: IREDA (1987) Housing: NHB (1988) SMEs: SIDBI (1989)	• IDFC (1997) • IIFCL (2006) • IL&FS (limited operations now) • L&T Infra Finance, SREI Infra Finance (insolvency proceedings initiated) • IDBI and ICICI (turned into commercial banks) • NIIF (2015)

Source: Gulzar (2020).

---

[5] José de Luna-Martínez and Carlos Leonardo Vicente. 2012. *Global Survey of Development Banks* (https://openknowledge.worldbank.org/bitstream/handle/10986/3255/WPS5969.pdf?sequence=1&isAllowed=y).

exclusively the preserve of the DFIs until the mid-1990s when the function was opened up to commercial banks. The DFIs also provided term finance to industry.

There was logic to the creation of the DFIs. Private investment needed to be supported with suitable finance as the capital markets were in their infancy at the time of independence and were slow to develop in the decades that followed. Banks were not equipped for the role as they had neither access to long-term funds nor did they have the expertise to evaluate projects. DFIs were created to fill the gap. It was important that they provided finance at rates that were consistent with the return to capital on long-gestation projects. There was recognition that this meant making available finance to industry at concessional rates, that is, rates lower than market-determined rates for such loans.

It followed that the DFIs themselves needed access to low-cost finance. This was made possible in several ways. The most significant was the provision of a concessional line of credit by the RBI under the National Industrial Credit Long-Term Operations Fund. Further, the DFIs issued bonds that were often guaranteed by the government. Thirdly, they had access to foreign-currency funds available through the concessional window of international multilateral institutions. They were also able to tap long-term finance because of a provision in the Companies Act that allowed long-term funds such as provident funds, superannuation funds, and gratuity funds to invest in notified 'Public Financial Institutions'.[6]

However, the DFIs started facing problems with the liberalization of the Indian economy in the 1990s. The Narasimham Committee on the Financial Sector (1998) was of the view that, in the changed context, DFIs should convert themselves into banks or NBFCs. This was followed by the report of the SH Khan Working Group on 'Harmonising the Role and Operations of Development Financial Institutions and Banks' (1998). The RBI came up with a paper in 1999 on universal banks, that is, banks that could meet the entire range of customer requirements. All these contributed to an intellectual climate in which DFIs were seen as no longer relevant. With the closing of access to low-cost finance, competition from

---

[6] Ministry of Finance, Government of India. 2020. *Draft Report of Sub-Group on 'Expanding Institutional Finance for Infrastructure' Constituted under IMSC for Enabling Financing of Infrastructure Projects under National Infrastructure Pipeline.*

traditional banks and the concentration risk of infrastructure financing, the DFIs converted themselves into universal banks (except IFCI, which became a NBFC and is performing poorly anyway).

An assessment of India's experience with DFIs

An assessment of the performance of these institutions reveals a mixed picture. They have contributed to term lending, project finance, and financial consultancy services. However, unlike peers in Latin America and East Asia where DFI lending to infrastructure constituted 25–50 per cent of their disbursements, in India it constituted less than 5 per cent of total disbursements. Industrial lending formed the major share of lending by Indian DFIs.

On the back of the establishment of several DFIs in the late 1960s and 1980s, disbursements by all DFIs rose from a measly 2.2 per cent of gross capital formation in 1970/71 to 15.2 per cent in 1993/94. In fact, the early 1990s could be described as peak-DFI period in India. Post-liberalization there was a squeeze on development finance. By 2011–2012, the share of DFIs had declined to just 3.2 per cent of gross capital formation. As a share of the financial system as a whole, DFI loans have been in continuous decline, falling to l.7 per cent after 2004.

The quality of such loans has often been found to be poor. This has been borne out by recent events surrounding a DFI, Infrastructure Leasing and Financial Services (IL&FS), which has limited operations now. As public support and concessional finance declined following economic liberalization (the bonds that were issued qualified as Statutory Liquidity Ratio (SLR) securities for banks up to the early 1990s, which implied preferential access to long-term funding),[7] their competitiveness was adversely affected.

The profile of their portfolio points to a largely passive role in contributing to the efficient crowding-in of infrastructure investments as apparent from the negligible share of projects that are commercially unviable in their project portfolio. For example, in the case of IDFC, more

---

[7] K. V. Kamath. 2021. Right Time for a New DFI in India.

than three-quarters of its investments have gone into the power, transportation (mostly roads), and telecom sectors which are largely de-risked and commercial. Also, IIFCL mandate confines it to financing only commercially viable projects, including those made viable after getting viability gap funding from the Government of India. Instead of crowding - in private capital, IIFCL is actually displacing private capital from commercially viable assets by competing in the market with other private investors. Their portfolio also suffers from the concentration risk of lending to infrastructure.

The NIP aims at infrastructure investment of about US$1.5 trillion in the six-year period ending in 2024/25. Because of the ongoing difficulties in infrastructure financing in India, it has been suggested that India needs a new DFI on the lines of BNDES of Brazil and the China Development Bank. However, it has also been opined that in the current times, the government does not have the resources (both financial and human) to capitalize a DFI. Besides, there are many sectoral DFIs that have come up (e.g. PFC and REC in the power sector, IRFC in the railway sector, HUDCO in the housing sector, NABARD in the agriculture sector, etc.). In addition, there is IIFCL, with its portfolio of projects extending across infrastructure sectors, which can function as a DFI. For all these reasons, it has been opined that the idea of a public-sector-promoted new DFI in current times may not be opportune, while a private-sector DFI may be considered. Let us examine this point of view.

Rationale for a new DFI

The NIP, with its huge investment target of Rs.111 lakh crore ($1.5 trillion) by FY 2025, has budgeted 2–3 per cent of this outlay to come from the new DFI. The counter-cyclical role of a new DFI becomes even more important in the current scenario to kick off the next cycle of growth. The international and Indian experience with DFIs shows the following:

- DFIs are typically instituted to address 'market failures', hence, the mandate of DFIs needs to be carefully crafted accordingly.
- There is a separation of ownership and the supervisory role of government to ensure that the DFI functions independently.

- Almost invariably, DFIs are principally owned by the government. Government ownership helps in raising cheaper resources and assuming first-loss risk.
- Although debt remains the principal product offering, the product suite of DFIs is wide enough to enable the institution to play an influential role in catalysing private-sector participation.
- As the pre-eminent institution of infrastructure finance and cluster of infrastructure expertise, DFIs play an instrumental role in crafting and creating bankable project pipelines for the country.

Given the above analysis, a new DFI can be set up under the Differential Licensing Regime of RBI (Wholesale and Long-term Finance Banks).[8] However, the following issues should be resolved before doing so:

  i. It is important to take stock of India's existing DFIs (Table 12.1). Such an exercise would help understand the quantum of infrastructure currently financed, its efficacy, financing mechanisms, funding constraints, governance, capacity, instruments, and project pipeline. Stock-taking of the existing DFIs would enable gaps to be identified which would then help make a case for the new DFI to cover any gap not bridged by existing DFIs. This would clarify whether the DFI would be universal or sectoral, for example. There is a need for financing infrastructure in up-coming areas like start-ups, climate change, and social sectors (such as health), which lack any sector-specific financing intermediary.

 ii. Setting up a new DFI is not a short-term solution as it requires careful design around funding, governance, business plan, staffing, and so on. This entire process would mean that the new institution would likely take two or three years before it could commence financing specific infrastructure projects. However, there are immediate needs for financing infrastructure. Therefore, it needs to be assessed if the DFI would address a temporal or a structural need.

iii. Regulation and supervision, and governance: The following questions need to be clarified: whether the DFI would be set up within

---

[8] Reserve Bank of India. 2017. *Discussion Paper on Wholesale and Long-term Finance Banks.* Available at https://www.rbi.org.in/Scripts/PublicationReportDetails.aspx?UrlPage=&ID=866#3.

the existing framework or would it need a new regulatory framework (e.g. the characteristics of DFIs are closer to the existing AIFIs (All India Financial Institutions) that are currently operating in India; therefore, the extensive prudential regulations for AIFIs may be adopted for the new DFI); structure of the DFI's board (the board can have equal representation of independent and government-nominated directors expected to facilitate independence, transparency, professionalism, and accountability); would the DFI operate under market principles or provide credit at lower-than-market costs; compliance to ESG criteria would expand financing for the DFI.

These questions are also related to the governance of the institution which needs to be of a high order. Specific elements of good governance practiced by successful DFIs include: operating within an agreed strategy and mandate (e.g. the DFI may provide financing to infrastructure as defined in the 'Harmonized Master List of Infrastructure Subsectors' issued by the MoF; the DFI should prioritize funding projects with positive externalities; periodic reviews of the mandate would be desirable to ensure that the institution remains relevant in changing times); separation of ownership and the supervisory role of government; independent and objective operational management; and maintaining public confidence through transparency.

   iv. A new institution would also entail a large and concessional public-funding requirement (whether from the government budget, MDBs, or state guaranteed bonds) at a time of constrained fiscal space. The issues around funding would be related to initial investors, mix of public/private/multilateral capital, institutional long-term finance from pension and insurance funds (on the lines of BNDES, Brazil, and the Industrial Development Bank of Turkey), intentions for leverage, key sources of debt funding (including state-guaranteed bonds), low-cost funding and concessionality, and so on.

Two models have emerged: Model I—Fiscal transfers from government: BNDES, for example, was largely financed by fiscal transfers; and

Model II—Direct government equity contributions: KfW, and DBSA (Development Bank of Southern Africa, South Africa) were given direct government equity contributions to leverage capital raised in national and international bond markets, typically with different forms of sovereign guarantees, including call-able capital.

    v. Product portfolio: The DFI is expected to address the principal market failure of absence of low-cost, long-term finance in the infrastructure space in the country. Therefore, long-term project finance debt should be the principal product offering of the institution. This should be complemented with alternate product profiles or structured credit (e.g. subordinate debt, mezzanine funding, and credit guarantees) that are very critical in today's context. The institution may also consider taking equity exposure on a case-by-case basis. The DFI should also assist in structuring a bankable project pipeline for the government.

    vi. Indian infrastructure sector experiences not just a financing gap but also a significant shortfall in non-financial services such as project management, project appraisal, credit monitoring, advisory services, project pipeline development, and so on. In existing DFIs, there is a deficit of the required skill mix in the manpower and capacity for undertaking complex financing of projects. The institution would need skilled operating staff with competitive market-driven compensation packages.

Current status

In 2021/22 Budget, the finance minister announced the setting up of a new DFI with Rs.20,000 crore as government equity to provide, enable, and catalyse infrastructure financing.[9] Subsequently, the National Bank

---

[9] Para 45 of the Budget Speech 2021/22 reads: 'Infrastructure needs long-term debt financing. A professionally managed Development Financial Institution is necessary to act as a provider, enabler and catalyst for infrastructure financing. Accordingly, I shall introduce a Bill to set up a DFI. I have provided a sum of Rs.20,000 crores to capitalise this institution. The ambition is to have a lending portfolio of at least Rs.5 lakh crores for this DFI in three years time' (https://www.indiabudget.gov.in/doc/budget_speech.pdf).

for Financing Infrastructure and Development (NaBFID) Bill (2021) was passed in March 2021 and NaBFID has since commenced operations. The new DFI is a body corporate with an initial Government of India holding of 100 per cent (with provision for more than 26 per cent ownership at all times). This will help finance the envisaged 3 per cent of the NIP outlay of Rs.111 lakh crore. However, the expectation is that it can do more and leverage about Rs.5 lakh crore in three years in the form of long-term funds for infrastructure projects. The government will give a grant of Rs.5,000 crore to the DFI—to provide for a hedging cost if borrowings are in foreign currency, subsidize a guarantee fee, lower the cost of funds, and make bonds tax free to subscribers. There would be ten-year tax exemption to funds invested in DFI to attract institutional investors. DFI will have thirteen board members, including a chairman, two government nominees, and four full-time directors. The legislation provides for private sector DFIs to come up. However, unless the above issues (i–vi) are addressed, the DFI may not be able to deliver on its expectations.

Is There a Need for a New Credit-Rating System for Infrastructure Projects?

Infrastructure projects are characterized by high upfront investments and a steady revenue stream over the long term. Besides, they have comfort from a signed concession agreement, which secures their revenue streams. Therefore, it has been suggested that a Loss Given Default (LGD) scale may be better than a Probability of Default (PD) scale for credit rating of infrastructure projects. This section discusses the issue to arrive at a reasoned recommendation.

Infrastructure projects are characterized by high upfront investments, and a steady revenue stream after completion over the long term. Besides, they have comfort from a signed concession agreement by the public authority and the private company which secures their revenue streams. Therefore, it has been suggested that an LGD scale may be better than a PD scale for credit rating infrastructure projects in that the proposed scale incorporates the unique risk characteristics of the infrastructure sector projects in ratings. These unique characteristics of infrastructure projects are:

- Incorporating the benefit of asset recovery prospects (or loss given default analysis) into the conventional rating scale. Internationally this is done by providing notch-ups to issuer rating for high recovery (or low loss given default) to arrive at an issue rating that could be higher than the issuer rating;
- Internationally, it has been found that recovery rates are higher for project finance transactions than for plain-vanilla corporate issuers. Therefore, several large banks, which actively participate in infrastructure financing share their default and recovery rates in a central depository, which can be accessed by rating agencies to fine-tune their criteria and factor the benefit of higher recovery into the ratings;
- Establishing the enforceability and transferability of the concession agreements through step-in rights to lenders is expected to get better ratings for infrastructure companies;
- Long-tenor (ten years to thirty years) amortizing capital market instruments: Longer-tenor instruments help achieve higher ratings, due to better debt service coverage ratios. The critical supporting factors for rating agencies to provide full benefit of the longer tenors include: legal frameworks that enable enforceability and transferability of long-term concession and off-take agreements; and, adoption of financial metrics like project life-cycle cover or loan life-cycle cover that allow agencies to take a life-cycle view of the cash flows.

The existing credit-rating methodology and scale used by rating agencies is more suitable for corporate ratings but not for infrastructure project ratings as it considers PD (which implies assessing the likelihood of a default on the agreed repayment obligations and even a 'single day, single rupee' delay in the case of bank facilities or borrowing programmes with pre-defined repayment schedules is treated as a default) but largely ignores LGD (infrastructure debt recovery rates are higher, at 84 per cent, than those of other assets like corporate debt and bonds at 50–60 per cent; infrastructure debt exhibits an increasing cumulative default risk during the initial years of the loan, but the risk goes down as the loan matures and then stabilizes by year eleven, after which the debt performs as an investment-grade security. Non-infrastructure debt exhibits a similar cumulative increase in default risk, but with higher marginal default rates during the initial years of the loan until it stabilizes and performs as an investment-grade security by year sixteen; in other words, infrastructure assets are less risky than non-infrastructure assets, corporate debt, and bonds)[10] applicable for infrastructure projects. For infrastructure entities, the credit ratings anyway tend to be more conservative on account of the following: non-recourse (or limited recourse) financing nature; high exposure to execution risks (during implementation phase); operation and maintenance risks; concentration on single asset cash flows; shorter debt tenure compared to the overall economic life of the project; unpredictable ramp-up periods; risks pertaining to counterparties; and regulatory risks. Due to these multiple risks, infrastructure projects get projected as having vulnerable and volatile cash flows. This results in lower credit ratings on the conventional PD rating scale.

Infrastructure projects tend to have some positive features which are ignored in the PD rating scale. Post-completion and stabilization, they tend to generate a steady stream of long-term cash flows. They often have a nearly monopolistic market position, steady demand growth, stable pricing formats, and low technological obsolescence risk. Further, PPP infrastructure projects have additional features like the availability of termination payments, contractual protection through some form of non-compete clause, sovereign counterparty (say, in renewable energy solar projects, there is SECI as the quasi-sovereign counterparty), and so on. Structural features such as ring-fencing of cash flows, covenants ring-fencing the infrastructure asset SPV (or a group of SPVs) from the sponsors, well-defined payment waterfall mechanism, and low incremental capex risk also act as risk mitigation factors. These strengths are well corroborated by the high number of successful resolution plans (under the RBI's restructuring scheme) implemented for operational infrastructure projects, where many had shown up as 'defaulters' at some early stage due to some short-term blips or inappropriate loan structuring. Given the focus on timely servicing of financial obligations (single rupee, single day), the conventional PD rating scale has its limitations in taking cognizance of these positive characteristics, thereby resulting in undeserved lower ratings for infrastructure projects. Such lower ratings consequently

---

[10] Global Infrastructure Hub. 2021. *Infrastructure Monitor*.

constrain participation from a wide range of long-term investors who are mandated to invest in or lend to only higher-rated projects.[11]

Due to the inappropriateness of the existing rating methodology, the Government of India in its Union Budget 2016/17 announced its intention to upgrade to a new credit-rating system which gives emphasis to various in-built credit-enhanced features in an infrastructure project, like a signed concession agreement in which the public authority promises to pay the stated amount to the PPP operator even in the event of concessionaire default, generally captured in LGD methodology. Thereafter, an expert group was constituted in the Ministry of Finance to develop a revised rating mechanism more suited to infrastructure projects for the guidance of rating agencies. Subsequently, the three main rating agencies, CRISIL, CARE, and India Ratings, developed a superior rating methodology which captures the conventional PD as well as LGD approach, giving the 'Expected Loss' (or EL) rating scale. The revised rating methodology is in sync with the principles of IndAS (Indian Accounting Standards) mandated by Ministry of Corporate Affairs for all companies registered under the Companies Act. IndAS is India's equivalent of the internationally accepted International Financial Reporting Standards.

The new EL rating scale extends from EL1 to EL8. CRISIL has suggested EL2 as the threshold for insurance companies and pension funds for investment (as against AA under the old scale, which assigns AAA to D ratings). It may be noted that not all A-rated projects under the old scale would get the EL2 rating; only A-and-above projects with a high estimated recovery rate, that is, projects with low LGD, would qualify for EL2. Therefore, the new methodology would bring additional infrastructure projects into the ambit of 'eligible investments' of insurance companies and pension funds, without increasing the overall credit risk or expected loss of these institutional investors.

While in the project's initial stage, there may not be much difference in the conventional PD and the EL-based ratings, the latter will be less volatile and not susceptible to sharp downgrades as is the case in the conventional rating system. This will be useful in the case of

---

[11] Vinayak Chatterjee and Shubham Jain. 30 August 2021. Credit Ratings of Infrastructure Entities: Go the Whole Hog on Adoption of New System.

infrastructure projects facing temporary cash-flow mismatches as the ratings on an EL basis will also factor in the project fundamentals and other mitigating factors. As the project progresses to the operational stage, with the stabilization of its cash flows, both PD and LGD are expected to reduce in an ideal situation, thus benefitting the EL-based rating of the project.

To operationalize this, and for infrastructure projects to get financing from banks and institutional investors like pension and insurance funds, the following changes could be considered:

- RBI Master circular—Basel III Capital Regulations, dated 1 July 2015

Existing provision: Banks rely upon the ratings assigned by the external credit-rating agencies chosen by the RBI for assigning risk weights for capital-adequacy purposes as per the mapping furnished in these guidelines. The risk weights assigned under the said regulations are currently based on a standard rating scale based on PD methodology with ratings of AAA to D.

Recommended change: Apart from the PD-based rating, RBI can specifically ask banks to mandatorily consider EL-based rating for infrastructure projects and accordingly RBI should clearly specify the risk weights for the EL-based ratings so that the banks can calculate the capital charge for the respective infrastructure project. Infrastructure projects have unique features such as predictability of cash flows over the life of the project, which are better captured through an EL assessment over the life of a debt instrument. External rating agencies have already formulated a rating structure for infrastructure projects based on the Expected Loss method. However, it is not being used frequently by lenders/developers.

In the meetings convened by the MoF on this issue, RBI has conveyed that it needs to follow the international (Basel) norms, so far as risk weights and capital adequacy are concerned, that are based on the PD scale and not on the EL scale.

- 'Rating Criteria for investments under New Pension System (NPS) scheme' of Pension Fund Regulatory and Development Authority

(PFRDA) and Master Circular 'Investment regulations' of Insurance Regulatory and Development Authority (IRDA).

Existing provision: As per the circular dated 8 May 2018, PFRDA permits specified NPS schemes to invest in corporate bonds/securities which have a minimum of an A rating or equivalent; IRDA Master Circular mandates a minimum of an AA rating for investments in corporate bonds and AAA for securitized paper. However, there has been a change and IRDA has recently allowed insurance companies to invest in debt issued by infrastructure companies, rated not-less-than A (on the conventional scale) along with an Expected Loss rating of EL1 (highest rating on the EL scale).

Recommended change: PFRDA and IRDA may modify the permissible rating to EL2 and above under the new rating methodology, together with PD rating of investment grade (BBB– and above under the existing rating scale), when applicable for infrastructure projects. So, the prudential norms governing investment in infrastructure by insurance and pension funds could provide the option of either a minimum AA-or A rating requirement as already stipulated in their guidelines or a minimum of EL2 subject to the PD rating being investment grade (BBB– and above under the existing rating scale). EL2-rated exposure has been found to have annualized EL levels comparable to what is being priced by investors for AA-rated papers under the PD scale. Besides globally, BBB– rating is investment grade under the PD scale and therefore presents a reasonable degree of comfort for investors.

Since the new rating methodology is applicable only for projects, the existing rating methodology and threshold of AA may continue for investments in bonds issued by all 'non-projects' including financiers.[12] These changes would enable institutional investment (investment from pension and insurance funds, which does not suffer from the asset–liability mismatch typically associated with bank financing of infrastructure) to flow into infrastructure projects.

---

[12] Ministry of Finance, Government of India. 2020. *Report of Project Finance/Refinance Sub-Group Constituted under IMSC for Enabling Financing of Infrastructure Projects under National Infrastructure Pipeline.*

Should India Have a 3P Institution for Shepherding PPPs in the Country Like the United Kingdom and Australia?

An issue that is not directly connected with infrastructure financing, but one which regularly comes up in policymaking circles is whether India should have a 3P institution for shepherding PPPs in the country just like the United Kingdom and Australia. There are many questions that come up regularly while dealing with private participation in infrastructure, for example, hybrid annuity model (HAM) may be poor value for money to the government and should be discontinued; in evaluating bids for private infrastructure projects, do we evaluate both the technical and financial capacity of bidders, or only the financial capacity, given that bidders with the required financial capacity can hire the best technical capacity available to implement the project?; is it time to use least-present value of revenues (LPVR) as a bidding parameter in PPP projects as it would mitigate traffic risk? Answers to these questions would have an important bearing on private participation in infrastructure. Therefore, there may be a need for an institution like 3P India to systematically deal with these questions. This section expands on this point of view.

Background

Providing adequate and quality infrastructure is a prerequisite for rapid and sustained economic growth. In 2020, the Government of India announced its first ever NIP envisaging infrastructure investment of about US$1.5 trillion in over 6,800 projects over a six-year period up to 2024/25. With a GDP of US$2.8 trillion, India needs to spend about US$250 billion (~8 per cent of GDP) on infrastructure on a per annum basis. In the past decade (2008–2017), India invested more than US$1.1 trillion on infrastructure, out of which more than a third came from the private sector. Given the competing demands on fiscal resources, PPPs are critical for meeting the infrastructure investment targets through resource augmentation as well as improving the efficiency of infrastructure service delivery. Investment of this order will ensure that infrastructure does not become a binding constraint to the growth of the Indian economy.

Need for 3P India

India runs the second-largest PPP programme in the developing world (as per the Private Participation in Infrastructure database of the World Bank) but has no specialized and dedicated 3P institution. There are a number of issues that come up on a regular basis, where there is a need for impartial advice: for example, clarity on invocation of the *force majeure* clause in the current Covid-19 pandemic; HAM projects may be poor value for money to the government and therefore should be discontinued; in evaluating bids for private infrastructure projects, do we evaluate both the technical and financial capacity of bidders, or only the financial capacity under the logic that technical capacity can easily be purchased if a prospective bidder has the required financial capacity; is it time to use LPVR as a bidding parameter in transport PPP projects as it would mitigate traffic risk?; developing new Model Concession Agreements (MCAs) for new sectors and new PPP models. A dedicated 3P India institution can provide impartial advice on these issues. Further, market leaders like the United Kingdom (Infrastructure and Projects Authority) and Australia (Infrastructure Australia) have such institutions, making the proposed 3P India, an international best practice.

The finance minister in his 2014/15 Budget speech, inter alia, stated that: 'PPPs have delivered some of the iconic infrastructure like airports … But we have also seen the weaknesses of the PPP framework, the rigidities in contractual arrangements, the need to develop more nuanced and sophisticated models of contracting and develop quick dispute redressal mechanism. An institution to provide support to mainstreaming PPPs called 3P India will be set up with a corpus of Rs.500 crores.'

The Kelkar Committee (2015) set up to revisit and revitalize PPPs, endorsed the 3P India to function as a centre of excellence on PPPs, to enable research, review, and roll out activities to build capacity and support more nuanced and sophisticated models of contracting and dispute redressal. 3P India can support a dynamic process of infrastructure design, build, and operate in India and thereby help deliver on the promise of reliable infrastructure services for all citizens.

Objectives of the proposed 3P India

In this context, the objectives of the proposed 3P India would be:

- Policy support—provide integrated and holistic institutional support to PPPs in infrastructure (including up-coming infrastructure sectors and PPP models) and to address related issues from time to time;
- Capacity-building and technical assistance for project preparation to central ministries and state governments, which will help in developing a steady pipeline of well-structured PPPs;
- Quality control—half-baked projects need not be brought to the market and therefore, the institution would help in developing well-prepared projects;
- Standardization—Prepare model concession agreements across infrastructure sectors;
- Repository of knowledge, maintain PPP database, and disseminate project information and best practices to stakeholders. India currently has no institution which maintains a unified database on quantum of infrastructure or PPP investment in the country.

Functions of 3P India

- Policy support:
  o Provide expert inputs on infrastructure policy considering international best practices, for example, renegotiation framework across infrastructure sectors; should there be independent sectoral regulators for each infrastructure sector or options like 'regulation by contract' or multi-sectoral regulators may also be considered?
  o Provide advice on increasing sectoral spread and PPP models with balanced risk-sharing between public and private sectors—social sectors like health, education, solid waste management, waste-water treatment and water supply are high priorities;

  o Recommend sectors that can be considered 'infrastructure' by including them in the Harmonized Master List of Infrastructure.
- Capacity-building and technical assistance—3P India would develop knowledge material on infrastructure and PPPs; would conduct training programmes for officials at central/state/and local levels, where the focus would be on lagging states and line agencies;
- Prepare and disseminate guidance material on PPPs, for example, integration of value-for-money analysis in PPP project appraisal, contingent liabilities and guarantees, service quality and performance standards, efficient contract management, framework for brownfield asset monetization, and so on;
- Prepare model concession agreements across infrastructure sectors;
- Promote PPP project quality by bringing only well-prepared projects to the market. The finance minister in the Budget speech 2020/21 proposed setting up a project preparation facility (PPF). The PPF would address issues of lack of appropriately structured projects due to inadequate preparatory work, unbalanced risk allocations, contractual frameworks, poor demand assessment, and so on, and ensure an adequate flow of capital from the private sector. A dedicated PPF set up for project development activities would assist in translating the demand for infrastructure into credible projects which could help the investor in weighing the risk–return trade-off. Project preparation includes the work required towards taking projects from concept to award of contract. Key underlying principles of PPF may include:
  o Due diligence and identification of associated risks and its mitigants;
  o Balanced risk-sharing between government and private investor;
  o Understanding the investor requirements and structuring the project to suit the requirements, to the extent possible given the need for balanced risk sharing between public and private sectors;
  o Making sure that the project is bankable and would attract interest from potential bidders.
- Prepare and update the NIP. The government has already announced the NIP, envisaging investment of Rs.111 lakh crore up to FY 2025. 3PI would update this document every year;
- Prepare and update the financing plan of NIP including recommending new institutions and instruments;

- Develop a PPP database: Provide authentic data on PPPs in India, including data on project sponsor, year of financial closure, concession period, total project cost, current status of the project, and so on;
- Convene investor conferences with participation from line ministries, state governments, regulators, private investors, pension, insurance, and sovereign wealth funds.

Staffing 3P India

3P India would be a Section 25 company under the Companies Act and would have a staff strength of twenty-five by the end of year three. It will be headed by a CEO (acknowledged PPP expert), and would have twenty technical professionals (project finance, contracts, procurement, legal, and sector experts in energy, transport, water, urban, health, and education) and would have four administrative staff. Since the quality of personnel needs to be of a high order, 3P India would be permitted lateral hiring along the lines of staffing at Invest India/NITI Aayog. 3P India would be free to develop its own HR and compensation policy to attract and retain quality talent. Depending on the workload, a review of the staffing pattern may be necessary at the end of year three.

Funding 3P India

An amount of Rs.100 crore should be sufficient for the first three years of 3P India's existence (including staffing costs, furnishing of office space, lease rents, etc.). Thereafter, it may raise funds based on project appraisal fees, capacity-building charges, and so on. Bilateral and multilateral organizations (like the World Bank and ADB) are also likely to contribute. Care may be taken to ensure against conflict of interest in 3P India in terms of its mandate and fund-raising (say from the private sector).

Elements of success

Effective 3P Institutions in parliamentary systems are attached to treasury departments (MoF). However, an arms-length relationship with government needs to be maintained to enable unbiased inputs and prevent conflict of interest. 3PI units with executive power tend to be more effective than those that are purely advisory. 3P India needs a mandate to promote and facilitate good PPPs, which may imply the need for 'veto power' through a gateway process that allows PPPs to be monitored throughout the project life cycle (with an ability to stop PPP projects following due process in contracts at any stage in its life cycle). So, the 3PI institution may be set up as an independent institution seated in the MoF. Over time, increased expertise and capacity-building could result in better structured and financed projects, enabling lower NPAs and better-quality infrastructure assets.

Bibliography

Abadie, Richard. 2020. COVID-19 and Infrastructure: A Very Tricky Opportunity (https://blogs.worldbank.org/ppps/covid-19-and-infrastructure-very-tricky-opportunity).

Acharya, Shankar. 2021. *An Economist at Home and Abroad—A Personal Journey*. Noida, India: Harper Collins.

Airports Authority of India. 2020. *Annual Report 2019–20*.

Airports Council International. 2020. Best Airport by Size and Region (https://aci.aero/customer-experience-asq/asq-awards-and-recognition/asq-awards/current-winner-2019/departures/best-airport-by-size-and-region/#between-25-and-40).

Almeida, Miguel, Lionel Mok, and Krista Tukiainen. 2020. *Sustainable Debt Global State of the Market H1 2020: Climate Bonds Initiative*, p. 4 (https://www.climatebonds.net/system/tdf/reports/cbi-sustainable-debt-global-sotm-h12020.pdf?file=1&type=node&id=54589&force=0).

Asian Development Bank. 2020. *An Updated Assessment of the Economic Impact of COVID-19.* (https://www.adb.org/publications/updated-assessment-economic-impact-covid-19)

Asian Development Bank. 2021. *Covid-19 and Public–Private Partnerships in Asia and the Pacific Guidance Note* (https://www.adb.org/sites/default/files/publication/681536/covid-19-ppps-asia-pacific-guidance-note.pdf).

B20 Italy. 2021. *Finance and Infrastructure Policy Paper* (https://www.b20italy2021.org/wp-content/uploads/2021/10/B20_FinanceInfrastructure.pdf)

Blanchard, Olivier. 2019. *Public Debt and Low Interest Rates*. Peterson Institute of International Economics (https://www.piie.com/system/files/documents/wp19-4.pdf).

Bloomberg. 2021. European ESG Assets Shrank by $2 Trillion after Greenwash Rules (https://www.bloomberg.com/news/articles/2021-07-18/european-esg-assets-shrank-by-2-trillion-after-greenwash-rules?sref=hyzKRfwE).

Bombay High Court Order. 2017. *Mumbai Metropolitan Region Development Authority vs The Fare Fixation Committee and Others* (https://indiankanoon.org/doc/140387429/)

Bombay Stock Exchange (BSE) website. *Larsen & Toubro Ltd share price* (https://www.bseindia.com/stock-share-price/larsen--toubro-ltd/lt/500510/)

Boston Consulting Group. 2013. Bridging the Gap—Meeting the Infrastructure Challenge with Public-Private Partnerships (https://www.bcg.com/documents/file128534.pdf).

Boston Consulting Group and Sovereign Investment Lab. 2019. *The Rise of Collaborative Investing—Sovereign Wealth Funds' New Strategies in Private Markets* (https://image-src.bcg.com/Images/Sovereign-Wealth-Funds-Co-Investments-Approach_tcm9-227441.pdf).

Boston Water and Sewer Commission. *Current Water and Sewer Rates Effective from January 1, 2020 (Residential)* (https://www.bwsc.org/residential-customers/rates) .

Business Standard. 2021. The Slip Is Showing—India's Gender Gap Is Wider Than Ever, 2 April.

Business Standard. 2021. Acuite Ratings 1st Rater in India to Sign Up for ESG, 30 September.

Canada-India Business Council. 2022. *Why India? Unlocking Canada's Opportunity in the Indo-Pacific* (https://canada-indiabusiness.com/why-india).

Cartlidge, Duncan. 2006. *Public Private Partnerships in Construction* (https://vdo cuments.mx/reader/full/public-private-partnerships-in-construction).

Census of India. 2011. http://censusindia.gov.in/2011-prov-results/paper2/data_fi les/india/paper2_1.pdf.

Chao, Jenny and Jason Zhengrong Lu. 2020. Using Government Guarantees Carefully as the Private Sector Redefines Bankability (https://blogs.worldbank.org/ppps/ using-government-guarantees-carefully-private-sector-redefines-bankability).

Chatterjee, Vinayak and Shubham Jain. 2021. Credit Ratings of Infrastructure Entities: Go the Whole Hog on Adoption of New System. *Financial Express*, 30 August.

Chaudhary, Archana. 2021. Extreme Weather Puts Rs.6.2 Trillion Bank Debt at Risk. *Business Standard*, 4 March.

Choudhary, Sanjeev. 2020. Kerosene Subsidy Removed via Small Price Hikes over 4 Years. *The Economic Times*, 13 March. (https://economictimes.indiatimes.com/ industry/energy/oil-gas/kerosene-subsidy-removed-via-small-price-hikes-over- 4-years/articleshow/74601660.cms?from=mdr).

Christensen, Clayton M., Michael E. Raynor, and Rory McDonald. 2015. What Is Disruptive Innovation? *Harvard Business Review* (https://hbr.org/2015/12/what- is-disruptive-innovation).

Comptroller and Auditor General of India. 2021. Report of the Comptroller and Auditor General of India on Implementation of Phase-III of Delhi Mass Rapid Transit System by DMRC. (https://cag.gov.in/uploads/download_audit_rep ort/2021/Report%20No.%2011%20of%202021_DMRC_English-061a88483a1f 130.47012068.pdf)

Concession Agreement of the L&T MRHL project. 2010. https://www.pppinindia. gov.in/documents/20181/34422/5.+Hyderabad+Metro+Rail+project.pdf/7fd98 761-d514-4087-b56f-33db56472cb8?version=1.0

Credit Suisse Research. 2021. *CS Gender 3000.* (https://www.credit-suisse.com/ about-us/en/reports-research/studies-publications.html)

CRISIL. 2021. *Yearbook on the Indian Debt Market* (https://www.crisil.com/en/home/ our-analysis/reports/2021/02/crisil-yearbook-on-the-indian-debt-market-2021. html).

Cruz, C. O. and R. C. Marquez. 2013. Exogenous Determinants for Renegotiating Public Infrastructure Concessions: Evidence from Portugal. *ASCE Journal of Construction Engineering and Management.* Volume 139 Issue 9

DeJongh, Taylor. 2009. *Assessing the Impact of Recent Credit Constraints on Energy Sector Investment Requirements in Bangladesh.* A study commissioned by the World Bank. Washington, DC: World Bank.

Delhi Jal Board. 2018. Revised Water Tariff, 1 February. http://www.delhijalboard.nic. in/sites/default/files/AllPDF/Revised%2BWater%2BTarif%2Bwef%2B01022018_0.pdf.

Delhi University (Faculty of Law). 2020/21. Schedule of Fees. http://www.du.ac.in/ du/uploads/COVID19/pdf/adm2020/Notice_Admission%20in%20Faculty%20 of%20Law.pdf.

Delmon, Jeff and Andy Ricover. 2020. Rebalancing Airport PPPs, Even As the COVID-19 Winds Still Blow (https://blogs.worldbank.org/ppps/rebalancing-airp ort-ppps-even-covid-19-winds-still-blow).

Department for Promotion of Industry and Internal Trade (DPIIT), Government of India. 2021 https://dpiit.gov.in/sites/default/files/FDI_Factsheet_March%2C21.pdf.

Department of Telecommunications, Government of India. 2020. *Annual Report 2019–20.*

Diletta Giuliani. 2019. *Securitisation as an Enabler of Green Asset Finance in India: Climate Bonds Initiative*, p. 17 (https://www.climatebonds.net/files/repo rts/securitisation-as-an-enabler-of-green-asset-finance-in-india-report-15052 020.pdf).

Diop, Makhtar. 2020. What Can AI Tell Us about COVID-19's Impact on Infrastructure? (https://blogs.worldbank.org/ppps/what-can-ai-tell-us-about-covid-19s-impact-infrastructure).

Diop, Makhtar. 2021. Private Sector's Retreat Jeopardizes Recovery, 26 February (https://blogs.worldbank.org/ppps/private-sectors-retreat-jeopardizes-recov ery?CID=WBW_AL_BlogNotification_EN_EXT).

DMRC, Journey Planner. 2021 http://www.delhimetrorail.com/metro-fares.aspx)

Eckstein, David, Vera Künzel, and Laura Schäfer . 2021. *Global Climate Risk Index 2021*. Germanwatch, p. 8. (https://germanwatch.org/sites/default/files/Global%20 Climate%20Risk%20Index%202021_1.pdf)

Economic Times, The. 2021. Ola Electric Raises $200 mn at over $5 bn Valuation: Sources, 8 October (https://auto.economictimes.indiatimes.com/news/two-wheel ers/ola-electric-raises-200-mn-at-over-5-bn-valuation-sources/86872969).

Ministry of Finance, Government of India. 2010. Record of Discussion of the 12th Meeting of Empowered Committee (https://www.pppinindia.gov.in/documents/ 20181/22340/12+EC+minutes+29.07.2010-+HMR.pdf/a3ee67fc-a0a0-4c07-aaad-a47b9eb7bd57?version=1.0)

Ministry of Finance, Government of India. 2013. Record of Discussion of the 17th Meeting of Empowered Committee (https://www.pppinindia.gov.in/documents/ 20181/22340/17th+EC+Minutes++06.05.2013.pdf/7672db31-d525-483d-8d0f-239a7d4a0ade?version=1.0).

Ministry of Finance, Government of India. 2019. Record of Discussion of the 32nd Meeting of Empowered Committee (https://www.pppinindia.gov.in/documents/ 20181/22340/RoD+of+32nd+EC+Meeting/7b4160ee-1405-4c2a-b637-3993a d6e6ce9?version=1.0).

Ministry of Finance, Government of India. 2019. Record of Discussion of the 34th Meeting of Empowered Committee (https://www.pppinindia.gov.in/documents/ 20181/22340/Record+of+Discussions+of+the+34th+EC+Meeting.pdf/68979 c66-0498-4d39-9d33-834cf38b6c91?version=1.2).

Ernst & Young. 2020. *Risk, Returns and Resilience: Integrating ESG in the Financial Sector.* (https://assets.ey.com/content/dam/ey-sites/ey-com/en_in/topics/climate-change/2020/ey-risk-returns-and-resilience-integrating-esg-in-the-financial-sector.pdf?download)

Fakhoury, Imad N. 2022. New Data Shows Private Investment Lends a Hand as Public Debt Looms Large (https://blogs.worldbank.org/ppps/new-data-shows-private-investment-lends-hand-public-debt-looms-large?CID=WBW_AL_BlogNotifica tion_EN_EXT).

Farquharson, Edward, Clemencia Torres de Mastle, and E. R. Yescombe with Javier Encinas. 2011. *How to Engage with the Private Sector in Public-Private Partnerships in Emerging Markets.* Washington, DC: World Bank.

Foster, Vivien and Cecilia Briceño-Garmendia (eds). 2010. *Africa's Infrastructure—A Time for Transformation.* Washington, DC: World Bank.

Foster, Vivien, Maria Vagliasindi, Nisan Gorgulu. 2022. The Effectiveness of Infrastructure Investment as a Fiscal Stimulus: What We've Learned (https://blogs. worldbank.org/ppps/effectiveness-infrastructure-investment-fiscal-stimulus-what-weve-learned?CID=WBW_AL_BlogNotification_EN_EXT).

G20 *Principles for Quality Infrastructure Investment.* 2019 (https://www.worldbank. org/en/programs/quality-infrastructure-investment-partnership/qii-princip les#1)

Garg, Subhash Chandra. 2021. Monetisation Plan Too Ambitious, No Likelihood of Getting Done: Subhash Garg, Former Finance secretary. *The Economic Times* (https://economictimes.indiatimes.com/news/economy/finance/monetisation-plan-too-ambitious-no-likelihood-of-getting-done-subhash-garg-former-fina nce-secretary/articleshow/85648859.cms?from=mdr).

Ghani, Abha Joshi. 2020. How COVID-19 Will Impact our Cities in the Long Term (https://www.weforum.org/agenda/2020/11/what-will-our-cities-look-like-after-covid-19/).

Ghani, Ejaz, Arti Grover Goswami, and William R. Kerr. 2012. Highway to Success: The Impact of the Golden Quadrilateral Project for the Location and Performance of Indian Manufacturing, November (https://academic.oup.com/ej/article/126/591/317/5077429).

Ghosh, Saurabh, Siddhartha Nath, Abhinav Narayanan, and Satadru Das. 2022. Green Transition Risks to Indian Banks. *Reserve Bank of India Bulletin* (https://rbidocs.rbi.org.in/rdocs/Bulletin/PDFs/03AR_17032022266D3EFB505B744DB9B32A37C162E0680.PDF).

Global Impact Investing Network. 2020. *Annual Impact Investor Survey 2020 (Executive Summary)*, pp. 5 and 7 (https://thegiin.org/assets/GIIN%20Annual%20Impact%20Investor%20Survey%202020%20Executive%20Summary.pdf).

Global Infrastructure Hub. Meet Four Women Leaders Who Are Transforming Infrastructure Development in Latin America (https://www.gihub.org/blog/women-in-infrastructure-in-latin-america/).

Global Infrastructure Hub. 2020. *Infrastructure Monitor 2020*, p. 13 (https://cdn. gihub.org/umbraco/media/3241/gih_monitorreport_final.pdf).

Global Infrastructure Hub. 2021. *Infrastructure Monitor 2021* (https://www.gihub. org/resources/publications/infrastructure-monitor-2021-report/)

Global Infrastructure Hub. 2022. *Transformative Outcomes through Infrastructure* (https://transformativeinfratracker.gihub.org/overview/?utm_source=PR&utm_medium=media&utm_campaign=FTpaid_May22)

Global SWF Data Platform. *Sovereign Wealth Funds & Public Pension Funds* https://globalswf.com/.

Gombar, Vandana. 2021. Offshore Wind, Jobs, Hydrogen. Business Standard, 5 May.

Government of NCT of Delhi. 2020. *Economic Survey of Delhi 2019–20* (http://delhiplanning.nic.in/content/economic-survey-delhi-2019-20).

Guasch, J. L. 2004. *Granting and Renegotiating Infrastructure Concessions: Doing It Right.* Washington, DC: World Bank.

Haldea, Gajendra. 2010. Sub-prime Highways—An Issues Paper (gajendrahaldea.in/download/Sub-prime_Highways-An_Issues_Paper.pdf)

Halder, A. 2018. Narendra Modi's 'Metro' Vision: 50 Cities to Be Covered through 700 km Network in Coming Years, Says Hardeep Singh Puri. Financial Express, 6 March (https://www.financialexpress.com/infrastructure/railways/narendra-modis-metro-vision-50-cities-to-be-covered-through-700-km-network-in-coming-years-says-hardeep-singh-puri/1089085/).

Harris, Clive and Kumar V. Pratap. 2009. *What Drives Private Sector Exit from Infrastructure—Economic Crises and Other Factors in the Cancellation of Private Infrastructure Projects in Developing Countries.* Washington, DC: World Bank (https://openknowledge.worldbank.org/bitstream/handle/10986/10569/478840BRI0Grid10Box338868B01PUBLIC1.pdf?sequence=1&isAllowed=y).

Hart, Oliver. 2017. Incomplete Contracts and Control. *American Economic Review Vol. 107, NO. 7*

Hetzner, Christiaan. 2020. Germany Doubles EV Incentives, Excludes Internal-combustion Cars from Stimulus Program (https://www.autonews.com/sales/germany-doubles-ev-incentives-excludes-internal-combustion-cars-stimulus-program). Crain Communications Inc, Detroit.

IJ Global. Project Finance League Report: Full Year 2020 and PF Charts. 2021 (https://ijglobal.com/reports).

Inderst, Georg. 2021. Institutional Investors: Time to Get Involved in Development and Blended Finance, 12 May (https://blogs.worldbank.org/ppps/institutional-investors-time-get-involved-development-and-blended-finance?CID=WBW_AL_BlogNotification_EN_EXT).

India Infoline. 2016. Impact of the Telecom Sector in the Year 2015 and the Year Ahead (https://www.indiainfoline.com/article/news-top-story/impact-of-the-telecom-sector-in-the-year-2015-and-the-year-ahead-116010400208_1.html).

India Investment Grid (IIG). 2022. https://indiainvestmentgrid.gov.in/opportunities/nip-projects.

India Today. 2021. Distress Signals, 23 August.

Indian Institute of Management, Ahmedabad. 2020. *IndiGrid: Creating India's First Power Transmission InvIT* (https://sk.sagepub.com/cases/indigrid-creating-india-first-power-transmission-invit-a)

Infrastructure and Projects Authority, Government of the United Kingdom. 2016. National Infrastructure Delivery Plan, March (https://assets.publishing.service.gov.uk/government/uploads/system/uploads/attachment_data/file/520086/2904569_nidp_deliveryplan.pdf).

Infrastructure Australia. 2016. Australian Infrastructure Plan, February (https://www.infrastructureaustralia.gov.au/sites/default/files/2019-06/Australian_Infrastructure_Plan.pdf).

Infrastructure Australia, Government of Australia. 2021. Reforms to Meet Australia's Future Infrastructure Needs—2021 Australian Infrastructure Plan, August (https://www.infrastructureaustralia.gov.au/sites/default/files/2021-09/Exec%20Summary%20%28standalone%29.pdf).

Institute for Energy Economics and Financial Analysis. 2021. Green Bonds Are Driving Cost-effective Finance to Clean Energy in India (https://ieefa.org/ieefa-green-bonds-are-driving-cost-effective-finance-to-clean-energy-in-india/).

Insurance Regulatory and Development Authority of India. 2020. *Annual Report 2019–20*.

Insurance Regulatory and Development Authority of India. 2020 *Annual Report 2019–20*, p. 212 (https://www.irdai.gov.in/admincms/cms/uploadedfiles/annual%20reports/IRDAI%20Annual%20Report%202019-20_English.pdf)

International Council on Clean Transportation. 2020. *Electric Vehicle Capitals: Cities Aim for All-electric Mobility*, p. 1 (https://theicct.org/sites/default/files/publications/ev-capitals-update-sept2020.pdf).

International Energy Agency. 2021. *Global EV Outlook 2021*, p. 5 (https://iea.blob.core.windows.net/assets/ed5f4484-f556-4110-8c5c-4ede8bcba637/GlobalEVOutlook2021.pdf)

International Energy Agency. 2021. *India Energy Outlook 2021*, p. 169 (https://www.iea.org/reports/india-energy-outlook-2021).

International Finance Corporation. 2020. *Growing Impact—New Insights into the Practice of Impact Investing* (https://www.ifc.org/wps/wcm/connect/8b8a0e92-6a8d-4df5-9db4-c888888b464e/2020-Growing-Impact.pdf?MOD=AJPERES&CVID=naZESt9).

International Monetary Fund. 2021. *Fiscal Monitor Report*. Washington, DC: IMF.

International Monetary Fund. 2021. *Strengthening Infrastructure Governance for Climate-responsive Public Investment*. Washington, DC: IMF.

International Monetary Fund. 2021. *World Economic Outlook*, April. Washington, DC: IMF.

IQ Air. 2021. *World Air Quality Report* (https://www.iqair.com/world-most-polluted-cities/world-air-quality-report-2021-en.pdf)

Jena, Labanya Prakash and Dhruba Purkayastha. 2020. *Accelerating Green Finance in India: Definitions and Beyond*. Climate Policy Initiative. (https://www.climatepolicyinitiative.org/wp-content/uploads/2020/07/Accelerating-Green-Finance-in-India_Definitions-and-Beyond.pdf)

Kamath, K. V. 2021. Right Time for a New DFI in India. in *New Generation DFI in India: Opportunities and Challenges*. Research and Information System (RIS) for Developing Countries. New Delhi.

Kerala Water Authority. 2021. Water Tariff (https://kwa.kerala.gov.in/water-tariff/).

Keshavdev, V. 2021. SBI Loan to Adani's Coal Project Stuck. Fortune India.

Kowarski, Ilana. 2020. See the Price, Payoff of Law School before Enrolling (https://www.usnews.com/education/best-graduate-schools/top-law-schools/articles/law-school-cost-starting-salary).

KPMG. 2012. *Infrastructure 100* (https://assets.kpmg.com/content/dam/kpmg/pdf/2012/11/Infrastructure100.pdf)

KPMG. 2020. *Analysing the Concept of Stock Exchange in India*, p. 5 (https://assets.kpmg/content/dam/kpmg/in/pdf/2020/07/analysing-the-concept-of-social-stock-exchange-in-india.pdf).

Ladley, Herb. 2020. COVID-19 and Infrastructure: Why Governments Must Act to Protect Projects (https://blogs.worldbank.org/ppps/covid-19-infrastructure-why-governments-must-act-protect-projects).

L&T Metro Rail (Hyderabad) Limited. 2017. Fare Notification issued by L&T MRHL, November (http://corpwebstorage.blob.core.windows.net/media/35991/press-release-25th-november-2017-fare-chart-hyderabad-metro-rail.pdf)

L&T Metro Rail (Hyderabad) Limited. 2018. *Annual Report 2017–18* (https://corpwebstorage.blob.core.windows.net/media/38559/annual-report-2017-18-ltmrhl.pdf)

L&T Metro Rail (Hyderabad) Limited. 2018. *Annual Report 2017–18*, p. 65 (https://corpwebstorage.blob.core.windows.net/media/38559/annual-report-2017-18-ltmrhl.pdf)

L&T Metro Rail (Hyderabad) Limited. 2021. Website https://www.ltmetro.in/about-us/about-lt-metro-rail-limited/.

Lam-Frendo, Marie and Morgan Landy. 2021. If You Issue It, They Will Come: Lessons from Recent Infrastructure Bonds, 23 September (https://blogs.worldbank.org/ppps/if-you-issue-it-they-will-come-lessons-recent-infrastructure-bonds?CID=WBW_AL_BlogNotification_EN_EXT).

Larsen & Toubro. 2019. *Annual Report 2018–19.* (http://investors.larsentoubro.com/upload/AnnualRep/FY2019AnnualRepFull%20Annual%20Report%202018-19.pdf)

Larsen & Toubro. 2019. *Annual Report 2018–19*, p. 265 (http://investors.larsentoubro.com/upload/AnnualRep/FY2019AnnualRepFull%20Annual%20Report%202018-19.pdf)

Lok Sabha. 2021. Unstarred Question No. 1702 answered on 11 February. (http://10.246.55.105/Loksabha/Questions/QResult15.aspx?qref=20613&lsno=17)

Lok Sabha. 2021. Unstarred Question No. 1786 answered on 11 February. (http://10.246.55.105/Loksabha/Questions/QResult15.aspx?qref=20619&lsno=17)

Lu, Jason Zhengrong. 2020. A Simple Way to Close the Multi-trillion-dollar Infrastructure Financing Gap (https://blogs.worldbank.org/ppps/simple-way-close-multi-trillion-dollar-infrastructure-financing-gap).

Luna-Martínez, José de and Carlos Leonardo Vicente. 2012. *Global Survey of Development Banks*. Washington, DC: World Bank (https://openknowledge.worldbank.org/bitstream/handle/10986/3255/WPS5969.pdf?sequence=1&isAllowed=y).

Maharashtra Water Resources Regulatory Authority. 2018. Review and Revision of Bulk Water Rates for Domestic, Industrial and Agriculture Irrigation Use in Maharashtra State, Order 1/2018 (https://mwrra.org/wp-content/uploads/2020/10/BWT-Order-English.pdf)

Manila Water Press Release. 2022. Manila Water in Historic Win as First Philippine Company to Be Named 'Water Company of the Year' at the 2022 Global Water

Awards (https://www.manilawater.com/corporate/sustainability/agos/2022-05-20/manila-water-in-historic-win-as-first-philippine-company-to-be-named--water-company-of-the-year--at-the-2022-global-water-awards).

Mass Transit Rail Corporation. 2019. *Annual Report 2019*, p. 20 (http://www.mtr.com.hk/archive/corporate/en/investor/annual2019/E09.pdf).

Mass Transit Rail Corporation. n.d. Financial Highlights of MTR (http://www.mtr.com.hk/archive/corporate/en/investor/10yr_stat_en.pdf).

Mauricio Franco Mitidieri. 2020. *The Evolution of the YieldCos Structure in the United States, 13 April*. Sean T. Wheeler Latham & Watkins MLP Practice.

McKinsey Global Institute. 2017. Bridging Infrastructure Gaps: Has the World Made Progress? (https://www.mckinsey.com/business-functions/operations/our-insights/bridging-infrastructure-gaps-has-the-world-made-progress).

McKinsey & Company. 2020. The ESG Premium: New Perspectives on Value and Performance (https://www.mckinsey.com/business-functions/sustainability/our-insights/the-esg-premium-new-perspectives-on-value-and-performance?cid=other-eml-ttn-mip-mck&hdpid=b62e2c93-e9a5-425d-8a55 12e52d307fa6&hctky=9579620&hlkid=43078758859542b2923b61248e74a845).

McKinsey & Company. 2020. Restoring Public Transit amid COVID-19: What European Cities Can Learn from One Another, 5 June (https://www.mckinsey.com/industries/travel-transport-and-logistics/our-insights/restoring-public-transit-amid-covid-19-what-european-cities-can-learn-from-one-another?cid=other-eml-alt-mip-mck&hlkid=bcb6a521d0c54555a7405ffef83c0651&hctky=9579620&hdpid=d3f2a42e-78f6-452b-a794-bb46dbc15100).

McKinsey & Company. 2021. Built to Last: Making Sustainability a Priority in Transport Infrastructure (https://www.mckinsey.com/industries/travel-logistics-and-infrastructure/our-insights/built-to-last-making-sustainability-a-priority-in-transport-infrastructure?cid=other-eml-dre-mip-mck&hlkid=608129efd7bb4 39e998c6e67ff9bca12&hctky=9579620&hdpid=1f11f87d-0534-4c99-99b7-d818a 439acb6).

McKinsey & Company. 2022. The Role of ESG and Purpose (https://www.mckinsey.com/capabilities/strategy-and-corporate-finance/our-insights/the-role-of-esg-and-purpose)

Metro Railway (Operation & Maintenance) Act. 2002. http://mohua.gov.in/upload/uploadfiles/files/MetroRail_Act_2002.pdf.

Miller, Alan S. 2021. A Brief Introduction to the Critical, Complex World of Climate Finance (https://alanmiller-64880.medium.com/a-brief-introduction-to-the-critical-complex-world-of-climate-finance-120001f4ca61).

Ministry of Finance, Government of India. 2013. *Scheme and Guidelines for Financial Support to Public–Private Partnerships in Infrastructure (VGF Scheme)*. (https://www.pppinindia.gov.in/documents/20181/21751/VGF_GuideLines_2013.pdf/999e4386-9623-47bb-b372-38246ede1a0f)

Ministry of Finance, Government of India. 2013. Format of Tripartite Agreement. In *Scheme and Guidelines for Financial Support to Public–Private Partnerships in Infrastructure (VGF Scheme)*, p. 21 (https://www.pppinindia.gov.in/documents/20181/21751/VGF_GuideLines_2013.pdf/999e4386-9623-47bb-b372-38246 ede1a0f).

Ministry of Finance, Government of India, Government of India. 2020. *Economic Survey 2019–20.*

Ministry of Finance, Government of India. 2020. *Report of the Task Force on National Infrastructure Pipeline.*

Ministry of Finance, Government of India. 2020. *Report of the Task Force on National Infrastructure Pipeline, Volume 1*, p. 26 (https://dea.gov.in/sites/default/files/Rep ort%20of%20the%20Task%20Force%20National%20Infrastructure%20Pipel ine%20%28NIP%29%20-%20volume-i_1.pdf).

Ministry of Finance, Government of India. 2020. *Recommendations of the Report of the Sub-group on Capital Markets for financing of National Infrastructure Pipeline.*

Ministry of Finance, Government of India. 2020. *Report of Project Finance/ Refinance Sub-Group Constituted under IMSC for Enabling Financing of Infrastructure Projects under National Infrastructure Pipeline.*

Ministry of Finance, Government of India. 2020. *Draft Report of Sub-Group on 'Expanding Institutional Finance for Infrastructure' Constituted under IMSC for Enabling Financing of Infrastructure Projects under NIP.*

Ministry of Finance. 2020. *Strategic Asset Recycling Initiative (SARI): Draft Report by Sub-Group on Asset Recycling and Infrastructure Equity.*

Ministry of Finance. 2020. *National Infrastructure Pipeline: Draft Report by Sub-Group—Urban and Social Infrastructure Finance.*

Ministry of Finance, Government of India. 2021. *Economic Survey 2020–21.*

Ministry of Finance, Government of India. 2021. *Monthly Review of the Indian Economy,* November.

Ministry of Finance, Government of India. 2021. *Updated Harmonized Master List of Infrastructure Sub-sectors* (https://dea.gov.in/sites/default/files/updated%20%20 Harmonized%20Master%20%20List%20%20of%20%20Infrastructure%20%20 Sub-sectors%20dated%2024-8-2020_1.pdf).

Ministry of Finance, Government of India. 2021. *Finance Minister's Budget Speech 2021/22*

Ministry of Finance, Government of India. 2022. *Finance Minister's Budget Speech 2022-23* (https://www.indiabudget.gov.in/doc/Budget_Speech.pdf)

Ministry of Heavy Industries and Public Enterprises, Government of India. 2020. *Annual Report 2019–20,* p. 107.

Ministry of Housing and Urban Affairs, Government of India, (n.d.), *Value Capture Finance Policy Framework* (http://mohua.gov.in/upload/whatsnew/59c0bb2d8f1 1bVCF_Policy_Book_FINAL.pdf).

Ministry of Jal Shakti, Department of Water Resources, River Development and Ganga Rejuvenation. 2019. *National Compilation on Dynamic Ground Water Resources of India, 2017.*

Ministry of Power, Government of India. 2019. *Annual Report 2018–19,* p. 46 https:// powermin.nic.in/sites/default/files/uploads/MOP_Annual_Report_Eng_2 018-19.pdf.

Ministry of Power, Government of India. 2020. Rajya Sabha Unstarred Question No. 1421 Answered on 3 March 2020 on Transmission and Distribution Losses of DISCOMs (https://pqars.nic.in/annex/251/AU1421.pdf).

Ministry of Railways, Government of India. 2020. *National Rail Plan—India: Draft Final Report, Volume 1.*

Ministry of Statistics and Programme Implementation, Government of India. 2021. *Women and Men in India.* (https://www.mospi.gov.in/publication/women-and-men-india-2021)

Ministry of Water Resources, Government of India. 2016. *Draft National Water Framework Bill, 2016*, p. 20 (http://www.mowr.gov.in/sites/default/files/Water_Framework_May_2016.pdf).

MNRE, Government of India. 2014. Implementation of a Scheme for Development of Solar Parks and Ultra Mega Solar Power Projects in the Country Commencing from 2014–15 and onwards (i.e. from the year 2014–15 to 2018–19), p. 5 (https://mnre.gov.in/img/documents/uploads/d9f99dc08abd4b6988ba7ee3be288ee1.pdf).

Modak, Samie. 2021. India Inc Does Well on ESG. *Business Standard*, 29 June (https://www.business-standard.com/article/economy-policy/india-inc-fares-well-on-environmental-social-and-governance-disclosures-121062800371_1.html).

Mohan, Rakesh. 2021. New Development Finance Institution and Infrastructure Financing in India. In *New Generation DFI in India: Opportunities and Challenges. 2021. Research and Information System (RIS) for Developing Countries.* New Delhi.

Morris, Sebastian. 2019. *The Problem of Financing Private Infrastructure in India Today.* (https://vslir.iima.ac.in:8080/jspui/handle/11718/23859)

Mukherjee, Andy. 2021. Australia Has Lessons for India's Asset Recycling Plan. *Business Standard.*

Mukul, Jyoti. 2021. EV Start-ups Feel the Spark of Recovery. Business Standard, 25 March.

Mukul, Jyoti. 2021. Giants Hitch a Ride on the Green Road. *Business Standard*, 29 December.

Mutambatsere, Emelly and Maud de Vautibault. 2022. Blended Finance Can Catalyze Renewable Energy Investments in Low-income Countries (https://blogs.worldbank.org/ppps/blended-finance-can-catalyze-renewable-energy-investments-low-income-countries?CID=WBW_AL_BlogNotification_EN_EXT).

Natarajan, Gulzar. 2020. Designing a New Development Finance Institution for Infrastructure. https://papers.ssrn.com/sol3/papers.cfm?abstract_id=3517980.

National Audit Office. 2002. *The PFI Contract for the Redevelopment of West Middlesex University Hospital* (https://www.nao.org.uk/report/the-pfi-contract-for-the-redevelopment-of-west-middlesex-university-hospital/).

National Highways Authority of India (NHAI). 2021. Toll Information System. *Snapshot of tolling as on 31 March 2021 under NHAI Projects.* (accessed on 28 July 2021) (https://tis.nhai.gov.in/faq.aspx?language=en)

National Investment and Infrastructure Fund. 2021. National Investment and Infrastructure Fund Limited (NIIFL) announces USD 100 million investment from New Development Bank (NDB) into the NIIF Fund of Funds (FoF), 11 February. Available at https://www.niifindia.in/uploads/media_releases/Press%20Release%20-%20NIIFL%20announces%20USD%20100%20million%20investment%20from%20New%20Development%20Bank%20(NDB)%20into%20the%20NIIF%20Fund%20of%20Funds%20(FoF)%20(2)-converted.pdf.

National Pension System Trust (Government of India). 2021. *Annual Report 2020–21*, p. 31. Available at: http://npstrust.org.in/sites/default/files/Annual%20Report%20 of%20NPS%20Trust-%20FY%202020-21%20%281%29.pdf.

National Securities Depository Limited, Government of India. *FPI Net Investment Details (Financial Year)* (https://www.fpi.nsdl.co.in/web/Reports/Yearwise. aspx?RptType=5)

National Securities Depository Limited, Government of India. *FPI Net Investment Details (Calendar Year)*
(https://www.fpi.nsdl.co.in/web/Reports/Yearwise.aspx?RptType=6)

National Securities Depository Limited, Government of India. *Fortnightly Sector-wise FPI Investment data* (https://www.fpi.nsdl.co.in/web/Reports/FPI_Fortnightly_Se lection.aspx)

National University of Singapore, Tuition Fees Per Annum (Applicable for Academic Year 2020/2021) (http://www.nus.edu.sg/registrar/docs/info/administrative-polic ies-procedures/ugtuitioncurrent.pdf)

New South Wales Treasury. 2005. *New Schools Privately Financed Project—Post-implementation Review* (https://www.treasury.nsw.gov.au/sites/default/files/pdf/ trp053_New_schools_privately_financed_project_-_POST_IMPLEMENTA TION_REVIEW_dnd.pdf)

NITI Aayog. 2021. *National Monetization Pipeline, Volume 1: Monetization Guidebook* (https://www.niti.gov.in/sites/default/files/2021-08/Vol_I_NATIONAL_ MONETISATION_PIPELINE_23_Aug_2021.pdf).

NITI Aayog, Government of India. 2017. Appraisal Document of Twelfth Five Year Plan (2012–17), pp. 178–9 (https://niti.gov.in/writereaddata/files/document_publ ication/Appraisal%20Document%20Five%20Year%20Plan%202012%20-%2017-Final%20%281%29.pdf).

NITI Aayog, Government of India. 2019. *Composite Water Management Index* (http:// niti.gov.in/sites/default/files/2019-08/CWMI-2.0-latest.pdf).

NITI Aayog and World Energy Council. 2018. *Zero Emission Vehicles (ZEVs): Towards a Policy Framework*, p. 4 (https://niti.gov.in/writereaddata/files/document_publ ication/EV_report.pdf).

OECD. 2018. *Roadmap to Infrastructure as an Asset Class* (https://www.oecd.org/g20/ roadmap_to_infrastructure_as_an_asset_class_argentina_presidency_1_0.pdf).

OECD. 2020. Draft Progress Note on Asset Recycling. Paris: OECD.

OECD. 2020. *Green Infrastructure in the Decade for Delivery: Assessing Institutional Investment*, ch. 2 (https://www.oecd-ilibrary.org/sites/f51f9256 en/1/3/2/index. html?itemId=/content/publication/f51f9256-en&_csp_=7d5d22ec82800d8235fe1 f2706f7224f&itemIGO=oecd&itemContentType=book).

OECD. 2020. *Pension Markets in Focus* (https://www.oecd.org/daf/fin/private-pensi ons/Pension-Markets-in-Focus-2020.pdf).

OECD. 2021. *The Application of ESG Considerations in Infrastructure Investment in the Asia-Pacific*. Paris: OECD.

Orekhova, Svitlana and Guillermo Diaz-Fanas. 2020. Bouncing Back Is Not Enough. Let's Bounce Forward to Infrastructure Resilience (https://blogs.worldbank. org/ppps/bouncing-back-not-enough-lets-bounce-forward-infrastructure-res ilience).

Pangestu, Mari Elka and Mats Granryd. 2020. Equal Access to Digital Technologies: A Key to Resilient Recovery (https://blogs.worldbank.org/voices/equal-access-digital-technologies-key-resilient-recovery).

Parameswaran M. P. 1979. Significance of Silent Valley. *Economic and Political Weekly*, 14(27): 1117–19 (https://www.jstor.org/stable/4367757?read-now=1&refreqid=excelsior%3Ab71944efafa8baee999d8c1a54c5da96&seq=1).

Paris Public Transport. 2021 (https://en.parisinfo.com/practical-paris/how-to-get-to-and-around-paris/public-transport) .

Patel, Urjit R. 2021. Central Banks Must Stop Pussyfooting on Climate. *Business Standard*, 9 September.

PIB. 2021. Budget 2021/22 Augments Capital of SECI and IREDA to Promote Development of RE Sector (https://pib.gov.in/PressReleaseIframePage.aspx?PRID=1696498).

Planning Commission, Government of India. 1992. *Eighth Five Year Plan* New Delhi: Planning Commission

Planning Commission, Government of India. 2001. *Approach Paper to the Tenth Five Year Plan (2002–2007)*.New Delhi: Planning Commission

Planning Commission, Government of India. 2001. *Indian Planning Experience—A Statistical Profile*. New Delhi: Planning Commission

Planning Commission, Government of India. *Various Five Year Plan documents* (https://niti.gov.in/planningcommission.gov.in/docs/plans/planrel/fiveyr/welcome.html) New Delhi: Planning Commission

Popov, Vladimir. 2019. *Infrastructure Investment and Growth: Market Failures Can Be Corrected by the Government*. Available at https://carleton.ca/vpopov/wp-content/uploads/Infrastructure-investment-and-growthMarch-2019.pdf.

Power Finance Corporation. 2020. *Report on Performance of State Power Utilities, 2018–19* (https://www.pfcindia.com/DocumentRepository/ckfinder/files/Operations/Performance_Reports_of_State_Power_Utilities/Report%20on%20Performance%20of%20State%20Power%20Utilities%202018-19.pdf).

Prasad, R. U. S. 2008. *The Impact of Policy and Regulatory Decisions on Telecom Growth in India*. Stanford, CA: Stanford Center for International Development.

Pratap, Kumar V. 2015. User Fees and Political and Regulatory Risks in Indian Public-Private Partnerships. *Economic and Political Weekly*, L(36) (5 September): p. 24-26 (http://www.epw.in/commentary/user-fees-and-political-and-regulatory-risks-indian-public%E2%80%93private-partnerships.html).

Pratap, Kumar V. 2020. A New Normal in Infrastructure—Barring the Onset of Second Covid Wave, the Worst Is behind Us. *Financial Express* (https://www.financialexpress.com/opinion/a-new-normal-in-infrastructure-barring-the-onset-of-second-covid-wave-the-worst-is-behind-us/2033384/).

Pratap, Kumar V. 2020. Power Play: How Renewables' March Could End State DISCOM Era. *Financial Express*, 27 October (https://www.financialexpress.com/opinion/power-play-how-renewables-march-could-end-state-discom-era/2114342/).

Pratap, Kumar V. 2020. Renewing Faith in Public Private Partnerships. Financial Express, 12 June (https://www.financialexpress.com/opinion/renewing-faith-in-public-private-partnerships/1988892/).

Pratap, Kumar V. 2021. Are We Creating Outcomes Similar to Power Sector by Proliferating Metro Rail across Cities in India? *Vikalpa*, 46 (1): 7–12 (https://journ als.sagepub.com/doi/full/10.1177/02560909211015455).

Pratap, Kumar V. and Rajesh Chakrabarti. 2018. *Public–Private Partnerships in Infrastructure: Managing the Challenges.* Singapore: Springer Science and Business Media Singapore Pte Ltd. (http://www.springer.com/la/book/9789811033544).

Pratap, Kumar V. and Manshi Gupta. 2022. *The Role of Reasonable User Charges in Financing the National Infrastructure Pipeline. Vikalpa*, 47(3): 1–6 (https://journ als.sagepub.com/doi/pdf/10.1177/02560909221117698).

Pratap, Kumar V. and Mira Sethi. 2019. Infrastructure Financing in India—Trends, Challenges and Way Forward. In Rajat Kathuria and Prateek Kukreja (eds). 2019. *20 Years of G20—From Global Cooperation to Building Consensus.* p. 183–198 Singapore: Springer.

Press Information Bureau. 2001. *Golden Quadrilateral Project*, 28 November.

Press Information Bureau. Government of India. 2014. *Establishment of Model Schools under Public-Private Partnership Mode* (https://pib.gov.in/newsite/Print Release.aspx?relid=106778)

Press Information Bureau, Ministry of Heavy Industries & Public Enterprises, Government of India. 2019. Implementation of National Electric Mobility Mission Plan, 8 July (https://pib.gov.in/newsite/PrintRelease.aspx?relid=191337).

Press Trust of India. 2020. User Fee Collection through FASTag Crosses Rs 80 cr per Day with Record 50 lakh Transactions: NHAI. *The Economic Times*, 25 December (https://economictimes.indiatimes.com/news/economy/infrastructure/user-fee-collection-through-fastag-crosses-rs-80-cr-per-day-with-record-50-lakh-trans actions-nhai/articleshow/79955960.cms#:~:text=NEW)

PRS Legislative Research. 2021. *The National Bank for Financing Infrastructure and Development (NaBFID) Bill, 2021* (https://prsindia.org/billtrack/the-national-bank-for-financing-infrastructure-and-development-bill-2021).

PUB (Singapore's National Water Agency). 2017. Water Price Revisions (https://www. pub.gov.sg/sites/assets/PressReleaseDocuments/WPR2017-AnnexA.pdf).

Public–Private Infrastructure Advisory Facility (PPIAF), 2015. Case Study: Hong Kong MTR Corporation (https://ppiaf.org/sites/ppiaf.org/files/documents/toolk its/railways_toolkit/PDFs/RR%20Toolkit%20EN%20New%202017%2012%20 27%20CASE5%20HK%20MTR.pdf).

Rastogi, Anupam and Vivek Rao. 2011. *Product Innovations for Financing Infrastructure: A Study of India's Debt Markets.* Asian Development Bank South Asia Working Paper Series No. 6.

Ravenhorst, Ivo and Dirk Brounen. 2022. *Why Infrastructure?* (https://papers.ssrn. com/sol3/papers.cfm?abstract_id=4154640)

Ministry of Urban Development, Government of India . 2011. Report on Indian Urban Infrastructure and Services (https://icrier.org/pdf/FinalReport-hpec.pdf).

Reserve Bank of India. 16 September 2013 and 15 September 2021. *Handbook of Statistics on Indian Economy* (Industry-wise Deployment of Gross Bank Credit) (https://www.rbi.org.in/scripts/AnnualPublications.aspx?head=Handbook%20 of%20Statistics%20on%20Indian%20Economy).

Reserve Bank of India. 2017. *Discussion Paper on Wholesale and Long-term Finance Banks.* Available at https://www.rbi.org.in/Scripts/PublicationReportDetails.aspx?UrlPage=&ID=866#3.

Reserve Bank of India. 2018. *Financial Stability Report* (https://www.rbi.org.in/Scripts/FsReports.aspx)

Reserve Bank of India. 2018 and 2021. *Handbook of Statistics on Indian Economy* (https://www.rbi.org.in/Scripts/AnnualPublications.aspx?head=Handbook+of+Statistics+on+Indian+Economy)

Reserve Bank of India. 2019. India's Corporate Bond Market: Issues in Market Microstructure. *RBI Bulletin*, 73(1): 21. Available at https://rbidocs.rbi.org.in/rdocs/Bulletin/PDFs/BULLETINJANUARY2019_FBB1F301E2A264F8E8999CED9F9117658.PDF

Reserve Bank of India. 2021. Green Finance in India: Progress and Challenges. *RBI Bulletin* (https://www.rbi.org.in/Scripts/BS_ViewBulletin.aspx?Id=20022).

Reserve Bank of India. 2021. RBI Releases the Financial Stability Report, July 2021. (https://rbi.org.in/Scripts/BS_PressReleaseDisplay.aspx?prid=51832) Mumbai: Reserve Bank of India

Reserve Bank of India. Press Release *RBI joins Network for Greening the Financial System.* April 29, 2021 2021–2022/131. (https://www.rbi.org.in/Scripts/BS_PressReleaseDisplay.aspx?prid=51496)

Roy, S. 2020. Covid-19 Pulls the Chain: Delhi Metro Loses Rs 10 Crore/Day. *Times of India*, 16 May (https://timesofindia.indiatimes.com/city/delhi/covid-pulls-the-chain-metro-loses-rs-10cr/day/articleshow/75906591.cms).

Rundell, Sarah. 2020. *India's NIIF gathers steam* (https://www.top1000funds.com/2020/02/indias-niif-gathers-steam/).

Rundell, Sarah. 2020. *The Rise of the Sovereign Wealth Fund* (https://www.top1000funds.com/2020/03/the-rise-of-the-sovereign-wealth-fund/).

Sankhe, S., Vittal, I., Dobbs, R., Mohan, A., Gulati, A., Ablett, J., ... and Setyy, G. 2010. *India's Urban Awakening: Building Inclusive Cities, Sustaining Economic Growth.* McKinsey Global Institute.

Sasikala A. S. 2014. *Gandhi and Ecological Marxists: The Silent Valley Movement.* (http://www.satyagrahafoundation.org/gandhi-and-ecological-marxists-the-silent-valley-movement/).

Seattle Government. 2019 Residential Drinking Water Rates Effective from January 1, 2020 (Residential Commodity Charges) (http://www.seattle.gov/utilities/your-services/accounts-and-payments/rates/water/residential-water-rates).

Securities and Exchange Board of India (SEBI). 2020. *Consultation Paper on the Format for Business Responsibility and Sustainability Reporting* (https://www.sebi.gov.in/reports-and-statistics/reports/aug-2020/consultation-paper-on-the-format-for-business-responsibility-and-sustainability-reporting_47345.html).

Security and Exchange Board of India. 2020. Report of Working Group on Social Stock Exchange (https://www.sebi.gov.in/reports-and-statistics/reports/jun-2020/report-of-the-working-group-on-social-stock-exchange_46751.html).

SEBI. 2021. Registered Infrastructure Investment Trusts (https://www.sebi.gov.in/sebiweb/other/OtherAction.do?doRecognisedFpi=yes&intmId=20)

Shyam, Radhey, Dilip Nigam, Anindya S. Parira, and Sunil Kr Gupta. 2019. The Evolution of Solar Parks in India: A Comprehensive Analysis. *Infraline Plus*, 8(4): 26 (https://www.researchgate.net/publication/336261442_The_Evolution_of_Solar_Parks_in_India_A_Comprehensive_Analysis/link/5d973b2da6fdccfd0e7653b9/download).

Singapore MRT/LRT Fare Calculator, Travel Time and Route Guide. 2021 (https://mrt.sg/fare)

Smith, Adam. 1776. An Inquiry into the Nature and Causes of the Wealth of Nations, Book IV, Chap. 2. London: Methuen and Co Ltd

Solar Energy Corporation of India. 2020. *Annual Report 2019–20*.

Srivastava, Vikas and V. Rajaraman. 2018. *Project and Infrastructure Finance: Corporate Banking Perspective*. Oxford University Press: New Delhi.

Subramanian, Arvind. 2018. *Of Counsel—The Challenges of the Modi-Jaitley Economy*. Gurgaon, India: Penguin Random House India.

Sulser, Patricia. 2021. Scaling up PPPs by Engaging Impact Investing Charities and Foundations (https://blogs.worldbank.org/ppps/scaling-ppps-engaging-impact-investing-charities-and-foundations?CID=WBW_AL_BlogNotification_EN_EXT).

Swiss Re Institute. 2021. *Closing the Infrastructure Gap* (https://www.swissre.com/dam/jcr:3f5e2757-f08b-4fb2-8805-fdc479dd7c20/swiss-re-institute-publication-closing-the-infrastructure-gap-2021.pdf)

Tandon, Amit. 2021. An Over-engineered Social Stock Exchange? *Business Standard*, 21 December.

Tax Policy Centre, Urban Institute and Brookings Institution. 2020. *What Are Municipal Bonds and How Are They Used* (https://www.taxpolicycenter.org/briefing-book/what-are-municipal-bonds-and-how-are-they-used).

Telecom Regulatory Authority of India (TRAI). 2017. *A Twenty-Year Odyssey 1997–2017* (https://trai.gov.in/sites/default/files/A_TwentyYear_Odyssey_1997_2017.pdf).

Telecom Regulatory Authority of India (TRAI). *Annual Report* (various years)

The Economist. 2021. Regulators Want Firms to Own Up to Climate Risks, 13 March (https://www.economist.com/business/2021/03/13/regulators-want-firms-to-own-up-to-climate-risks?utm_campaign=the-climate-issue&utm_medium=newsletter&utm_source=salesforce-marketing-cloud&utm_term=2021-03-22&utm_content=ed-picks-article-link-4&etear=nl_climate_4).

The Economist. 2021. Lithium Battery Costs Have Fallen by 98% in Three Decades, 31 March 2021 (https://www.economist.com/graphic-detail/2021/03/31/lithium-battery-costs-have-fallen-by-98-in-three-decades).

The Economist. 2021. Joe Biden Unveils America's Most Ambitious Infrastructure Plan in Generations, 1 April (https://www.economist.com/united-states/2021/04/01/joe-biden-unveils-americas-most-ambitious-infrastructure-plan-in-generations).

The Economist. 2021. *The Climate Issue*, 3 May.

The Economist. 2021. Climate Finance—The Green Meme, 22–28 May.

The Economist. 2021. How Green Bottlenecks Threaten the Clean Energy Business, 12 June.

The Economist. 2022. Three Letters That Won't Save the Planet, 29 July.

The Economist. 2022. Asset Managers—The Saviour Complex, 29 July.

The Economist. 2021. Hot Take—Could Climate Change Trigger a Financial Crisis? 10 September.

The Economist. 2021. Why Nations That Fail Women Fail, 11 September.

The Economist. 2021. Ford and General Motors Fight It Out to Electrify, 28 September.

The Economist. 2021. Pension Funds—Building Bridges, 8 October. (https://www.economist.com/middle-east-and-africa/2021/10/02/african-pension-funds-have-grown-impressively).

The Economist. 2021. Climate Investing—The Virtues of Green Government Bonds May Be More Political Than Economic, 15 October.

The Economist. 2021. Pollution—Baby, It's Toxic Outside, 12 November.

The Economist. 2022. Green Investing—A Dirty Secret, 18 February.

The Economist. 2022. A New Formula. 14 May (https://www.economist.com/briefing/2022/05/14/india-is-likely-to-be-the-worlds-fastest-growing-big-economy-this-year).

Thinking Ahead Institute. 2021. *Global Pension Assets Study*, pp. 9. Available at https://www.thinkingaheadinstitute.org/content/uploads/2021/02/GPAS__2021.pdf.

Times of India. 2021. Shackled Momentum, 13 May.

Times of India. 2021. HDFC Bank, TCS Aim for Carbon Neutral Tag, 4 June.

Times of India. 2021. Finance Minister Unveils Rs 6 Lakh Crore National Asset Monetisation Plan, 24 August.

Times of India. 2021. Women at Work—Industrial Jobs Can Tackle a Key Gender Imbalance, 18 September.

Times of India. 2021. Record FASTag Collection Points to Recovery Road, 1 November.

Times of India. 2021. RIL Makes Green Finance Debut with $736 mn Loan, 7 December.

Times of India. 2021. Ind-Ra: Ratings to Have ESG Factor, 11 December.

Times of India. 2022. In EV Push, Govt Eases Rules to Set up Charging Stations, 16 January.

Times of India. 2022. Follow the Clouds, 20 June.

Times of India. 2022. CIL's $970 mn Deal to Add Solar Cap, 15 October.

Tokyo Metro. 2021. Regular tickets (https://www.tokyometro.jp/en/ticket/regular/index.html).

Tremolet, Sophie, and Niraj Shah. 2005. "Wanted! Good Regulators for Good Regulation: An Evaluation of Human and Financial Resource Constraints for Utility Regulation." Report by Environmental Resources Management and Tremolet Consulting for the World Bank, Washington DC

UN Office for Project Services (UNOPS), UN Environment Programme (UNEP) and University of Oxford. 2021. *Infrastructure for Climate Action* (https://www.unep.org/news-and-stories/press-release/new-report-reveals-how-infrastructure-defines-our-climate).

Vaze, Prashant, Sandeep Bhattacharya, Neha Kumar, Monica Filkova, and Diletta Giuliani. 2019. *Securitisation as an Enabler of Green Asset Finance in India: Climate Bonds Initiative*, p. 17 (https://www.climatebonds.net/files/reports/securitisation-as-an-enabler-of-green-asset-finance-in-india-report-15052020.pdf).

Vikas, Namita, Sourajit Aiyer, and Cymoran Vikas. 2021. *4 Ways to Scale up Finance for India's Water Sector* (https://www.weforum.org/agenda/2021/05/4-ways-to-scale-up-finance-for-indias-water-sector/).

Viswanathan, N. S. 2016. *Issues in Infrastructure Financing in India*. Mumbai: Reserve Bank of India

Volz, U., Böhnke, J., Knierim, L., Richert, K., Röber, G.-M., and Eidt, V. 2015. *Financing the Green Transformation: How to Make Green Finance Work in Indonesia*. Basingstoke: Palgrave Macmillan.

Walsh, James P, Chanho Park, and Jiangyan Yu. 2011. *Financing Infrastructure in India: Macroeconomic Lessons and Emerging Market Case Studies*. IMF Working Paper. Washington, DC: IMF.

Waqar, Maria and Jade Shu Yu Wong. 2021. Making Gender Matter in Infrastructure PPPs (https://blogs.worldbank.org/ppps/making-gender-matter-infrastructurepps?CID=WBW_AL_BlogNotification_EN_EXT).

Warrieron S. Gopikrishna. 2018. Silent Valley: A Controversy That Focused Global Attention on a Rainforest 40 Years Ago. (https://vikalpsangam.org/article/silent-valley/).

Wells, L. T. and Gleason, E. S. (1995) Is Foreign Infrastructure Investment Still Risky? *Harvard Business Review 73, no. 5*

Wendt, Karen. 2017. *Social Stock Exchanges—Democratization of Capital Investing for Impact*. 30th Australasian Finance and Banking Conference, 2017 (https://papers.ssrn.com/sol3/papers.cfm?abstract_id=3021739).

Wharton School, University of Pennsylvania. 2020. *What Will It Take for India to Reach Its Infrastructure Goals?* (https://knowledge.wharton.upenn.edu/article/will-take-india-reach-infrastructure-goals/).

Willis Towers Watson. 2021. *Global Pension Assets Study*, pp. 7, 9. Available at https://www.thinkingaheadinstitute.org/content/uploads/2021/02/GPAS__2021.pdf.

World Bank. *Private Participation in Infrastructure Database* (http://ppi.worldbank.org).

World Bank Indicators *Net Official Development Assistance Received* (https://data.worldbank.org/indicator/DT.ODA.ODAT.CD).

World Bank. 2018. *What Do We Do/Projects and Operations: India Energy Efficiency Scale-up Program*

World Bank. 1994. World Development Report—Infrastructure for Development. Washington, DC: World Bank.

World Bank. 2008. The Growth Report: Strategies for Sustained Growth and Inclusive Development, p. 35. Washington, DC: World Bank (https://openknowledge.worldbank.org/bitstream/handle/10986/6507/449860PUB0Box3101OFFICIAL0USE0ONLY1.pdf?sequence=1&isAllowed=y)

World Bank. 2015. What Are Green Bonds? p. 23 (http://documents1.worldbank.org/curated/en/400251468187810398/pdf/99662-REVISED-WB-Green-Bond-Box393208B-PUBLIC.pdf).

World Bank. 2017. Contribution of Institutional Investors to Private Investment in Infrastructure (https://ppi.worldbank.org/content/dam/PPI/documents/PPI_InstitutionalInvestors_Update_2017.pdf)

World Bank. 2019. *Gender Equality, Infrastructure and PPPs—A Primer* (https://library.pppknowledgelab.org/documents/5720/download).

World Bank. 2020. *Doing Business 2020: Comparing Business Regulation in 190 Economies*. Washington DC: World Bank (https://openknowledge.worldbank.org/handle/10986/32436 License: CC BY 3.0 IGO).

World Bank. 2021. Global Economic Prospects (https://openknowledge.worldbank. org/handle/10986/34710).

World Bank. 2021. India Takes a Quantum Leap in Building New Freight Corridors (https://www.worldbank.org/en/news/feature/2021/01/12/india-takes-a-quan tum-leap-in-building-new-freight-corridors?cid=SHR_SitesShareLI_EN_EXT)

World Bank. 2021. *Private Participation in Infrastructure 2020 Annual Report*

World Bank's Ease of Doing Business rankings, 2020 (https://www.doingbusiness. org/content/dam/doingBusiness/country/i/india/IND-LITE.pdf)2020

World Bank and RTSC (Railway and Transport Strategy Centre) at Imperial College London. 2017. The Operator's Story: Emerging Findings. Presented at the 'International Transport Forum'. Paris: OECD.

World Economic Forum. 2017. Recycling our Infrastructure for Future Generations (http://www3.weforum.org/docs/WEF_Recycling_our_Infrastructure_for_Fut ure_Generations_report_2017.pdf).

World Economic Forum. 2019. *The Global Competitiveness Report 2019* (https:// www3.weforum.org/docs/WEF_TheGlobalCompetitivenessReport2019.pdf).

World Economic Forum. 2020. *Six of the World's Ten Most Polluted Cities Are in India* (https://www.weforum.org/agenda/2020/03/6-of-the-world-s-10-most-pollu ted-cities-are-in-india/#:~:text=6%20of%20the%20world's%2010,include%20De hli%2C%20Hotan%20and%20Raiwind).

World Economic Forum. 2021. *4 Big Infrastructure Trends to Build a Sustainable World* (https://www.weforum.org/agenda/2021/01/four-big-infrastructure-trends-for-2021/).

World Meteorological Organization. 2021. *State of the Global Climate Report..* Geneva, Switzerland: World Meteorological Organization.

Wu, Xun and Nepomuceno A. Malaluan. 2008. *A Tale of Two Concessionaires: A Natural Experiment of Water Privatisation in Metro Manila. SAGE journals*

Name Index

For the benefit of digital users, indexed terms that span two pages (e.g., 52–53) may, on occasion, appear on only one of those pages.

Tables, figures, and boxes are indicated by *t*, *f*, and *b* following the page number

Subject Index

For the benefit of digital users, indexed terms that span two pages (e.g., 52–53) may, on occasion, appear on only one of those pages.

Tables, figures, and boxes are indicated by *t, f*, and *b* following the page number

9 780198 884934